STORY

AND

FAITH

A GUIDE TO THE OLD TESTAMENT

◆

James L. Crenshaw

Vanderbilt University

MACMILLAN PUBLISHING COMPANY
New York

COLLIER MACMILLAN PUBLISHERS
London

ACKNOWLEDGMENTS

The Scripture quotations contained herein are from the Revised Standard
Version of the Bible, copyrighted 1946, 1952, 1971 by the Division of
Christian Education of the National Council of the Churches of Christ in the
U.S.A., and are used by permission. All rights reserved.

Photos pp. 13, 22, 23, 24, 48, 121, 151, 154, 167, 177, 178, 187, 207, 216, 224,
250, 269, 309, 349, 356, 368 reproduced by Courtesy of the Trustees of the
British Museum.

Photos pp. 15, 20, 83, 123, 156, 157, 261, 263, 271, 444 by Professor Douglas
A. Knight, Vanderbilt Divinity School.

Photo p. 116 courtesy of Israel Tourist Agency.

Courtesy of Shlomo Gafni, G.G. The Jerusalem Publishing House, Ltd.:
Photos pp. 176, 228; photos pp. 11, 54, 112, 150, 153, 353, 377 by Zev
Radovan; photo p. 30 by David Harris.

Macmillan Publishing Company
866 Third Avenue, New York, New York 10022

Collier Macmillan Canada, Inc.

Library of Congress Cataloging-in-Publication Data

Crenshaw, James L.   (date)
    Story and faith.

    Bibliography: p.
    Includes index.
    1. Bible. O.T.—Introductions. I. Title.
BS1140.2.C74   1986   220.6'1   85–18756
ISBN   0–02–325600–1

Printing: 3 4 5 6 7 8   Year: 6 7 8 9 0 1 2 3 4 5

ISBN 0-02-325600-1

To Walter Harrelson
Mentor, Colleague, and Friend

◆ PREFACE ◆

THIS book is written for everyone who wishes to undertake serious study of the Old Testament, whether at a college or university or in any other setting where inquiry into ancient literature takes place. The text is prepared for beginners; *Story and Faith* does not presuppose any prior knowledge of biblical literature. The organization of the discussion derives from the Hebrew Bible itself; I offer a guide to each book in the Old Testament. My reason for this is to emphasize the written text rather than any number of important—though from my viewpoint secondary—concerns: ancient history, archaeology, sociology, and the like.

Because I believe most beginning students will be unfamiliar with ancient Israelite history, I offer a concise summary of the significant epochs from the beginning in Egypt to the time of Roman domination from 63 B.C.E. onwards. My aim is to enable readers to imagine the socioreligious setting within which various biblical writings came into being. In addition, I have written a short introduction to the three divisions of the Old Testament, as well as one for the Apocrypha (the fourteen extra books in the Greek Bible).

The primary aim of this guide to the Old Testament is to communicate an appreciation for the beauty and profundity of the sacred text—hence the title *Story and Faith*. I have paid special attention to the literary craft, the art of storytelling, and the choice of vocabulary and imagery. Not for one moment, however, have I forgotten that these texts originated as religious literature and continue to function in this manner to the present day. Therefore, I have been especially sensitive to the resources within the Bible for anyone who believes that life is fuller when one acknowledges transcendence.

There is no single method of studying the Old Testament; scholars use several approaches to the Bible. For this reason I adopt an eclectic method that combines the strengths of all the different perspectives. At all times I have tried to present the various alternative theories, though openly suggesting which ones seem to have the most merit. I hope I have honestly and fairly described views different from my own, for I am fully aware of my limitations and of the presuppositions I bring to the text.

Two special features of this guide to the Old Testament deserve a few words. The first concerns its scope. *Story and Faith* offers a comprehensive introduction not only to the Old Testament but to the Apocrypha as well. These additional books were, after all, sacred texts in Alexandrian

v

Judaism and in the early Christian church. A knowledge of these texts is essential for understanding the religious situation in the time of Jesus. The second concerns the kind of bibliographical assistance I have sought to provide. I offer descriptive comments about important articles and books that beginners can read with profit. I list these references by topic, hoping thereby to increase their usefulness. In a few cases I mention studies that are somewhat more advanced, but these references are specially noted. I believe this annotated bibliography will greatly help readers explore in depth virtually any subject that comes to mind.

My debt to other scholars is immense, as they will readily perceive. But two people deserve special mention: Gabrielle Robinson, associate professor of English at Indiana University at South Bend, and G. I. Davies, University Lecturer in Divinity and Fellow of Fitzwilliam College, Cambridge University, Cambridge, England, both of whom read the entire manuscript and made many valuable suggestions for its improvement. I wish to thank them for their kindness in making this a better book than it would otherwise have been.

Since it was during a sabbatical at St. Edmund's House, Cambridge, that I first met both of these scholars, I would be remiss if I did not thank the Master, Fellows, Research Fellows, Visiting Scholars, students, and staff of St. Edmund's House for providing a congenial environment for research as well as warm space in their library in which to complete the writing of this book. As always, I am grateful to the library staff at Vanderbilt Divinity School for their unselfish and expert assistance. Finally, I wish to thank Christine Scannaliato and Marie C. Khair for typing much of the manuscript, as well as Paula McNutt for reading portions of it and for her valuable help in preparing the maps.

James L. Crenshaw
Cambridge, England

◆ CONTENTS ◆

Introduction

THE words *story* and *faith* in the title of this book focus attention on two aspects of the Hebrew Scriptures:* their literary artistry and their religious power. My governing conviction is simple: the Old Testament is first and foremost religious literature. Its several books proclaim the human response to what was perceived to be an encounter with the holy one; however, the sacred story also purports to convey the divine word, albeit concealed within human utterances. Thus the words are broken testimony, requiring an act of faith for ordinary discourse to achieve the status of revelation. Because the language of the Bible is religious, it often uses hyperbole, singularly appropriate to love and worship. Furthermore, the discourse gives voice to the full range of human emotions and sentiments, though certain polarities of expression—for example, divine presence and absence, justice and mercy, and order and chaos—exercise a unifying force.

The claim that sacred discontent characterizes the Old Testament vis-à-vis the cultures of the ancient Near East is only partly correct.† Nevertheless, it is possible to understand vast sections of the Hebrew Scriptures

---

*In this book the expressions Hebrew Scriptures, Hebrew Bible, and Old Testament are used interchangeably. None is entirely satisfactory. The first two lack precision because (1) for Judaism the Torah, the first five books of the Bible, is scripture par excellence, whereas the Prophets and the Writings have derivative authority; and (2) certain portions of the Bible are written in Aramaic (Dan. 2:4b–7:28; Ezra 4:6–6:18 and 7:12–26; Jer. 10:11; and two words in Gen. 31:47). The third expression, Old Testament, is a Christian convention that offends many Jews because it may imply that the Jewish scriptures have been supplanted by a New Testament (in Greek the word used means covenant and will; translated into Latin it becomes testament). This usage, Old Testament, has been retained in the title of the book because it has become a literary convention that communicates over a wide spectrum.
†Herbert Schneidau, *Sacred Discontent* (Berkeley: University of California Press, 1976) has argued that Israelite religion constitutes a radical break with ancient ways of viewing reality.

1

as literature of dissent if one broadens the discussion to include rival viewpoints within the Bible itself.* Here one finds competing views from first to last, whether within the separate divisions or beyond the narrow confines of Torah, Prophets, and Writings. Priests, prophets, sages, visionaries—all tell their "story" in poetry or prose, and distinct parties within each sociological group struggle to advance their own particular insights and prerogatives. In so doing they give birth to literary conventions—a sacred garden, a holy mountain, an exodus, a chosen city, a deliverer—that function for generations to unite past and present.

Although the vitality of the literature ensured its survival, it also obscured the history of intellectual and spiritual development in ancient Israel. Earlier "stories" were updated again and again, each one frequently reinterpreted in the light of new circumstances. In every sense of the words, the Bible is made up of living tradition.† Legal collections grew over the centuries, as did prophetic oracles and proverbial sayings. In most cases the authorship of the material was of little consequence and quickly disappeared from memory. Later editors and contributors to the growing body of texts added their own insights without bothering to claim proprietary rights over their thoughts. Often an individual paid the ultimate compliment to an earlier thinker by commenting on the predecessor's ideas and developing them along different lines.

As a consequence, a purely historical analysis of the literature cannot yield satisfactory results. Efforts to specify exact dates for biblical books and to examine them according to their historical sequence are doomed from the start. It has become increasingly clear that no satisfactory history of the literature can be written, for the various texts that make up the Old Testament cannot be dated with any certainty. Thus far, no suitable criteria exist by which to separate later glosses from early writings, and every indication points to extremely active editorial work in updating ancient traditions. Because of this uncertainty, this book will follow the order of the books in the Hebrew Bible.

How do the words *story* and *faith* function in this analysis? To illustrate the concerns of my particular approach to the Bible, I have chosen a brief incident in the larger narrative about the judge, Gideon, found in Judges 6:11–24. Here we read that the angel of the Lord appears to Gideon and recites traditional belief; the dubious judge-to-be challenges the messenger's credal affirmation on the basis of harsh reality and is convincingly answered by a miracle. In this encounter one confronts the peculiar nature of all religion: it can only be affirmed. People like Gideon may question faith assertions, such as "The Lord is with you," because religious convictions cannot be verified; thus the challenge arises: "Pray, sir, if the

---

*I have developed the idea about the Bible as dissent in "The Human Dilemma and Literature of Dissent," in *Tradition and Theology in the Old Testament*, edited by Douglas A. Knight (Philadelphia: Fortress Press, 1977) 238–258.
†*Tradition and Theology in the Old Testament* illustrates this point well.

Lord is with us, why then has all this befallen us? And where are all his wonderful deeds which our fathers recounted to us. . .?" In short, the telling of the sacred story, achieved here largely through dialogue, elicits faith or disbelief,* depending on the personal circumstances and disposition of the hearer. In this particular instance, the sense of realism, communicated by a series of questions, vanishes in a flame when the angel disappears from sight during an act of worship, the offering of a sacrifice. Only by directly encountering mystery does skepticism change into awe, now transformed into belief and action.

This little episode covers the vast range of possibilities that accompany sacred narrative. The Old Testament is also testimony to past religious experience (story) to which hearers long ago, as they do today, responded in faith or disbelief. Those of us whose lives have been dedicated to understanding that story and faith can identify with Gideon. Some hearers find it impossible to advance beyond doubt to faith; others bow in awe before the mystery of life. Both responses are authentic ones within the Hebrew Bible, for they are integral to its story and faith.

Although I emphasize the literary and theological dimensions of the Bible, my analysis uses the many currently practiced methods of interpretation. These include textual criticism, source criticism, form criticism, tradition history, literary criticism (sometimes called aesthetic criticism or a close reading of the text), theological interpretation, structuralism, canon criticism, and sociological analysis. The primary concern of textual criticism is to establish the actual text of a given book or smaller unit. Its domain consists of ancient manuscripts, translations, versions and any other reliable source that assists in the difficult and painstaking task of determining the most accurate Hebrew text and of explaining variants of all sorts. Source criticism addresses the question, What literary sources have actually contributed to the final composition of, for instance, the Book of Genesis? Source critics concentrate on inconsistencies, repetitions, linguistic patterns, and vocabulary that indicate multiple authorship within a given literary work. Form criticism focuses on the oral or preliterary stage of a text, analyzing it on the basis of its constituent genres and seeking to elucidate the form, function, and social setting of small units. Tradition history treats the development of larger complexes that cohere to a particular theme or place. Both form criticism and tradition history probe into the oral stage of a text, seeking to understand who its guardians were and how they used the material in society at large. Aesthetic criticism, or literary analysis, studies the art of expression, whether poetic or prosaic, and endeavors to appreciate the rhetoric of a text in terms of Hebrew usage. It asks how a text achieves its goal–that is, how its argument is structured and how language furthers this purpose. The-

---

*The word *faith* is used here in its wider sense of obedient response rather than in an exclusively intellectual sense.

ological interpretation aims at understanding the moral and cognitive dimensions of the religious viewpoint within a text. To succeed in this task, it engages in comparative studies of other religions in the ancient Near East. Structuralism studies the linguistic patterns beneath the surface of the text that represent cultural constraints on writing itself. Canon criticism examines the way in which a normative body of texts shapes the reader's understanding. Sociological analysis endeavors to perceive the different social contexts governing the concerns expressed.*

Most interpreters use a range of approaches, though inclining in one direction or another for their basic method. Moreover, all their work depends in large measure on the adequacy with which they translate the Hebrew, and in doing so two different principles may be used: formal correspondence and dynamic equivalence. In the formal correspondence method, translators strive to reproduce in the target language the exact linguistic usage of the source language, for example rendering an infinitive by an infinitive or a participal by a participal. In dynamic equivalency the goal is to reproduce the sense of the source language in the idiom of the target language without regard to actual grammatical constructions. Examples of the first method are the King James Version and the Revised Standard Version (RSV); the New English Bible and Today's English Version use the second method. The quotations cited in this book are taken from the RSV.

For more than twenty years in the classroom I have endeavored to combine the two emphases, story and faith. This has been my way of offering an alternative to the excessive emphasis on history during this period. The recent burst of energy directed toward understanding narrative art within the Bible and the assertions, however accurate, that a shift from the historical to the literary has taken place in the discipline suggest that others, too, have found the dominant mode of interpretation in the textbooks unsatisfactory.† While I have learned much from these literary interpretations, I do not believe the gains of historical criticism should be set aside so readily. What I envision, therefore, is an eclectic approach that draws on the research of countless interpreters and many methods. Nevertheless, I hope to emphasize the literary and religious comprehensions of reality within the Bible. Over the years my own students have unfailingly responded enthusiastically to the approach I have developed; their encouragement has spurred me on to write this book for a wider audience.

This book is intended for beginning students. Experience in the classroom has taught me that students by and large no longer bring a knowl-

---

*Beginning students will find convenient introductions to these different methods of interpretation in the Guides to Biblical Scholarship that have been published under the general editorship of Gene M. Tucker for Fortress Press, Philadelphia.
†See the Selected Bibliography under "The Bible as Literature."

edge of the Bible with them. For this reason, I have chosen to guide them through a reading of the twenty-four books in the Hebrew Bible as well as the additional books in the Septuagint (the translation of the Bible into Greek, third century B.C.E. and later). My goal is to lift out the essential themes of each biblical book and to provide contextual information that illuminates the material. I have studiously avoided anything that might hinder students from acquiring an appreciation for the Bible as religious literature. My debt to other scholars is immense, but I have made a conscious decision to omit citations that would only confirm what is already known to the scholars involved. In this way the curious meanderings of scholarship will not get in the way of students' initial study of the Hebrew Bible. Furthermore, I have tried to practice a necessary "suspension of disbelief" rather than burden the discussion with frequent qualifying expressions, such as "the writer believed." My aim is to let the literature generate its own response; in order to do so, it must first be heard in all its power and grandeur, insofar as that is possible today. I have chosen to include a limited bibliography, mostly in English, since unfortunately I cannot assume extensive knowledge of other languages among the students who will read this book. However, these works will contain references adequate to satisfy almost any interest that may express itself in the course of reading the Bible. For this reason as well as to enhance the book's readability, I have kept footnotes to a minimum. Perhaps it is necessary to add that the book is written to be used in conjunction with the Bible.

THE LAND

Since I believe the Bible cannot properly be understood apart from its ancient Near Eastern setting, a few words about the land and the people of this area are imperative. Acquaintance with the material in this section will greatly enrich the reader's grasp of the events that gave rise to the Bible in the first place.

The Mediterranean Sea forms the western border for the entire length of the country. Here the coastal plain makes up the valuable area occupied by Phoenicians and Philistines for most of Israel's history. Important coastal towns to the north, Ugarit* and Byblos, had existed long before Israelites entered the land. Below Byblos were Sidon and Tyre, whence ships traveled to all parts of the world and brought back valuable cargo. Mount Carmel jutted out into the sea just below the plain of Accho (Acre), and the coastal town of Joppa nestled between the fertile coastal plains

---

*Ugarit (Ras Shamra) is the site of the discovery, beginning in 1929, of numerous Canaanite texts. The most important ones for our purposes are the following: *Baal and Anat, The Legend of Keret,* and *Dan'el and Aqhat.*

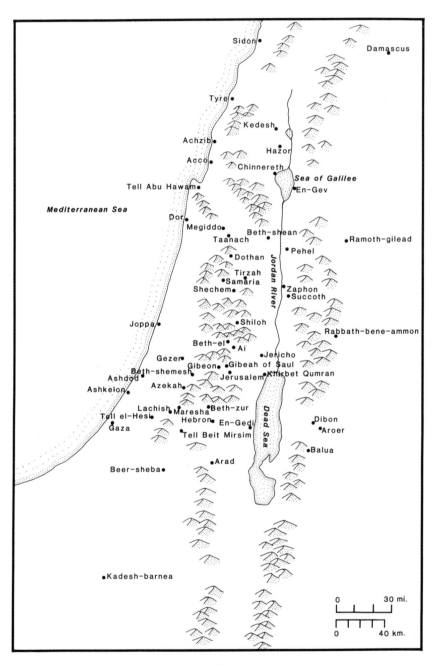

Sidon•

Damascus

Tyre•

Kedesh•

Achzib•

Hazor•

Acco•

Chinnereth•

Tell Abu Hawam•

Sea of Galilee

•En-Gev

Mediterranean Sea

Dor•

Megiddo•

Beth-shean•

•Ramoth-gilead

Taanach•

•Pehel

•Dothan

Tirzah•

•Samaria

Shechem•

Zaphon•

•Succoth

Jordan River

Joppa•

Shiloh•

Rabbath-bene-ammon•

Beth-el•

•Ai

Gezer•

•Jericho

Gibeon•

•Gibeah of Saul

Beth-shemesh•

Jerusalem•

•Khirbet Qumran

Ashdod•

Azekah•

Ashkelon•

Lachish•

•Beth-zur

Tell el-Hesi•

•Maresha

Hebron•

•En-Gedi

Dead Sea

•Dibon

Gaza•

Tell Beit Mirsim•

•Aroer

•Balua

•Arad

Beer-sheba•

0   30 mi.

•Kadesh-barnea

0   40 km.

The Israelite Period (c. 1200–587 B.C.E.*)*

6

The Sea of Galilee, flanked by date palms. Modern day Golan Heights are in the distance.

of Sharon and Philistia to the south. A Latin form of the latter has yielded a name for the entire land, Palestine. The lowlands (Shephelah) separated this area from the hill country of Judah, and farther south was the desert region known as the Negeb.

The central highlands were made up of three regions, Galilee in the north, Samaria in the center, and Judah in the south. The plain of Esdraelon broke through the mountain range to separate Samaria from Galilee. Like the plain of Philistia, this region was extremely fertile; it was especially suited for the cultivation of grain. Mount Tabor in the northeast and Mount Gilboa stand on the northern and southern side of the plain, respectively. Two mountain peaks, Ebal and Gerizim, also overlook the city of Shechem. The Judean mountains eventually taper off into the Negeb and the Sinai Peninsula. South of them to the west is the Shephelah, where grain, figs, dates, and olives thrived. On the western slopes of the Judean hills, the cultivation of grapes became the main agricultural pursuit. To the south is the dry region known as the Negeb.

The Jordan rift begins in upper Syria, flanked on either side by the Lebanon and Anti-Lebanon mountains. The Jordan River winds its way back and forth in the valley floor. Beginning in the foothills of Mount Hermon, it flows through lake Huleh, then the Sea of Chinnereth (Galilee), and finally into the Salt Sea (Dead Sea). At this point it is 1,290 feet below sea level. Because the Dead Sea has no outlet, it collects so

A desolate area of the Negeb.

many chemicals that it cannot sustain life. Farther south is a gorge extending to the Gulf of Aqaba which is known as [Wadi] Arabah. The Jordan rift is very fertile in some areas and boasts one of the oldest cities in the world, Jericho.

The eastern highlands, or Transjordan, make up the territories of Bashan, Gilead, Ammon, Moab, and Edom. The mountains rise sharply out of the Jordan rift, and a wide area receives sufficient rainfall for cultivation. The highest mountain in the east is Nebo. Four rivers flow from the eastern highlands into the Jordan gorge: the Yarmuk, Jabbok, Arnon, and Zered. The first two flow into the Jordan river between the Sea of Galilee and the Dead Sea, and the last two empty into the Dead Sea.

The biblical description of the land as one flowing with milk and honey was true only to seminomads accustomed to the struggle for survival on the fringes of civilization. Nevertheless, certain areas of Palestine were quite fertile, amply justifying the glowing description. The importance of this land,* however, in shaping Israel's ideas about the Deity rests in its exposure to contact with the great nations of the second and first millennia B.C.E. In large measure, Israel's history was determined by the strength or weakness of the great nations to the south and east.

*Walter Brueggemann, *The Land* (Philadelphia: Fortress Press, 1977), has examined the religious significance of sacred space in ancient Israel.

THE PEOPLE ISRAEL

There is considerable uncertainty about the proper starting place in writing a history of Israel. One answer to the difficulty is to begin with the first known datable reference to Israel. That is the Merneptah stele (c. 1220 B.C.E.), which mentions various Canaanite cities conquered by the pharaoh Merneptah. The name Israel occurs in this list, but without the ideogram for land; in its place is the sign for people, presumably because they did not occupy a specific territory at the time. Of course, this ideogram could be a scribal error, but a city named Israel has not shown up elsewhere. As a matter of fact, the word Israel has four senses in the Hebrew Bible: (1) the patriarch, Jacob; (2) a group of tribes immediately after the settlement in Canaan; (3) the monarchy in the time of Saul and the northern kingdom after Solomon's death; and (4) a religious entity, particularly after the fall of Samaria in 722 B.C.E. On the basis of this reference to Israel on the Merneptah stele, it is reasonable to assume that a group of people calling itself Israel occupied the land of Canaan in 1220 B.C.E.

Origins

According to its recorded memory, this group identified its origins with Ur in southern Mesopotamia, although Haran in northern Mesopotamia appears prominently in these recollections as well. One text (Deut. 26:5) associates Jacob with the Aramaeans, and scholars have tried unsuccessfully to reinforce this link linguistically. Another important clue about Israel's origins occurs in the word Hebrew, which seems to have some connection with 'Apiru, the name for a socioeconomic class of people. The Israelites recall a period when their ancestors tended livestock, specifically sheep and goats. An earlier identification of these patriarchs as nomads overlooked the fact that camels are essential to nomadic existence, but this animal is rarely mentioned in the texts. The alternative theories that they were ass nomads and seminomads are not entirely satisfactory because the former implies that the patriarchs bred asses, and the latter suggests that they were in the process of settling down permanently. The stories associate them with areas just outside cities, usually in a single region. Since the patriarchs were herdsmen, they stayed reasonably close to water holes. Therefore, the frequent strife over water in the biblical stories is quite understandable.

All attempts to date the partriarchs have failed.* Earlier arguments based on Nuzi customs have collapsed under close examination. These

---

*For this presentation of Israel's history I have found H. Jagersma, *A History of Israel in the Old Testament Period* (Philadelphia: Fortress Press, 1983), especially useful.

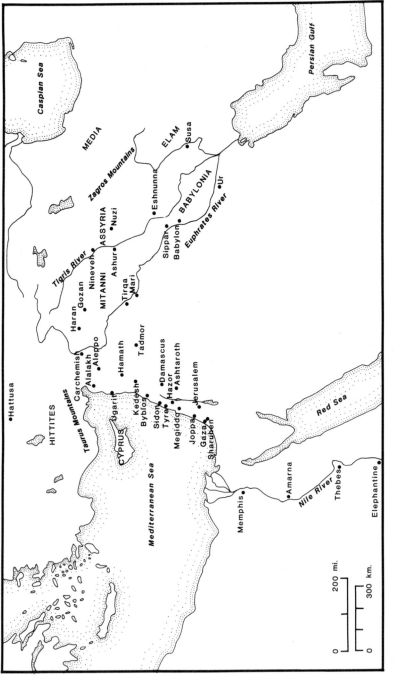

The Ancient Near East (mid-second millennium B.C.E.*)*

Caspian Sea

MEDIA

Zagros Mountains

ELAM

Susa

Eshnunna

Nuzi

BABYLONIA

Ur

ASSYRIA

Tigris River

Nineveh

Ashur

Sippar

Babylon

Euphrates River

Gozan

MITANNI

Tirqa

Mari

Haran

Tadmor

Carchemish

Aleppo

Alalakh

Hamath

Damascus

Ashtaroth

Hattusa

Taurus Mountains

Ugarit

Kedesh

Hazor

Jerusalem

HITTITES

Byblos

Sidon

Tyre

Megiddo

Joppa

Gaza

CYPRUS

Sharuhen

Mediterranean Sea

Red Sea

Persian Gulf

Memphis

Amarna

Nile River

Thebes

Elephantine

200 mi.

300 km.

0

customs include adoption of an heir (Abraham's reference to Eliezer, his slave, as an heir, and Laban's relationship to Jacob), adoption of a slave girl (Abrahan/Hagar; Jacob/Bilhah and Zilpah), Hurrian practice (at marriage the husband adopted his wife as sister, giving her a higher social and legal position; cf. Abraham's treatment of Sarah), Hittite real estate practices (Abraham's purchase of the cave of Mach-pelah), and general ideas shared by Mari and Nuzi (the right of the firstborn). The association of the patriarchs' move to Canaan with an Amorite invasion of the land (c. 1900–1700 B.C.E. is based on dubious archaeological evidence. An identification of Amraphel (Gen. 14:1–24) with Hammurabi, which seemed to support this early dating, has also proved untenable. Understandably, some scholars have argued for a later date (1600–1400 B.C.E.). This approach requires them to treat the biblical reference to 480 years (1 Kings 6:1) between the Exodus and the building of the Temple as artificial. Because the Bible gives different calculations itself, the supposition that 480 is symbolic (12 × 40) seems reasonable.

However, some features of the patriarchal narratives point to a very early date. For example, the association of the god El with a person, rather than a place, and the nonpriestly character of patriarchal religion are distinctive. The patriarchs erected sacred pillars *(matstseboth)* and

A Canaanite altar for burnt offerings dating from 2600–2300 B.C.E. at Megiddo, one of the major cities of ancient Canaan and Israel.

worshipped at sacred trees; they also built altars in recognition of a holy place. In their practice, circumcision was associated with marriage (cf. Gen. 34:13–24). The absence of polemic against Baal and the exclusive use of El names for deity may point to a period before 1500, when Baal worship began to supplant El in the Canaanite pantheon.

Where does this leave us in trying to assess the patriarchal period? It seems entirely possible that Israel's ancestors migrated from southern Mesopotamia through the region of Haran, eventually arriving in Canaan. This history is clouded in devotional legend, where single individuals represent larger groups. This is especially transparent in the stories about Jacob, the one person who has the most claim to historicity. This obscure period must have occurred at some time during the second millennium, perhaps earlier than 1400. Nevertheless, the narratives that preserve these memories were composed much later, and it is therefore difficult if not impossible to reconstruct this earlier period with any confidence. Consequently, some critics insist that Israel's history really began with the settlement in Canaan, together with the Exodus, the decisive event that made this occupation of the land possible.

The Exodus

The Exodus from Egypt presupposes a stay in the land of the Nile. Two distinct traditions offer opposing explanations for the initial entrance into Egypt, although both accounts indicate that foreigners sold Israel's ancestors as slaves. In each case, the foreigners are kinship groups: Ishmaelites and Midianites. Because non-Egyptians achieved high positions in Egypt at various periods, this clue does not require us to put Joseph in the Hyksos period, as some scholars think. The Hyksos invaders, who introduced horse-drawn chariots, seized control of Egypt about 1720 and were not driven out until 1570, when Ahmose, the founder of the Eighteenth Dynasty, managed to regain the government for his people. Joseph's marriage to the daughter of a priest of On makes this dating of Joseph in the period of the Hyksos unlikely, for they worshipped Seth. Descent into Egypt during times of economic hardship, occasioned by famine, is attested in a report that a certain official sent to Merneptah; it states that the official has admitted into Egypt an Edomite group with its cattle. Some scholars think the troubled Amarna period (Akhnaton ruled from 1364 to 1347) provides the most likely time for the descent into Egypt, as well as explaining certain features of Moses' religion. A text from the time of Ramses II (c. 1290–1224) refers to 'Apiru who were forced to carry stones for fortifications, and some personal names in the biblical story are authentic to the Egyptian locale (the midwives Shiphrah and Puah, Hophni, Phinehas, Merari, Moses). Even the Passover rite that is so closely associated with the Exodus testifies to the antiquity of

Akhnaton, the pharaoh of the Amarna revolution (1380–1362), a short-lived religious reform.

these traditions, for it was an old shepherd festival, commemorating the movement of herds to new pastures in the spring.

When did the Exodus take place? Perhaps the first thing that must be said is that Israel recalls two occasions of exodus from Egypt, which have coalesced in the tradition. One group was driven out and traveled northward; after a stay in Kadesh it entered Canaan from the south. Another group fled from Egypt eastward, and wandered in the Sinai Peninsula and thence through the regions of Edom and Moab into Canaan. The biblical record is equally ambiguous about the chronology. (It mentions the fourth and seventh generations after Abraham as those who came out of Egypt, and it also gives different calculations of years, 430 and 400.) Firmer evidence comes from the allusion to a new ruler whose policy represented a change of attitude toward the ancestors of Israel. If this allusion implies a long rule prior to the change, it may suggest that Ramses II had been replaced by Merneptah. At this general period the Egyptians were occupied with repelling the Peoples of the Sea, and forced laborers may very well have seized this opportunity to escape. If the mention of Israel on the Merneptah stele actually refers to the oppressed peoples who managed to escape into Canaan, an exodus under Ramses II or Merneptah is certainly possible.

At least one group that departed from Egypt retained sacred memory of Sinai as a region of religious pilgrimage. The association of Kadesh with Sinai leads some critics to believe that the two places were in the same area; if this hypothesis were true, Sinai would be located somewhere in the southern region of the Negeb. Thus far all attempts to identify the sacred mountain have failed to generate a consensus, partly because the biblical materials are themselves so ambiguous. The link between Yahweh and Sinai seems firmly established in early poetry and in prose accounts (Judges 5 and Exodus 19–24). This period of Israel's early existence has left entirely contradictory impressions on those who later reported its sacred story. In the tradition that is by far the most vigorous, these days were remembered as characterized by constant strife over leadership, whereas now and again prophets looked back on the period as one of obedience to the Deity. This latter understanding, which seems to have represented the viewpoint of many who found the harsh realities of urban society inimical to Yahwism, may represent the heritage of people like Jonadab, the founder of the tent-dwelling Rechabites. But a spiritualization of the wilderness came to prominence in Isaiah 40–55 and flourished among the community at Qumran.* The alternative view, that the wilderness period was marked by murmuring, is equally shaped by theological apologetic. In any event, it seems likely that the references in these ancient stories to an ark and a tent, or tabernacle, reflect authentic memory, although the ark was probably a box into which religious objects were placed, and the tent functioned as a portable sanctuary.

An early twelve-tribe confederation has been postulated on the basis of a Greek amphictyony, but that claim has gradually eroded. The biblical material suggests that the coalitions of tribal groups varied in number, some of the individual tribes disappearing completely. In the old song of Deborah (Judg. 5:14–18) two names appear that do not normally occur in the lists of twelve tribes (Machir and Gilead, although the latter may be a corruption of Gad). The Simeon group may have vanished early,

---

*The Qumran Scrolls, generally called the Dead Sea Scrolls because they were found in caves near the Dead Sea, include biblical manuscripts, commentaries on biblical books, and special writings belonging to a sectarian community, presumably the Essenes, from about 200 B.C.E. to 135 C.E.

The well-preserved ruins of the Essene community settlement at Qumran dating from the second century B.C.E. to the first century C.E. The Dead Sea lies in the background.

and Levi may have also, if there ever was such a secular tribe. Quite possibly there never were tribes who called themselves Joseph and Levi. There is some indication that Judah may have entered the coalition of tribes after the time of Deborah's battle with Sisera, but other explanations for Judah's absence from this poem are possible. Furthermore, there were groups other than the ten tribes mentioned in the song of Deborah (Ephraim, Benjamin, Machir, Zebulun, Issachar, Reuben, Gilead, Dan, Asher, and Naphtali). These additional groups were Kenites, Calebites, Jerahmeelites, Othnielites, and perhaps also a clan calling itself Israel.

The Occupation of Canaan

When and how did these groups occupy Canaan? If we assume that two groups moved from Egypt into Canaan by different routes and at different periods, several strange features in the biblical account become meaningful. Two things, in particular, are illuminated by this hypothesis. First, the obscurities of the route from Egypt to Canaan receive an explanation, and second, the silence with regard to military conflict in the area of Shechem is understandable, because at the time of the conquest led by Joshua this area was already occupied by kindred groups. If the second group left Egypt under Ramses II or Merneptah, then the first group must obviously have departed some time prior to that. Archaeological evidence at Jericho and Ai has failed to confirm the biblical story, for neither of these cities was occupied during the thirteenth century, having been destroyed long before. However, it is a different story in the hill country of central Canaan, where Israelite towns seem to have emerged in the thirteenth century. In fact, a large-scale attack on Canaan seems to have occurred during this time, although nothing conclusively links this invasion with the Israelites.

The Exodus was part of a larger migration in the ancient world, and the unsettled circumstances from the fifteenth to the twelfth centuries aided Israelite clans to escape. Egypt's control over Canaan ceased during the Amarna period; the turmoil in Canaan is clearly represented in the Amarna correspondence between various Canaanite officials and Akhnaton. These letters, discovered in Amarna, were prompted by a threat from 'Apiru and request immediate assistance. Various city-states (Hazor, Megiddo, Shechem, Jerusalem, Lachish) are mentioned, but the pharaoh was too occupied with religious reform to attend to such matters. Slightly later, the Hittite kingdom came to rival Egypt, and the battle at Kadesh, though indecisive, left Egypt's hold over Canaan seriously weakened. The worst blow of all came from the Peoples of the Sea, who invaded coastal areas; the Philistines belonged to the latest stages of this wave. An account of Ramses III's successful resistence of the Sea Peoples, the inscription of Medinet Habu, witnesses to the gravity of this threat. In the course of three centuries, Egypt's control in Canaan had diminished appreciably. The departure from Egypt during this troubled time by those who later called themselves Israel is imaginable; this supposition also explains the mixed population that came to make up Israel. Those fleeing from Egypt found similar groups in Canaan, many of whom eventually linked themselves with the Israelites through intermarriage and covenants. The precise manner in which these people occupied Canaan is unclear, but there is probably some truth in all the theories that have been proposed. These include (1) a peaceful settlement, (2) a swift and decisive conquest, and (3) a peasant revolt.* The extrabiblical evidence for the last theory is hardly compelling, because the country population was not always at odds with city-states. No single answer therefore deals fully with the evidence. Perhaps the separate groups who later constituted Israel entered the land and settled it in various ways. Some, like the Benjaminites, occupied Canaan by force; others did so by less hostile means. At least two groups, Dan and Machir, demonstrated a willingness to move to more congenial territory because of pressure from surrounding

*The theory that the Israelites originated as a peasant revolt against Canaanite city-states has been proposed by George E. Mendenhall, *The Tenth Generation* (Baltimore and London: Johns Hopkins University Press, 1974). See also Norman K. Gottwald, *The Tribes of Yahweh* (Maryknoll, N.Y.: Orbis Books, 1979).

peoples. In truth, the Philistine threat did more than anything else to bring the various groups together.

The Period of the Judges

The period of the judges was characterized by frequent conflicts with neighboring peoples (Canaanites, Philistines, Midianites, Edomites, and so forth). The introduction of iron into the area by Philistines changed the power base over the years, for it made possible a more efficient cultivation of the hill country, ideally suited for the cultivation of grapes. The dominance of the Philistines and Canaanites during this period is recognizable behind the stories about judges, despite their apologetic character. These judges were local warriors who stepped forward in times of peril and delivered endangered groups. Consequently, the warriors have been called charismatic figures, because they acted on the basis of personal gifts, *charisma*. During this early period an effort at kingship came to naught; Abimelech ruled over Shechem for a short time, but opposition from a mixed populace sealed his doom. Perhaps the destruction of Shechem in the twelfth century took place in connection with Abimelech's experiment at monarchy. Another kind of authority seems to have arisen during this general period, that of a religious sanctuary and its priest. Other religious centers existed, of course, but Shiloh soon took precedence over the rest, perhaps because of such leaders as Eli and Samuel.

The Monarchy

Eventually, the prestige of this sanctuary at Shiloh appears to have brought about a return to the monarchical experiment. Saul's rise to power resembles that of other judges, for he delivered the inhabitants of Jabesh-gilead from a horrible fate at the hands of an Ammonite army. Despite Saul's success, the Philistine presence in Canaan soon became so threatening that religious sanction was bestowed on the kingship, perhaps amid protests from an opposition party. Saul was an able warrior, achieving a measure of success against the Philistines in a skirmish at Michmash, but he was no match for these peoples and fell mortally wounded in a battle at Gilboa. His kingship was a simple one; he had no palace and seems only to have boasted a fortress at Gibeah. He did possess one thing, however; the loyalty of the people. Even the biblical story about this king, which is written as a defense of David's usurpation of the throne, does not conceal this fact. One can hardly understand David's vassalage under the Philistines apart from the supposition that Saul's popular support left David no alternative. It follows that the description of Saul as a king who was mentally unstable arose from apologetics rather than from reality. In all likelihood, Saul's kingdom was quite small, embracing the regions of Benjamin, Gilead, and Ephraim. For some reason, possibly personal jealousy, Samuel withdrew religious support from him, but the people remained loyal to the end. That loyalty is difficult to explain if Saul actually suffered from fits of madness. With his defeat, the position of the Philistines was even stronger, for they captured the stronghold of Beth-shan.

David

With David's rise to power, the tribe of Judah began to replace Benjamin as the center of political activity. In many respects this new hero was unscrupulous and merciless. By clever marriages with Abigail and Ahinoam he gained support from Calebite families in southern Judah, and through outright deceit and cruelty he gained Philistine confidence, thus allowing him to live in close proximity with the enemies of Israel. During these years when David and his gang of mercenary soldiers engaged in guerrilla warfare, he raided cities and left no one alive who might identify him as their attacker. After Saul's death David became king over Judah at Hebron. Shortly thereafter, he communicated that fact to the loyal followers of Saul at Jabesh-gilead: "The house of Judah has anointed me king over them." The information was in fact a warning that the people of Jabesh-gilead would be well advised to acknowledge his authority. After Saul's son Ish-bosheth* reigned two years, he incurred the wrath of his general, Abner, who quickly threw his support to David. To cement his relations with Saul's supporters, David demanded that Saul's daughter Michal be returned to him. Then Israel proclaimed David king.

Choosing a Capital

The first issue facing the new king of these two regions, Israel and Judah, was to select a capital. Between the two lands sat the city of Jerusalem, which had as yet resisted efforts to capture it. David and his mercenary troops, who were largely of foreign extraction, took the city, evidently by climbing through its water tunnel and gaining access to the inner city. Jerusalem then became David's personal city, and this choice of a capital meant that it was outside the realms of Israel and Judah. Here in Jerusalem, David surrounded himself with non-Israelite professional soldiers (Uriah the Hittite, Cherethites, Pelethites) and functionaries (Zadok and Ahithophel). By now the Philistines recognized David's betrayal of trust, but it was too late. He defeated them in successive battles and then proceeded to widen his territory by conquering large areas in Transjordan,

---

*In some instances names that had the *Baal* form were changed to *Bosheth* (shame). Eshbaal thus became Ish-bosheth, and Merib-baal was written Mephibosheth.

the site of important copper mines. By bringing the ark to Jerusalem, David enhanced the city's religious prestige. To supervise cultic matters in the capital, he appointed two priests, Abiathar and Zadok. Eventually a court prophet, Nathan, provided divine legitimation for the Davidic dynasty, and Jerusalem's cult soon became the focal point of all religious activity.

David's skill as an organizer and his ability to prepare for any eventuality were missing in his relationship with his sons. The Israelites never fully endorsed David as their king, and Absalom was quick to take advantage of their unrest. By carefully courting their favor, he stole their hearts; therefore, Absalom dared to approach some of David's trusted officials, and two of them, Ahithophel and Amasa, joined him in rising up against his father. Although David's personal bodyguards put down this revolt, it was costly, for he had to make economic concessions to Judah and even made Amasa leader of his army. Such extreme action failed to prevent a rebellion by the Israelites under Sheba's leadership. The third revolt was far less damaging, except to David's own family. Once more a son, Adonijah, rebelled against his father and declared himself king, but quick action by Zadok, Nathan, and Bathsheba manipulated the aging ruler into naming Solomon as coregent. It is significant that the people had chosen Saul as king, and exercized choice in the naming of David as ruler, whereas they were completely disregarded in the selection of Solomon. His rule continued this total disregard for the will of the people, and indeed for their well-being.

Solomon

The era of Solomon was one of expansion, both political and economic. Under this absolute monarch the kingdom of Israel and Judah achieved its maximum size, and wise use of politically motivated marriages linked Solomon with important ruling families as far as Egypt. Trade agreements with Phoenicia gave him access to vital Mediterranean seaports, and expansion into Transjordan provided Solomon with a valuable port at Eziongeber in the Gulf of Aqaba. Trade thus flourished, with an Israelite monopoly on many items. To make effective use of his subjects, Solomon divided the kingdom into twelve tax districts and introduced forced labor, chiefly in the many building works that he funded. These included the Temple; his own palace, which required nearly twice as long to build; a house for his wife, the pharaoh's daughter; and fortifications at Megiddo, Hazor, and Gezer, and also in the Negeb. It appears, too, that a major temple was built at Arad during this period. The era of Solomon is remembered as a time of peace and prosperity, but alongside such unparalleled wealth went considerable poverty. The distinction between rich and poor grew sharper, and unrest increased until it resulted in a revolt instigated by a certain Jeroboam. This opposition to Solomon was cen-

Steps leading to the shaft that goes down to the water tunnel at Hazor (first half of the ninth century B.C.E.*). The tunnel is about 100 meters long.*

tered in Shiloh and its religious personnel, and it probably represented resentment over the increasing role Jerusalem came to play in religious life. Nevertheless, Solomon's grip on his kingdom was secure at this time, and Jeroboam was forced to flee beyond the border into Egypt. There he bode his time until the situation was right to raise a flag once more.

The Divided Kingdom

Jeroboam's opportunity arose after Solomon's death, largely because of his successor's resolve to continue his father's burdensome policies. Rehoboam sought advice from opposing generations, youth and elders at Shechem, and opted for the young people's counsel. His announced intention to introduce even more stringent taxation measures fomented open revolt. In no time at all, Rehoboam had succeeded in alienating himself from the northern tribes, so that he retained only Judah, a rump state. Even this kingdom was placed in peril during his fifth year, when Shishak of Egypt invaded Judah and captured a number of cities. Scholars generally assume that Rehoboam purchased Jerusalem's continued existence by handing over the treasury from the Temple. Otherwise the absence of Jerusalem in the list of conquered cities that appears on the wall of a temple of the god Amon in Karnak is strange.

Jeroboam wasted no time in securing his kingdom to the north. He instituted the worship of Yahweh at two major cult centers, Bethel and Dan. To rival David's brilliant strategem in using Israel's ancient sacred object, the ark, Jeroboam introduced golden bulls as the invisible Deity's sacred symbol. These cult centers and sacred objects could boast an equal place in early worship, a fact that is obscured in the present biblical text by polemic against this cult. But Jeroboam's choice of a capital was less successful than David's; the first choice, Shechem, eventually gave way to Penuel and that, in turn, to Tirzah. After reigning for twenty-two years, Jeroboam was succeeded by his son Nadab, who was slain by Baasha in the first of nine successful attempts to overthrow a ruling family in the northern kingdom. By contrast, the Davidic line continued in Judah until the very end, with a single exception (the queen Athaliah). Rehoboam was succeeded by his son Abijam, and Asa followed him. Armed conflict between Baasha and Asa further depleted the treasury in Jerusalem's Temple, for Baasha's occupation of Ramah so threatened Jerusalem that Asa paid Ben-hadad of Damascus to come to his assistance. In the north, the kingdom passed from Baasha to his son Elah, but he was quickly murdered by Zimri, who fell to Omri after seven days. This event marked the beginning of a powerful dynasty in Israel, one that was so influential that Assyrian royal inscriptions referred to Israel as the house of Omri long after his dynasty had vanished.

The Omride Dynasty

Like David, Omri soon saw the wisdom in possessing his own private capital and acted accordingly. He purchased the hill of Samaria and established his rule there, although Omri and his successors seem to have maintained an Israelite base at Jezreel as well. Ivories discovered at Samaria dating from this period demonstrate the remarkable prosperity of this city; various prophetic narratives, especially those dealing with Elijah and Elisha, imply that such wealth was acquired at the expense of countless citizens. But some of it also came through military expeditions, particularly in Moab. Although the biblical account does not mention it, the famous Moabite stone tells about King Mesha's later recovery from Omri's victory over Moab. By the time Ahab, Omri's successor, came to power, Assyria began to flex its muscles. Ahab aligned his kingdom with Phoenicia through marriage with Jezebel, the daughter of King Ethbaal, and when Shalmaneser III invaded Syria-Palestine, Ahab joined a coalition of kings, including the powerful Syrian ruler, and they successfully resisted Assyria's advance at the battle of Karkar in 853. In the Assyrian records Ahab is said to have contributed two thousand chariots and ten thousand foot soldiers to the battle. The wealth this Israelite king had at his disposal enabled him to strengthen Samaria and to build stables for his vast chariotry. It seems likely that the conflict between rich and poor was rivaled by hostility between Canaanite and Israelite inhabitants

The Sargon Prism refers to King Omri and his capital city, Samaria. Although the Hebrew Bible virtually overlooks Omri's achievements, they were sufficiently impressive to lead Assyrian annalists to refer to Israel as "the house of Omri."

of Ahab's kingdom. The intense opposition to the worship of Baal probably owes its existence to this struggle, and Ahab was caught in the middle. He wanted to maintain both types of worship in his kingdom, and the Yahwistic prophets refused to sanction such tolerance even by one whose children bore Yahweh names (specifically, Ahaziah and Jehoram).* It was one of these prophets, Elisha, who took an active part in Jehu's bloody coup d'etat that overthrew the Omri dynasty. During the rule of the Omrids, Judah's power was dwarfed by the giant to the north, and Judah's rulers may have been looked upon as vassals to their counterparts in Israel. Jehoshaphat managed to increase Judah's holdings in the south and in Transjordan, but an ambitious effort to restore the Solomonic merchant fleet from Ezion-geber ended in disaster. Jehoshaphat's son Joram married the daughter or sister of Ahab, with fateful consequences. Ahaziah's short reign was followed by five years of rule by Athaliah, an Omrid. The priest Jehoiada brought her to a grisly end with a dagger, largely through popular support.

---

*Ahaziah and Jehoram contain, respectively, the suffix and prefix *yah*. This is a short form of the divine name Yahweh, which was used freely throughout the Hebrew Bible. Eventually, the name became so sacred that the word *Lord* was substituted for it during the reading of the Bible in synagogue worship. The vowels for the word *Lord* were written when vowels were added to the consonantal text, giving rise to the strange form Jehovah.

Jehu, King of Israel, is depicted on his knees before Shalmaneser III, the victorious sovereign to whom the spoils of war are being brought.

Jehu and the Rise of Assyria

Jehu's rule in the northern kingdom aimed at stamping out Baal worship, but subsequent events show how persistent this religion was in Israel. As late as a decade or two before Samaria's fall in 722, the prophet Hosea launched a vigorous campaign against Baalism. To secure his rule against all claimants to the Omrid dynasty, Jehu slaughtered all seventy sons of Ahab. However, Jehu's mightiest foe was to the east. By this time Assyria was becoming the dominant force in the ancient Near East. In 841, Shalmaneser III marched through Syria and Israel, taking vast sums of wealth from these countries. The Black Obelisk of Shalmaneser pictures Jehu prostrate before the Assyrian king. A few years later Adad-nirari III made a similar foray into Israel, receiving tribute from Jehoahaz or Jehoash. The latter of these kings plundered Jerusalem during Amaziah's kingship in Judah, and Jeroboam, successor to Jehoash, was able to expand the northern borders at Aram's expense. The reason was that Aram had its hands full with Hamath and Assyria. In the early years of Jehu's dynasty, Hazael of Aram had attacked Jerusalem and required Joash to empty the Temple of its gold as the price of sparing the city. Joash's successor in Judah, Amaziah, fought successfully against Edom, and his successor

This figure of Tiglath-pileser III (744–727) comes from the palace at Nimrud.
The Old Testament calls this Assyrian king Pul.

Azariah (Uzziah) made significant advances in southern Transjordan. It
was during his long reign that the prophet Amos ventured northward in
order to prophesy in Bethel. At some point in his fifty-two-year reign,
Uzziah contracted leprosy, and his son Jotham became coregent. The
well-known vision in Isaiah 6 occurred in connection with Uzziah's death
(c. 740).

Tiglath-pileser III ascended to the Assyrian throne about this time
(744). He wasted no time in overcoming resistence from the kingdom of
Urartu; then Pul, as the Old Testament writers call him, turned toward
Syria and Israel, leaving a trail of horror wherever he went. His policy
of calculated frightening, mass slaughter, and wholesale deportation was
intended to remove all opposition as speedily as possible. Israel at this
time suffered from internal unrest, one ruler replacing another in rapid

succession. Shallum killed Zechariah and lasted a month; his murderer, Menahem, paid tribute to Tiglath-pileser III, according to the Assyrian records. Opposition to Menahem led to his murder by Pekah, who, together with Rezin of Damascus, tried to persuade Ahaz of Judah to join them in resisting Assyria. Isaiah the prophet urged Ahaz to trust in Yahweh, but the king chose to enlist the aid of Tiglath-pileser. The result was disastrous for Israel, but in the process Judah's king became an Assyrian vassal. As for Israel, a large number of people were deported to Assyria. The so-called Syro-Ephraimite war left Israel greatly diminished in size and population. Hoshea became king and paid tribute to Shalmaneser V, before revolting against Assyria. This act of rebellion spelled Israel's doom. Shalmaneser besieged the city, and after a siege of about three years Samaria fell, either to Shalmaneser or to his successor, Sargon II. Assyrian records state that 27,290 inhabitants of Israel were deported, and in their place came people from Babylon, Hamath, and Cuthah.

Sennacherib's Invasion of Judah

Judah escaped deportation, but its rulers were wholly subordinate to Assyria's wishes and paid dearly in revenues. In 705, Hezekiah joined a coalition of Canaanite kings who revolted against Assyria. Four years later Sennacherib invaded Syria and Canaan, capturing the Philistine strongholds of Ashdod and Ashkelon and laying waste forty-six cities in Judah, including the important fortress at Lachish. Sennacherib's annals state that he shut up Hezekiah like a bird in a cage and that the king purchased Jerusalem's survival at tremendous cost. All his elaborate precautions to bring water into the city through a secret tunnel did not work out as planned; the Siloam Inscription gives an account of this remarkable engineering achievement. As late as 663, Assyria's long arm extended beyond Judah, even beyond Egypt's borders, for in this year Thebes fell to Assyria. As for the people of Judah, they watched while refugees from Israel fled into their midst and Assyrian forces occupied the city of Lachish and remained there for some time. Furthermore, this period was one of extensive religious syncretism; for some reason Judah's kings, Manasseh and Amon, actively promoted Assyrian worship. The former was summoned to Assyria during the reign of Esarhaddon; later speculation envisioned a repentance by Manasseh, whose long reign required some justification for the sake of those people who believed in divine justice. These pious people of the land placed a youthful Josiah on the throne when Assyria's star seemed to be fading.

The Decline of Assyria

A combination of things contributed to Assyria's decline. To begin with, it had overextended its reach. On the periphery, Psammetichus took the first step toward restoring Egypt to its former glory, and a few years later (c. 630–625) the Scythians invaded Syria. But the decisive force was nearer to home. The Babylonian Nabopolassar joined hands with the Medes, and together they captured Nineveh in 612. Assur-uballit II maintained a rump state at Haran until 609, a fateful year for Judah as well. The young king Josiah, who in 622 had inaugurated a sweeping religious reform aimed at centralizing worship in Jerusalem and at political autonomy, tried to prevent Necho of Egypt from going to Assyria's assistance or from plundering the spoil. The two kings met in the valley near Megiddo, and Necho slew Josiah. This Judean king's legacy was the destruction of all sanctuaries except Jerusalem and the elevation of the priests in the central place of worship at the expense of all other local priests. All of these measures were carried out in a conscious effort to establish a state on the model of a written constitution, presumably an early form of Deuteronomy. These measures, however, did not survive Josiah's death by very long. In these eventful years, the prophets Jeremiah and Habakkuk openly resisted royal policy. Nevertheless, the nationalist prophet Nahum described Nineveh's fall in extraordinarily powerful imagery. Zephaniah, too, spoke of the Deity's wrath in unforgettable poetic symbolism.

Judah's Fall to Babylon

Assyria's demise was hardly the good news Nahum thought it was, for Judah's destiny lay in the hands of Egypt and Babylon. After Josiah's death, the people appointed Jehoahaz king, but three months later Necho deposed him and placed Eliakim, whom he named Jehoiakim, on the throne. This king incurred Jeremiah's contempt, both for his pro-Egyptian policy and for his cruel measures of taxation that enabled him to pay Egyptian assessments and to build himself a grand palace. In 605, Nebuchadnezzar defeated the Egyptians at Carchemish, but the tide seemed to turn a few years later, prompting Jehoiakim to renew his allegiance with Egypt. In 598, Nebuchadnezzar besieged Jerusalem. Jehoiakim died, and Jehoiachin, his successor, was taken into exile in Babylon. With him also went large numbers of Judah's leading citizens, including the prophet Ezekiel. Nebuchadnezzar placed Mattaniah on the throne in Jerusalem, changing his name to Zedekiah. The vast wealth and sacred vessels that Nebuchadnezzar took from the Temple are mentioned in the Babylonian Chronicle, which also states that he named a new king over Jerusalem. This ruler, Zedekiah, remained loyal to Babylon for a few years, but in the end a misplaced trust in Egypt prompted him to revolt. Nebuchadnezzar moved into Judah and besieged the country. Lachish, Azekah, and Jerusalem held out for some time. A soldier's correspondence from Lachish reveals the desperate situation in those last days of the kingdom. He could no longer see the signals of Azekah, perhaps because the town had already fallen. Jerusalem did not survive very long, and Zedekiah's punishment was severe. The city fell in the spring of 587 or 586, and opportunistic Edomites profited from the events occasioned by this fall. Again inhabitants of Judah were taken to Babylon, and a rump state was set up by Nebuchadnezzar at Mizpah. Jeremiah accompanied the governor, Gedaliah, to this site, but a certain Ishmael soon murdered Gedaliah. Fearing reprisals from Babylonian officials, these terrified citizens then fled to Egypt, forcing Jeremiah to accompany them. On Egypt's frontier a colony of Israelites had already settled; official documents from this community at Elephantine have thrown considerable light on Israelite religion during the fifth century. Here in Egypt they worshiped two deities alongside Yahweh. Many of those citizens who were exiled from Judah to Babylon soon prospered, a fact that archives from Nippur confirm. They list the names of prominent Judeans involved in business transactions. The prophet Ezekiel carried on a prophetic ministry in Babylonia, where contact with new religious ideas gave rise to extensive theological reflection, greatly enriching biblical literature. Ancient traditions were now committed to writing, and a sacred history was composed. Here, too, the unknown author of Isaiah 40–55 announced the good news that gave renewed hope to those Judeans who longed for a return to Jerusalem.

The Rise of Persia

The return to Jerusalem was occasioned by the collapse of Babylon. Nebuchadnezzar was succeeded by Evil-Merodach, and he by Neriglissar, who in turn was followed by Labashi-Marduk. A more stable rule was inaugurated by Nabonidus in 555; he ruled until 539, when Babylon fell to Cyrus of Persia. Nabonidus was preoccupied with scholarly pursuits in his residence at Tema; his absence from Babylon created a situation in which priests of the god Marduk, angry because Nabonidus favored the worship of the god Sin, conspired against the king. When Cyrus advanced against Babylon he found the doors to the city wide open. Like Deutero-Isaiah,* these priests also proclaimed Cyrus their great emancipator. The events of this period are recorded on the Cyrus Cylinder.

With the coming of Persian rule (539–333) some distinct changes for the former inhabitants of Judah began to manifest themselves. According to the biblical account, the Edict of Cyrus commissioned the return of people and sacred vessels to Jerusalem and even made funds available for rebuilding the Temple. Because Cyrus's attitude toward other dispersed peoples accords with this account, scholars usually accept its accuracy. Thus began a long era of religious tolerance throughout the Per-

---

*Deutero-Isaiah is the name that scholars have given to the author of Isaiah 40–55. It means Second Isaiah, and refers to an unknown poet in Babylon about 540 B.C.E.

sian empire, which was divided into districts or satrapies, each with a governor who was responsible to the crown. Evidence is ambiguous about Judah; the area seems to have been included in Samaria until the time of Nehemiah, but Sheshbazzar is given a title that may imply that he was a governor. In any case, he assumed the task of reconstituting the community in Jerusalem. For some reason, he did not embark on the task of rebuilding the Temple, the stated reason for his return to Judah. That work did not begin until 521, when the prophets Haggai and Zechariah spurred the people to action despite economic hardship. The inspired workers completed the construction in short order, dedicating the new edifice in 516.

The Restored Community in Judah

The reconstitution of the community in Jerusalem was beset with difficulty from the outset. Very few people in Babylonia remembered Judah, and fewer still were willing to leave comfortable surroundings for an unknown future in faraway Judah. Those few who returned met stiff opposition from the people who had settled in Judah during the interval since Jerusalem fell to Babylonian soldiers. But the fiercest hostility came from the Samaritan community, which had extended its authority as far south as Jerusalem. Even the returning community seems to have been divided, to judge from apparent rivalry between Joshua and Zerubbabel alluded to in the Book of Zechariah. Priestly interests began to play an increasingly greater role in the life of the people. Zech. 6:9–15 even entertains the notion of a royal crown for the high priest Joshua. Perhaps the elevation of the Temple and its cult to the center of the universe was in part a response to a significant Persian innovation: temple personnel were required to pay revenues into the royal treasury rather than the other way around. Perhaps, too, the introduction of coins throughout the Persian empire facilitated the rise of a powerful priestly group in society, which amounted to a hierocracy.

The biblical attitude to Cyrus is puzzling. On the one hand, Deutero-Isaiah sings his praises and designates him the servant of Yahweh. On the other hand, Haggai and Zechariah are completely silent about Cyrus's part in rebuilding the Temple. The same goes for their attitude to Darius, who came to power in 521, precisely when the two prophets began their work. The story is very different in Ezra and Nehemiah, where great reliance on royal support is reported.

The sequence of these two figures in Jerusalem is a matter of debate. Nehemiah arrived in Judah in 445; his appointed mission was to rebuild the walls of Jerusalem, a feat that he accomplished in short order. At issue is Ezra's date; the problem arises from the fact that there were two rulers named Artaxerxes, one of whom is mentioned in the story about Ezra. Therefore two possible dates for Ezra's arrival in Jerusalem have been proposed: 458 and 398. His primary mission was to introduce the law of the Deity into daily life, particularly in cases of marriage between Judeans and foreigners. Ezra appealed to the written law in the Pentateuch prohibiting intermarriage. Accordingly, he forced the dissolution of such marriages regardless of the suffering this caused. Naturally, the narrow views represented by Ezra and Nehemiah brought them into open conflict with the Samaritan community, which broke off relations with the Jewish community at about this time, boasting a rival temple at Mount Gerizim and a rival version of the Law.

The Jewish Colony at Elephantine

Some documents from the Israelite colony in Elephantine help clarify this period. A temple of Yahu, a short form of Yahweh, Israel's God, existed on this island, but the people also worshipped the god Bethel and the goddess Anath. A letter from 407 to Bagoas, the Persian governor of Judah, reports on the destruction of their temple in 410 and requests permission to rebuild it. This letter states that a letter has also been sent to Sanballat the governor of Samaria. This information seems to suggest that Samaritans had not yet broken completely with the Jews in Jerusalem. Another letter mentions Johanan as high priest in Jerusalem in 408; according to Neh. 12:22 he was the grandson of the high priest Eliashib. This letter permits us to date Nehemiah with confidence.

The Hellenistic Empire

For the Jews, the Persian period was a time of flourishing literary activity, but a new power soon made its presence known, bringing about a conflict between East and West, Orient and Occident. Philip of Macedon was succeeded by his son Alexander, who crossed the Hellespont and defeated the Persian army under Darius II at Issus (333). Alexander proceeded to capture the important seaport of Tyre, and after that Egypt. It seemed that nothing could stop him when he went as far as the Indus River. Alexander's premature death in 323 left a vast empire in the hands of four successors who emerged to the forefront after two decades of fighting: (1) Cassander (Macedon); (2) Lysimachus (Asia Minor); (3) Ptolemy Lagi (Egypt); and (4) Seleucus Nicator (Syria and Mesopotamia). The Ptolemaic rule extended as far north as Judah until 198, when the Seleucids gained control. During the Ptolemaic era the Jews were unmolested though heavily taxed; according to a legendary account in the Epistle of Aristeas it was in Ptolemy II Philadelphus' reign that translation of the Torah into Greek (the Septuagint) was inaugurated. In 198, Antiochus III defeated the Ptolemies at Paneas. Then began a massive campaign to Hellenize the Jews, an effort which sharply divided the Jewish community. Antiochus IV Epiphanes increased the pressure to integrate

Judaism into the dominant culture. He sold the office of high priest to the highest bidder (Menelaus over Jason), and in 168 he offered swine to his god on the altar in the Temple at Jerusalem. The author of the Book of Daniel calls this act the abomination of desolation. Antiochus IV further proscribed the practice of Judaism; anyone caught with a copy of the Bible or observing rites such as sabbath and circumcision was executed. To enforce his decree Antiochus stationed his own troops in a section of Jerusalem, the Akra.

The Maccabean Revolt

The Maccabean revolt originated in the little village of Modin, when Mattathias, a priest, killed a Jew who was preparing to offer a sacrifice to the Syrian god, and a Syrian officer as well. Mattathias and his four

Clay jars in which some of the Dead Sea Scrolls were deposited for safekeeping during an unknown emergency. Many of these texts were written in the last two centuries B.C.E.

sons led the Jews in successful guerrilla warfare that eventually won complete independence. In December 165, the Maccabees celebrated the Feast of Dedication, which has been observed ever since as Hanukkah. A party of Hasidim supported these efforts to secure the survival of Judaism. Mattathias was succeeded by his son Judas, and he in turn was followed by his brother Jonathan, who supported various contenders for the Syrian throne. As reward, Jonathan was appointed high priest in 152, and ten years later Jerusalem's political freedom was assured. In 140, Simon was made high priest and commander of the army, thereby effectively uniting religion and politics. This was his compensation for the treacherous murder of his brother. Another assassination left John Hyrcanus on the throne from 134 to 104; during the period of his successor, Alexander Jannaeus (103–76), Judah waged wars to enlarge the kingdom to its former glory under David. Salome Alexandra ruled from 76 to 67, a time of prosperity for the Pharisees, one of two religious parties that had recently emerged to prominence. The other party was the Sadducees, who were more priestly in attitude. From 67 to 63, Hyrcanus II and Aristobulus contended for the Hasmonaean kingdom (Antipater, the father of Herod, supported Hyrcanus). Both Hyrcanus and Aristobulus offered a bribe to Pompey, who promptly moved to annex Judah into the Roman empire. Following Herod's rule and that of later procurators, two revolts against Roman rule (66–70 C.E.; 132–135 C.E.) brought the Jewish state to an end. But the literature that these people had composed continued to influence an emerging rabbinic community as well as a new group that arose in its midst, the Christians.

◆ PART ONE ◆

THE TORAH

T HE first division of the Hebrew Bible—called the Torah, the Pentateuch, or the Law—consists of five books: Genesis, Exodus, Leviticus, Numbers, and Deuteronomy. As early as the first decade in the second century B.C.E. this division was called the Torah. Although this word is often translated "law," it has a much broader connotation. Its origin is connected with the Hebrew verb which means "to throw," and by extension the noun form suggests something that is cast in a particular direction, namely, instruction for learners. Hence, "teaching" is an appropriate translation for the word *torah* in many of its contexts. Therefore, it will be helpful to examine both senses of the word before moving on to the individual books in this initial division of the Bible.

LAW IN THE ANCIENT NEAR EAST

The origins of law antedate Moses by more than a thousand years. Various economic texts from Shuruppak and Lagash reflect Sumerian legal procedures from the middle of the third millennium. From about the same time comes an account of a reform by Urukagina (twenty-fourth century), and four centuries later a law code has survived in fragmentary form (the code of Ur-Nammu, c. 2000 B.C.E.). Legal documents from Mari (1800–1700) and the law codes of Lipit Ishtar (c. 1870) and Eshnunna (eighteenth century) are rivaled only by the famous law code of Hammurabi (c. 1700). Hurrian economic and legal texts from Nuzi derive from two centuries later, as also do Hittite laws and Kassite legal texts from Assyria. Then there are numerous Middle Assyrian laws from about 1200–1100, as well as later comparable Neo-Babylonian texts. Eventually law codes were associated with Shamash, the sun god, although the laws themselves provide many indications that they sprang from custom and legal precedents within society. No law code has survived in Egypt, but the "Ad-

33

monitions of an Egyptian Sage" report that law books were thrown into
the streets during a revolution, a fact which suggests that codes of law
did in fact exist there. However, it is significant that the distinctive role
of the pharaoh would have made law codes irrelevant, because it was
believed that the deity ruled the land. This belief naturally meant that
the divine will for society did not have to be reduced to written form.
The conservative nature of Egyptian culture may also have militated
against the creation of law codes, which often were associated with reform
movements.

The law codes within Exodus, Leviticus, and Deuteronomy derive
from many different settings and periods. Much of the material comes
from a time before the Israelites occupied the land of Canaan and seems
largely to have been borrowed from the people who lived there prior to
Israel's entry. Other law codes reflect priestly interests in later Israel,
and still other laws are characterized by strong humanitarian concerns.
In some respects—for example, the *lex talionis* ("an eye for an eye and
a tooth for a tooth")—Israel's law resembles ancient codes such as Hammurabi's. The Assyrian laws were harsher in one instance, the practice
of physical mutilation, but Israel's laws are generally rather severe.

It is this aspect of law that eventually prevailed within certain Christian
circles, the Pauline, as opposed to those traditions associated with James,
the brother of Jesus. In Paul's view the Law was a heavy burden that
weighed down the believer, and Jesus offered deliverance from the bondage of a salvation through works. The attitude to the Law that one encounters in the Psalms and in Sirach (Ecclesiasticus) does not have the
slightest element of such negative thinking. Instead, this material celebrates the giving of the Law as a happy occasion, and expresses un-
ceasing gratitude for this matchless gift. Indeed, certain psalmists meditate on the joy of keeping the Law, which bestows life and happiness.
In later Judaism a desire to build a hedge around the Law manifested
itself, for the sages did not want to break the Law in any manner what-
soever. Even the author of the Gospel of Matthew has Jesus say that he
came not to destroy the Law but to fulfill it, however that Greek verb is
to be understood.

LIBERATION

Perhaps it is important that the Sinaitic legislation through Moses is
placed after an account of liberation and thus represents an expression
of the redeemer's intention for a rescued society. At the heart of the Torah
lies this decisive event, the deliverance from bondage in Egypt. Here,
as in certain aspects of biblical prophecy, the central theme of liberation
shines through, so that wherever there are oppressed people the Bible
addresses them with a word of hope. That message is the assurance that
the Deity hears their cry of affliction. The Law came later as a sign of

continued presence on the part of the savior; it represents the condition on which divine favor depends in the future.

The liberation event was more than an exodus from Egypt, for it represented the fulfillment of ancient promises of a land and progeny that would enable the people of God to bless humanity. Hence the act of liberation served to demonstrate divine integrity; by this deliverance from bondage into the land of promise, the Deity showed faithfulness against strong resistence. The refusal to submit to divine leadership, however, was not restricted to the oppressor, for it also characterized those people who came out of Egypt. This theme occupies a prominent place in the story of salvation, which reports that the Israelites complained constantly during their journey from bondage into freedom.

The promise was first given to the ancestors of these oppressed people, and it gave birth to sacred memory. This family history had its dark moments, like all family histories, and there seems to have been no conscious effort at covering up such unpleasant recollections. What is astonishing is that the people who called themselves Israel admitted to being latecomers on the historical scene. Thus there was a long period when Israel was absent from the table of nations. Because the nation Israel rarely played a significant part in the course of events that engulfed the Fertile Crescent, this admission seems particularly apt.

Nevertheless, Israel's Deity was believed to have created the arena within which the drama of liberation played itself out. Like its neighbors, Israel understood this creative event in two different ways, perhaps in three ways. Either the universe came into being as a result of a battle against the forces of choas, or it was created by a transcendent One who merely spoke the world into existence. A third concept in Egypt, Mesopotamia, and Canaan depicts the Deity as "begetter" of heaven and earth. That is the widespread belief that male and female principles conjoined to procreate the universe.

The Torah is the scripture par excellence in modern Judaism, and the other two divisions simply reflect its radiance to a greater or lesser extent. Perhaps that is true to some degree in Christianity as well, for it is precisely in this arena that the battle has been waged over the appropriateness of using the critical approach to scripture. To the extent that such controversies arise from a desire for power, conscious or otherwise, it is merely carrying on the struggle represented by various priestly groups who sought to elevate Aaron within the Torah, even at Moses' expense.

◆ 1 ◆

Genesis

THE first book of the Hebrew Scriptures is appropriately called Genesis, for it deals with beginnings. The scope of the book extends from creation to the death of Joseph in Egypt. Between these two events, the beginning of all things and the end of the patriarchs, come stories of alienation, self-aggrandizement, lust, divine punishment, and compassion. The initial eleven chapters embrace all humanity, giving the appearance of universality and even timelessness, whereas the remaining chapters focus on the special history of a single family. Nevertheless, that narrowing down of the narrator's interest did not remove the events from the scene of world history, but in the end it thrust the father and sons into the Egyptian royal court where history was made. This unlikely place became the crucible within which a religion and a nation were forged.

Significant episodes in the primeval history (chapters 1–11) include murder (fratricide), a story about a bigamist who sought revenge, a tale about lustful heavenly beings, an account of a flood, and a narrative about frustrated efforts to build a tower to heaven. The patriarchal narratives (chapters 12–36) consist of three cycles: stories about Abraham, Sarah, and Lot; stories about Isaac; and stories about Jacob, Esau, and Laban. The final chapters of the book describe the experiences of Jacob's children, with special attention to Joseph (chapters 37 and 39–50) and Judah, or more correctly Tamar (chapter 38). The opening verse affirms a creative act that gave shape and light to chaotic matter, and the closing verse reports on the last of the patriarchs who lies in a dark coffin in Egypt, the country that became a symbol for chaos in later literature.

This story of the human race, which becomes ever more focused until one married couple and their descendants occupy center stage, is structured by a series of genealogical formulas (Gen. 2:4; 5:1; 6:9; 10:1; 11:10; 11:27; 25:9; 25:12; 36:1,9; 37:2). In some cases these formulas occur at decisive turning points—for example, creation, the flood, the confusion

37

of languages, the selection of Abraham, the divergent line from Abraham, and the transition to the second level of patriarchs. Other instances of the formula seem to reaffirm the genealogical line that has already been given. Occasional stories underline the concern for purity in the blood line, as when Abraham takes great care to secure a wife for Isaac from his own larger family in Mesopotamia rather than choosing a local Canaanite woman, or when Esau, ever eager to please his father, avoids union with Canaanites by marrying Ishmael's daughter.

AUTHORSHIP

This attempt to give a meaningful structure to the book has failed to conceal the many indications of multiple authorship: doublets, contradictions, and differences in style, vocabulary, and theology. To be sure, the entire Pentateuch (Genesis through Deuteronomy) was attributed to Moses by the late fifth or early fourth century B.C.E. when the Chronicler* lived, and this tradition of Moses' authorship is further attested in the Septuagint. This view prevailed during the New Testament era, when the Law (Torah) was almost automatically associated with Moses. Occasional reservations about the appropriateness of Moses describing his own death were made by Jewish writers (Philo, Josephus) and sharp attacks came from pagan polemicists (Celsus, Porphyry), but the situation had changed little as late as the Middle Ages when the Jewish scholar Ibn Ezra cautiously drew attention to features of the text that clearly reflected a situation long after Moses' death. With the birth of modern criticism, these troublesome aspects of the text soon made the traditional view of Mosaic authorship untenable.

Some things about the Pentateuch cause one to wonder how it was ever possible to think of Moses as the author. Of first importance is the frequent expression "until this day." Similarly, the author, who always speaks about Moses in the third person, observes that the Canaanites were then in the land, which obviously reflects a time long after Moses when David and Solomon had finally succeeded in defeating the original inhabitants of the land. Furthermore, the narrator's orientation is invariably that of someone who is living west of the Jordan River. Events that are located across the river take place in Transjordan, although Moses is said never to have set foot on the western banks. Moreover, anachronisms occasionally demonstrate the lateness of the text in question. For example, references to kings in the land and allusions to towns like Dan can only have arisen after these phenomena became reality, events which occurred considerably later than Moses.

*The Chronicler is the unknown author of First and Second Chronicles and possibly also of Ezra and Nehemiah.

Doublets and Inconsistencies

There is much within Genesis itself that points to multiple strata. Perhaps the presence of doublets and contradictions is most damaging to the claim of unitary authorship. At the outset two distinct creation stories confront the reader, each with its own peculiar vocabulary, style, and view. Even within the first account of creation (1:1–2:4a) earlier traditions remain unassimilated, for eight acts of creation are here forced into a strange pattern calling for seven days, and creation by a word vies with creation by deed. The perspective is altogether different from that of the second creation narrative (2:4b–25). Water is the antagonistic element in the first creation story, and it is the catalyst in the narrative about life emerging at a desert oasis; the former story has "male and female" emerge in divine likeness as the final creative act, apart from the institution of the sabbath, but the latter story has the man precede the forming of animals and woman. In the first account the creator pronounces a solemn assessment of each creative work, culminating in the emphatic assertion that everything was exceptionally good. The second creation story has the man utter an ecstatic shout over the suitability of woman for his needs. In the first account the Deity is transcendent, removed from any contact except verbal, whereas the second story emphasizes divine nearness in very concrete ways: the Lord God shapes man from dust, breathes life into his nostrils, performs the first surgical operation, and eagerly provides for the needs of the first earth creature.

Doublets also occur within the patriarchal narratives, and they do not always seem to function to give literary emphasis. Abraham receives what appear to be two divine calls, Sarah drives Hagar and son into the wilderness twice, the name Beer-sheba is explained in two different ways, and Abraham passes Sarah off as his sister twice. In themselves these apparent doublets do not mean very much, but when contradictions are also taken into account, it is difficult to think that a single author could have written such an inconsistent narrative. Two different versions about Joseph's initial misfortune lie behind the surviving tale, a situation which is confusing, to say the least. Who tried to rescue Joseph? Judah or Reuben? And who eventually laid hands on him, and by what means? Ishmaelites or Midianites? Within the primeval history doublets occur most noticeably in the flood story, the details of which are hopelessly confused. How many animals was Noah commanded to take on the ark? Two of each kind or seven pairs of all clean animals? And how long did the flood last? Forty days or 150 days? What brought on the flood? Rain or a combination of rain and the upsurging of underground springs? Sometimes the different combined traditions produce ludicrous results, as when Hagar is depicted as placing Ishmael in her arms and then leaving the thirteen-year-old "infant" by a bush to die, or when an old Abraham who is beyond hope for progeny becomes rejuvenated sufficiently to propel him in search of a new wife. At times the laughter is more like that of Sarah, who is described as having laughed on two different occasions when hearing that she would again have pleasure that would fulfill the promise of a son.

Inconsistencies sometimes extend over more than one book. According to Gen. 4:26 people began during Enosh's time to address the Deity in prayer with the name Yahweh, but the second creation story had already made use of the name, coupled with the more general word for deity. Between this story of creation and Enosh's day, the narrator freely uses the name Yahweh and even places it in Eve's mouth: "I have gotten a man with the help of the Lord" (4:1).* However, the Book of Exodus has two entirely different pronouncements about the first use of the name. In the story about the divine manifestation to Moses in a bush that was not consumed by fire the name Yahweh is first revealed, and a firm link with older terminology is made. However, in Exod. 6:2–3 it is specifically stated that the name Yahweh was withheld from the patriarchs and was first made known to Moses: "And God said to Moses, 'I am the Lord. I appeared to Abraham, to Isaac, and to Jacob, as God Almighty, but by my name the Lord I did not make myself known to them.' " This notice that links the divine name Yahweh to Moses is probably correct historically, for there is some evidence that Moses' father-in-law may have introduced him to the worship of Yahweh, the deity of the Kenites. Prior to Moses' adoption of this name and the religion that accompanied it, El Shaddai is said to have been the normal designation of the Deity.

Differences in Style and Theology

Besides these indications of diverse strata within Genesis and throughout the Pentateuch, stylistic differences and theological divergences also betray the hands of more than one author. Lively description and energetic dialogue find their opposite in dull prose that amounts to little more than a series or list; more importantly, certain topics such as genealogies, cultic ritual, and laws dealing with clean and unclean things always occur where this sort of style does. When clear differences in theology also correspond to stylistic divergencies, the natural conclusion is that more than one tradition is present. That supposition seems irrefutable where precise preferences of vocabulary also characterize these literary strata, such as different names for the Deity, for the sacred mountain on which Moses received the law (Sinai and Horeb), for Moses' father-in-law (Hobab and Jethro), for the inhabitants of the land (Canaanites and Amorites), and even different Hebrew words for the same maidservant.

Two Strata

These significant features of the book suggest that at least two basic literary strata are discernible. Here and there indications of yet another

*The Revised Standard Version translators render the name Yahweh as Lord.

stratum manifest themselves, but seldom with sufficient force to demand the hypothesis of a continuous independent tradition as opposed to supplementary editing on the part of an unknown individual. Stated another way, this incomplete stratum has been combined with the more comprehensive layer similar to it, so that often it is difficult to distinguish the one from the other. As for the third stratum, its style is so distinctive that its scope has been fixed with a great degree of certainty. These strata do not confine themselves to Genesis, but extend throughout Exodus, Leviticus, and Numbers. One of them, the livelier prose stratum, seems to reach into the opening chapter of Judges, and the other has been attached to the Book of Deuteronomy (chapters 32–33), which constitutes still another literary stratum. Modern scholarship labels these strata the Yahwist, the Elohist, the Priestly stratum (or source), and the Deuteronomist. The first two are distinguished from one another by the divine names they use. Although the Priestly stratum also uses the name Elohim, it has seemed better to designate it by its main emphasis. Because the remaining stratum coincides with the Book of Deuteronomy, except for the two chapters mentioned above, it goes by the siglum D. Abbreviations for the others are widely used as well: J for the Yahwist, E for the Elohist, and P for the Priestly stratum. The J derives from the initial letter of the German word for Yahwist,* and it also signifies Judah as its place of origin, just as E stands for Ephraim as its original setting. In other words, the two strata arose in separate geographical areas, J in the south and E in the north.

The Oldest Layer

Scattered clues here and there have given rise to the suggestion that the oldest stratum (J) arose shortly after the death of Solomon and offered a defense of the Davidic kingship. This argument rests on an assumption that poetic allusions to David's dynasty and to specific incidents like the suppression of Moabites and Edomites reflect the author's actual historical situation. Similarly, an enigmatic reference to Edom's attempt to shake free from Judean dominance is understood as an event during Solomon's reign, and the divine promise to make Abraham's name great is related (dubiously) to the prophecy by Nathan assuring David a dynasty. These obscure clues are supported by arguments about the grand view of history that permeates the story and by an understanding of events that is said to reflect court ideas of all Israel as a single nation. Because there is no awareness of an Assyrian threat, it is generally thought that the Yahwistic layer took shape before the battle of Karkar (853). None of this evidence is decisive, and the admission that a later bloc of material has entered the Yahwistic layer (Genesis 18) raises the possibility that such allusions to specific events in David and Solomon's day may be redactional glosses. It is even possible that these two layers of tradition

*The classic source theory was developed by German scholars, who have done pioneer research in many areas of biblical studies over the last two centuries.

had already come together prior to David's ascension to the throne. Although the characteristic hostility toward Canaanites that occurs in this tradition is similar to the exclusivism of the postexilic community, it also fits the period described in the Elijah stories when a sharp separation between followers of Baal and those of Yahweh was required. Critics therefore usually date the Elohist about 750, largely because of a prophetic ethic that resembles views of eighth-century figures like Amos, Hosea, and Isaiah. Naturally, the assumption of a northern origin requires a date before 722.

The Latest Layer

The Priestly layer presupposes Deuteronomy, which usually is associated at some stage with Josiah, for it takes for granted a single sanctuary at Jerusalem. Because the story leaves the Israelites on the eastern side of the Jordan, it seems to point to exiles who also were poised to enter the land once more. Furthermore, the centrality of the high priest in this stratum seems to reflect a situation later than Zechariah, where governor and priest are thought to be functioning jointly. The fully developed cultic system that this layer presents is the product of many centuries, and Ezra is often said to have carried the Priestly legislation "in his hand." For these reasons, the usual dating of this stratum is the sixth or early fifth century, certainly before the Samaritan schism, because this religious community accepted the Torah as scripture.

Nevertheless, a distinction between the age of composition and the age of the material within the stratum is essential, for there is much within the Priestly stratum that is quite early. The same goes for the other strata, each of which contains very old material that circulated orally for centuries. Perhaps some of the specific traditions were actually written down prior to their collection into the greater strata indicated here by J, E, D, and P. The advantage rested with the final redactor, insofar as shaping the entire literary complex is concerned. The Priestly editor achieved a structure largely by means of an artificial chronology, at first devoted to family lineage and later arranged according to an itinerary, the journey from Egypt to the land of promise. It is usually claimed that this author developed a scheme of four covenants (creation, Noah, Abraham, Moses). Only two of these are actually associated with a covenant, the Noachian covenant that speaks of the rainbow as its sign, and the covenant with Abraham, symbolized by circumcision. The first was universal, hence the visible sign the world over, and the second was restricted to the Jewish people, at least as a special religious act. The sabbath was linked with creation, and the Mosaic law with Sinai. These four things distinguished Israel from the other peoples during the exile and later: the Mosaic Torah, circumcision, sabbath observance, and an assumption that the rest of the world also stood in a special, although different relationship to Yahweh.

The Possibility of Supplementation

The preceding observations have by no means resolved all the problems that Genesis poses on its own, or in combination with the four books immediately following. As a matter of fact, it is entirely possible that the various strands of tradition came together in circles where they were preserved and that separate literary sources never actually existed. In that case, one would speak of strata with their own vocabulary and style, and the Torah would have arisen by a process of accumulation, one stratum supplementing another. In favor of ever smaller strands of tradition is the fact that both the Yahwistic stratum and the Priestly stratum drew upon divergent traditions. It therefore follows that a complex tradition of growth lies behind the larger strata, and many different traditions have left their mark on the Pentateuch. In many instances respect for other traditions has resulted in the preservation of conflicting material that must surely have been just as obvious to later redactors as it is to modern readers. In some instances, such doublets and even divergent accounts gave an entirely different perspective and were therefore deemed worthy of retention. An excellent example of this use of doublets is found in the two different stories about creation. Who would dare to claim that the Book of Genesis would be richer by dropping one of these narratives? Nevertheless, this literary response to the presence of inconsistencies hardly resolves the problem treated above, for a certain unevenness exists that only a supposition of diverse strata adequately explains.

COMPOSITION

So far the actual process of growth that produced the Book of Genesis and the other books in the Torah has not occupied our attention. How did this larger complex of traditions take shape? The place to begin is the tradition complex—those larger blocks of material that together make up the Pentateuch, or as some scholars prefer, Tetrateuch (alternatively, Hexateuch).* In brief, the tradition complexes are the primeval history, patriarchal narratives, the Exodus, wilderness, Sinai, and conquest traditions, Deuteronomy remaining an entity unto itself. There seems to be general consensus that these traditions comprise the Torah, but considerable controversy surrounds all efforts to explain how these separate complexes arose and came together.

Cultic Confessions or Collections of Stories?

One theory, which until recently has enjoyed wide support, is that the traditions dealing with patriarchs, the Exodus, wilderness, and conquest

---

*The prefixes imply a collection of five books (*Penta*teuch), four (*Tetra*teuch), or six (*Hex-ateuch*).

emerged in a context of cultic confession at the sanctuary in Gilgal in connection with the Feast of Weeks and that the Sinai tradition arose separately at the cult in a covenant feast at Shechem, until the Yahwist eventually joined these together and inserted the primeval history as a preface to the story of promise and fulfillment that this creative theologian fashioned from independent tradition complexes. This view is partially supported by a variant interpretation that emphasizes the merging of the several tradition units prior to the Yahwist and denies the existence of a conquest tradition to all Israel. According to this approach, the first four books of the Bible are considered a unit, and Deuteronomy is joined to the four books that follow. For both views, the cult played the dominant role in shaping the tradition complexes. Another view, much older, is that the narratives in Genesis were conceived in the imaginations of professional storytellers and achieved final form through constant telling and retelling of sages. Recently, a proposal to attribute the literary fusion of these tradition complexes to the Yahwist has been marshalled, thus reinforcing the explanation for the Torah in terms of saga. This interpretation extends beyond the sagas in Genesis to the traditions of Midian and the Exodus. In short, the cult played a vital role in one theory, saga in the opposing view.

The former hypothesis has become problematic for two important reasons. First, the confessional statements in Deut. 26:5b–6 and 6:20–25 and in Josh. 24:2b–13 (also appearing in Psalm 136) are now known to represent the final stage in the development. Hence, the outline of the events that comprise the Hexateuch which appears in these cultic texts actually derives from the sacred story rather than giving rise to it. Second, the Sinai bloc, which clearly was inserted into its present context and interrupts the natural flow of the story, cannot realistically be separated from the other tradition complexes. The absence of a primeval history from the creeds presents less of a problem, for it does not belong to the specific history of Israel that is recited in the cult. Two explanations for the missing Sinai material have arisen, neither of which is satisfactory. The first suggests that the Sinai tradition belonged to a separate feast, but all memory of it has vanished. This explanation merely points to the basic flaw in the theory, for such an important festival would certainly have left traces in the literature. The other explanation begins with parallels from ancient treaties, where a historical prologue often set out the context in which the treaties became binding. According to this view, the confessions in Deuteronomy and Joshua function like these specific elements in vassal treaties; they therefore provide the historical prologue of an agreement that becomes explicit in the Sinai legislation. But in these parallels from vassal treaties the actual stipulations follow the prologue, thus destroying the analogy.

Each attempt to explain the origin of the tradition complexes is useful, even if neither provides an adequate account of the final literary product.

Although the particular creeds alluded to above represent the culmination of a process, there can be little doubt that liturgical compositions arose in various sanctuaries and developed into complex traditions through frequent recital. The Priestly account of creation and the passover narrative in Exodus seem to reflect extensive liturgical use, and other examples easily come to mind. A similar judgment also applies to the explanation for the tradition units as the result of sagas. Many stories, especially in Genesis, give little indication of use in liturgical circles, whereas they have all the markings of professional narration with entertainment as the primary goal. Originally, these sagas functioned to give pleasure, often at the expense of neighbors, and to express an awareness of family history. Some of the stories sought to offer explanations for various unusual phenomena, and therefore they constitute elementary teaching.

An Original Thinker?

If, indeed, both of these explanations for tradition complexes possess a measure of validity, the decisive question then becomes, how did such disparate traditions as those centered in cultic sanctuaries and those comprising a storyteller's repertoire come together? It seems essential to posit the existence of at least one individual who wove the various independent units into a single account of destiny shaped by divine action. This conviction that history from the very beginning resisted its real goal and was rescued only by divine intervention may well have grown out of cultic apologetic for a given political regime, but many elements from ancient sagas paved the way for this elevation of a single dynasty. Together, cult and saga constructed a story of the past that placed the present at a favorable point in the arc that joined together promise and fulfillment.

Traditional answers to the question about creative personalities behind the final literary work have isolated three figures who shaped the Genesis material, although as we have seen one of these is hardly more than a shadow. Whether these three are understood as individuals or as circles of thought matters very little in the long run. In any event, distinctive styles and theologies point to characteristics of these three dominant influences, and a closer examination of the Yahwist, Elohist, and Priestly writer is essential to an adequate understanding of Genesis.

THE YAHWIST

The Yahwistic stratum understands history in global terms. Its scope begins with the entire human race, narrows down to a single family, and follows the course of history as it unfolds to implement a divine promise of land, progeny, and blessing. In Genesis the threat to this promise is a central motif; this threat assumes various forms. The patriarch abandons the land in search of food, and while in Egypt he entrusts his wife to the pharaoh, who makes her a member of his harem, thus endangering the promise of descendants. Abraham's moral impoverishment constitutes a curse for the pharaoh and endangers the blessing. Unwilling to wait patiently for the fulfillment of the promise about progeny, Abraham introduces strife into the family scene by fathering a son by a concubine. Similar threats arise in the strife between Jacob and Esau, who threatens to kill the legitimate heir, who in turn forsakes the land in search of sanctuary. The Joseph stories combine both types of threat, fraternal hostility and abandonment of the land.

Within the primeval history the Yahwist's own theological understanding achieves unparalleled heights. Creation promptly ensued in a fall, and sin spread rapidly throughout the land until decisive action to check it was required. The extent of sin's pervasiveness can be seen in Cain's murder of his brother Abel, Lamech's cry for seventy-seven-fold revenge, and the seizure of human mates by heavenly creatures (the only example of unassimilated mythic material in the Hebrew Bible). The flood is presented as the Lord's attempt to stop this spread of sin that had invaded even heaven, but the story about what seems to be a homosexual act on Canaan's part ("he gazed on his father's nakedness," a euphemism) and the narrative about the tower of Babel show how recalcitrant sin is, even when the Deity tries to eradicate it.

Ancient parallels to the general scheme of the Yahwist exist in the Atrachasis epic and Sumerian King List.* Nevertheless, the Yahwist often moves beyond the simple presentation of the Deity to include elements of compassion and mystery. The two sides, human worth and divine justice, are held in tension, and care is taken to communicate the compassion of the Lord for oppressed people. Because of this feature in the narrative, characters such as Lot, Jacob, and Joseph possess freshness and realism. Lot may have been greedy, but he took the hospitality code with utter seriousness: once he had invited someone into his house, he was willing to go to any lengths to protect that guest, even to sacrificing his daughters' virtue. Jacob was indeed a trickster, but he was also treated unjustly by Laban, who substituted his less desirable daughter in marriage for the one whom Jacob loved and who cheated him out of his wages. While Joseph lacked tact where his brothers and father were concerned, he did not deserve the harsh treatment that the brothers and Potiphar extended to him. In short, the Yahwist manages to paint both sides of the story rather than giving simple characterizations. The Deity is also far more mysterious than one might gather from the picture of a Deity who molds

*W. G. Lambert and A. Millard, *Atra-hasis: The Babylonian Story of the Flood* (Oxford: Oxford University Press, 1969).

dust into a human and breathes life into the earthling. Nowhere is this fact clearer than in the story of the first sin.

The Fall

The clever link between the second narrative about creation and the story of the Fall, a play on the words for naked and subtle, functions to remove any temporal distance between the two chapters. Creation and fall belong together, with no long period of dreaming innocence between the two. Dialogue and narrative alternate until the episode ends in a divine reflection about fallen human nature, an observation that breaks off and is replaced by narrative. This story of the first sin demonstrates unusual psychological and religious insight, together with a subtlety of language. The opening dialogue between the woman and the serpent establishes the parameters of the discussion: is the Deity tyrannical? That problem is the implication of the serpent's question, and the overstatement is calculated to make the woman think she has nothing to fear from this uninformed serpent. Nevertheless, her response indicates that she feels the necessity of adding further strictures to the divine prohibition, lest she be sorely tempted. So the prohibition against eating has now become one against the mere touching of the fruit. The serpent's response plants the seed of doubt in the woman's mind: "You will not die." Opposing assertions now require her to choose between the two, which necessitates a careful assessment of the advantages and disadvantages of each. In this rational assessment, the Deity's threat fades into oblivion when the fruit's desirability is examined from various perspectives—the sensual, the aesthetic, and the cognitive. Naturally, she acts on this considered judgment, and so does her passive male partner, whose role demonstrates sin's generosity and sociality.

The immediate consequence of this act seems to indicate that the two made the right choice, for their eyes were indeed opened and they became conscious of being exposed. If the serpent had divulged only partial truth, the Deity had actually departed from the truth, for death did not come that day. Instead nakedness and shame made their appearance, so that when the Deity came down for a stroll in the cool of the evening, the two disobedient humans hid in the midst of the trees where their sin had occurred. Dialogue then surfaces once more, this time with the Deity as a partner in conversation. Curiously, the divine summons comes to the man, who quickly implicates himself in guilt by an admission of nakedness and shame. When his offense becomes known, the man shifts the blame to the woman, who in turn accuses the serpent. Because the hidden implication of the man's answer is an implicit accusation against the Deity who brought the woman to him, the serpent has no one on whom to cast the blame.

A series of curses follow, here presented as punishment for disobe-

A cylinder seal from the third millennium. It has the image of a tree flanked by a god and a woman, behind whom is a snake. In the ancient Near East snakes represented the mysterious powers of procreation and rejuvenation (healing).

dience. They reverse the order of the dialogue; the first curse falls on the serpent, the second on the woman, and the last on the ground from which man was taken and to which he will return. Each one of these curses seeks to answer the child's question, "why?" In other words, why does a serpent crawl on its belly, and why do humans dread snakes so much? Why do women retain sexual desire despite dominating husbands and pain during childbirth? Why is the earth so resistant to human efforts toward cultivation? And most importantly, why do people die and decay? The human response to these curses hovers on the thin line between defiance and submission. The man calls the woman Eve, which contains a play on the word *life*. The anomaly is that the one who is thought to have brought death has lost no stature in her husband's eyes. Still, the narrator reports, a compassionate Deity provides a means of concealing nakedness and thereby reduces the sense of shame, although this act of mercy costs an animal its life.

The story concludes with the Deity's solemn declaration that the serpent's claim about open eyes making one like the gods was a correct reading of the situation. A deeper sense lurks behind this phrase about becoming like God, knowing good and evil (presumably everything). In the episode about Enkidu, which appears in the *Gilgamesh Epic*, a harlot lass, successful at seducing this creature who preferred animals as companions to humans, declares that through the sexual encounter Enkidu has become like the gods. In Genesis virtually all traces of a sexual understanding of the first sin have disappeared, and the offense is presented as much broader, although certainly less specific. The final act on the Deity's part seems less intended to protect divine prerogatives than to prevent humans from living forever in their alienated state. Hence, the exclusion of the man, here used collectively, from the garden of Eden is actually an expression of divine compassion.

The Mesopotamian Flood Story

The narrative that follows the Fall justifies the assessment that alienation must not be allowed to become eternal. Brother slays brother over an arbitrary choice on the Deity's part; revenge consumes wronged individuals; lust engulfs the "sons of God," until the Deity intervenes. Despite the sinful display, Yahweh matches it with compassion. Even Cain receives an identifying sign that protects him from wanton slaying. Eventually punishment falls on a sinful world, virtually extinguishing humankind. This flood story has its prototype in the *Gilgamesh Epic*, where the hero of this narrative goes in search of eternal life, ultimately arriving at the residence of Utnapishtim, the survivor of the flood. This worthy figure, having been granted unending life, tells Gilgamesh about the deluge that the gods sent as punishment for excessive noise. One deity, the god of wisdom, leaked the information to Utnapishtim and urged him to build a boat. In this account the eventual resting place of the ship was Mount Nitsir, and Utnapishtim offered a sacrifice after the waters receded. The parallels between the two stories extend to the sending out of birds, but decisive differences also occur. Whereas the Mesopotamian deities crowd like flies around the sacrifice, Yahweh is content to smell the aroma; whereas the biblical story sets the flood in the context of judgment for sin, the Mesopotamian account emphasizes the need for sleep on the part of the older gods. One significant difference concerns the survivor of the flood and an occasion of divine favor; Noah found favor in the Deity's eyes but remained mortal, but Utnapishtim acquired a twig from the tree of life. The mighty Gilgamesh, who managed by superhuman effort to reach the tree of life, was not so lucky. The hero plucked a branch from this rejuvenating source, only to have a serpent steal it from him in an unguarded moment. Had Gilgamesh devoured the branch at the time of acquisition, as the serpent did, he would not have been forced to watch as the thief shed its skin and slithered away.

The Tower of Babel

In the Yahwist's view, drastic punishment for sin failed to achieve its goal, and the Deity swore never to repeat this response to disobedience. The rainbow is taken as a visible sign that life can go on despite human sinfulness. The story about Noah's drunkenness indicates that evil has survived the deluge, and that point is repeated in the narrative about the confusion of languages. The background for this story is a special kind of temple tower in Mesopotamia, which was called a ziggurat. Since the people being described in the story originally came from the mountains, they built temple towers for worshipping their gods. An echo of this building activity is heard in the biblical story, which interprets such endeavors as manifestations of pride. Humans achieve unity and aspire to make a name for themselves by constructing a tower to heaven. Twice they summon helpers with the words, "Come, let us . . . ." Their success alarms the Deity, who concedes that a united people can accomplish whatever they wish. Therefore the Lord takes up their cry, "Come, let us," but here the purpose is to descend to earth and confuse their language. In this divine response to human ambition, an answer is given to a child's natural curiosity about the existence of several different languages, which are associated with dispersion into many different geographical areas. It is ironic that the name of these people is obscured, and their futile effort at fame has left only a mistaken pun, Babel.

Sodom and Gomorrah

The Yahwist's desire to call attention to divine mercy reaches its zenith in the story about Abraham's intercession for the inhabitants of Sodom and Gomorrah (Gen. 18:16–33). Because of its advanced ethical views and subject matter, this passage is often taken as a late addition. In one respect it matters very little whether this text is attributed to the Yahwistic stratum or not, for it certainly coincides with an authentic strain throughout this material. Nevertheless, the concern to justify the Deity is considerably more overt in this dialogue between Abraham and the Deity; hence, the suspicion that exilic or postexilic concerns have found expression in Genesis is warranted. The loose connection between this unit and preceding verses seems to confirm this suspicion, for the observation that the men turned or set out from there occurs twice (verses 16 and 22). The patriarch's intercession for Lot and his fellow citizens of doomed cities is a superb example of linguistic excess that appeals to the emotions.

Abraham begins by stating the decisive issue in question form:

> Wilt thou indeed destroy the righteous with the wicked? Suppose there are fifty righteous within the city; wilt thou then destroy the place and not spare it for the fifty righteous who are in it? Far be it from thee to do such a thing, to slay the righteous with the wicked, so that the righteous fare as the wicked! Far be that from thee! Shall not the Judge of all the earth do right? (Gen. 18:23–25)

The Deity's answer makes known a willingness to withhold punishment, which seems to be the implicit reason for divulging the divine intention in the first place. Once Abraham has established the principle that a few innocent people suffice to rescue many guilty ones, he proceeds to determine just how large the former group must be: fifty, forty-five, forty, thirty, twenty, ten. Each time the Deity answers that the presence of the specified number of innocent persons would bring about a cancellation in the plans to destroy the cities. Abraham's self-consciousness in this exchange is just as excessive as his language. Asserting that he has presumed to question the Deity's decision, Abraham acknowledges his own frailty ("I who am but dust and ashes") and pleads for patience on the

Jagged cliffs in the vicinity of the Dead Sea near the area that is thought by some to have been Sodom and Gomorrah.

Lord's part toward him. The formula for presumption occurs twice ("Behold, I have taken upon myself to speak to the Lord"), as does the plea for patience ("Oh, let not the Lord be angry, and I will speak"). Although the Deity readily agrees to spare the cities for the sake of the righteous, in the end the Lord breaks off discussion and sets out for the doomed cities. Naturally, the memory of destruction in the remote past prevented the narrator from allowing Abraham to press the issue all the way to a single innocent person. As the story unfolds, it turns out that even the three persons who survive hardly deserve the adjective "righteous." Of course the tale about a drunken father and two desperate daughters directs scathing polemic against two of Israel's neighbors, the Ammonites and Moabites.

THE ELOHIST

The Elohistic stratum rivals the Yahwistic in ethical sensitivity and psychological sophistication. Indeed, one could even say that the Elohist demonstrates superiority on both counts. The Yahwist was content to record the ugly story about Abraham's readiness to let Sarah fall into alien hands (Gen. 12:10–20), whereas the Elohist retells the story to absolve the patriarch of blame (20:1–18). According to this version, Abraham's description of his wife as a sister is said to be a true statement. Furthermore, Sarah's virtue is not compromised in this story, a matter that the Yahwist had left unclear, although the implication is certainly that she became a member of the pharaoh's harem. In addition, Abraham is called a prophet and is credited with intercession on behalf of a king who had been prevented from sexual relations with Sarah by divine watchfulness. Here, too, the question of justice arises, this time in the anxious question of King Abimelech: "Lord, wilt thou slay an innocent people?" One feature of this narrative is the emphasis on dreams as the medium of revelation; often the dreams occur in pairs. For example, two dreams are mentioned here, and in the Joseph narrative this seems to be the norm. He has two dreams that, when told, antagonize his brothers and father (the brothers' sheaves of grain bow to his; the sun, moon, and stars bow down before him); the baker and butler have parallel dreams; the pharaoh has two dreams (seven thin cows devour seven fat ones; seven thin ears of grain swallow seven full ears). Single dreams also communicate the divine will in this literary stratum (Jacob's ladder to heaven, Laban's warning against interfering with Jacob). In one instance a vision informs Abraham that his descendants will be innumerable: "Look toward heaven, and number the stars, if you are able to number them. . . . So shall your descendants be" (15:5). This assurance is then strengthened by a covenant that preserves ancient treaty procedures in which a sacrificial animal was cut in half and the two contracting persons walked between the pieces. According to the biblical narrative, Abraham succumbs to a deep sleep and in a nocturnal vision beholds a smoking fire pot and a flaming torch as they pass between the pieces. Here the Deity assumes full responsibility for transforming the promise of descendants into tangible reality.

The Offering of Isaac

The masterpiece of the Elohistic narrative is the offering of Isaac (Gen. 22:1–19).* The Deity's command to sacrifice the child of promise comes to Abraham by night, presumably in a dream or vision, although this is not stated. The story is linked with the Yahwistic account of Abraham's call in two ways: it recalls the words that prompted Abraham to leave family and country in search of an unknown place, and it actually reiterates the accompanying promises. In this manner two acts of sacrifice are juxtaposed, an initial abandoning of parents and a later giving up of

---

*The literature on this story is vast, but none is more provocative than Shalom Spiegel, *The Last Trial* (New York: Schocken, 1967). Gerhard von Rad, *Das Opfer des Abraham* (Munich: Kaiser Verlag, 1971), reproduces excerpts from classic attempts to understand this text in literature, philosophy, and art. My own analysis is found in *A Whirlpool of Torment* (Philadelphia: Fortress Press, 1984), pp. 13–29.

The mosaic floor in the synagogue at Beth Alpha is richly decorated with Jewish and Greco-Roman symbolism (the offering of Isaac and the zodiac, respectively).

a son. The poignant account of a divine test is also juxtaposed with a narrative about an earlier abandonment of another son, this one by a handmaiden. The antecedents for this superb example of narrative art are therefore provided by the Yahwistic stratum, but the story about an aborted sacrifice possesses its own capacity to attract poets, artists, and composers. Furthermore, this unusual story continues to fascinate interpreters from various disciplines (philosophy, literature, psychology, theology).

The narrator specifically states that Abraham is being subjected to a test, although this information is not divulged to either of the individuals affected by the divine command. The final verse in the story has opened the door to speculation about what actually occurred on the sacred mountain, for Abraham returns alone. (Later Jewish interpreters reflected on this story at length, concluding that Abraham actually offered up his son, whose ashes the Deity transported to Eden where the dew revived the son of promise.) Between the announcement of a test and the curious note that remains wholly silent about Isaac, a father demonstrates his radical obedience, here identified as faith, and a last-second reprieve delivers him from wielding a knife against his own son. The conversation between father and son forms the center of the story, and their speech is bracketed by a refrain: "So they went both of them together."

And Isaac said to his father Abraham, "My father!" And he said, "Here am I, my son." He said, "Behold, the fire and the wood; but where is the lamb for a burnt offering?" Abraham said, "God will provide himself the lamb for a burnt offering, my son." (Gen. 22:7–8)

Soon the lad who carried the wood for the fire finds himself bound on that same wood, and the father whose early start toward the distant place demonstrated his religious zeal now goes about his task like a sleepwalker. Even the language and style call attention to the rapidity with which Abraham prepares to slay Isaac. Then at the last second an angel stops him.

A portion of the mosaic floor at Beth Alpha. This scene depicts the moment just before an angel stopped Abraham from sacrificing Isaac on an altar (Gen. 22: 1–18).

> But the angel of the Lord called to him from heaven, and said, "Abraham, Abraham!" And he said, "Here am I." He said, "Do not lay your hand on the lad or do anything to him; for now I know that you fear God, seeing you have not withheld your son, your only son, from me." (Gen. 22:11–12)

Only at this moment does Abraham become aware that God has indeed provided a ram for the sacrifice, and he substitutes it for Isaac. This scene contains two additional characteristic features of the Elohistic stratum, a fondness for angels and an emphasis on the fear of God.

Behind this story lies a significant transition within ancient sacrificial custom, one that witnessed the abandonment of the earlier practice of human sacrifice (Exod. 22:29b–30). Naturally, a rationale for this change was required, particularly to prevent a return to the earlier practice during times of peril. This story argues that the inner intention suffices to demonstrate fear for the Deity, who reckons such an attitude as tantamount to the actual performance of the sacrifice. To be sure, traces of generational conflict lie beneath the surface of the text, but that element is almost completely suppressed. Perhaps the most noteworthy aspect of the entire story is its restraint, the economy of language that has given rise to the expression "fraught with background." In this instance the narrator chooses to leave much to the imagination, a technique that works especially well in a culture that seems to have encouraged effusive speech.

Joseph

Such restraint and moral fervor characterize another fine example of the Elohistic stratum, the story about Joseph's temptation (Gen. 39:6–23). Joseph successfully resists the temptation, but fares less well initially than Abraham did in Egypt. Use of euphemistic language threatens to obscure the natural associations in this story. The food that the master ate, which alone was withheld from Joseph, is an allusion to Potiphar's wife. The accuracy of this interpretation can be seen by noting two things: the natural thought progression from the expression to the comment about Joseph's sexual appeal, and the explicit clarification that only the wife has been kept back from Joseph. The woman's amorous advances evoke a mighty declaration of the ethical position advocated by the Elohist: "How then can I do this great wickedness, and sin against God?" Constant availability and persistent offers of sensual pleasure fail to alter Joseph's resolve, until the woman's aggressive seduction strips him of his outer garment and sends him in hasty retreat. The spurned wife then delivers a masterful speech to her servants, in which she accuses the Hebrew slave and implies that he intended harm to them as well. By the time her husband returns, this practiced speech seems to incriminate the husband as well as Joseph.

As is well known, this story is quite similar to the Egyptian *Tale of*

Two Brothers, the younger of whom spurns the advances of his brother's wife and suffers for his integrity. This angry wife disfigures her appearance so as to give the impression that she has been raped, and when her husband asks who violated her she names the younger brother. The husband waits behind a stable door, hoping to slay his brother when he brings the cows home, but a cow warns the intended victim and he escapes, whereupon a chase ensues, ending when the wronged brother castrates himself and declares his innocence. Although scholars have compared the two texts and have claimed literary dependence for the biblical account, the motif is too common to require actual acquaintance with a literary document. Of course, it is possible that mythic use of the Egyptian tale became known in Canaanite centers, particularly in the years before the Amarna revolution, which inadvertently produced the important correspondence between the Pharaoh Akhnaton and local Canaanite chieftans.

In a single statement by Joseph to his brothers, the moral and religious sensitivities of the Elohist come together beautifully:

> Fear not, for am I in the place of God? As for you, you meant evil against me; but God meant it for good, to bring it about that many people should be kept alive, as they are today. So do not fear: I will provide for you and your little ones. (Gen. 50:19–21)

It was not Joseph's place to seek revenge for all the hardship the brothers caused him; rather his responsibility was to forgive them and to provide for their needs. The rationale for this behavior is theological: Joseph recognizes a hidden purpose for the events of his life, one that is orchestrated by the Deity. The implications of this thinking are spelled out in a related passage: "And now do not be distressed, or angry with yourselves, because you sold me here; for God sent me before you to preserve life. . . . So it was not you who sent me here, but God" (45:5, 8a). Nevertheless, Joseph's treatment of his brothers shows the powerful effect of divided consciousness.

THE PRIESTLY WRITER

In Genesis the Priestly stratum is limited to four narrative blocks: creation, the flood, the covenant with Abraham, and the burial of Sarah. Elsewhere within the book this layer is present in genealogies, which serve a sociological function by legitimating a given dynasty or group in authority and by reflecting changes in societal patterns. Their role in the Book of Genesis is a thoroughly religious one; the genealogies trace the line of a chosen family. The artificial distinction in life span between the individuals who preceded the flood, on the one hand, and those who followed it, on the other hand, seems to reflect a theological assumption that the spread of sin affected longevity (the size of humans was also believed to have dwindled). Ancient Sumerian parallels exist, for in the King List antediluvian rulers are said to have lived as long as 240,000 years, whereas postdiluvian kings are thought to have lived only a tenth that long. The ratio in the biblical material is roughly the same; whereas Methusaleh is believed to have reached the ripe age of 969, by Genesis 11 the maximum age declined to about 200, and less by the time of Joseph and Moses (147 and 120, respectively). This feature in the Priestly narrative therefore functions in the same way the story of the fall does in the Yahwistic narrative.

Genealogies

For the Priestly stratum chronology performed a theological function, and for this reason a genealogy traces the saving history to the beginning of time. Periodically new beginnings occurred, and these were marked by covenants (Noah, Abraham). Each of these covenants introduced eternally valid cultic ordinances, the first for humanity in general and the second for the group of people who believed that the Deity had chosen them for special destiny. Essentially, the covenant with Noah came to signify a kind of fundamental religiosity (abstaining from murder and from eating food with blood in it). The covenant with Abraham required the practice of circumcision, which received a profoundly religious interpretation. Later elevation of this ritual, which applied only to males, is but one of many symptoms that patriarchal ideas shaped Israel's thinking to a large degree.

The Babylonian Creation Story

For the most part, genealogies consist of one name after another in unrelieved monotony. However, when the Priestly stratum takes up other types of subjects, the dull style persists, making its contributions to Genesis easily recognizable. In the case of the creation account in 1:1–2:4a, the repetitive style achieves a high degree of solemnity, perhaps through frequent liturgical use. Conscious polemic underlies the narrative, as if its aim were to replace the familiar Neo-Babylonian version of creation to which Israel's exiles were subjected. In this story, entitled *Enuma elish* ("When from above") from its opening words, creation is the result of conflict. Actually, the mythic drama seems to reflect seasonal patterns, the torrential spring rains that sweep silt toward the Persian Gulf and deposit it on the shore, forming new land. According to the story, Apsu and Tiamat, who represent fresh water and salt water, exist in the beginning, and from their union derive other deities who eventually anger their father. Apsu's plan to slay the younger gods becomes known and he is slain. In due time Tiamat ventures forth looking for revenge and the search for a champion among the gods settles on Marduk, the patron deity of Babylon. An older version told of Enlil's championing the cause of the gods. Having demonstrated his ability to bring something into existence from nothing, Marduk promises to deliver the gods if they will grant him sole rule. They agree to these conditions, and, after a mighty struggle, Marduk slays Tiamat in battle. From her body he forms heaven and earth, and as an afterthought Marduk creates humans from the blood of the slain god Kingu, Tiamat's lover. To the newly created humans Marduk assigns the cultic task of feeding the gods.

In the biblical version several things stand out when one reflects on this Babylonian account as its prototype. First, the creation of male and female in God's image is the goal toward which the story moves, with, of course, the institution of the sabbath. Second, certain polemical features occur in the narrative—for example, the designation of sun and moon as greater and lesser lamps. Because the words for these luminaries were names for deities, the Priestly narrative relegates these gods to nonentities. Third, creation results from a spoken word by a transcendent Deity, and the sole link between this Deity and humans is the spoken word. To be sure, echoes of the older version persist: a mighty wind stills the waters, just as the spring rains were dried up by the strong winds that followed; the earth is formed from preexistent matter, and even the Hebrew word for the deep resembles the name Tiamat; and God converses with a heavenly council ("Let us make man in our image, after our likeness"). One further indication of polemic is the ambiguity over the actual meaning of the initial words. Does the account presuppose a temporal beginning or an absolute one?* The textual evidence yields both, or neither, for the actual vocalization is ambiguous. The probability is that the narrative intends a temporal beginning: "When God began to create the heavens and the earth, the earth was without form and void." As for the concept of the divine image, the text suggests that it implies dominance, just as God rules over heaven. In addition, the narrative seems to suggest resemblance in appearance and in communicative capacity. Nevertheless, the Priestly stratum zealously guards divine transcendence. Humans only resemble deity; they do not possess divine features or divine blood.

Nature's Part in Creation

It is entirely proper to use the term *evolution* with reference to the Priestly creation account. Nature itself participates in the creative work; seeds produce new plants, and all creatures multiply, replenishing their kind. Even the sequence of life forms begins with sea creatures and moves

---

*The usual translation, "In the beginning God created the heavens and the earth," presupposes an absolute sense of the verse, whereas a temporal understanding would assume that matter already existed when God began the creative work.

to those that dwell on land and fill the sky. Human beings are the last to be formed, and their sexuality is assumed. This is a significant point, for the biblical understanding of sexuality in this narrative, especially the divine declaration that everything is very good, desacralizes sex. This achievement was far-reaching in the ancient world, for it ruled out the worship of sex or fear of its hidden powers. The battle to maintain such an understanding of sexuality was fought long and hard, and the Priestly narrative's sober announcement is the result of centuries of conflict in this vital area. The divine charge to be fruitful and master the earth is not a justification for willful abuse of natural resources; to the contrary, the restriction on food that follows indicates that responsible dominion is implied. The first humans are commanded to become vegetarians, and that requirement remains in force until after the flood.

The Priestly account of the flood has merged with the Yahwistic one, and certain inconsistencies have naturally resulted. In general, the Priestly account emphasizes a single pair of clean and unclean animals and offers a different chronology for the length of the flood. The reason for the former distinction is the Priestly view that the Sinaitic legislation about what was clean and unclean did not arise until the Deity revealed it to Moses. The Priestly narrative also introduces a covenant with Noah, which is then followed by a genealogy. In this instance the genealogy is more lively than elsewhere, for here a conscious theological statement appears: "The sons of Noah who went forth from the ark were Shem, Ham, and Japheth. Ham was the father of Canaan. These three were the sons of Noah; and from these the whole earth was peopled" (Gen. 9:18–19). The contrast with the table of nations in chapter 10, or the Priestly genealogy in chapter 5 is noteworthy.

Beyond Genesis

The Priestly stratum extends beyond Genesis, and as a matter of fact dominates within Exodus, Leviticus, and Numbers where levitical privilege and legal codification are concerned. The assumption of a great distance between deity and humans gives rise to a theology of deity who dwells in mystery. Cherubim, a pillar of cloud and a fire, thick smoke, the ark—all these and more serve to protect the holiness of God. The cult alone provides the means whereby sin's spread can be checked, and priests occupy center stage in this drama of atonement. Competing traditions have left traces of a struggle for power and privilege, and some interpreters understand the resulting inconsistencies as proof that two strata exist within the Priestly material. (The name Adam is used as a proper name; it is a collective term. Only Aaron and the High Priest are anointed; all priests are anointed. Levites begin service at age twenty-five; they begin at age thirty.) On the basis of the cultic data within this narrative, interpreters usually assume that the high priest has usurped the role earlier attributed to kings. The Priestly stratum in the Torah became identified with the Deity's will for the restored community in Judah after the exile; its importance in shaping the character of life can hardly be overestimated.

Theology and History

Insofar as Genesis is concerned, the Priestly layer has given the book a distinctive quality, for it has applied the notion of history to material that was ill-suited for such an understanding. Bishop James Ussher's well-known seventeenth-century C.E. attempt to fix a precise date for the creation of the world (4004 B.C.E.) is based on a literal reading of chronology that functioned theologically for the Priestly stratum. This confusion between theology and history has persisted, particularly in discussions of the patriarchal narratives. Whereas the biblical stories allow for the possibility that the various figures are eponymous heroes (a single individual representing an entire nation)—for example, in the cases of Jacob, Ishmael, Esau, Moab, and Ammon—many modern believers insist that the narratives tell the actual history of individuals. The Priestly writer is in no small measure responsible for creating this confusion, which will only ease when readers appreciate the nature of the sagas underlying Genesis. Perhaps then the anxiety over locating the patriarchs in a specific period of history will disappear, so that the theological and aesthetic dimensions of the book can be fully appreciated. Then exquisite narration such as the story about Eliezer's journey in search of a wife for Isaac (Gen. 24:1–67) and the episode about Tamar's refusal to accept injustice from her father-in-law (38:1–30) will take their place alongside lesser tales in which conventional motifs are brought together into a coherent story (strife over a well, an ancestress in danger, hero legends such as the story in chapter 14 in which Melchizedek appears briefly, strife between brothers, parental preference for one son over another, success stories with magical elements, barren wives, and much more).

AN ALTERNATIVE THEORY

Recent literary analyses of Genesis offer an alternative to the three-strata theory of composition. The two accounts of creation are taken to be complementary, one stressing theological concepts and the other moral and psychological issues. Since the deity is both transcendent and immanent, the author chooses appropriate names, Elohim and Yahweh, to connote both concepts. Furthermore, reality itself is both ordered and unpredictable; hence, two different notions of creation are essential to describe the world as it is known. A purely linear presentation is deemed inappropriate inasmuch as the world is essentially contradictory. The two creation accounts deal with two spheres, an upper and a lower. Moreover, even within the Priestly account there is complete symmetry—for example, the mention of plants on the third day arises from the desire to restrict the fifth day to things that move about.

Unity is claimed for the entire Pentateuch, not just for Genesis. This argument rests on subtle links between Genesis and Exodus as well as on broad themes. The centrality of the seventh day is linked with the story about the Tabernacle in Exodus 39–40. But the similarities are also thought to derive from the arrangement of the primeval history (Genesis 1–11), which is believed to be a polemic against mythic concepts in the ancient world. The narrative emphasizes population growth, as opposed to control by natural barrenness, high infant mortality, and artificial barrenness by cultic practices. The primeval history is structured as follows: creation; three threats; resolution (creation; Adam, Cain, Noah; dispersion). Its intent is to reject civilization; the genealogy in 4:17–26 indicts the civilized world by deriving most peoples from the incestuous Ham. The same pattern occurs in Exod. 1:1–2:15 (genealogy; three threats; resolution), in which the shorter section replicates the larger. This structure is also perceived on a wide scale. Two examples suffice: the first five books of the Bible and the book of Genesis. The macrostructure is seen in this way: Genesis; three wilderness books; Deuteronomy. Within Genesis the pattern is described as follows: primeval history; Abraham, Isaac, Jacob; Joseph.

Although the linguistic links are minimal in these larger comparisons (a blessing in Genesis 49 and in Deuteronomy 33; people filling the face of the whole earth in Genesis 1–11; the spirit of God in Genesis), many involved verbal connections within Genesis are put forth as proof of unitary authorship. Perhaps the most intricate scheme of interconnection concerns the Jacob-Esau cycle in 25:19–35:22. It is claimed that perfect symmetry appears here: ABCDEFE'D'C'B'A'. The links are as follows: AA' (25:19–34 and 35:1–22); BB' (26 and 34); CC' (27:1–28:9 and 33); DD' (28:10–22 and 32); EE' (29 and 31); F (30). This kind of intricate connection is also believed to underlie Genesis 1–11, which is united by five genealogies, and the final episode about the tower of Babel is thought to have a symmetrical design. Similar patterns are isolated in Exodus 1–4, where links with Genesis are recognized (Joseph being fruitful and filling the earth), as well as in Exodus 5–19, where twelve connections with Exodus 1–4 are discovered. The same kind of bond is posited between Genesis 3 and 4:1–16; the account of the first sin is an inner psychic drama, whereas the story about Cain and Abel is its sociological extension.

Even the apparent contradictions in the flood story are attributed to one author and are explained as variety for variety's sake or as the result of necessity (Noah needed more than two animals, or else he could not have sacrificed to the Deity after the waters subsided). The narrative reports that Noah entered the ark twice for emphasis. The shift in divine names presents no difficulty in this analysis; the narrative moves back and forth between Yahweh and Elohim until the final reference to God, where both names are combined into Yahweh Elohim. The same explanation is given for the three accounts of divine institution of the covenant. Since three aspects of the covenant are mentioned (land, progeny, and Abraham), it is established three times, each with a different emphasis. The troublesome "intrusion" of the story about Judah and Tamar (Genesis 38) is explained as more than an interlude to allow time for Joseph to arrive in Egypt. Actually, linguistic connections ("this . . . recognize") link the Joseph story with the Tamar episode, where garments become occasions of erroneous perception and correct identification.

Repetition is explained as the storyteller's means of communicating with large audiences, some of whom would have missed the words in their first reciting. But repetition is also understood as foreshadowing and as the result of type-scenes. An example of a type-scene is the thrice-repeated story of the ancestress in danger. Another is the frequently repeated betrothal scene, which consists of the following elements: a foreign country, a well, barrenness, and announcement of a changed status. Another reason for repetition is to allow for slight changes in the story, which provide glimpses into characterization. When Potiphar's wife addresses her husband, she changes the story ever so slightly from what she had said to her maidens. The minor shifts in emphasis reveal important aspects of her personality.

It remains to be seen whether this literary approach to the Torah will offer adequate answers to the vexing questions that produced the hypothesis of literary strata in the first place. In the meantime readers will be presented with competing theories and different readings of the text, many of which are fresh and provocative. A single example demonstrates the potential of the literary approach. The story about Abraham's journey to Egypt in Gen. 12:10–20 is an inversion of the exodus theme, one that recurs in Genesis 21. Here an Israelite (Sarah) deals harshly with an Egyptian (Hagar) and drives her and her son (Ishmael) into the wilderness, where the Lord watches over them both.

◆ 2 ◆

Exodus

T HE Book of Exodus begins with a dramatic conflict between the Lord and Pharaoh (Exod. 1:1–15:21), describes a brief journey into the wilderness (15:22–18:27), and concludes with an account of the covenant at Sinai (chapters 19–40). The prevailing mood is one of strife and its resolution; it is significant that two images of the Deity come to prominence in the presentation of this drama: warrior and healer. The first image surfaces in the victory song attributed to Moses after Pharaoh's army succumbs to the waves of the Reed Sea: "The Lord is a man of war; / the Lord is his name" (15:3). The second comes at the beginning of the journey into the wilderness; its function is to assure the people who have fled Egypt that their God not only is capable of causing disaster, as they had witnessed among the Egyptians, but also can bring well-being. The promise of healing is conditional; it will come to the people if they observe the statutes and ordinances of the Lord. Then they will escape the diseases that afflicted the Egyptians, and the reason given is that "I am the Lord, your healer" (15:26).

STRIFE AND HARMONY

The two categories, strife and harmony, are useful rubrics in examining the contents of this book, particularly because the artificial schemes of chronology and itinerary are rendered useless by the insertion of material out of context and by the "suspended time" resulting from the extended description of the sanctuary and its contents. The former of the two, strife, takes place on four levels: (1) Yahweh versus Pharaoh; (2) Yahweh versus Moses; (3) Yahweh versus the people who fled from oppression; and (4) Moses versus Aaron. In the first conflict the Deity prevented a resolution, and the struggle is described as sport, as if Yahweh were playing a cat-and-mouse game. Here the pharaoh is helpless in the Deity's hands, and

63

whenever the stricken ruler tries to work toward a solution Yahweh hardens his heart. Moses' wife achieves a resolution of the struggle between the Deity and her husband, whereas Moses and the Levites bring about harmony between the people and a wrathful Deity bent on destroying them. The tension between Moses and Aaron occurs at the redactional stage, and it therefore lacks resolution because such harmonization would have exposed the polemic concealed within the text. But the issue is more complex than this lack of a resolution might suggest, for between the tale of strife and murmuring stands Moses' intercession. Consequently, harmony is achieved when Moses dwells on the mountain with the Deity and when the people's representative talks with God face to face in the tent of meeting. Furthermore, in bringing more than enough gold and fabric to equip the tabernacle and its furnishings, the people demonstrate their willingness to be a kingdom of priests and a holy nation. Moreover, Aaron's intrusion into the limelight is made to appear less a struggle for power than a consecration for service when Moses anoints him, together with the Levites, and sprinkles them with the blood of sacrifice.

COMPETING DEITIES

The conflict between Moses' God and Pharaoh falls under the category of competing deities, for the pharaoh was believed to embody divine qualities. Therefore, the story deals with the issue of sovereignty; it demonstrates Yahweh's superior might over the dominant force of the time. A single refrain echoes through the halls of the palace: "Let my people go!" The drama exposes the pharaoh's gradual change from a defiant rejection of the request to full acquiescence in what by then had become a demand. The following stages make up this shift in attitude: (1) who is the Lord, that I should let the people miss three days of work? (5:2–5); (2) you and the people may worship *within* the land of Egypt (8:25); (3) the men may go beyond the border, but they must leave their families and possessions (10:11); (4) all may go, but they cannot take their cattle or possessions with them (10:24); and (5) all may go, and they are free to take their cattle as well (12:31–32). The easing of the pharaoh's defiance is accompanied by an increasing severity in the plagues that strike the country and its inhabitants, except for the oppressed residents of Goshen.

The legend about Moses' rescue from the Nile River locates the source of conflict within the royal household. A similar tale is preserved about King Sargon of Agade, who was placed in a basket and set afloat on a river. The story about the Hebrew infant offers an explanation for the name Moses, which resembles an Egyptian word in such names as Thutmose. There is irony in the narrative when Pharaoh's daughter is unknowingly persuaded to let Moses' actual mother nurse the child. The tale of Moses' rash action in defending a Hebrew from cruelty functions to explain how he later came to be in Midian, but it also implies that life at the court did not make him an Egyptian. Having demonstrated an inability to stand idly by while Hebrews suffered at the hands of cruel taskmasters or while young women were oppressed by shepherds at the watering hole, Moses became a prime candidate to assist in a far greater deliverance. The divine commission to a reluctant Moses set the stage for decisive battle; Yahweh's representative faced the pharaoh's agents, magicians whose powers failed them after initial success.

THE PLAGUES

The ten plagues have been explained in purely natural terms, but they are represented as extraordinary. The usual explanation runs something like this: the Nile River became polluted in its overflow, and on receding left numerous small ponds in which frogs and mosquitos reproduced; once the water dried up, the frogs died, and flies multiplied; the flies spread disease to cattle; a hailstorm followed; a swarm of locusts invaded the country; the hot chamsin winds (which come in March or early April) darkened the sky; and death struck every household. The extent of the calamity is described once as ranging from Pharaoh's house to the maidservant behind the mill; in another instance the scope is said to go from the royal household to the captive in the dungeon. The narrative turns ordinary natural calamity into a mythic confrontation between two deities, with a people's fate hanging in the balance. For the Egyptians and their subjects this confrontation was weighty business, but for Yahweh it is described as making sport of Pharaoh.

THE DEITY VERSUS THE PEOPLE

Just as an act of murder offered a foretaste of things to come in the struggle between two deities, so Moses' resistance to divine summons points to further conflict. The reasons Moses gives for refusing Yahweh's commission move from the legitimate to the fabricated. He argues that his lips are uncircumcised, that they are sealed to the extent that he is slow of speech. The Deity's response renders such argument worthless.

> Who has made man's mouth? Who makes him dumb, or deaf, or seeing, or blind? Is it not I, the Lord? Now therefore go, and I will be with your mouth and teach you what you shall speak. (Exod. 4:11–12)

Moses' other excuse is simply an unwillingness to venture forth on faith, which prompts divine anger against him, as well as the introduction of Aaron's name into the story. Whereas Moses will be like God, putting words in Aaron's mouth, Aaron will be the spokesman in his stead. The story that follows, in which the Lord sought to kill Moses but was prevented from doing so by quick action on the part of Zipporah, Moses wife, seems to relate to an ancient period when circumcision was connected with puberty and marriage. If so, it must also have merged with a tale about the Deity's right to the initial sexual encounter. The presence of a child in this obscure account presents a problem for this interpretation, because marriage preceded the coming of a child in the natural sequence.

The strife between the Deity and a murmuring multitude is occasioned by Moses' absence from the camp while he was receiving the Ten Commandments. An impatient people resolved to fashion gods to replace Moses in advancing toward their destination, and Aaron readily obliged them. Once a golden bull (calf) became the object of their adoration, fertility worship quite naturally followed, because a bull represented sexual powers in ancient thinking. Thus the people rose up to dance and play, but their play was less innocent than one might think. This behavior explains Moses' intense anger that compelled him to throw the two tablets of the Law onto the ground, breaking them literally as the people were doing so figuratively. Harmony is achieved in this narrative by two things: first, the Levites slaughter about three thousand people, and second, a plague breaks out among the guilty people. The latter is probably meant to be associated with the "trial by ordeal," according to which Moses pulverized the golden bull and made a potion for everyone to drink. The assumption was that guilty persons would become sick and die after drinking the mixture.

MOSES VERSUS AARON

The struggle between Moses and Aaron operates on a different level of the text. Ostensibly, everything is reasonably harmonious between the two leaders, even when Aaron lies about his own involvement in the episode about the golden bull. However, there is considerable tension within the story that seems to suggest that Aaron was not originally involved in the larger conflict at all. Later priestly interests have introduced him into the story and relegated to him the task that the Deity had earlier entrusted to Moses. Hence, Aaron wields the magic rod and earns a place alongside Moses, his younger brother, in the story about deliverance from Egyptian bondage. Nevertheless, the final portrayal of Aaron is less favorable than that of Moses, whose uniqueness is signaled by the belief that he conversed with Yahweh as humans talk, face to face. The tradition about his shining countenance that had to be covered by a veil leaves no question about the awe in which the narrator held Moses. Still, when the Deity rewarded him by passing over and allowing the goodness to be seen, Moses is prevented from beholding the actual figure of God. This author refuses to compromise the mystery of the Lord, even for one who catches a glimpse of the receding Deity and hears the proclamation of divine attributes:

> The Lord, the Lord, a God merciful and gracious, slow to anger, and abounding in steadfast love and faithfulness, keeping steadfast love for thousands, forgiving iniquity and transgression and sin, but who will by no means clear the guilty, visiting the iniquity of the fathers upon the children and the children's children, to the third and the fourth generation. (Exod. 34:6–7)

For his own protection Moses is sheltered in a cleft of rock, and the Deity's hand covers him so that he will not behold God and die. This favored one who enjoys divine protection himself stood in the breach and sheltered a sinful people from intended destruction. The story about Moses' readiness to sacrifice his own standing before the Deity introduces the idea of a book of life into which the names of God's people are entered.

> Alas, this people have sinned a great sin; they have made for themselves gods of gold. But now, if thou wilt forgive their sin—and if not, blot me, I pray thee, out of thy book which thou hast written. (Exod. 32:31–32)

Such selfless intercession fails to move the Deity wholly from punishing the people, although it does evoke a decision to limit that punishment to the guilty individuals. There appears to be some inconsistency within the story, inasmuch as two different forms of punishment obliterate the sinners (the Levites' sword; the potion of gold and water, which brings about a plague).

DRAMATIZATION

One feature of the book is the way the dramatic events of the past are reactualized for a later community. The dramatic struggle between Pharaoh and Yahweh is represented as a battle between good and evil, order and chaos. The victory over ever-present forces of evil is celebrated in two songs, one quite brief and another more extensive. Miriam's victory song is often taken to reflect the excitement of an eyewitness: "Sing to the Lord, for he has triumphed gloriously; / the horse and his rider he has thrown into the sea" (15:21). This judgment about the antiquity of the song can scarcely be verified, because the mark of any skillful poet is an ability to write realistic verse. The poem attributed to Moses begins with this short song of Miriam, but goes on to reflect about Yahweh's cosmic battle with the sea and to extol the Lord for guiding the people into Canaan. Although certain features of the poem require a much later date than the actual time of Moses (the Philistines did not occupy the land until much later), Canaanite imagery fills the poem, specifically the battle between the deity and the sea and the notion of Canaan as a holy abode, which echoes the language about Mount Zaphon.* When the poet endeavors to speak about Yahweh's incomparability, another image intrudes that fits rather badly with the wonder being celebrated.

> *Who is like thee, O Lord, among the gods?*
> *Who is like thee, majestic in holiness,*
> *terrible in glorious deeds, doing wonders?*
> *Thou didst stretch out thy right hand,*
> *the earth swallowed them. (Exod. 15:11–12)*

The result of these two songs is to encourage later generations to celebrate Yahweh's marvelous victory as timeless.

The same impulse seems to characterize the narrative about the passover. Here two ancient celebrations, a spring nomadic festival and a feast of unleavened bread identified with the barley harvest, have received historical anchorage in the story about the Exodus from Egyptian bondage. Great care is taken to turn this account into an instructional device, and the mode of observance is calculated to invite questions from children. Why do we eat this strange food in haste and while dressed for traveling?

> And when your children say to you, "What do you mean by this service?" you shall say, "It is the sacrifice of the Lord's passover, for he passed over the houses of the people of Israel in Egypt, when he slew the Egyptians but spared our houses." (Exod. 12:26–27)

The intention is to retain a fresh memory of the deliverance from death that the blood from a sacrificial animal made possible. Hence the curious ritual that will surely evoke questions in later times is portrayed as far more than a trivial agricultural festival and is firmly set within Israel's history of salvation.

NARRATIVE TENSION

The attempt at reactualization has led to some unevenness in the story; for example, the explanation for the Passover ritual assumes that the deliverance lies in the past, although it still is in the future when the narrator introduces the justification for strange actions. Other indications of inconsistency exist as well. Perhaps the most noteworthy is the presence of both inflated and reduced numbers. In the spirit of mythic contest, the oppressed males are said to number 600,000, whereas the story about Moses' rescue from the river implies that only two midwives existed

*Mount Zaphon is the mountain on which Baal was believed to have resided in Canaanite myth. According to Isaiah 14 and Job 26, it was the mountain of the gods generally.

among the Hebrews. If the Exodus story is actually grounded in a historical event, as seems likely, the number of people who fled from Egypt must have been quite small, and the mention of only two midwives fits very nicely. However, the naming of these women, Shiphrah and Puah, may simply derive from its literary genre, the folktale. In all likelihood, the reference to the fruitfulness of the Israelites is a conscious allusion to the divine commission to multiply and fill the earth (Gen. 1:28).

Other indications of unevenness also appear, and these are usually taken as proof that at least the Yahwistic and Priestly strata persist in the Book of Exodus. There are opposing views about the precise moment when the Deity revealed the name Yahweh, whether on the occasion of the burning bush or three chapters later. Furthermore, the narrative seems somewhat confused about the exact location of Moses' wife. According to chapter 4, she accompanies him to Egypt, but she later comes with her father-in-law to meet Moses in the wilderness. Similarly, the nature of the miracle at the sea varies, and the Priestly account heightens the event by describing the waves as forming a wall on either side of the caravan. The alternative account understands the miracle as an east wind driving the water in a single direction, until the Egyptian army pursued the fleeing subjects into the marsh bed and the wind shifted directions. Again, the natural flow of the story is broken by the effort to place Aaron alongside Moses, and this procedure seems to have replaced a report of Moses' return to Egypt (Exod. 4:27–31). Here Aaron performs wonders, and the people believe.

THE DESPOILING OF THE EGYPTIANS

An important ingredient in the story concerns the despoiling of the Egyptians. Perhaps this theme functions to explain how slaves happened to have more than enough gold, which they put to base and sublime use. Because the people are supposed to have fashioned a bull from gold, they must have obtained the precious metal somewhere. But the elaborate description of the tabernacle, the ark, the table, the lamp, and the lampstands could become reality only if the people possessed vast quantities of gold, linen, precious stones, and so forth. Therefore, the despoiling of the Egyptians renders this fanciful account of a tabernacle plausible. It matters little that the result is a strange assessment of Moses' esteem in the eyes of Egyptians.

> And the Lord gave the people favor in the sight of the Egyptians. Moreover, the man Moses was very great in the land of Egypt, in the sight of Pharaoh's servants and in the sight of the people. (Exod. 11:3)

The curious qualification of Moses by the adjective "man" shows how much at home in mythic confrontation this story is, for his actions have propelled him headlong into a cosmic struggle for justice. Here is the secret behind the appeal of the cry for liberation; it is anchored in a distinct time and place, but it transcends both and universalizes the struggle for freedom.

Once the issue of power is settled and Yahweh's deliverance of the oppressed people has established a bond between subjects and their king, it is proper that they learn what is expected of them. The remaining chapters of the book describe the conduct that offends or pleases the Deity. The first part of this section concerns laws; the second part concentrates on worship. Two very old law codes are incorporated into the discussion: (1) the Covenant Code and (2) the ritual Decalogue. In addition, the Decalogue is given here in a slightly different version from that preserved in Deuteronomy.

THE COVENANT CODE

The Covenant Code (Exod. 20:22–23:33) seems to reflect customary law from the Canaanites; at any rate, it presupposes an agricultural community with people living in houses and engaging in ordinary business transactions. These earlier laws are adapted to covenant faith; the very first law, the prohibition of graven images, is distinctively Yahwistic. The prohibition is immediately followed by instructions about building an altar; two things stand out: (1) it must not be profaned by tools, and (2) it must not have steps that would reveal the nakedness of priests. For the most part, the laws deal with issues that arise in everyday life: treatment of slaves and punishment for murder, theft, and sexual crimes. A distinction is made between voluntary and involuntary manslaughter, as well as between various sorts of theft and disposition of stolen goods. The ancient requirement that the firstborn be sacrificed appears here in its stark form.

> The first-born of your sons you shall give to me. You shall do likewise with your oxen and with your sheep: seven days it shall be with its dam; on the eighth day you shall give it to me. (Exod. 22:29b–30)

Moreover, the death sentence is required for sorceresses and for persons guilty of sodomy. Influence of covenant faith has produced a concern for strangers, and this compassion is grounded in the people's experience in Egypt. The interest in widows and orphans—and the poor, which occurs here as well—is not distinctive of Yahwism, but it is readily found in Canaanite texts and Egyptian wisdom literature. However, the concern for the poor does find concrete expression in the Covenant Code, specifically in the provision that creditors must return garments taken in pledge lest night fall on poor people whose only protection from the cold has been taken from them. The fallow law, according to which the land shall be allowed to rest every seventh year, also receives its rationale

Canaanite high places like this one are thought to have served as places of animal sacrifices. The practice of offering animals to the Deity was continued by ancient Israelites.

from concern for the poor who are permitted to glean in unworked fields. Finally, the Covenant Code stipulates that all males shall appear before the Lord at an unspecified sanctuary three times each year: the feast of unleavened bread, the feast of harvest, and the feast of ingathering.

CULTIC LAWS

The ancient cultic decalogue (Exod. 34:10–26) seems to be a variant of the covenant ratification, but it is presented as a renewal of the broken covenant. This cultic material emphasizes Yahweh's jealous nature and even identifies the Deity's name as Jealous. Accordingly, this Yahweh demands that all Canaanite altars and sacred objects be demolished. The laws prohibit images, the mixing of leaven and sacrificial blood, and fertility rites like boiling a kid in its mother's milk. Positive injunctions include observance of the feast of unleavened bread, the sacrifice of all firstborn (with the important provision that unclean animals, for example, the ass, can be redeemed; sons may also be redeemed), observance of the sabbath, the keeping of three annual festivals, and the offering of the first fruits of the ground.

THE TEN COMMANDMENTS

Minor differences between the Decalogue in Exod. 20:1–17 and the version in Deut. 5:6b–21 concern the rationale for sabbath observance (here it is based on God's resting after six days of creation) and the placing of the neighbor's wife first in the final commandment. Not all religious traditions divided the ten commandments in the same way. Judaism understands the statement, "I am the Lord your God, who brought you out of the land of Egypt, out of the house of bondage," (verse 2) as the first commandment, and views the prohibitions of other gods and graven images as a single commandment. Protestants and Catholics also differ with respect to these verses (3–4) and the last verse (17), which Catholics divide into two different commandments. Some scholars believe that the original Decalogue consisted of short prohibitions and commands without any elaboration. Because the explanatory comments clearly reflect later circumstances, the Decalogue in its present form cannot be Mosaic. Without these additions, the commandments are thought to possess nothing that prevents a connection with Moses. Not all critics accept the thesis that the Decalogue was originally a unified list of short prohibitions or commands, and even among those who do, there is no general agreement that the laws came from Moses. Nevertheless, it is worth noting the conjectured short form.

1. You shall have no other gods before me.
2. You shall not make for yourself a graven image.
3. You shall not take the name of the Lord your God in vain.
4. Remember the sabbath day, to keep it holy.
5. Honor your father and your mother.
6. You shall not kill.
7. You shall not commit adultery.
8. You shall not steal.
9. You shall not bear false witness.
10. You shall not covet.

Whether the Decalogue ever existed in such a form is doubtful.

THE TABERNACLE

The elaborate description of plans for building the tabernacle and equipping it, together with the provision of appropriate clothing for Aaron and the Levitical priests, occupies a large segment of the Book of Exodus. Priestly interests dominate, and the whole discussion strikes readers as completely removed from reality. It appears that later features of worship in the Solomonic temple are projected back into the period of the wilderness journey. The total picture is one of a Deity who is withdrawn from ordinary people; consequently, they rely on priests to carry out the necessary daily ritual on their behalf. It is often thought that the Priestly stratum lacked an account of the Sinaitic legislation but that the elaborate means of atonement enabled the people to escape divine wrath.

SUMMARY

To recapitulate, conflict and its resolution characterize the Book of Exodus. The corresponding images of the Deity, warrior and healer, gather up these opposing themes. Their prominence in various episodes of the book indicates that the author used the images thematically. We have not attempted to examine every episode in which the Deity appears as warrior and healer. One thinks of the story about the battle with Amalek, when Moses held up his hand and Israel prevailed and when Aaron and Hur devised a means by which to assist Moses in keeping his hands raised. After the battle the warrior Deity instructed Moses to write the following sentiments in a book: "I will utterly blot out the remembrance of Amalek from under heaven" (Exod. 17:14). This hostility for Amalek and his descendants is particularly strong in the Book of Samuel, where King Agag becomes the occasion for Saul's offense, and in the Book of Esther, where Haman the Agagite conceives a scheme to destroy the Jews. The other image of Deity as healer is not limited to the story about Moses' sweetening of waters by putting a certain kind of tree in it but is also present in the account of divine solicitude for a hungry throng. The book abounds in stories about the Deity's provision for the peoples' needs: water from limestone rock, manna, quail. In all three instances scholars have offered natural explanations. Water lies just beneath the surface of limestone rocks in the area involved; Moses simply made a crack in the rock and allowed the water to flow freely. The manna was a honeydew substance that forms on twigs of the tamarisk bush when scalelike insects are present. It is claimed that quail land in the area after an exhausting flight over the sea, and they can easily be caught. But for the narrator the presence of life-preserving sustenance in the wilderness was nothing less than a miracle.

· 3 ·

Leviticus

THE Book of Leviticus specifies the precise manner by which a holy God can be worshipped by an elected people who are called to be holy also. The divine summons to be like the Deity occurs again and again.

> For I am the Lord your God; consecrate yourselves therefore, and be holy, for I am holy. . . . For I am the Lord who brought you up out of the land of Egypt, to be your God; you shall therefore be holy, for I am holy. (Lev. 11:44–45).

To safeguard the people from contamination and thus to assure the working of the cult, exact specifications are provided about the sacrificial system (chapters 1–7), the service of ordination (chapters 8–10), laws of impurity (chapters 11–16), conduct (chapters 17–26, the Holiness Code), and gifts to the sanctuary. Although these stipulations about purity and holiness are thought to derive from the divine legislation at Sinai, the connection with the Book of Exodus is a loose one. Chapter 8 seems to continue the discussion in Exodus 29, which describes the ceremony of anointing priests for service at the altar. The material that has come together in this legislation about purity and impurity derives from several strata, but the Priestly viewpoint has shaped its present form.

THE ORIGIN OF LAWS AND INSTITUTIONS

This Priestly perspective has obscured the fact that many of the laws arose from concerns for health. Experience had taught the people to avoid pork and various other foods that presented health hazards in a hot climate. Other laws sprang up as illustrations of moral principles, while still others arose in the process of teaching. Nevertheless, all of these laws are attributed to the Deity and are said to be a part of the revelation

74

to Moses on Mount Sinai. The point seems to be that Israel's sacrificial cult is not its own invention of a means to salvation but a gift of the Deity. Because much of the sacrificial terminology in Leviticus is identical with a similar phenomenon in Canaanite literature, this insistence on a divine origin for these laws is understandable.

A variety of sacrifices existed to cover every kind of inadvertent sin. It should be noted that the cult did not provide a means of dealing with intentional sin. For such willful acts against fellow humans and deity, punishment was swift and merciless. In matters concerning purity and impurity, neither innocence nor prior knowledge really counted. Contamination had occurred and needed immediate attention. The different kinds of offerings (for example, sin offering, peace offering, burnt offering, cereal offering, drink offering) aimed at reconciliation between a holy God and an impure people. The descriptions of these sacrifices and priestly responsibilities in chapters 1–7 reflect a later period when a complex sacrificial system characterized daily life at the Solomonic Temple. Considerable attention is paid to the special privileges that accrue to the descendants of Aaron, whose livelihood depended on a thriving sacrificial system. The laws therefore reflect a high degree of vested interest on the part of priests, who stood to gain from a scrupulous conscience on the people's part. Nevertheless, the laws made allowances for poor persons who could not afford to donate sheep and goats but who sought forgiveness for unwitting sins. In this way Israel's priests demonstrated a readiness to consider personal circumstances, even though such concessions lessened their own revenues from official duties.

The old regulations concerning purity and impurity embrace a wide range of topics from personal hygiene to mildew that grows on walls within houses. The food laws specify exactly what types of animals, fowl, and insects, were considered clean and therefore edible. The law of purification after giving birth makes a distinction between the length of impurity and purification following male and female children. After the birth of a son, a mother was unclean for a week and her purification lasted thirty-three days; where a daughter was concerned, these figures were doubled. The procedures for determining whether a skin disease was leprosy or not are given in great detail. The priest played a decisive role in this diagnosis, and his decision was final, even to banishing a person from life within the community. In such matters the welfare of the group took precedence over the rights of a single individual, who was relegated to existence as an outcast. However, such banishment was not necessarily permanent, and provision was made for purifying lepers and therefore allowing their return to society. A similar rule applied to houses where mildew began to grow; if all evidence of the fungus disappeared, the house could be occupied once more. Otherwise the affected building had to be demolished. In matters of personal hygiene—specifically, discharges such as nocturnal emissions or regular sexual encounters—procedures were laid down about overcoming temporary impurity. This concern for discharges also specifies procedures relating to the menstrual period.

These rules about purity and impurity end abruptly with a curious ritual by which a goat is chosen to bear the sins of the community. The priest places his hands on this animal and symbolically transfers to it the guilt of the people; then the scapegoat is sent away into the wilderness. Presumably, this animal was offered as a sacrificial victim to Azazel, an evil spirit. This solemn ritual of atonement is fixed in the liturgical calendar, as if to assure that no guilt slips through the cracks and defiles the people who diligently bring their respective offerings to the holy Deity.

THE HOLINESS CODE

The Holiness Code (chapters 17–26) modifies earlier laws in quite distinct ways. For example, because it presupposes a central sanctuary at Jerusalem, this code demands that animals for food be sacrificed there. The older Covenant Code had permitted the slaughter of animals at any sanctuary. The central theme of the Holiness Code is that the holy God demands that the people be holy. The stipulations indicate the precise conduct that falls under the rubric of holiness. They cover all kinds of relationships, with particular emphasis on sex. Accordingly, specifications about appropriate sexual partners are given. These rules prohibit incest and sexual relations with a woman during her menstruation. Although there are stories of patriarchs who married two sisters, and even one who married a half-sister, such relationships are prohibited in this code. The laws also reject certain Canaanite types of worship (offering children to Molech by fire), homosexuality, and sodomy.

Ritual observances occur alongside exalted notions of ethical conduct. Here one finds the remarkable requirement to love a neighbor as oneself; in addition, one discovers laws about looking after the welfare of poor people and sojourners. Many of these laws occur elsewhere in other legal codes within the Bible: prohibition of idols, theft, lying, sorcery, unjust business practices, and so forth. Other laws resemble the humanitarian emphasis in Deuteronomy—for instance, the specification that food should be left in the fields and vineyards for the poor in society, and the stipulation that fruit trees should be given four years to thrive before eating their fruit. But some laws held in common lack this humane legitimation—for example, the requirement that cattle breed with their kind and similar kinds of seed be used on a field, and that only one kind of cloth be used on a garment.

Two laws are of particular interest. According to one, the people are prohibited from making their daughters harlots, and another seeks to legislate an attitude of respect for age: "You shall rise up before the hoary head, and honor the face of an old man, and you shall fear your God: I am the Lord" (Lev. 19:32). In one case a law resembles some old curses in Deuteronomy 27, but the form in Leviticus is different: "You shall not curse the deaf or put a stumbling block before the blind, but you shall fear your God: I am the Lord" (19:14). One section (19:26–31) contains open polemic against Canaanite practices: witchcraft, mourning customs in which cuttings and tatoos marred the flesh, sacred prostitution, and necromancy (consulting the spirits of the dead).

In instances of sexual misconduct the death penalty is enjoined. This rule extends beyond cases of adultery to incest and sexual relations during a woman's menstrual flow. Special rules apply to priests, who are forbidden to marry harlots or divorced women. The chief priest is a special case, for he is permitted to marry only a virgin of his own people. Even children of priests are subjected to rigorous laws. Any daughter who plays the harlot is to be removed from the people by burning. Care is also taken to rule out the possibility that a blemished priest might approach the altar and incur wrath. The list of ineligible priests is large: those suffering from a blemish, a blind or lame priest, one who has a mutilated face or a limb too long, a man who has an injured foot or hand, a hunchback, a dwarf, a man with a defect in sight, a person with an itching disease, or scabs, or crushed testicles.

The Holiness Code places emphasis on a jubilee year, every fiftieth year, in which all slaves are to be set free and all land returned to its original owner. An exception is made for houses in walled cities, which remain in the hands of their owners. A system of prorating is introduced for the land and indentured slaves; its purpose is to prevent businessmen from refusing to transact business in years when the jubilee is approaching. The code prohibits slavery by fellow Hebrews, and the same goes for charging interest on loans within the ranks of Israel. The premise behind this jubilee year, which seems never to have existed in reality, was that the land belonged to God and could not be sold outside family groups who leased it from the Deity.

The Holiness Code concludes in the same way the Covenant Code and the Deuteronomic Code do, namely, with promises and warnings. Obedience will bring the annual rains in their proper time, and therefore bountiful crops will follow. The resulting prosperity will not be threatened by wild beasts or their human counterpart, molesting soldiers, so that the people of God will multiply and dwell in peace. Disobedience will bring crop failure, oppressive rule, drought, plagues, wild beasts, and the sword. An ancient futility curse increases the horror of this threat: "you shall eat, and not be satisified." This description of the ravages of war reflects accurate remembrance of Assyrian practices, specifically the transporting of whole populations to other locations within the empire.

The allusion to eating one's own children echoes the worst memory of all, the extreme measures of survival adopted during siege.

REDEEMING PERSONS OR ANIMALS

The book closes with an appendix that deals with the cost of redeeming persons who have been promised to the Deity and of redeeming tithes. The value of humans at different stages of life is interesting, and seems to relate directly to their function and potential for work in the household. A woman's price relative to a man's worth increases with advanced age (three fifths from twenty to sixty years of age, two thirds in cases involving people over sixty). The percentage varies in other age brackets too. From a month to five years old, girls are valued at three fifths the worth of boys; from five to twenty years old, girls can be redeemed for half the price of boys. As for the redemption of firstborn animals, which belong to the Deity, it sufficed to add one fifth to the worth of that tithe. The same rule applied to the tithe of the land, seed, and fruit.

SOME LOOSE ENDS

Here and there the book shows signs of disarray. For example, an anecdote about a son who was of mixed parentage, an Israelite woman and an Egyptian man, interrupts the discussion of festivals (Lev. 24:10–23). This story tells about the son's grievous offense, blaspheming the Name, and indicates that Moses obtained a special divine ruling on this case. For this offense death by stoning was deemed an appropriate punishment. In this context rules about an exact payment for crimes, the so-called *lex talionis,* are repeated. Here the law appears in the form, "fracture for fracture, eye for eye, tooth for tooth; as he has disfigured a man, he shall be disfigured" (24:20). This restriction on the extent to which revenge might be pursued is associated with an indication of further human concern, this time for sojourners. Thus it is specifically stated that one law applies to Israelites and to sojourners. In this way a response was given to what must have increasingly been a problem: the presence of children of marriages between Israelites and foreigners, with competing ideas about right and wrong. In another instance, as well, historical circumstances seem to have produced a situation that required a special word. Quite simply, the priestly lineage did not follow the expected course but went through Aaron's third son, Eleazar. To explain this departure from the customary ancestry through the firstborn, the traditionist tells a story about Aaron's first two sons, Nadab and Abihu, who offered unholy fire on the altar and were consumed by the flames.

PROTECTING HUMANS FROM HOLINESS

As the story about Nadab and Abihu demonstrates, holy people were subject to contamination from all kinds of impurities. Often the taint was unavoidable, as when one suddenly came into contact with the dead, and often it was concealed from view, and therefore both unconscious and inadvertent. For the tradition behind this book, both were equally reprehensible. Guilt had been incurred and required atonement. Expiating guilt was the function of the sacrificial cult associated with the royal court. The Book of Leviticus gave a theological rationale for this expensive ritual. In due time this justification for the sacrificial cult became wholly superfluous, for the Temple fell and other forms of worship superseded the ancient ones. Traditional Judaism retains the hope that the Deity will restore the Temple cult at some time in the future, but for the present it substitutes other forms of worship. Christianity quickly dispensed with any idea that the sacrificial cult belonged to true worship, although Christian theologians freely employed language and concepts from that ambience. As a result, many Christians have difficulty appreciating the Book of Leviticus. That difficulty is unfortunate, although understandable; nevertheless, it is worth remembering that the injunction to love a neighbor as oneself appears in this context where the holiness of God and the people is central. To be sure, the ethical component of holiness is by no means dominant here, but it is present nevertheless. That is no small achievement.

• 4 •

Numbers

THE title of the Book of Numbers derives from the initial section, which records the results of a census, supposedly taken in the wilderness but probably based on figures from a considerably later period after the establishment of the monarchy. At any rate, the numbers are highly inflated, because one can hardly imagine a contingent of more than 600,000 males, besides women and children, surviving in the wilderness for any length of time. The title in Hebrew, "In the Wilderness," is more appropriate to the contents of the book, which recounts the peoples' experiences during their journey in the wilderness. As one might expect, the only indication of structural arrangement concerns geographical areas (Num. 1:1–10:10, the wilderness of Sinai; 10:11–21:9, north of Sinai and west of the Wadi Arabah; and 21:10–36:13, east of the Wadi Arabah). A few chronological references occur, but these do not seem to represent a conscious effort to structure the book along temporal lines.

MOSES' AUTHORITY

Much of the discussion concentrates on a single issue, the legitimate possessor of authority. At least five episodes take up the problem of authority and offer rationales for the prominence of various persons, particularly Moses and Aaron, although Aaron challenges Moses' authority in one episode and is rebuked. In the story of the seventy elders on whom the spirit of Moses fell, causing them to prophesy near the sacred tent, the emphasis is on shared ministry. Indeed, when two others outside the circle, Eldad and Medad, begin to prophesy also, Joshua rises to limit the number of inspired individuals. Moses' response endorses a principle that reaches out to ever-widening circles: "Are you jealous for my sake? Would that all the Lord's people were prophets, that the Lord would put his spirit upon them!" (11:29). Nevertheless, the story clearly subordinates the seventy-two elders to Moses, whose inspiration came directly from the Deity.

This point stands out even more noticeably in the episode that records a challenge of Moses' authority by those closest to him, Aaron and Miriam. The occasion for their resentment is Moses' Egyptian wife, although the exact nature of the complaint is not disclosed. In one sense this episode concerns a family squabble, with the older brother expressing resentment against a younger brother, and with a sister lending her support to the elder of the two. The narrator characterizes Moses as "very meek, more than all men that were on the face of the earth." Already the language of devotional legends indicates who will win this fight. The Deity promptly summons the three to the sacred tent and addresses them as follows:

> Hear my words: If there is a prophet among you, I the Lord make myself known to him in a vision, I speak with him in a dream. Not so with my servant Moses; he is entrusted with all my house. With him I speak mouth to mouth, clearly, and not in dark speech; and he beholds the form of the Lord. Why then were you not afraid to speak against my servant Moses? (Num. 12:6–8)

The ending to this family dispute seems somewhat disjointed; only Miriam suffers for her part in the drama. One can easily imagine why Aaron's reputation was salvaged here, for if he had contracted leprosy his priestly function would have been in jeopardy. Therefore, the present text limits the punishment to Miriam, and, thanks to Moses' intercession, the illness lasts only a short time. Nevertheless, she is excluded from the camp for a week. The divine justification for excluding Miriam from the people for seven days is an interesting example of analogy: "If her father had but spit in her face, should she not be shamed seven days?" (12:14a). In this ancient account dreams and visions are accepted as authentic media of revelation, albeit less immediate and therefore inferior to direct speech. Furthermore, they are more subject to misunderstanding, because the language of dreams and visions is enigmatic, requiring interpretation. However, direct revelation of the kind Moses receives is crystal clear. Perhaps this distinction between immediate revelation and disclosure of the divine will in dreams and visions explains the later hostile attitude of prophets like Jeremiah to his fellow prophets who relied heavily on visionary experiences.

Rebellion against Moses' authority was not restricted to members of his immediate family. A certain Levite named Korah led a group of 250 respected men who carried Moses' principle of egalitarianism to its logical conclusion. These men objected to Moses' function as a prince among them, and reminded him that their quality of life in Egypt was better than anything they had experienced in the wilderness. Their language is fraught with irony: Egypt is described as a land flowing with milk and honey, an expression that normally applies to the land of promise. Moses recognizes the real purpose behind Korah's complaint and rebukes the rebels for aspiring to the priesthood when they had already received great honor by being set apart as Levites. Chafing from the charge that he has acted like a prince, Moses objects that he has never profited from his role nor has he acted oppressively against anyone. The outcome of this conflict is far more deadly than a brief stint of leprosy. The earth swallows Korah and his two allies, Dathan and Abiram, while fire consumes the remaining Levites who had joined in the rebellion. The occasion for their death shows that they were presumptuous to claim priestly prerogatives, for they die in the act of offering incense. This story also presents Moses as intercessor, pleading for the entire congregation that was endangered by the rebels themselves. But here Moses is accompanied by his brother Aaron. "O God, the God of the spirits of all flesh, shall one man sin, and wilt thou be angry with all the congregation?" (16:22). When a plague breaks out among the people and threatens the whole congregation, Aaron quickly acts to make atonement. Confirmation of his priesthood comes when his rod alone among the twelve, representing all the tribes of Israel, sprouts. The buds, blossoms, and ripe almonds leave no doubt about the Deity's choice of a priestly representative.

REBELLION IN THE WILDERNESS

Several narratives describe the rebellion against Moses' leadership as widespread. At Meribah the contention so infuriates Moses that he strikes a rock twice to extract water from it, although the Deity has specifically instructed him to speak to the rock. For this disobedient act Moses is condemned to die without ever entering the land of promise. On another occasion the people complain against God and Moses, with the result that fiery serpents are sent to punish them. Once again Moses intervenes by fashioning a bronze serpent and lifting it up for all the people to behold and therefore to benefit from its healing power. Remnants of this cult survived in Israel until the late eighth century B.C.E., when King Hezekiah removed the bronze serpent from the Temple. Possibly the most notable example of rebellion took place at Peor, where the people succumbed to the worship of Baal. According to this tradition, the leaders were hanged and all participants in this fertility worship were slain. An anecdote tells how Phinehas distinguished himself in Levitical service by piercing an Israelite and his Midianite wife with his spear, presumably while they were joined sexually. Because the Midianites posed a temptation to the Israelites, a vendetta against this nation receives the Deity's endorsement, with the stipulation that only virgin daughters may be spared.

A small oasis on the eastern side of the Sinai Peninsula.

BALAAM'S CHALLENGE TO DIVINE AUTHORITY

Thus far the challenge of authority has concentrated on Moses and Aaron. In many ways the most interesting story in the book enlarges that discussion of human authority to divine supremacy. This account concerns the professional curser Balaam, whom Balak king of Moab summoned to strengthen his cause against the Israelites. The narrative is rich in humor, although it has been turned into a serious theological document by the mixing of variant strata. An unevenness has resulted that has the Deity command Balaam to go to Balak but also reports that God's anger was kindled because he obeyed. A similar ambiguity has accompanied Balaam's reputation, which is tarnished elsewhere in the biblical tradition despite his honorable conduct in this narrative. Extrabiblical testimony to the prominence of this Balaam tradition has recently appeared from excavations at Tell Deir-'Alla in Transjordan.

The biblical narrative reports that Balak sent messengers to Balaam twice. The first emissaries were told that the Lord refused to let him go with them. When the second group promised Balaam great reward, he spurned the offer, even if it were a house full of silver and gold. Absolute obedience to the Lord and accuracy of speech are the qualities that Balaam holds dear. The sequel presents a far less worthy diviner, one who sees less than his ass does. Here we have a vivid depiction of a man on an ass encountering an angel with drawn sword. The ass tries to get around the angel, and in doing so bruises Balaam's foot. An angry seer strikes the ass, who asks what he has done to deserve such treatment. Balaam answers that the ass has made sport of him, to which the ass responds that he has always been a faithful ass. Balaam is thus forced to concede this fact, whereupon his eyes are opened and he sees the angel with drawn sword. Now the angel rebukes Balaam for mistreating the ass, and allows the diviner to proceed on his journey. But he instructs Balaam to speak only what is spoken to him—which is exactly what Balaam had insisted that he would do anyway. After elaborate preparations and sacrifice, Balaam pronounces his words about this horde of people whom Balak fears.

The oracles of Balaam are in poetic form;* they consist of four speeches from different periods. The first is characterized by synonymous parallelism:

> From Aram Balak has brought me,
>   the king of Moab from the eastern mountains:
> "Come, curse Jacob for me,
>   and come, denounce Israel!"
> How can I curse whom God has not cursed?
>   How can I denounce whom the Lord has not denounced?
> For from the top of the mountains I see him,
>   from the hills I behold him;
> lo, a people dwelling alone,
>   and not reckoning itself among the nations!
> Who can count the dust of Jacob,
>   or number the fourth part of Israel?
> Let me die the death of the righteous,
>   and let my end be like his! (Num. 23:7–10)

A second attempt at cursing is no more successful, and Balaam can only acknowledge the Deity's inability to lie.

> God is not man, that he should lie,
>   or a son of man, that he should repent. . . .
> The Lord their God is with them,
>   and the shout of a king is among them. (Num. 23:19,21b)

Further elaborate ritual and sacrifice achieved the same result. The third oracle is enormously important because of the information it provides about the revelatory experience.

---

*The most noticeable feature of Hebrew poetry is the division of a line into two parallel halves. It is generally thought that this parallelism is synonymous, antithetic, or climactic (ascending in stair-step fashion). Scholars have not yet determined the exact nature of Hebrew meter, and scansion of biblical poems is largely subjective. The problem is caused by the great diversity of meter within the Bible.

> *The oracle of Balaam the son of Beor,*
> *the oracle of the man whose eye is opened,*
> *the oracle of him who hears the words of God,*
> *who sees the vision of the Almighty,*
> *falling down, but having his eyes uncovered. . . . (Num. 24:3–4)*

This time Balaam envisions a nation that will defeat its enemies and thinks of an exalted kingship that will bring prosperity and peace. An angry Balak warns Balaam to flee, because the Lord has held him back from honor. Then Balaam utters a prophecy about the future Davidic dynasty.

> *I see him, but not now;*
> *I behold him, but not nigh:*
> *a star shall come forth out of Jacob,*
> *and a scepter shall rise out of Israel;*
> *it shall crush the forehead of Moab,*
> *and break down all the sons of Sheth.*
> *Edom shall be dispossessed,*
> *Seir also, his enemies, shall be dispossessed,*
> *while Israel does valiantly.*
> *By Jacob shall dominion be exercised,*
> *and the survivors of cities be destroyed! (Num. 24:17–19)*

The survival of this anticipatory perspective in the Priestly material demonstrates its powerful appeal. The language clearly reflects familiarity with the Davidic empire and its victory over Moab and Edom.

In the midst of so many incidents of conflict it is refreshing to discover an altogether different kind of text, although its subject is similar to the utterances by Balaam. An ancient priestly blessing has been preserved in this setting, and has found its place in the liturgical tradition of Judaism and Christianity.

> *The Lord bless you and keep you:*
> *The Lord make his face to shine upon you,*
> *and be gracious to you:*
> *The Lord lift up his countenance upon you,*
> *and give you peace. (Num. 6:24–26)*

In pronouncing this blessing, Israel's priests put the Deity's name on the people and thereby claimed divine favor. Whereas this blessing and the Balaam story stress the power of a spoken word, elsewhere it is explicitly stated that in some instances even solemn vows were not binding. For example, a husband had the power to abrogate a vow that his wife made, and a father could nullify a vow that issued from his unmarried daughter's lips. Nevertheless, if either the husband or the father remained silent on the occasion when the vows were made, then nothing could be done to abrogate them. The word of widows and divorced women was binding, for no male exercised authority over these two classes of women.

THE ORDEAL OF JEALOUSY

A curious ordeal of jealousy arose to satisfy suspicious husbands, and this procedure too indicates the subservient status of a wife at this time. Whenever a husband suspected his wife of unfaithfulness, he could require the accused woman to drink a special mixture of water and dust from the sanctuary under priestly supervision. The assumption was that guilty persons who pronounced a curse on themselves would suffer the grievous consequences of drinking this potion. Women who were unjustly accused would suffer no harm beyond public humiliation. Nothing is said about cases in which wives suspected husbands of infidelity.

THE NAZIRITE VOW

Another old tradition concerns the Nazirite vow, which implied separation from the product of the grapevine and from corpses; it also required that one refrain from cutting the hair. This vow was not limited to men but rather applied to both sexes. Persons who set themselves apart for the Deity by this special vow were expected scrupulously to avoid not only strong drink, but also less potent products like grapes and even their seeds or skins. At the end of the specified period, Nazirites shaved their hair and burned it in the sacred fire at the tent of meeting. Then they were permitted to drink wine. In cases where Nazirites broke the vow through no fault of their own, they had to start over anew. These old traditions take divine ordinances with utmost seriousness. For example, when a man was observed gathering sticks for firewood on the sabbath, no one knew what to do. The Deity issued a verdict, and the man was executed. The command to sew tassels and a blue cord on the corners of garments is placed within this setting; even the clothes one wears therefore serve as a reminder of a higher authority.

PURIFICATION

Since the people were always in danger of encountering a corpse and hence becoming defiled, it was imperative to devise a means of purification. The old ritual in which a red heifer was burned and its ashes were gathered for mixing in the water for impurity addresses this problem straightforwardly. Various specifications assured the effectiveness of this ritual, which was intended to protect the people from the Deity's wrath. In these ancient stories divine anger flashes with considerable frequency, despite lip service to the old liturgy about the Deity's long suffering. Even the arrangement of the people was motivated by the desire to insulate the camps from divine destructiveness. Accordingly, the people camped in ever-widening circles, with the tent of meeting as the focal point. The presence of holy persons in the inner circles meant that only they were exposed to the intensity of holiness, supposedly because these persons could survive such proximity to the Deity.

This wish to provide safe places for the people extended to those who accidentally killed someone. Thus it is said that six cities were set aside to which such murderers could flee, and no avenger of blood would be allowed to pursue them into these cities. Furthermore, as long as they remained within these places of refuge, they were safe. However, if they ventured outside the cities, then they lost immunity from the avenger. It is further stated that the death of the chief priest changed things appreciably, so that at that time the person who had been in hiding could go forth freely. This old tradition also refers to forty-eight Levitical cities, together with their pastureland, as the Levites' share in the promised land. No family was allowed to miss out on its share of the inheritance, even if it meant giving land to surviving daughters. Demonstrating that rule is the point of preserving the anecdote about the daughters of Zelophehad. However, these women are required to marry cousins, and this special provision is intended to guarantee that the land will remain within the family.

One feature of this book strikes readers as strange. Elsewhere the selection of seventy elders is understood as Moses' sharing of the heavy burdens imposed on him, and the initiative for this delegation of responsibility is attributed to Moses' father-in-law. The Book of Numbers explains the elevation of the seventy elders quite differently, and ultimately suggests that the Deity simply removed some of Moses' spirit and distributed it among the seventy, as well as on two others outside the inner circle. To be sure, this explanation occurs in a setting that emphasizes the heavy burden resting on Moses' shoulders, a load that was exacerbated by the people's hunger. Nevertheless, the attitude of this book to Hobab, as he is called here, is far from transparent. Moses invites his father-in-law to "serve as eyes for us," which made good sense when one considers the old man's familiarity with the area. Hobab's intention is to return home to his own kindred rather than set out for the unknown land which the Deity had promised the people. The story leaves the issue unresolved, although one could assume that Hobab agreed to lead Moses over unfamiliar terrain. What can explain this ambivalence? Quite possibly it derives from the vigorous hostility toward Midianites. After all, Moses' father-in-law was a Kenite, a clan of the Midianites.

◆ 5 ◆

Deuteronomy

THE name Deuteronomy has resulted from a mistranslation in Greek. The Hebrew expression in Deut. 17:18 for a copy of the law was rendered "a second law" (*deuteronomion*) by the Septuagint. According to Deut. 4:13 and 9:7–10:5, only the Decalogue was given to Moses on Mount Horeb (Sinai). The nature of the book resists description by either of the two expressions, "a copy of the law" or "a second law," for strictly speaking there is very little pure law in Deuteronomy. Rather, an exposition of law generally occurs, and this hortatory feature is placed within a framework of historical retrospect. Moses, the great lawgiver, recounts Israel's journey from Egypt and characterizes the people as rebellious and therefore worthy of divine curses. But he offers the Deity's blessings to the new generation poised to take the promised land, provided that they will keep the statutes and ordinances of this law with complete faithfulness.

STYLE

The style of direct address pervades the book, and therefore its language is often characterized by stereotypical expressions, many of which occur again and again. This repetitious feature makes Deuteronomy stand out as distinctive in its manner of expression. Instead of economical language, the author prefers full, rich, one could even say effusive, rhetoric. For that reason it is appropriate to speak of Deuteronomy as the law proclaimed, and to use the analogy of a sermon. Certain expressions occur often: "the word which I command you this day"; "the place which Yahweh has chosen, to make his name dwell there"; "with all your heart and with all your soul, and with all your might"; "with a mighty hand and an outstretched arm." Such language appeals to the emotions, sup-

88

ported as it is by frequent reference to mighty deeds on Israel's behalf and terrible threats of dire consequences for refusing to keep this law.

A curious aspect of the style, the shift from second person singular to plural, has occasioned much comment. Whatever this alternating audience suggests, whether different sources or editorial carelessness, the result is a splendid example of addressing both the individual Israelite and the entire community with a word of the past that had fresh claim to be heard in present circumstances. The style emphasizes continuity between past and present, while contributing to the notion of one people without obviating the need for personal decisions. This link with the past is both comforting and terrifying, because the history of Israel includes the consciousness of divine election and a story of sustained rebellion.

The Law Preached

In a sense Deuteronomy constitutes Moses' divine charge to the people, delivered at second hand. The law is here placed in the hands of the laity, rather than being zealously guarded by priestly groups. Better still, the law is committed to human hearts, and fervent appeals accompany the teaching of divine statutes and ordinances. The form in which the Decalogue appears demonstrates just how important this hortatory dimension was to the author. Great care is taken to assure the present generation that these laws apply to them: "Not with our fathers did the Lord make this covenant, but with us, who are all of us here alive this day" (Deut. 5:3). Whereas the version of the Ten Commandments in Exod. 20:1–17 based sabbath observance on the allusion to God's resting after six days of creation, the rationale within Deuteronomy is firmly tied to historical memory. The sabbath is an occasion of rest for every creature, including slaves and domestic animals, for the following reason:

> You shall remember that you were a servant in the land of Egypt, and the Lord your God brought you out thence with a mighty hand and an outstretched arm; therefore the Lord your God commanded you to keep the sabbath day. (Deut. 5:15)

Concern for the well-being of slaves, sojourners, and animals is no accidental feature of Deuteronomy; indeed, a humanitarianism pervades the book. At times this spirit crops up in altogether unexpected places—for example, within rules governing warfare. Thus the people are enjoined to spare fruit trees during a prolonged siege, for obvious reasons, but also because poor people rely on them for food. The same spirit underlies the laws about harvesting one's crops, for it is specifically noted that grain, olives, and fruit must be left so that unfortunate victims of society's indifference will have something to nourish them. This principle is extended to oxen, which should not be muzzled while they tread grain, and to Hebrew slaves, who are to be set free after six years of service and given a generous supply of daily necessities.

Utopian Character

Many of the stipulations in the Book of Deuteronomy strike the modern reader as utopian. Indeed, in one instance the author attempted to combat realism, where creditors refused to lend money during the sixth year because the debt would be considered paid in the next year, the year of release. A practice of wiping the slate clean every seventh year, whether releasing slaves or absorbing all loans, could hardly have commended itself to any society. The same judgment goes for the rules about partic- ipation in warfare, even if psychological reasons can be offered for the categories of exclusion: the person who has built a house without ded- icating it, the man who has married a wife without consummating the union, the one who has planted a vineyard without enjoying its fruit, and the individual who is frightened by the prospect of facing enemy soldiers. Perhaps the least useful rule of all was the one that offered a criterion by which to distinguish authentic prophecy from bogus proc- lamation in the Deity's name. Elsewhere the author recognizes the in- adequacy of fulfillment as the decisive means by which to decide whether to execute a prophet or not. Here it is acknowledged that prophets whose word does not derive from Yahweh may indeed predict something ac- curately (Deut. 13:1–5; contrast 18:15–22). The understanding of proph- ecy as essentially prediction is characteristic of Deuteronomy and the books that display its influence (Joshua, Judges, Samuel, and Kings). Naturally, the phenomenon of prophecy is far richer when the prophetic books are allowed to characterize it.

The so-called law of the king also has an unrealistic quality (17:14– 20), although it seems to have arisen with a specific king in mind, namely, Solomon. The stipulation that the king shall be an Israelite, as opposed to a foreigner, is altogether unnecessary, because the issue never arose in the sources that have survived. However, it may have been intended to maintain the need for independence from foreign rule, for example, by Assyria. As for warnings against acquiring horses, wives, and wealth, they either repudiate kingship as it was known or they represent extreme naiveté. The idealism of this text reaches a pinnacle in the injunction that the king write a copy of Deuteronomy in a book and read it regularly to retain humility and to assure permanence in his rule, a reward for faithful obedience to the law.

One result of such idealistic thinking is a degree of timelessness, as if the people are suspended between a sordid past and an open, unknown future. A note of urgency thus fills the air, and this potential for good is accentuated by language of decision. Moses offers the people a choice between life and death, blessing and curse. Moreover, he assures them that the supreme gift of grace is accessible to one and all without elaborate physical effort or superhuman intellectual achievement.

> For this commandment which I command you this day is not too hard for you, neither is it far off. It is not in heaven, that you should say, "Who will go up for us to heaven, and bring it to us, that we may hear it and do it?" Neither is it beyond the sea, that you should say, "Who will go over the sea for us, and bring it to us, that we may hear it and do it?" But the word is very near you; it is in your mouth and in your heart, so that you can do it. (Deut. 30:11–14)

But a suspicion of being out of touch with reality colors the description of the past as well, particularly the ordinances about wholesale slaughter of the inhabitants of the land that the Deity has given Israel lest their religious practices corrupt Yahwism. Naturally, women and children from distant lands could hardly be expected to forget their ancient religion when being absorbed into their captor's household. A single argument, issued as the rationale for the Deity's failure to exterminate the native population all at once, shows how far the author will go: the gradual victory is said to have been dictated by the need to prevent rapid increase of wild beasts in the land, lest they vex the Israelites.

Structure

The actual structure of the book contributes to the sense of suspended time. Two introductions (chapters 1–4, 5–11) and various concluding incidental fragments (chapters 27–34) enclose what is loosely taken to be a body of laws (chapters 12–26). The two introductions rehearse the events during the sojourn in the wilderness and draw some important conclusions from history that ought to enter into the thoughts of the people who confront the demands of this law once more. The fragments at the end describe the consequences of wise and foolish decisions, exhort the people to choose wisely, and give a report of Moses' death. In addition, they include two poetic texts, the Song of Moses (32:1–43) and the Blessing of Moses (33:2–29). Chapter 27, which contains among other things a series of curses, interrupts the natural flow of the book, although its content is in itself remarkable. The people respond "Amen" to the following curses spoken by Levites.

> Cursed be the man who makes a graven or molten image, an abomination
>   to the Lord, . . . and sets it up in secret. . . .
> Cursed be he who dishonors his father or his mother. . . .
> Cursed be he who removes his neighbor's landmark. . . .
> Cursed be he who misleads a blind man on the road. . . .

> Cursed be he who perverts the justice due to the sojourner, the fatherless,
>   and the widow. . . .
> Cursed be he who lies with his father's wife. . . .
> Cursed be he who lies with any kind of beast. . . .
> Cursed be he who lies with his sister, whether the daughter of his father
>   or the daughter of his mother. . . .
> Cursed be he who lies with his mother-in-law. . . .
> Cursed be he who slays his neighbor in secret. . . .
> Cursed be he who takes a bribe to slay an innocent person. . . .
> Cursed be he who does not confirm the words of this law by doing them. . . .
>   (Deut. 27:15–26)

This catalogue of secret offenses delves into areas that normally escape
detection, and would therefore go unpunished. The assumption is that
people who place themselves under the power of these curses will shun
the condemned behavior lest the curses be activated against them.

To some extent the structure of Deuteronomy corresponds to the material in Exodus that relates to Sinai, including a historical presentation,
recital of the law, commitment to the covenant, and enumeration of
blessings and curses. Within the legal code, Deuteronomy 12–26, the
Decalogue seems to have influenced the actual sequence and complexion
of ordinances and statutes. Two types of law have been distinguished:
apodictic and casuistic. The former, also called absolute or categorical
law, is exemplified by the Decalogue and curses, whereas the casuistic
or hypothetical law begins with the expression, "If a person does so and
so," and ends with the statement about specific forms of punishment to
follow. The earlier supposition that apodictic law was unique to Israel
has not held up under closer examination, although its frequency of occurrence in the Hebrew Bible is noteworthy. Distinction between sacred
and profane laws is even less useful, because the sacral and secular dimensions of life were closely intertwined.

Nevertheless, the Book of Deuteronomy witnesses to the gradual ero-
sion of the sacral in one special area, the slaughtering of animals. Because
the author calls for the destruction of all sanctuaries throughout the land
with a single exception, the Temple at Jerusalem, it was impossible to
maintain a sacral understanding of the simple slaughter of animals for
food. Naturally, everyone who killed an animal could not make the long
journey to Jerusalem in order to sanctify the act. Therefore, a new rule
of conduct was necessary, and it concentrated on what was to be done
with the animal's blood. Similarly, the law regarding the tithe was ad-
justed in a fascinating way: tithes of animals and grain were to be eaten,
and on special occasions three times each year when the trip to Jerusalem
was made, these tithes were to be converted to money and then spent
on food and drink. Here is a remarkable secularization of previous practice. Understandably, these rules came into open conflict with priestly
prerogative, and care was also taken to assure the Levites ample payment
to make up for their lack of a share in the land.

The floor plan of what is thought to have been a Canaanite temple at Hazor. The orthostats with two holes are believed to reflect Hittite influence.

COMPOSITION

How did the Book of Deuteronomy with its highly unusual style, tone, and structure come into existence? Modern interpreters subscribe to at least five different answers to this question, and a consensus does not appear to be forming. The book is (1) a cultic liturgy from ancient Shechem, (2) a covenant formulary patterned after ancient political treaties, (3) a last will and testament, (4) a legitimation for a royal reform, and (5) an expansion and revision of an earlier law code. The question of origin is complicated further by the identification of Deuteronomy, in some form, with the law book that was discovered by Hilkiah the priest while repairing the Temple during Josiah's reign. In other words, if this book actually played a role in Josiah's reform, and if it was not written specifically for the occasion, then an origin prior to the late seventh century B.C.E. in Judah must be postulated. The issue then becomes one of method: can one properly establish the date of a book by a reference outside it, particularly when taking into consideration the tendentious character of the Deuteronomistic history.

Cultic Origin

One theory that has enjoyed wide acceptance focuses on the cultic origin of Deuteronomy in the ancient northern sanctuary of Shechem. Traditions of a legal sort combined with a conquest liturgy at Gilgal to produce a covenant form that was regularly recited in the sanctuaries. This view emphasizes the living traditions that shaped the people's character and stirred their imaginations. Hence, the expository dimension adheres to the earliest layers of tradition, although it was enhanced in later appropriation of the old book during Josiah's day. In this particular theory the people of the land played a significant role, along with the Levites, of course.

Vassal Treaty

Others have noted many similarities between ancient Hittite suzerainty treaties and the Book of Deuteronomy. These affinities extend to the following features: a preamble, the history of the relationships between the two parties, a basic declaration of the future relationship, a specification of the privileges and responsibilities resulting from the relationship, an invocation of divine witness(es), and the recitation of blessings and curses. To some extent these features might be expected to appear in any circumstance where two parties enter into contractual agreement, so that many critics have refused to attribute much importance to such similarities, especially when differences in time and place are taken into account. In short, for them, the literary link between ancient international treaties and Israelite sacred literature has yet to be traced satisfactorily. In addition, it is often noted that blessings are largely missing from Deuteronomy and that the curses are intrusive. In any case, the similarity between the treaties and Deuteronomy is merely formal, for it does not extend to content. Furthermore, on the semantic level it seems that the Hebrew word *b^erith* signifies obligation rather than covenant, and the precise history of the notion of a covenant is unclear. Recent denials that the covenant idea antedates the seventh and sixth centuries, as an explanation for the fall of the two kingdoms, rest on questionable literary criticism. In principle, however, the argument may be sound.

Last Will and Testament

An obvious category for describing Deuteronomy occurs within the text itself, which is presented as Moses' testament to Israel. This literary type is well known in the ancient world, both within the canon and outside it. Aged leaders leave their accumulated wisdom to posterity, and the sum total of their knowledge comprises a legacy, their last will and testament. Accordingly, Moses looks back over the last forty years when he led a rebellious people on a hazardous journey that kept them suspended between the land of bondage and the promised land. As one who was thought to have enjoyed a unique relationship with the Deity, who according to tradition spoke with him face to face, Moses would naturally have possessed rare insight into reality. Consequently, his testament addressed the people with unprecedented authority. The utter seriousness of his words is revealed in the warrants for them, especially in the futility curses* that mention almost every conceivable calamity. Here the crudity of the language reinforces the horror of siege, when delicate women secretly eat their afterbirth and refuse to share the flesh from their children with husbands who are dying of starvation.

Josiah's Reform

Only those scholars who view Deuteronomy as a pious fraud think the book actually was compiled in Josiah's day, but many others also subscribe to the theory that the book functioned to legitimate a royal reform, although its traditions are considerably older. It follows that some critics who explain Deuteronomy in another way also subscribe to the view that Proto-Deuteronomy was the lost book mentioned in 2 Kings 22–23. The reasons for identifying Deuteronomy with this lost book are persuasive: the reforms that Josiah introduces coincide with the demands in Deuteronomy, including the centralization of worship at one place and the destruction of all high places throughout the land, hence the suppression of all astral cults, worship of Molech, or syncretism of any kind. However, it should have meant the exalting of Levites to places of equality with the other priests in Jerusalem, but this important feature of Deuteronomy did not achieve actuality. This failure of Josiah to elevate Levites to equal authority with Jerusalemite priests is unthinkable to some interpreters, but others see the discrepancy as a result of vested interests on the part of a powerful priestly establishment and as decisive proof that the reform was carried out in a real situation where compromise was indispensable.

On the other hand, Jeremiah's failure to refer to threats from Deuteronomy in his denunciation of Jerusalem and Judah is strange if the book actually had formed the basis for Josiah's reform. Furthermore, the actual date of Josiah's reform may have been ten years earlier, if a note in 2 Chron. 34:2–7 is trustworthy. This association of the reform with the decline in Assyrian power and the move to break away from foreign control is entirely credible. If a lost book had actually functioned as the account in 2 Kings 22–23 implies, one must wonder how it came to be lost in the first place and, even more importantly, how it came to be ignored by the Jerusalem priests and by a prophet like Jeremiah, who can hardly be accused of vested interests where his threats against Jerusalem are

*It was customary in the ancient Near East to threaten potential violators of political treaties with futility curses. For examples, the speaker mentioned numerous endeavors that would issue in nothing of worth: you shall plant vineyards but not eat or drink their produce; you shall build houses but not live in them; you shall marry but not consummate the marriage; you shall become pregnant but not give birth. In other words, one's efforts would be entirely futile.

concerned. It is significant that those who identify Hilkiah's discovery
with Deuteronomy acknowledge that its form was quite different, because
the book was read several times in a single day and consisted largely of
threats. Some critics insist, nevertheless, that some narrative material
would have been required to instill terror in Josiah's contemporaries.
For a few interpreters the second-person-singular texts serve to identify
the scope of Proto-Deuteronomy. If in truth a lost law book achieved
immediate constitutional authority for a government, providing justification for destructive acts against all manner of sacred places, its content
must have been terrifying beyond description. An alternative view, to
be sure, is to attribute the whole story about the discovery of a law book
to the imagination of the Deuteronomistic historian.

Revisions of Law Codes

A fifth explanation for the origin of the book takes its clue from the similarities between the earlier Covenant Code and Deuteronomy. In this
view the natural process of revising and expanding laws has produced
a law code that was eventually placed within a sermonic literary context.
The book is therefore the result of the accretion of earlier laws, and the
final composition occurred during the period of restoration under Ezra
and Nehemiah, or perhaps their predecessors. This setting offers an explanation for the militaristic spirit that is present in Deuteronomy, a feature that may first have emerged to validate Josiah's strong nationalism.
One curious aspect of the book, which those scholars who date its origin
after 587 have difficulty explaining, is the positive attitude toward
Edomites. The events associated with Jerusalem's destruction left a feeling of contempt for the citizens of Edom, who betrayed fleeing Judeans
and aided Babylonians in maximizing their cruelty.

Circles of Tradition

Almost as many theories exist about the actual circle within which the
book took shape. Because it champions the Levites' cause, their sponsorship is generally acknowledged, but this concession does not furnish
much specific information. Were these country Levites in the north or
southern Levites? Or did the book emerge in prophetic circles? It is well
known that the style and many of the values advanced in the book have
their closest parallels in prophetic theology. Even the harsh law about
prophets who led Israel astray may understandably have arisen in the
bitter conflicts among prophets themselves. The remarkable thing is that
Moses is depicted as a prophet, and a promise is made that another
prophet like him will arise periodically, or at some time in the future.
"The Lord your God will raise up for you a prophet like me from among
you, from your brethren—him you shall heed" (Deut. 18:15). Like Moses,
this unknown prophet will utter the Deity's words to a people who are
afraid to risk getting too close to holiness. One other circle has recently

been proposed as the source of Deuteronomy, specifically a scribe in Josiah's court who was trained in Israelite wisdom. This individual is said to have been acquainted with Assyrian vassal treaty forms, because he studied international wisdom, and he patterned the book on this foreign material. This hypothesis is supposed to explain the presence of a humanitarian spirit within the book, as well as the notions of fear and faith. Regrettably, this thesis does not deal adequately with the differences between court and clan wisdom, nor does it really demonstrate affinities between Deuteronomy and wisdom literature in general. While some obvious similarities between the two exist, a much closer kinship between Deuteronomy and prophecy seems to require clarification.

The variety of theories about the origin of Deuteronomy has served to call attention to the complexity of a book whose appearance is deceptively simple. It is likely that many circles have contributed to its final form and that just as many perspectives have merged to produce a document that bears witness to the vitality of tradition, even when it concerned legal matters. A northern origin for the nucleus of materials appears probable, and a powerful prophetic sponsorship is also likely. Some direct connection with Levites is reasonably certain, especially when their threefold task as described in the Blessing of Moses is heeded:

> Give to Levi thy Thummim,
>   and thy Urim to thy godly one. . . .*
> They shall teach Jacob thy ordinances,
>   and Israel thy law;
> they shall put incense before thee,
>   and whole burnt offering upon thy altar. (Deut. 33:8a, 10)

Nevertheless, weighty arguments against the identification of Deuteronomy with the law book in 2 Kings 22–23 caution against facile acceptance of the traditional view first proposed by several early church fathers.

MESSAGE

Yahweh Only

A much clearer answer can be given to the question, what is the message of Deuteronomy? First and foremost it is the affirmation that Yahweh alone is Lord.

> Hear, O Israel: The Lord our God is one Lord; and you shall love the Lord your God with all your heart, and with all your soul, and with all your might. And these words which I command you this day shall be upon your

---

*The Urim and Thummim were dice that priests used in order to determine the Deity's will for the moment. It is believed that the small stones had two letters of the Hebrew alphabet written on them. The letter *aleph* signified no, and *taw* meant yes. Priests would ask questions that could be answered with a simple yes or no, and then they would cast the dice until two negative or two positive signs appeared.

heart; and you shall teach them diligently to your children, and shall talk of them when you sit in your house, and when you walk by the way, and when you lie down, and when you rise. And you shall bind them as a sign upon your hand, and they shall be as frontlets between your eyes. And you shall write them on the doorposts of your house and on your gates. (Deut. 6:4–9)

This text, which in Hebrew is called Shema ("Hear"), from the first word, has become a devotional text of immense significance to Judaism. The crucial affirmation about God's oneness can be translated in a number of ways—for example, "The Lord our God, the Lord is one"; "the Lord is our God, the Lord is one"; and "the Lord is our God, the Lord alone." The initial commandment in the Decalogue requires exclusive loyalty to Yahweh and grounds this demand in historical memory: "I am the Lord your God, who brought you out of the land of Egypt, out of the house of bondage" (Deut. 5:6).

Perhaps the adjective *holy* belongs to this affirmation, although it is missing from the Shema. In any event, Moses' unique role as divine spokesman derives from the idea that the holiness of God terrified the people, who requested their leader to commune with the Deity on their behalf. The occasion of divine manifestation is described as a consuming flame within which a voice was audible, but no visible form appeared. Naturally, holiness also signified purity, and this is the sense that occurs most often in Deuteronomy. The laws regulating clean and unclean presuppose divine holiness, and occasionally the notion seems quite strange to modern readers. For instance, the concept of holy war in which an entire population was devoted to the ban, hence destroyed, and the injunction to cover one's excrement so that the Lord will not see it while walking in the midst of the camp strike us as highly immoral and ridiculous, respectively.

The demand for exclusive worship set Israel and its Deity apart in the ancient world, which possessed a tolerance akin to enlightened twentieth-century attitudes about religious claims. For Yahweh there was to be absolutely no relaxing of this demand, and the goal of eradicating rival forms of worship justified any act, however barbaric. Of course, such extreme measures were considered appropriate because of the character of paganism, especially its practice of human sacrifice and the elevation of the fertility dimension, with male and female cultic prostitutes assisting in this form of worship. Since Yahweh had no consort, such an expression of adoration as sexual cohabitation with sacred cultic personnel was meaningless. Yahweh was unique in yet another way, the refusal to permit images as an aid to worship. The belief that the Deity could not be adequately represented by any likeness, whether earthly or heavenly, arose from a desire to express divine freedom. No image, however exquisitely fashioned, gave its owner power over the Deity, who acted with complete sovereignty.

An Elect People

The second conviction that pervades the book of Deuteronomy is that the holy God has chosen Israel to be an elect people. That gracious act of choice was not earned by Israel's prior conduct but sprang from the Deity's desire to make a name, a reputation, for having formed a holy people from wholly unpromising seed. The author takes pains to deny any special worth in Israel that the Deity might have spotted.

> It was not because you were more in number than any other people that the Lord set his love upon you and chose you, for you were the fewest of all peoples; but it is because the Lord loves you, ... (Deut. 7:7–8a)

> Do not say in your heart, after the Lord your God has thrust them out before you, "It is because of my righteousness that the Lord has brought me in to possess this land"; whereas it is because of the wickedness of these nations that the Lord is driving them out before you. (Deut. 9:4)

Naturally, the people of God's own choosing were expected to regulate their lives by statutes and ordinances that the Deity made known. These included rules governing every aspect of life, from economic ventures to domestic relations. Therefore, a set of rules arose covering slavery, marital relations, divorce, commerce, warfare, things clean and unclean, and the like.

According to the Deuteronomic understanding of Israel's history, the people failed to live up to divine expectations. The punishment for such failure is the subject of much reflection in the book, suggesting to some interpreters that the book's purpose may very well have been to offer an explanation for the course of Israel's history and to provide a chance for a fresh start. Whether this is true or not, Deuteronomy certainly envisions captivity for the people whom the author characterizes as innately stubborn and rebellious. One intriguing prediction locates that enforced exile in Egypt and notes that in desperation the people will offer themselves on the slave market but no one will desire them (28:68). This reference need not be explained solely as a recollection of bondage under Pharaoh's mighty yoke, for a substantial community of Judeans migrated to Egypt in the sixth century. Even the small company of Judeans who fled from Mizpah, taking Jeremiah along with them to Egypt, may provide a historical referent for this allusion in Deuteronomy. This author assures scattered peoples that decisive action, here called circumcising the heart, will restore hope to those who lie in death's firm grasp (30:1–6).

A Single Sanctuary

A third aspect of Deuteronomy's message is the exclusive worship of the Deity at a single sanctuary, which is taken to mean Jerusalem, although originally it may have referred to a northern shrine.

> But you shall seek the place which the Lord your God will choose out of all your tribes to put his name and make his habitation there. . . . then to the place which the Lord your God will choose, to make his name dwell there, thither you shall bring all that I command you. . . . (Deut. 12:5, 11a)

Some interpreters have maintained that the expression means "in every place that the Lord chooses" rather than a single place, but this understanding of the texts has not convinced many critics. More persuasive has been the argument that the exclusive claims represent an addition to the original book, perhaps added by Josiah's supporters to legitimate his bold reforms. The move to centralize worship seems to be motivated by royal desire to exercise complete control over religion through an official priesthood. Naturally, priests from Jerusalem stood to gain much from this change, both in wealth and in prestige. The Deuteronomic legislation requires the people to go up to Jerusalem only three times each year, during the feasts of unleavened bread (Passover), weeks (Pentecost), and booths (Tabernacles). Proceeds from this influx of people would have greatly swelled the royal coffers and thus contributed to Josiah's military goals. But the shift also had a positive side, for religious syncretism could be effectively checked, at least in its overt expression. However, religious beliefs and practices have a remarkable capacity to survive regardless of efforts to stamp them out. The covert worship of other deities and their respective ritual probably continued unabated, sometimes in astonishing proximity to the holy of holies in the Jerusalem Temple. Evidence from Jeremiah and Ezekiel testifies to this resiliency within religious beliefs.

Deuteronomy's enumeration of the abominable practices that were to be eradicated covers a wide range. They include all altars at high places, those elevated areas on which sacrifice normally took place, and every kind of sacred object, whether wood or stone. The standing pillars (*mats-tseboth*) and sacred groves (Asherim), where fertility worship was encouraged, were to be hacked down and utterly destroyed. So, too, the sacred places where children passed through fire were condemned to extinction. The precise nature of this Molech worship is unclear, although the probability is that human sacrifice of firstborn sons and daughters occurred in this context. The horror of this practice evokes a strong protest in Deuteronomy against inquiring into the ways other nations serve their gods in order to do likewise.

> You shall not do so to the Lord your God; for every abominable thing which the Lord hates they have done for their gods; for they even burn their sons and their daughters in the fire to their gods. (Deut. 12:31)

Theology of the Name

Another ingredient in Deuteronomy's theology concerns the notion of a name, which means considerably more than what contemporary readers assume. The idea of the divine name as resident in the central sanctuary served to guard against assuming that the Deity actually dwelt in Jerusalem. The holiness of God, or transcendence, required that the Deity dwell in impenetrable darkness, and yet it was essential that the nearness of the Lord also be recognized. This aim was achieved in an ingenious manner: the Deity's name dwelt in Jerusalem and thus assured the people of divine presence. However, the subsequent defeat of the central sanctuary did not compromise the Deity's power because only the name resided in Jerusalem. The name constituted the being of Yahweh, everything the Deity stood for in the minds of the people. When the Deity's name was called over someone, it signified ownership and therefore a close relationship of trust.

This concept came to such prominence in Deuteronomy that the book is often equated with a theology of the name. The importance of the divine name is acknowledged in the Decalogue: "You shall not take the name of the Lord your God in vain: for the Lord will not hold him guiltless who takes his name in vain" (5:11). The intention here seems to be to protect the divine name from use by persons who wished to avail themselves of its unusual (magical) power. In a sense the prohibition arises out of a profound respect for divine sovereignty in a world where more than one story reports on a deity's fall from power through careless revelation of secret names to persons who pretended friendship but sought personal gain. In Deuteronomy the name comes to represent an actual manifestation of Deity, an invisible attribute, that functioned effectively as the Deity itself.

Fear and Love

A fifth ingredient in Deuteronomy's teaching concerns the human response to election by a holy Lord, who also chose Jerusalem as a central shrine in which the ineffable name would dwell. In brief, that response was fear and love. Negatively, the unique relationship between people and Deity evoked terror, but the positive side of that mutual bond was love. To be sure, fear arose from the concept of holiness, and it grew unchecked when sin entered the picture. But love prevailed over fear at its height, and the author seems never to have tired of celebrating divine love. Nevertheless, divine patience does not last forever, so Deuteronomy presents the people with a choice:

> I call heaven and earth to witness against you this day, that I have set before you life and death, blessing and curse; therefore choose life, that you and your descendants may live, loving the Lord your God, obeying his voice, and cleaving to him; for that means life to you and length of days, that you may dwell in the land which the Lord swore to your fathers, to Abraham, to Isaac, and to Jacob, to give them. (Deut. 30:19–20)

Such emphasis on divine love and human response in kind goes a long way toward combatting a legalistic understanding of the divine-human relationship.

A tendency toward external authority in a book emerges in connection with Deuteronomy, with mixed consequences. The elevation of this book as the constitutional authority to which even the king is subjected, if the story in 2 Kings 22–23 can be taken at face value, is a monumental step in the direction of a religion of the book. The occasional warnings against adding to or taking from individual codes soon applies to the entire book, as do the injunctions about copying and reading it. Similarly, the king is even subjected to its authority (Deut. 17:14–20), and he is instructed to read it all the days of his life. Moreover, periodic public readings are also enjoined, always with promises of well-being and threats of disaster as strong motivating forces.

Choose Life

Finally, Deuteronomy is characterized by a strong sense of actualization. The pretense of an address by Moses to an expectant people awaiting entry into the promised land functions to heighten the feeling of urgency the author seeks to foster. By emphasizing the divine covenant with the present generation, Moses effectively blots out centuries of Israel's history, once more placing the people in the context of decision. The Deuteronomist re-presents the past, hoping thereby to actualize the divine promises in the living present. This is the purpose of Moses' insistence that the covenant was made not with the fathers but with the present generation. The audience for whom this emotional appeal was written, presumably Josiah's contemporaries at one stage and probably also the later community who sought to restore Yahweh worship in Jerusalem after the exile, was being offered the chance to undo the mistakes of the past. Laxity in the realm of religious syncretism is identified as the essential cause for Israel's misfortunes, and a rigorous attitude toward extinguishing all foreign cultic practices is offered as the secret to success. Every effort to turn religion into an occult practice is therefore scorned: "The secret things belong to the Lord our God; but the things that are revealed belong to us and our children for ever, that we may do all the words of this law" (29:29). The reward for love and faithfulness with respect to the law here revealed is nothing less than life. That offer must surely have come as dew from heaven to a community whose survival was threatened by a hostile environment and whose efforts to reconstitute the people of God required immense personal sacrifice. "For what great nation is there that has a god so near to it as the Lord our God is to us, whenever we call upon him?" (4:7).

◆ PART TWO ◆

THE PROPHETS

I N the Torah, a single spokesman for the Deity came to prominence. In fact, one ancient text expresses the hope that a succession of leaders like Moses will appear on the scene from time to time.

> The Lord your God will raise up for you a prophet like me from among you, from your brethren—him you shall heed. (Duet. 18:15)

It was no light matter to speak with the Lord, and ordinary people stood in dread of being slain by the Holy One who could not countenance sin. Therefore, they greatly desired a mediator like Moses who would stand in their place and intercede for them. Moreover, the divine word required interpretation, for it was believed to come frequently in enigmatic form. Moses and his successors attended to the divine word and sought to apply it to daily life.

Israel's prophets were thought to have been related positively to the Torah, and their proclamations were sometimes grounded in specific aspects of the Mosaic legislation—for example, Amos's indictment of creditors' unscrupulous practice of holding garments taken in pledge rather than returning them in the evening to poor borrowers, who had no protection from the cold at night. However, like Moses, these prophets received inspiration from experiences that were conceived to be direct communication with the Deity. Hence their oracles were often introduced by a messenger formula, "Thus has the Lord spoken," or by an expression that was the equivalent of quotation marks, "Whisper of the Lord."

The belief that the Deity chooses special persons in the tradition of Moses and communicates the divine will to them is the fundamental basis of Israelite prophecy. To be sure, most ancient peoples recognized the importance of intermediaries, and similarities of thought and practice between Israelite prophets and those of neighboring countries occasion little surprise. In Israel, however, anticipation of a single messenger "like Moses" eventually produced messianic expectations of a deliverer who

103

would combine the best features of Moses and David. Because Israelite prophets flourished during the period of the monarchy, this particular combination is entirely appropriate. Nevertheless, these prophets did not sanction royal conduct either in Israel or in Judah but continually subjected it to the divine word. The prophets succeeding Moses changed considerably over the years, as might be expected, but even the latest prophets were still engaged in the awesome task of communicating the divine word to humans. The story of that activity unfolds in the Former and Latter Prophets.

The Former Prophets

URING the Middle Ages the second division of the Bible was further divided into the Former Prophets and the Latter Prophets, each comprising four books. Joshua, Judges, Samuel, and Kings made up the first group, and Isaiah, Jeremiah, Ezekiel, and the Book of the Twelve constituted the second group. The precise sense of the words *former* and *latter* is unclear. They may carry a local connotation and thus signify those books which come first and those which follow in a scroll, or *former* may imply temporal precedence, and *latter* then would suggest origin at a subsequent time. The expression "former prophets" already occurs in the Book of Zechariah, which seems to use it in a temporal sense. The two adjectives draw attention to the continuity of the prophetic witness from the very beginning of the people Israel to the cessation of canonical prophecy.

The unity of prophetic proclamation over the centuries is further documented in the character of the two subdivisions. The Former Prophets are predominantly narrative, with occasional short oracles. Although poetic oracle holds sway in the Latter Prophets, the narrative form survives in a number of books. In Isaiah and Jeremiah entire blocks of historiography exist alongside poetic oracles. The prevailing mode of presentation may differ, but both subdivisions advance a single understanding—to wit, that the nation's destiny is determined by its response to the prophetic word.

HISTORICAL CYCLES

The Former Prophets trace the history of Israel from the conquest of Palestine to the death of the last Davidic king shortly after 560 B.C.E. They characterize Israel's response to the prophetic explication of the Mosaic law as initial faithfulness throughout Joshua's leadership, followed

105

by alternating periods of obedience and disobedience. The description
of history therefore assumes a cyclical character, and this repetitious aspect is heightened by the frequent occurrence of standard formulas. In
the Book of Judges the cycle consists of four episodes: (1) the people
sin; (2) the Deity sends punishment at the hands of enemies; (3) a cry
for deliverance goes up, accompanied by repentance; and (4) relief (that
is, a warrior judge) arrives before it is too late, thus confirming divine
compassion. In Kings formulaic expressions identify reigning kings and
judge them on the basis of their conduct with regard to Deuteronomy's
demand for exclusive worship at a single sanctuary, which is understood
to mean Jerusalem. Naturally, this norm condemns every king who ruled
in the north, where royal sanctuaries at Bethel and Dan competed with
Jerusalem for prominence. Even kings in the south seldom came close
to complete obedience to the ancient provisions, and only two rulers
receive unqualified approval (Josiah and Hezekiah). Qualified approval
goes to Asa, Jehoshaphat, Joash, Azariah, and Jotham.

JOSIAH'S REFORM

In assessing Israel's history, one brief period is chosen as the closest
approximation to the divine will that has taken place. This high moment
occurred in 622 when King Josiah launched a thoroughgoing religious
reform based on the Deuteronomic demand for centralized worship. Although this understanding of proper worship arose only in the late seventh century, it is read back into the past, and kings are condemned for
failing to adhere to a perspective that they had never even encountered.
The result is a consistently negative picture of Israelite history. These
four books tell a story of failure which is dramatically juxtaposed with
an account of incredible success when a thousand Canaanites fled before
a single Israelite, according to Joshua's rhetoric.

An inevitable consequence of this manner of describing Israelite history is tendentiousness—biased story telling. The intention is not to
present what moderns generally call objective history, the unachievable
goal toward which many historians on the current scene rightly strive.
As is well known, to a certain extent all history is interpreted history,
for the very selection of facts to be recorded requires a subjective judgment. In addition, all interpreters work from a particular orientation,
whether consciously or unconsciously. The historiography in Joshua,
Judges, Samuel, and Kings lifts up theological issues as decisive in shaping Israel's destiny, whereas modern thinkers would naturally concentrate
on economic and political factors. Nevertheless, the essential concern in
these ancient narratives is to discern cause and effect and perhaps also
to profit from mistakes of the past.

The peculiar bias operating in these four books has produced a picture of the past that arose from ideals rather than describing what actually happened. To a large extent the resulting picture represents a theological construct, which existed only in the minds of the authors. This judgment applies both to the idealized account of the conquest of Palestine and to the subsequent history of failure. The intention was not to deceive, however, because evidence that is damaging to the theological construct is preserved as well. In some instances the religious stance has led to the obscuring of careers like that of King Omri, whose influence was felt far beyond Israel's borders but who is hardly mentioned in the biblical account. From this Deuteronomistic perspective, it mattered little that Ahab made his presence felt on the international scene, for he fell short when measured against the religious norm that these books advocate.

If this understanding of the Former Prophets is accurate, it means that the primary concern is theological rather than historical. For this reason, any discrepancy between the biblical narrative and historical fact should occasion little comment. Only those interpreters who refuse to allow the canonical authors freedom to apply religious judgments to historical events need worry. In any event, it is a serious methodological error to impose modern concepts of historiography on these narratives and to ignore their essentially religious character. To glean from these four books only those historically reliable accounts and to dismiss all else as worthless fiction represents irresponsible scholarship. So does its corollary, the insistence that the historicity of the biblical narrative be maintained at any cost.

A SINGLE VIEWPOINT

The religious viewpoint that pervades the Former Prophets links them together in such a way as to suggest the possibility of unitary authorship, or perhaps the activity of an editor who left an indelible mark on the material. Similarities between Deuteronomy and these four books have led to a supposition that together they constitute a single history, the product of a school of thought usually called Deuteronomistic. The editors have gathered together various sources, providing their own clue for understanding the individual accounts. In some instances the original material is preserved almost intact, with minor editorial additions here and there. In other cases the theological perspective has dictated the introduction of extensive blocks of material written specifically to expound the Deuteronomist's understanding of history. In Joshua and Samuel great blocks of such interpreted history are easily discerned, whereas the presence of editorial activity in Judges and Kings is much more dispersed throughout the earlier material. Evidence seems to point to at least three redactions of this Deuteronomistic history. The basic narrative was eventually subjected to a reworking by a person or group whose main interests derived from prophecy, and this edition was subsequently brought into line with legalistic thought of the time. A by-product of this editorial diversity is inner tension; contradictions have not been ironed out entirely, and opposing attitudes are allowed to stand in the same book. Nowhere is this as noticeable as the two quite distinct views of kingship, one favorable and the other unfavorable.

In spite of the presence of numerous independent accounts and at least three major editions of the whole work, the impression of unity dominates. The history of disobedience to the prophetic word is marked by a number of transitions, at each of which a speech in the Deuteronomic idiom or a theological statement occurs. Deuteronomy set the precedent for this feature with a farewell speech by Moses. The Deity addresses Joshua at the moment the leadership changes, and Joshua delivers a final speech at the end of his ministry. The prophet Samuel likewise sums up his activity just before the transition to kingship. When Solomon dedicates the Temple, he makes a similar speech before addressing the Deity in prayer. A shift takes place in the reporting of the northern kingdom's fall, for a theological statement functions in the way speeches do prior to this event. At the end of the narrative even theological statement virtually vanishes, and Judah's defeat evokes no comparable comment, presumably because the author understood this event as final.

PURPOSE

What was the purpose of presenting Israel's history in this manner? An adequate answer must take into consideration the devastating impact Jerusalem's fall and the accompanying exile must have made, particularly because this calamity came on the heels of a thoroughgoing religious reform. The issue of Yahweh's power must surely have arisen frequently, for the official cult at Jerusalem had promised in the Deity's name a permanent Davidic ruler. That era had now come to an end, and it appeared that the Babylonian deities had defeated Israel's God. The Deuteronomistic authors sought to combat such thinking. The fall of Samaria and Jerusalem occurred because the people refused to listen to the prophets and not because of Yahweh's impotence. As a matter of fact, the Deuteronomists argued, these two events demonstrate Yahweh's strength rather than weakness. Israel's Deity controls foreign armies, using them to punish disobedient Israelites.

Was there a purpose other than this defense of the Deity's power? In other words, did the authors envision any hope for the people whose guilt they so freely exposed? A slim basis for optimism has been seen in the release of King Jehoiachin from confinement in Babylon, but the reference to his death makes this view doubtful. It has been argued that the narrative was written in support of Josiah's reform and had to be quickly revised because of the disastrous events in 609 when Josiah's execution at the hands of a pharaoh dashed countless hopes. One further attempt to attach positive aims to this narrative focuses on the way for-giveness is related to divine judgment, concluding that the story en-deavors to create a situation in which divine forgiveness may reasonably operate. Despite the seemingly hopeless ending, it is difficult to imagine that so much effort would have gone into writing an indictment of a people if no positive result were entertained. After all, obedience subsequent to punishment does make a difference in Deuteronomic thought, ac-cording to a text that was specifically addressed to the exiles (Deut. 30:1–10).

DATE

When was this theological narrative completed? The events themselves extend to the period slightly after 561, when Jehoiachin's bondage was eased appreciably. But the basic narrative was much earlier, and the in-dependent sagas earlier still. Attempts to date the core narrative in the interval between the collapse of Solomon's empire and Ahab's rebuilding of Jericho in the eighth century may attribute undue weight to isolated references. The extreme emphasis on miracles* would seem to argue for a later date, as also would the ability of the imaginary account of the conquest to gain acceptance in the face of living memory about its real nature. In any event, even if an isolated verse yields precise dating, at least within a range of years, one can be sure only that this particular verse comes from that time. It is no less difficult to decide where this narrative arose, whether in exile or in Palestine. Both views are proposed, for a variety of reasons. Several things speak in favor of the exiles in Babylon as the original audience, not the least of which is the explanation in Joshua that the Jordan River floods its banks during the harvest season, information that would be unnecessary if the readers lived in Judah.

The choice of Josiah's era as the norm for obedient response to the prophetic interpretation of Mosaic law calls for additional comment. One can easily understand how such an assessment of the period might have characterized those individuals who were caught up in the excitement of religious reform during its actual heyday. What is puzzling, however, is the subsequent idealization of this period, given its abrupt termination, which seemed to cast a dark shadow over everything it stood for. How could anyone any longer subscribe to the theory of reward and punish-ment on which the Josianic reform rested? It may not be possible to

---

*The Elisha stories are marked by a heightened sense of the miraculous. It should be noted that such popular religious expression persisted into the New Testament period, flourishing in intertestamental literature as well. However, any use of this material for dating a text is suspect because such emphases may have existed from time immemorial.

answer this question. On the other hand, perhaps this tenacity of conviction offers an important clue about the power of religious texts in the ancient world. In these people's minds the Lord had declared a word to them through Moses, and that divine promise was reliable regardless of evidence that might appear to contradict it. Conceivably, the literary use to which this period of reform was put represented a conscious attempt to implement the divine promise of blessing as a reward for obedience. At the very least, this choice certainly suggests that for these authors the brutal facts of experience did not have the last word, and this acknowledgment requires the interpreter to listen attentively to theological statements.

The discussion thus far has focused on Joshua through Kings, although an occasional reference to Deuteronomy has appeared. The Hebrew canon clearly links Deuteronomy with the first four books, Genesis through Numbers. This situation prevailed in the third century B.C.E. when the Greek translators worked on the Torah, and also in the time of Sirach (Ecclesiasticus). These five books, the Torah, are later understood to be the divine revelation par excellence, and the rest of the Bible is a sort of commentary on it. Reasons for associating Deuteronomy with Genesis through Numbers and thus arriving at a Pentateuch are obvious, for without Deuteronomy the first four books are a torso. The important theme, promise and fulfillment, would lack its most important element if Genesis through Numbers were thought to be complete in themselves. However, it is strange that Deuteronomy has made no impact on these four books. Furthermore, there appear to be at least two introductions within Deuteronomy (chapters 1–4 and 5–11), one of which (1–4) provides a plausible introduction for the following four books, Joshua through Kings. When one considers the stylistic and thematic affinities between these books and Deuteronomy, it is difficult to avoid the conclusion that they form a single literary unit.

◆ 6 ◆

Joshua

THE Book of Joshua opens with a glance backward to the death of the incomparable leader Moses and concludes on a similar note, the death of Joshua. However, in the latter case, references to the deaths of two other persons, Joseph and Eleazar, vie for equal coverage. A subtle distinction therefore results and further enhances Moses' prestige. Between these significant deaths, a story unfolds that describes the conquest of Palestine and its allocation to the individual clans who made up the people Israel. The division of the newly acquired land also presents an opportunity for the selection of six towns in which unwillful murderers could take refuge from avengers of blood, as well as forty-eight Levitical cities to be the special inheritance of priests. Because the Jordan River separated two and a half tribes from the others, it seemed imperative that these Transjordanian peoples have decisive proof that they belonged to the larger entity. Hence the narrative tells how an altar was erected west of the river as a permanent witness that these Transjordanian clans were full participants in the religious history of the other clans. The story ends /with Joshua making a farewell speech and challenging all Israel to put away foreign gods, thereby renewing covenant loyalty.

CONQUEST

The account of the conquest emphasizes a quick military action in the central highlands, followed by a sweeping move to the south and then north, effectively taking possession of the entire country. (A curious silence about the central hill country has long been noted.) The only difficulty the Israelites encountered was said to be the consequence of greed by a certain Judahite named Achan. Otherwise, nothing hindered the Israelite army from vanquishing its foe. The reason for this success lay

111

The site of Jericho, one of the oldest cities in the world.

only partly in Joshua's cunning, according to the narrative, for the decisive factor in battle was the Lord, who is portrayed as eager to extinguish the Canaanites because their religious practices threatened the purity of Israelite religion. Indeed, the story actively involves the Deity in warfare, not just indirectly as the one who supervises miracles such as Jericho's crumbling walls, but also directly. The Lord is said to have hurled huge hailstones on the heads of the Canaanites, killing more by this means than the Israelite army massacred. Then there is the well-known story about the Deity's suspending of time, the halting of sun and moon from their appointed rounds, so that Joshua's soldiers would have sufficient daylight to slay the enemy. At one place in the narrative conscious reflection about the Deity's intentions occurs; here it is said that the Lord wanted to harden the hearts of Canaanites to provide a reason for exterminating them (Josh. 11:20).

GRADUAL INFILTRATION

The story of easy victory is not the only view of the conquest that surfaces in the Book of Joshua. Here and there the narrative concedes that the

Canaanites did not fall before the might of the invaders, that, in fact, large sections of the land remained in the hands of the native population. In these sources infiltration of the land was thought to have come gradually over a long period of time, and a religious cause for the delay is provided. A similar understanding of the initial settlement occurs in Judg. 1:1–2:5, a text that originally formed the conclusion of Joshua. A natural supposition is that an earlier view of the settlement has given way to the picture of a quick and thorough conquest.

Evidence of inner tension within the book is not limited to competing views of the precise manner in which Israelites occupied the land. The insertion of an independent account of covenant renewal at Shechem (chapter 24) has dictated the need for two reports that Joshua dismisses the people, and the removal of the earlier ending has resulted in two accounts of Joshua's death. Furthermore, there are opposing views on whether Jerusalem was captured or not, and similar alternating views about the character of the Israelites, who are said to have served Yahweh faithfully until Joshua's death and who are also accused of unfaithfulness that made complete victory over the Canaanites impossible. Further discrepancy appears in the chronology, especially where it is said that the people crossed the Jordan on the tenth day of the first month and celebrated Passover on the fourteenth, although wholesale circumcision is supposed to have occurred between these two dates.* Other indications of internal tension are the artificial attempts to arrive at twelve tribes and the awkward manner in which the sparing of Rahab's family has been tacked onto the narrative in Josh. 6:22–25. Indeed, the account of Jericho's fall seems to combine two different ideas of the way this feat is imagined to have occurred. The same statement applies to the curious story about memorial stones in the Jordan and at Gilgal. On the basis of such features of disharmony within the story, scholars naturally have sought an explanation in multiple sources and editorial activity.

EXPLANATIONS FOR THE TWO VIEWS

The nature of the material in the Book of Joshua has yielded competing explanations, one from the point of view of literary criticism and the other from the perspective of tradition history. The former approach focuses on various indications that at least three literary strands underlie the present narrative, although the exact scope of each is uncertain. The basic story line in chapters 1–11 is usually attributed to the Elohistic source, and the later Priestly hand is suspected in a few key passages

---

*The male population would thus have been in a state of ritual impurity, hence unable to participate in the Passover celebration.

(4:19; 5:10–12; 9:15b; and 9:17–21). The distinctive mark is that of the Deuteronomistic editor, who seems to have contributed 1:1–18; 8:30–35; 12:1–24; 21:43–22:6; and 23:1–6. Critics have not overlooked the fact that a concise delineation of sources has eluded the champions of literary criticism. Even the claim that the basic story derives from the Elohist has elicited surprise and skepticism that this author, who elsewhere possesses a scrupulous ethical concern, would have included the story about the harlot Rahab. A different analysis has come from tradition historians. Essentially, the theory goes like this: a collection of etiological sagas (chapters 2–9) and two hero legends (chapter 10 and 11:1–9) arose in connection with the sanctuary at Gilgal; later this Benjaminite material was linked with the name Joshua, and to this collection was attached a series of lists, one a quite old boundary list and another an administrative list from Josiah's time. After some unknown editor had replaced an earlier view of the settlement with an official version of conquest, the Deuteronomist added huge blocks of interpretative material at the beginning and at the end.

It appears that neither approach can explain all features of the narrative; perhaps the two perspectives are not mutually exclusive. The use of literary sources is beyond doubt, and the development of the traditions connected with Gilgal is equally certain. We are obliged to conjecture about the reason for bringing together such a wide variety of material. The date of the completed narrative cannot have been before the fifth century B.C.E. if the Priestly hand has really been at work. The text itself indicates that a time lapse has occurred between the recorded events and the reporting of them, for the formula, "until this day," is used often. Moreover, anachronisms occur in the story about the subservient role of the Gibeonites, and events subsequent to the settlement include a move north by the Danites and an allusion to a name change (Kiriath-sepher/Debir).

THE BOOK'S ORIGIN

To some extent the purpose of the book is related to its actual date of composition. Naturally, more than one explanation for the narrative comes to mind, depending on where one chooses to put the emphasis. The extreme animosity toward the Canaanites may suggest an origin in the circles that produced Ezra and Nehemiah. The intention of the book would therefore be to promote an exclusive attitude toward non-Israelites by offering an imaginary reconstruction of the settlement in Palestine. The argument appears to be that complete obedience in scrupulously avoiding the indigenous peoples brings divine blessing. Lands that have fallen into alien hands because of the enforced exile of Judeans will return to their former owners if they obey the Deity. This seems to be the implied message of the book.

A corollary of this line of reasoning is that the Deity has no special love for non-Israelites. Stated less generously, the book suggests that Yahweh required the complete eradication of Canaan's inhabitants. A natural conclusion would be that the task of extinguishing these peoples ought to be taken up anew. Whether such a mental leap ever occurred is not certain, but the grounds for it had surely been laid. The depiction of the past as an age of obedience must have forced many to wonder whether or not it would be possible to recreate a society from the past. The emotion-laden final challenge that Joshua thrusts on the people entertains such an eventuality. Joshua offers them an alternative and leaves no doubt about the direction he and his family will go. Such Deuteronomic speeches, which find their prototype in Moses' sermons, function to merge past and present. With a single touch of the pen, this author has blotted out centuries of disobedience and enabled the worshipping community to get a fresh start.

The reconstitution of the people of God here envisioned carries genuine risk. The preservation of the minority opinion on the conquest functions as a powerful reminder that even the original community of God failed to measure up fully to the rigorous demands placed on it. A danger arose from within, and not just from a desire to gain wordly goods like gold and silver. The people themselves lacked resolve to complete the task they began so faithfully. That failure had brought grievous consequences, and the extent of the danger could be seen in the secret niches where idols lay until circumstances dictated their use. This is the view that the author of the final chapter must have held, and Joshua's strong warning about the difficulty of serving the Lord burst any illusion that an ambivalent attitude toward the inhabitants of the land was permissible.

EXHORTATION

The hortatory dimension infuses quite a lot more than the final chapter, for some of the old sagas and hero legends exhort other people to action. It is possible that this preaching aspect of the stories derives from their character as liturgical material from a major sanctuary, presumably Gilgal. The command to meditate on the Mosaic law by day and night strikes readers as curious when the people are described as devoting their waking hours to fighting the Canaanites. Equally strange are the two passages that take pains to assure women that they will receive territory even if there are no brothers in the particular household. The homiletic features of the mysterious anecdote about an angel, the commander of the heavenly army, with drawn sword are transparent. This unusual story further develops the parallel between Moses and his successor by recalling the divine command from the unconsumed bush: "Put off your shoes from your feet; for the place where you stand is holy" (Josh. 5:15; cf. Exod. 3:5).

The excavated city of Jericho.

In one instance, it appears that two sagas have been juxtaposed because each one deals with cunning and deceit. Joshua made plans to get revenge on the citizens of Ai, who had drawn first blood against the Israelite army. To achieve this goal, he set an ambush and drew the enemy away from the city by pretending to be routed a second time. This clever ruse worked as anticipated, and Ai was razed. But the Canaanites were also capable of cunning, according to the story about the Gibeonites. After taking elaborate pains to give the appearance of having traveled for a long period of time, these clever individuals convinced Joshua and the rest of the Israelites that they were telling the truth. A covenant therefore followed, with assurance that the Gibeonites would not be killed. Even after the deceit had been discovered, the treaty remained intact, and the worst that befell the Gibeonites was servitude as woodcutters and water bearers. The background of this story is the Deuteronomic stipulation that covenants could only be made with people who lived a long way off, because it was assumed that remote inhabitants would not threaten

Israelite religion. Lest the obvious be missed, perhaps it should be noted that the dramatic story about Jericho's defeat is fraught with liturgical and homiletic features. Here the silent encircling of the city walls for six days and the sevenfold march on the seventh day contrast with the mighty shout at the very moment that the walls crumbled. The style of the story alone seems sufficient warning against taking this narrative as straightforward history. The episode is sermonic, and every aspect of the saga is chosen for its capacity to enhance the power of Israel's Lord.

APPLICATION TO A LATER PERIOD

The link between this homiletic feature of the book and a similar phenomenon in Deuteronomy has produced an episode in which Joshua and the people literally fulfilled Moses' instructions to read the law in the hearing of the people. Accordingly, the people gathered on two mountains, half on Gerizim and the other half on Ebal, while Joshua acquainted them with the complete law, including the blessings and curses (8:30–35). In narratives such as this one, the application is made to a later community that has been summoned to public reading of the Mosaic law. The primary concern was to motivate a later generation to obedience before the Torah, and the free rendering of the past in inspirational form sought to persuade readers to opt for the blessings associated with that Mosaic law. Those who ignore this obvious dimension of the text in pursuing clues that might enable them to reconstruct what really happened when the Israelites first made their presence known in Palestine, important as this task is, have consciously chosen to work on a level of the text that the Deuteronomistic editors relegated to the periphery.

With regard to this outer edge of the text, its actual historicity, three views have occasioned heated debate: conquest, gradual infiltration, and peasants' revolt. Many conservatives accept a modified version of the "official" view that the Israelites made an initial onslaught against the Canaanites and established themselves firmly in the land. Other interpreters opt for the alternative view that also has textual support; hence, they emphasize the gradual infiltration of the land through peaceful means, for the most part. The Canaanites allowed Israelites to take up residence in the uninhabited areas because this was to their advantage, especially because the newcomers had herds. As a result of intermarriage, treaties, land purchases, and the like, Israelites slowly expanded from the mountainous regions where they had originally settled. A recent attempt to offer a sociopolitical understanding of this period identifies Israelites as part of an indigenous population of peasants who revolted against oppressive rulers in the major Canaanite cities.

✦ 7 ✦

Judges

ENDLESS jockeying for position on the part of Israelite tribal groups generated friction, within their own ranks and outside those ranks as well. The story of this conflict has survived in independent sagas, heroic exploits, etiologies,* cultic legends, anecdotes, and similar literary forms that now make up the bulk of the Book of Judges. Happily, these narratives have been preserved for the most part without extensive rewriting by the Deuteronomistic editor who gave the book its distinctive tone through the addition of key formulaic expressions and a chronological framework, together with an occasional theological statement that interpreted Israel's history in a negative manner. The resulting account of this period leaves the impression that the individual episodes represent actions by all Israel, whereas they actually depict events in a limited area by a single tribe or a few tribes. Likewise, the judges whose function gives the book its name were really local figures, many of whom seem to have acted simultaneously in different parts of the country.

TWO KINDS OF JUDGES

The Hebrew root *shpt*, which is translated "judge," has an archaic sense: "warrior ruler," which is also the meaning of its Ugaritic equivalent among the Canaanites and of the cognate roots in Phoenicia and Carthage. This is the sense in which the word is used in this book about warrior chieftans, rather than its later judicial usage. Judges were first and foremost deliverers from oppression, not persons who adjudicated legal disputes. A distinction is necessary between major and minor judges. With

---

*An etiology is a story that attempts to explain some unusual feature: the presence of a rainbow; diverse languages; fear of serpents; or the peculiar shape of a geographical area, such as a salt formation resembling a woman. The Books of Genesis and Judges have numerous examples of such etiologies.

JUDGES

the exception of Jephthah, the Deuteronomist attached a chronological formula to the major judges: Othniel, Ehud, Deborah (and Barak), Gideon, Samson, and Jephthah. The minor judges include Tola, Jair, Ibzan, Elon, and Abdon. It has been thought that major judges were charismatic warrior rulers, whereas minor judges held an office of "law proclaimer" within the tribal league, but the evidence for this hypothesis of a legal institution is weak. It may nevertheless be correct that Canaanite law entered Israelite society mainly through minor judges who ruled cities and districts during the transition period.

WARRIOR RULERS

The present form of the stories about warrior rulers occasions surprise, for the editor allows the framework to exist, making no attempt to integrate it more fully into the actions of these notable men and women. In the first place, the book opens with a narrative that originally completed the Joshua complex of traditions. Here a completely different picture of the conquest passes before the eyes: the land was occupied gradually through a process of accommodation, and large pockets of Canaan remained outside Israel's grasp. Naturally, the Deuteronomist has given a theological interpretation of these unpleasant recollections, specifically that the failure completely to possess the land was punishment for disobedience. This remarkable list of nonpossessions concludes with an etiology about a place called Bochim (weepers), which recalls the appropriate response to this sad state of affairs. The book closes with a glance toward the future peril posed by the Philistines during Samuel's time, for the period of the judges properly ends with his anointing of the first king over Israel. The beginning and ending therefore bestow a Janus appearance on the book.*

The Deuteronomist did not entirely refrain from inserting his distinctive mark into the warrior stories, for the Othniel account seems to have been written from this perspective as a model for interpreting all the rest. This brief episode (Judg. 3:7–11) contains the Deuteronomistic theology in a few words. Israel sinned by worshipping Canaanite gods; God gave the people into the hands of an enemy for a specified time. they cried (repentantly) and God raised up a warrior to deliver them; then Israel had rest for forty years. The time frame varies, but 20, 40, and 80 years appear to be the Deuteronomistic author's favorite blocks of time. The intention was to allow 480 years to lapse between the Exodus from Egypt and the beginning of construction on the Solomonic Temple, but that aim was carried through poorly, resulting in unresolvable chronological confusion. Entirely consistent, however, is the cyclical view

*Janus was the two-faced Roman deity who was capable of looking backward and forward at the same time; for this reason, the name was used in the month January, which looks back over the previous year and anticipates the new year.

of history, both in this brief episode and in the entire book. The cycle consists of apostasy, oppression, repentance, and deliverance. Furthermore, the book opens with a judgmental comment on the state of religious loyalty and concludes with scandalous episodes that show how lax the divine law has become. As was true in the artificial chronology and cyclical view of history, here, too, a formula offers the interpretive clue. It reads: "In those days there was no king in Israel; every man did what was right in his own eyes."

A LAPSE

Structurally, this narrative about the lapse from almost pure obedience in Joshua's day consists of three segments: an introduction (Judg. 1:1–2:5), a central section (2:6–16:31), and an appendix (chapters 17–21). The combination of these separate parts documents the breakdown of Joshua's legacy, while at the same time emphasizing divine readiness to come to Israel's rescue time and again. The total impact of the book in its larger setting is to demonstrate the necessity for a more permanent form of leadership. However, the attitude toward kingship that seems to emerge in the several episodes is ambiguous, although the Deuteronomist certainly believed that kingship was a divine gift. It follows that two issues of primary importance arise in a discussion of the problems generated by this book: (1) the precise manner in which independent stories have contributed to a unified account and (2) the tensions within the book, particulary with regard to the monarchy.

DEBORAH AND BARAK

In one instance an exploit by a team of judges has survived in two forms, prose and poetry. According to general consensus, the poetic composition in chapter 5 is one of the oldest texts in the Bible. This celebration of victory by Deborah and Barak over the Canaanite foe, Sisera, is written in a style and diction that closely resembles Canaanite texts, making its translation enormously difficult. Like Psalm 68 and Habakkuk 3, this victory song gives evidence of a dialect quite distinct from the rest of the Hebrew Bible. Further indication of dialectal differences is offered in another episode in this book about warrior rulers, the conflict between Jephthah's Gileadite army and the Ephraimites. Here the fleeing Ephraimites betray their identity by the way they pronounce the word *shibboleth,* for they cannot form the *sh* sound, saying *sibboleth* instead (12:1–6). These unfortunate Ephraimites fared no better than the sleeping Sisera, who died at the hand of a woman bold enough to disregard strong

An ivory carving from Nimrud, in which a woman looks from a window. This motif is alluded to in the Book of Proverbs (7:6) and in Canaanite texts (cf. also Judges 5:28).

sanctions of hospitality in the ancient world. The poet displays rare insight into human nature when describing the thoughts of Sisera's mother, who permitted optimism to chase away disconcerting suspicions of disaster. The effect of juxtaposing two women in the poem is unforgettable; Jael hovers over the slain body of Sisera, whose mother waits anxiously for her son's return, while furtively looking out the window of her house. Particularistic sentiments (death for one's enemy) thus unite with universal experience ("Where can my boy be?"), and the latter is given an ironic turn, for the mother will soon put on mourning attire instead of the anticipated dyed stuffs. The repetition in describing Sisera's death leaves an eerie feeling, especially when one reflects on the poetic license operating here in portraying the death of a sleeping soldier.

> she struck Sisera a blow,
>   she crushed his head,
>   she shattered and pierced his temple.
> He sank, he fell,
>   he lay still at her feet;
> at her feet he sank, he fell;
>   where he sank, there he fell dead. (Judg. 5:26b–27)

This burst of poetic energy also has some strong condemnation for Israelites who refused to assist in the struggle that the Deity is thought to have brought to a decisive end by sending enough unseasonable rainfall to render Canaanite chariots useless. The poem is therefore an important witness to the absence of any strong sense of a tribal league that required concerted action by all members of the coalition. Levi, Judah, Caleb, and Simeon are not represented, and the Kenites are rebuked.

TRIBAL JEALOUSIES

Similar friction between kindred tribes has left its mark on several independent stories. Sometimes it takes the form of a feeling that others have snubbed a given group and must be dealt with by diplomacy or military action. Ephraim's complaint that Gideon had deprived the tribe of a chance to gain a reputation for valor against the Midianites was dealt with gently; Gideon described his achievements as of little consequence compared to Ephraim's execution of two Midianite princes, Oreb and Zeeb. In a similar situation Jephthah handled Ephraim's complaint with decisive force, silencing the vocal kin group. At other times mild polemic against a culpable tribal group surfaces in a story, for example, when Judahites are said to have preferred a policy of accommodation to confronting the Philistines in armed battle.

Some episodes depict a given group in a wholly negative light. For example, the Danites appear to lack courage and scruples when they find themselves unable to secure a position in their original place of settlement. The story about Micah's Levitical priest presents this religious representative in an unfavorable way, and spares no words in condemning the Danites who stole Micah's ephod and kidnapped a willing priest on their way toward massacring a peaceful village named Laish. Naturally, the polemic is directed against the northern sanctuary of Dan, despite its boast of a Levitical priesthood through Gershom, Moses' son. The brief note about priestly ancestry has apparently been added to this story, for it implies knowledge of a captivity, either Israel's or Judah's. In ad-

A twelfth- or eleventh-century B.C.E. *spiral staircase leading to a water source for the city of Gibeah (modern day Jib).*

dition, the note also looks back on the cult at Shiloh as a bygone era, the Deity having moved the divine dwelling place to another site.

The actions of Gibeah's citizens are reported with utter contempt; the rape of a concubine until she died and Benjamin's harboring of the criminals even elicits the following incredulous response from the general populace, each tribe of whom received by messenger one twelfth of a dismembered victim: "Such a thing has never happened or been seen from the day that the people of Israel came up out of the land of Egypt until this day" (19:30). Here, too, polemic against a venerable institution lies on the surface of the text. Gibeah, Saul's town, is characterized as a haven for barbaric people, and the unspoken reason for alluding to Jebus (Jerusalem) as the city in which the Levite chose not to seek lodging was to offer a contrast between two kingships as well, Saul's and David's.

STRIFE OUTSIDE KINSHIP GROUPS

Of course, not all conflict in the stories arose from competing kinship groups, for the Israelites frequently found themselves at odds with other inhabitants of the land. Indeed, the Deuteronomistic interpretation of history emphasized the punitive role played by Midianites, Ammonites,

Philistines, and the like. Occasionally the narrator introduces a comment to the effect that the Deity actively stirred up animosity between Israel and others—for example, Philistines—so that glorious victory against the enemy could ensue. In at least two instances, cities become occasions of controversy and bring about the destruction of their offenders—every man, woman, and child, with the exception of one significant category. That exception was every young woman who had remained a virgin, and the city involved was Jabesh-gilead, whose male population had neglected to avenge the rape of the Levite's concubine. The other city that came in conflict with an armed contingent was Succoth, whose officials refused to give food to a hungry army under Gideon's leadership. The story describes a painful pedagogy; Gideon whips the officials and elders of the city with briers and thorns. In the Samson saga, the strife is pictured as an ever-widening effort to get personal revenge, both Samson and the Philistines eagerly seeking to repay the other in kind. This point finds expression in Samson's final prayer, a request for renewed strength to enable him to obtain revenge for one of his useless eyes, but it has arisen many times in the course of Samson's struggle with the Philistines.*

One could attribute this portrayal of ceaseless fighting to the Deuteronomist, for the theological construct imposed on the stories requires some such animosity. But the more likely origin of this internecine strife was the constant struggle to secure territory already acquired and to expand wherever possible. The migration of the Danites, for instance, resulted from an insecure position in the general vicinity of powerful Philistines. That historical fact almost vanishes as a result of the explicit polemical thrust in the story preserved in chapters 17–18. Similarly, the crucial position of the valley of Jezreel in dividing Ephraim, Manasseh, and Benjamin from the northern tribal groups inevitably spelled trouble, and the celebration in song of Deborah's and Barak's decisive victory signaled the significance of controlling this vital region. Such tales of conflict therefore readily lent themselves to use in a unified treatment of the period of the judges that stressed Israelite disobedience and its serious consequences.

POPULAR TRADITIONS

For the most part the independent stories have been handed down with minimal editing. In isolated cases unrelated incidents have been incorporated into conflict narratives, specifically, explanations for peculiar geographic phenomena or strange customs. Thus a hill named Ramath-

---

*I have examined the Samson saga from a literary and theological perspective, with some attention to Milton's "Samson Agonistes," in *Samson* (Atlanta and London: John Knox Press, 1978, and S.P.C.K., 1979).

lehi (Hill of the Jawbone) is said to have received its name as a reminder of Samson's efficient use of a jawbone in killing Philistines, and a harvest dance is given a setting that relates it to a stratagem for replenishing the tribe of Benjamin. In this instance, parallels to the custom of seizing brides for a threatened group exist in the story about the rape of the Sabines. Occasionally, an anecdote offers an explanation for the name of a religious place. This kind of thing happens in the episode that describes an angel's appearance to Gideon and the accompanying conversation about the disparity between sacred story and living reality of the moment. The story concludes with a sacrifice and an angel vanishing in a flame, a motif that also occurs in the story about the angel's appearance to Samson's parents. In Gideon's case, he names the altar "Peace" to signify his survival after having seen the Deity. One other explanation for a custom is incorporated into the narrative about Jephthah's costly victory over the Ammonites. The sacrifice of his only daughter is preceded by a period of mourning for her virginity, and it is said that this incident gave birth to an annual custom of mourning four days for Jephthah's daughter. Moreover, Gideon is said to have possessed another name, Jerubbaal, which recalled his destruction of a Baal altar and a sacred Asherah, an action that prompted Gideon's father to defend him openly. The Deuteronomistic editor occasionally introduced explicit theology into earlier hero narratives. A good example of this practice is the dream oracle and its interpretation that served to allay Gideon's anxiety about facing a huge army of Midianites and relying on an element of surprise to spread panic among the enemy ranks. A dream about a barley cake that tumbled into the tent of Midian and caused it to fall was understood to mean that Gideon's sword was destined to strike a lethal blow against Midian. Another specific effort to offer a rationale for behavior occurs in the unlikely speech by the outcast Jephthah. Here the warrior, who resembles David in some respects, is compelled to counter a legitimate argument that on coming from Egypt the Israelites had taken Ammonite land, and the original owners now intended to repossess it. Jephthah proceeded to give a long account of Israel's journey during those difficult times, material that derives largely from Numbers 20–21, and ended the argument by putting a direct question to the Ammonites: "Will you not possess what Chemosh your god gives you to possess?" (Judg. 11:24). Having by this means disposed of all arguments based on right, Jephthah then asserted that the decisive issue was force, although this argument was cloaked in religious language. "And all that the Lord our God has dispossessed before us, we will possess." It is noteworthy that the narrative about David's confrontation with Goliath, the Philistine soldier par excellence, is also an occasion for theological instruction (1 Sam. 17:45–47). A third episode that is rich in religious teaching is the story about Gideon's twice-repeated test with fleece. This account magnifies the Deity by claiming that the natural elements are fully subject to the divine will, so that dew can be localized on a given fleece or just beyond its perimeter.

SAMSON

A comparable piety pervades the story about Samson's mother, who like Hannah in a subsequent story in 1 Samuel 1, is depicted as a remarkable individual. As a matter of fact, the admirable qualities of Samson's mother serve as a foil for the succeeding descriptions of women who enter this hero's life. It appears that the narrator intended to contrast an Israelite mother with Philistine women in a way that warned against erotic liaisons with foreigners. This theme comes to expression in the words of Samson's parents, who expressed surprise and dismay over his preference for a Philistine, however beautiful, and asked him to redirect his eyes on the women who belonged to his own kin group. Nevertheless, Samson found the erotic attraction of Philistine women irresistible, leading to betrayal of a secret about his hair and the breaking of a Nazirite vow.

To summarize, actual friction among Israelite tribes and between individual tribes and non-Israelites created the occasions for the exploits celebrated in the stories that make up the Book of Judges. The Deuteronomist used these accounts because they gave force to the special interpretation of history that characterizes his thought. By and large, the contributions of the Deuteronomist occur in discrete blocks of material, generally rather brief. It is probable that a religious spirit characterized some of the stories from their inception, although other narratives, such as the one about the left-handed Ehud, who murdered a king and left him in his boudoir, are coarse by modern standards and seem to have entertainment as their primary motive.

ATTITUDE TOWARD KINGSHIP

The second issue that these stories pose for modern interpreters concerns the ambivalence toward kingship that they display. From one perspective, it appears that the collected work pronounces a negative judgment on the period of the judges, and indirectly on the institution itself. Certainly, this is the view of the editor who is responsible for the present shape of the book. It is usually thought that the scandalous stories in chapters 17–21 function as a powerful argument for the monarchy, inasmuch as there was no central authority who could assure a law-abiding society. The thrice-used refrain about an absence of a king in those days, with the accompanying explanation in the final verse of the book ("every man did what was right in his own eyes"), seems to support this interpretation of the five chapters. Perhaps the stories do not discredit the significance of judges in dealing with external enemies, but they only indirectly imply the need for a form of government that can function as well in internal matters as in external ones. Because these stories focus on injustices that arose within the kin groups, whose greed and lust threaten the survival of elements within Israel itself, this hypothesis is a worthy one. In the society described by these stories, who could be trusted? A son steals from his mother; a priest who has earned a status of sonship readily spurns that relationship for fame and wealth; a clan robs and silences the victim by threat of death; a concubine is brutally raped until she dies; a host is forced to offer his virgin daughter to depraved men for their pleasure; a tribe is virtually extinguished; and marriage under certain circumstances is instigated by forceful seizure. There can hardly be a stronger indictment of the status quo than this collection of stories.

But the evidence in the central section of the book is less positive about pretensions to exercise dominion over human beings. The narrative concerning Abimelech's abortive attempt to establish a kingship looks on this episode as a grasping for power by an unscrupulous murderer. In the short span of three years this experiment was beset with cruelty, revolt, death. Launched by the execution of seventy rival brothers, kept afloat by razing a city and sprinkling salt on it and by burning a tower in Shechem and killing those in it, this local kingship came to an appropriate end. Like the Canaanite leader Sisera, this Shechemite was fatally injured by a woman, although an armor-bearer spared him the humiliation of having been killed by a woman.* The negative assessment of Abimelech's actions appears in the familiar fable attributed to Jotham, according to which the trees of the forest appointed a king to reign over them. Three trees declined the offer of kingship—the olive, fig, and vine—before the bramble agreed to rule over them. Although this fable is often believed to be a late interpolation deriving from wisdom instruction, the evidence is far from conclusive. The old narrative about Samson's riddle ("Out of the eater came something to eat. Out of the strong came something sweet") and the Philistines's answer ("What is sweeter than honey? What is stronger than a lion?"), which evokes a further riddling statement ("If you had not plowed with my heifer, you would not have found out my riddle"), suggests that these ancient storytellers were capable of composing a fable like the one placed in Jotham's mouth.

---

*Ancient Israelites believed that defeat at the hands of a woman was cause for disgrace. The implications of this attitude have been explored in various contexts by Phyllis Trible. See especially *God and the Rhetoric of Sexuality* (Philadelphia: Fortress Press, 1978) and *Texts of Terror* (Philadelphia: Fortress Press, 1984).

GIDEON'S RESPONSE TO THE PEOPLE

One further comment seems worth inserting into this discussion of kingship. It is entirely possible that Gideon's clever response to the offer of kingship was positive and that his pious words have been misunderstood. If so, Gideon agreed to institute a dynasty with the understanding that the real king was the Deity. Such a view of kingship was shared by later thinkers, and it conceivably underlies Gideon's words to the grateful Israelites. Then Gideon's son by a concubine, the daring Abimelech, would merely have acted to usurp the position of the claimant to the throne. In the opinion of the editor of these stories, still another warrior will exercise kingship over Israel before the legitimate heir to the throne, David, comes to prominence. This soldier who first obtained Samuel's blessing, Saul, will succeed in paving the way for his successor. For the subjects of a Davidic dynasty, this collection of stories about judges provides a cogent rationale for centralized authority, while at the same time refusing to overlook the dangers inherent in this form of government.

◆ 8 ◆

Samuel

IN ancient Hebrew manuscripts, Samuel and Kings filled a single scroll without any division into separate works. A division took place in the Septuagint because the addition of vowels required more space than could be accommodated on one scroll. The precise point at which the separation came between the four books of kingdoms is unfortunate, at least in one instance, for the natural break between First and Second Kings is at David's death (2 Kings 2). The principle of ending a book with the death of its main character was operative in Genesis (death of Jacob and Joseph), Deuteronomy (death of Moses), and Joshua (death of Joshua). Although the Greek translation designated Samuel and Kings as Kingdoms a, b, c, and d, a Hebrew manuscript relying on a much older precedent reduced this number to two books in 1448 C.E. This precedent was adopted by the Bomberg Bible (1517) and by most subsequent Protestant Bibles. Because the Vulgate followed the Greek practice but labeled the four books Kings I, II, III, and IV, many Roman Catholic Bibles continue to treat the four books as a single work.

DISUNITY

The unity of Samuel is compromised by the existence of duplicate and even triplicate accounts of certain episodes. Some of the most notable duplicates are the explanation for the origin of the popular saying, "Is Saul also among the prophets?"; the manner in which David first came to Saul's court and the flight from it; the exact circumstances surrounding Goliath's death and the actual name of the person who slew him; the deaths of Samuel and of Saul; and the account of David's refusal to slay King Saul when the opportunity presented itself. Perhaps the most notable thematic tension is the attitude toward the establishing of kingship in Israel, for some texts view this action as rejection of the Deity's rule,

129

but others describe the move as congruent with the divine will. Similar narrative incongruity occurs in the explanation for Saul's decline in the Deity's favor, which is attributed to disobedience in a matter related to holy war and to seizing prerogatives of priests.

These competing viewpoints and duplicate accounts of the same incident suggest that several strands of traditional material make up the book. Some of these strands are easily recognized—for example, a story about the ark, an account of Samuel's relationships with Saul, a narrative about David's relationships with Saul, a story about David's domestic difficulties, and some poetic compositions of considerable antiquity. The stories have not been subjected to an overarching perspective, so that it is difficult to sustain the hypothesis of a unified Deuteronomistic history in this book. Some passages do reflect the thinking that is typical of this supposed editor (1 Samuel 7 and 12; 2 Samuel 7), but the absence of an interpretive framework or a sustained ideology is puzzling. A few passages introduce later prophetic views into the book, particularly in the legends about Samuel. The author seems unable to decide whether to treat him as a Nazirite, priest, prophet, or judge.

The nature of these stories suggests to some critics that the authors may have been residents at the royal court in Jerusalem, but the uncomplimentary treatment of David in some episodes seems out of place in this context. If one disregards the features of the narrative that are unfavorable from David's perspective, a rationale for the collected stories certainly emerges. The material about the ark offers a legitimation for David's decision to place it in his newly acquired capital, whereas the collection about Saul and David exonerates the latter of any guilt in the power struggle that led to David's exercise of sovereignty over all Israel. It remains an open question whether the so-called succession document (2 Samuel 9–20; 1 Kings 1–2) provides a rationale for Solomon's ascendancy to the throne, or whether these narratives are better seen in some other way—for instance, as a depiction of David under the curse (preceded by a contrasting account of the king under the divine blessing, 2 Samuel 2–5).

Biased Defense of David

The preceding comments imply that a bias permeates these stories, whatever their original purpose. They function in the service of a cause, usually royal but occasionally religious ideology, and they present historical events in a selective manner. This point must be made because of frequent claims that the succession document, at least, is objective history. Even the word "document" used by earlier critics implies historical reliability, and much has been written about eyewitness reporting in these chapters and about their "secular" character that arose in an enlightened humanism associated with Solomon's court. That claim lacks substance, for much of this material consists of private conversations that no one would have heard except the participants. As was customary in the ancient world, authors made up speeches like these to communicate their story more effectively. In such stories we encounter historical royal novels of a type that is well known from ancient Egypt. The historical dimension is subsidiary to psychological and ideological dimensions; indeed, institutional concerns of a particular group dictate the actual presentation of valuable historical materials.

Nevertheless, these narratives are rightly called historiography, as it was practiced in the ancient Near East. They interpret the course of human events by a principle of cause and effect that applies to all human decisions. In varying degrees, the several collections emphasize human factors, as opposed to transcendent ones, that shape the destiny of the state. It is possible, then, to speak of an emerging nationalism in these stories, an attitude that is censured by prophetic sentiments interspersed throughout the narrative. The concept of history that surfaces in the succession narrative is rare in the ancient world, although a precedent for it occurred among the Hittites a few centuries earlier. The rejection of history as the fundamental category from which to view these stories must not obscure the extent of their contribution to the understanding of historiography. Still, the task of determining what actually happened, the residue of historical fact underlying literary fiction, is monumental. Furthermore, that task is complicated by the authors' capacity to write credible fiction, for the criterion of believability can lead to excessive optimism about historical reliability.

Narrative Art

The quality of writing in some of these stories is truly exceptional, rivaling if not matching the very best in the Bible. Often the imagery achieves heights that are unparalleled except in poetic compositions of unusual beauty. The wise woman from Tekoa, who is said to have uttered Joab's sentiments, described the death of her only imaginary son as a quenching of her coal, and she likened death to water being spilled on the ground. Abigail, Nabal's wife whom David later wooed successfully, expressed the wish that when enemies pursued David he would be bound in the bundle of the living in the care of the Lord, and that the Deity would sling out David's enemies as from the hollow of a sling. One can scarcely imagine more appropriate imagery for one who is reputed to have slain the Philistine giant with a sling and a stone. This hero, David, demonstrates the ability to express himself in powerful images when he asks Saul why he hunts him like a partridge. But the speeches of David's counselors, Hushai and Ahithophel, are filled with comparable imagery.

The latter likens an envisioned capture of a fleeing David to the return of a bride to her husband, whereas Hushai compares the valiant king to a bear robbed of her cubs. He continues:

> But my counsel is that all Israel be gathered to you, from Dan to Beer-sheba, as the sand by the sea for multitude, and that you go to battle in person. So we shall come upon him in some place where he is to be found, and we shall light upon him as the dew falls on the ground; and of him and all the men with him not one will be left. If he withdraws into a city, then all Israel will bring ropes to that city, and we shall drag it into the valley, until not even a pebble is to be found there. (2 Sam. 17:11–13)

The way in which the speaker pretends to be loyal to Absalom rather than to his father is noteworthy, for the plural pronoun "we" implies eagerness to implement the specific features of this battle plan.

Psychological Perception

A remarkable aspect of the story about Daivd's difficulties with his children is the knowledge of human nature that it demonstrates, especially in the episode about Amnon's uncontained lust for his sister Tamar. Incapacitating sickness gave way to contempt for the lovely woman who reminded him of his weakness, and the brother who had satisfied his lust brutally dismissed the victim of his lewdness with two words: "Up! Out!" Tamar's pitiful plea this time fared no better than an earlier imploring that her brother follow a legitimate path toward achieving his desire. Nevertheless, her words reveal insight into the implications of his conduct. His act of lust, however cruel, arose from something positive that had become debased, but the utter contempt of her signaled by his curt dismissal of a wronged sister sprang from hatred. That comparison is the basis for her observation that sending her away was worse than raping her. Tamar's pitiful protest in public view contrasts with Absalom's apparent trivializing of the act, although the words, "now hold your peace, my sister; he is your brother; do not take this to heart," mask a determined intention to avenge this loathsome deed in due time. Once that revenge took place, these words about not taking it to heart were directed to David himself, who waited anxiously to find out whether or not Absalom had extinguished all his brothers with one stroke. A subsequent note about the names of Absalom's children shows how much he really took the matter to heart, for he named his only daughter Tamar.

The description of David's behavior during Absalom's revolt also reflects accurate knowledge about the way love complicates power politics, and his indecisiveness sprang from that reality rather than from weakness. His poignant lament over Absalom's death* is entirely in character: "O my son Absalom, my son, my son Absalom! Would I had died instead of you, O Absalom, my son, my son!" (2 Sam. 18:33b; 19:1 in the Hebrew

---

*As is well known, William Faulkner borrowed the title of *Absalom, Absalom* (New York: Vintage Books, 1972), his powerful novel about the Old South, from this biblical account.

text). But such psychological insights are not restricted to the stories about David. The episode about Samuel's birth reveals an understanding of the pain inflicted on a barren woman by circumstances beyond her control. Elkanah's strong love for his childless wife was to a large extent nullified by custom, in this instance the precise offerings to be made at the yearly sacrifice, and by the heartless verbal abuse from a rival wife whose womb was fruitful. Hannah's fervent silent prayer for offspring, which the old priest mistook for drunken conduct, and her unselfish gift of that son to divine service are extraordinary examples of characterization. So is the description of a love between two men that prompted David to say that it surpassed the love of women. This unusual story about a bond between Jonathan and David that enabled Saul's son to ignore selfish considerations such as the crown and to turn his back on his father lacks the slightest hint of scandal. The story of David's relationship with Jonathan's sister is equally insightful. Initially enamored of her warrior husband, Michal eventually came to despise him for vulgar displays among the servant girls. Dignity appropriate to royal status does not seem to have penetrated David's thinking so powerfully that it prevented acts that would ingratiate him to ordinary citizens. The necessity for staying in touch with common people did not escape Absalom, whose calculated wooing of David's subjects is a superb study in political maneuvering for power.

Humor

The art of the narratives often manifests itself in humor, sometimes in polemical texts, and at other times even in near-tragic ones. The old story about the capture of the ark by Philistine soldiers and the resulting calamities that beset the uncircumcised nation pokes fun at worship of Dagon, whose statue is portrayed as falling on its face and losing its head and hands. This gentle mockery offers an opportunity to explain why Canaanites jumped over the thresholds of their temples. Naturally, this peculiar practice goes back to something more substantial than a pile of broken hands and a head, perhaps to the belief that evil spirits lurked at thresholds and emerged when someone was careless enough to wake them. A humorous episode in the story about Absalom's revolt tells about a runner who insisted on exhibiting his superior athletic prowess even though the news was bad. Although this speedy Ahimaaz outran the Cushite to whom fell the burden of announcing Absalom's death, prudence dictated that he stand aside and let the Cushite convey the full story of what had transpired. A breathless Ahimaaz could only announce, "I saw a great tumult, but I do not know what it was." Humorous features also crop up in palpably apologetic contexts—for example, the report that Saul entered a cave to relieve himself, and while thus occupied he gave David, who was hiding in the darkness of the cave, an opportunity to cut a piece from the king's garment. The humor occasionally becomes crude by modern standards, as when Saul promised his daughter in marriage to David if he would deliver one hundred Philistine foreskins to the king, and David promptly killed two hundred Philistines and handed over the desired bounty with plenty of foreskins to spare.

Economy of Expression

In a few cases these stories display a rare capacity to capture a significant character trait in a single phrase. David's unforgettable response to badgering by his older brother speaks volumes: "What have I done now?" How many times the younger brother had found himself the brunt of rebuke by older ones can only be imagined, but a pattern is implied that seems almost universal. Likewise, Jonathan's observation that good nourishment on the part of the Israelite army would have accomplished far more than a religious ban on eating prepares readers to expect him to distance himself from this father. The content of a song by merrymakers portends ill for Saul and promises glory for David: "Saul has slain his thousands, / and David his ten thousands" (1 Sam. 18:7). This poetic device serves much the same function as the later prosaic statement that "David grew stronger and stronger, while the house of Saul became weaker and weaker" (2 Sam. 3:1). A marvelous economy of language marks the brief report that Ish-bosheth, Saul's successor, sent and took Michal from her husband Palti-el so that she could be handed over to David, and Palti-el followed her, weeping as he went, until Abner spoke two words whose deeper meaning was unmistakable: "Go, return" (2 Sam. 3:16). In this regard, Palti-el showed more sense, but not more courage, than Asahel, who persisted in chasing Abner until it was too late. In one case a heinous deed, the willful murder of Uriah, was trivialized beyond belief; David advised Joab, the commander of his army: "Do not let this matter trouble you, for the sword devours now one and now another" (2 Sam. 11:25).

The prophet Nathan used the same idea to announce divine punishment on David for this act: "Now therefore the sword shall never depart from your house" (2 Sam. 12:10). Nathan's parable of the poor man's pet ewe lamb that a powerful rich man confiscated to feed a guest has remarkable evocative power, spoken as it was to a former shepherd whose fury rapidly turned to the shame of exposure generated by the courageous words, "You are the man." Just as this direct accusation plumbed the depths of shame and guilt, so David's resigned acceptance of his child's death acknowledged the grim finality of death: "I shall go to him, but he will not return to me" (2 Sam. 12:23). Although the full implications of the brief report in 1 Sam. 14:45 that, "the people ransomed Jonathan, that he did not die," escape modern readers, it is likely that ancients who heard or read this account understood the price in human life that must have been required to spare the king's son.

Poetic Texts

Alongside narratives whose literary artistry invite comment are some poetic compositions of considerable antiquity. Hannah's thanksgiving song (1 Sam. 2:1–10), which provided the model for the Magnificat (Mary's song of thanksgiving in the New Testament, Lk. 1:46–55) resembles Egyptian poetry about the reversal of fortunes that occurred in connection with social upheavals. The rich have become poor, and the poor have attained wealth. This poem was inserted into its context because it alludes to the barren person who has borne seven, although very little else really fits Hannah's circumstances. The praise of the Deity for killing and bringing to life is significant. The metaphor of Deity as a rock occurs here and in the poetic composition that virtually brings the Book of Samuel to a close (2 Sam. 22). This ancient poem is also preserved in Psalm 18; it describes the majestic appearance of the Deity, riding on a cherub in thick clouds and laying bare the foundations of the earth.

The permanency of the Davidic dynasty is the subject of a psalm in 2 Sam. 23:1–7. The form of this poem recalls Psalm 1, where a contrast between godly and wicked persons employs the image of trees with ample or inadequate root systems. David's final testament likens a just ruling house to the dawning of morning light, the sun shining on a cloudless day, and rain that brings lush growth. Such a dynasty, the poem contends, is David's. But the psalm concedes that godless persons are like thorns that inflict injury on those who touch them without adequate protection. The theme of a permanent Davidic house occurs elsewhere in 2 Samuel 7, a prose context that gives evidence of editorial retouching. David determined to build a house for the Deity, and Nathan, his prophetic spokesman, pronounced a blessing on the project. Later that night Nathan reached a different conclusion, based on past dealings with Israel on the Deity's part. Here the Lord reasoned that so far there had been no need for a house, and great things had been accomplished. However, the Deity promised to build a house for David, one that would last forever. Once that feat has occurred, an offspring of David will erect a suitable edifice for the Deity. This promise is followed by an unconditional one that the Davidic dynasty will be established forever. Saul's house is specifically recalled for contrast; even if a descendant of David sins, the Deity will chasten him but will not turn away from him as the divine favor abandoned Saul. Quite a different prophetic sentiment underlies the poetic oracle placed in Samuel's mouth on the occasion of Saul's failure to carry out the ban against the Amalekites:

> Has the Lord as great delight in burnt offerings and sacrifices,
>   as in obeying the voice of the Lord?
> Behold, to obey is better than sacrifice,
>   and to hearken than the fat of rams. (1 Sam. 15:22)

This ethical critique of ritual in favor of obedience of the heart has a parallel in Egyptian literature.

A sarcophagus from Bethshan, the city on whose walls the bodies of Saul and Jonathan were exposed.

Lament

David's lament over the heroic deaths of Saul and Jonathan is ascribed to the Book of the Upright (2 Sam. 1:19–27). Synonymous parallelism dominates this archaic text, which many interpreters take to represent David's actual feelings. A remarkable feature of the lyric is the admiration for Saul as well as for Jonathan, a sentiment that the anti-Saulide editor of the prose has left untouched. Canaanite features are present in the poem, particularly in the expression "the upsurging of the deep." The lament begins:

> *Thy glory, O Israel, is slain upon thy high places!*
> *How are the mighty fallen!*
> *Tell it not in Gath,*
> *publish it not in the streets of Ashkelon;*
> *lest the daughters of the Philistines rejoice,*
> *lest the daughters of the uncircumcised exult.* (2 Sam. 1:19–20)

Such lavish praise of Saul then concedes that he and his son fought valiantly. The further point that they were undivided in life and death does not reflect the perspective that survives in the stories. The poem calls on the women of Israel to lament over Saul, whose spoil had kept them well clothed. As for Jonathan, David himself provides the lament.

Jonathan lies slain upon thy high places.
I am distressed for you, my brother Jonathan;
very pleasant have you been to me;
  your love to me was wonderful,
    passing the love of women. (2 Sam. 1:25b–26)

The very different presentation of Saul and Jonathan in this lament from the account in the stories can be credited to the rhetoric of the moment, but it may alert interpreters to the presence of bias within the surviving stories, which clearly promote the Davidic cause at Saul's expense.

INTENTION

The presentation of Saul and David within the stories reveals the conscious intention of the book. That aim was to offer contrasting examples of rulers in such a way that David's supplanting of Saul's dynasty appears both reasonable and right. In order to make a credible case, the stories had to acknowledge Saul's admirable qualities while at the same time exposing a fatal flaw in his character, and they needed to exalt David without altogether glossing over some of his less desirable attributes. Because the selection of the material and the manner of its presentation serve a polemical end, it is impossible to say whether or not Saul really

The site of the ancient city Bethshan.

suffered from pathological jealousy and mental instability. Uncertainty also pertains to the portrait of David that emerges, for we cannot be sure that the character sketch existed anywhere but in the mind of the one who composed it. Nevertheless, the two examples are plausible, so that it is possible to render a favorable verdict on the literary achievement.

Saul

The king who came to the throne through a single deed of valor that earned gratitude from the inhabitants of Jabesh-gilead is subjected to the critical scrutiny of a religious leader, who anointed him to rule over Israel. Perhaps the explanation for Samuel's birth, which actually fits Saul's name rather than Samuel's, cleverly hints at the king's subordinate role where this prophet is concerned. Competing attitudes toward kingship have shaped these stories about Samuel's anointing of Saul. According to one, the move to monarchy constituted apostasy, a rejection of the Lord and of Samuel. The alternative perspective took its point of departure from the brutal fact of Philistine aggression, concluding that Israel's survival required an institutional government similar to that of this powerful foe. The extent of Philistine superiority surfaces in the incidental remarks about their monopoly on iron, which placed Israelites in the unhappy position of having to pay them for sharpening agricultural tools. Samuel's initial support of Saul's regime is rescinded for reasons that seem unwarranted to modern readers. Faced with desertion by his soldiers on the one hand and a mighty army poised to attack him on the other hand, Saul waited for Samuel as long as he dared. Then he acted in the prophet's place, and Samuel responded by withdrawing his support. Alternatively, Saul saw no sense in burning the Amalekite spoil when he had an army to feed, but Samuel insisted that the ban took priority over everything else. Samuel's ruthless execution of King Agag is therefore viewed as obedience to the Deity. From one perspective, then, Saul's collapse is brought on by Samuel's refusal to endorse his kingship any longer.

The other side of the story is equally appropriate to the ancient world, where ability to gain victory on the battlefield was the essential qualification for kingship. It follows that David's growing reputation for valor threatened Saul's position as king, for he could no longer defend himself against at least one pretender to the throne. A tendentious element has entered the story at this point, leaving the impression that David always remained a loyal subject. The unlikelihood of this presentation hardly needs defending, as anyone must acknowledge who reads the twice-told tale of David's sparing Saul. Here King Saul praises David for his superior virtue and confesses to be in the wrong: "behold, I have played the fool, and have erred exceedingly. . . . Blessed be you, my son David! You will

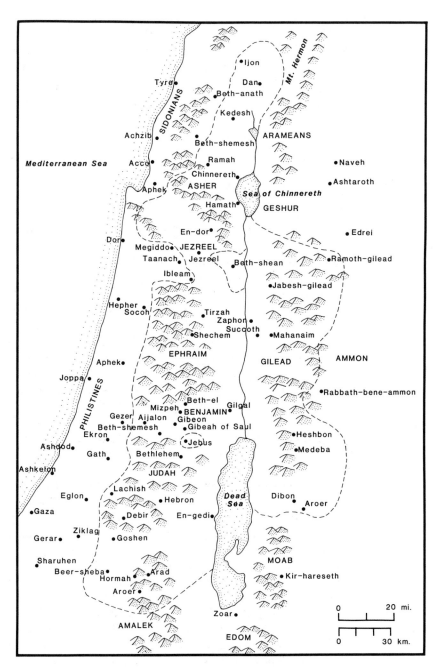

The Kingdom of Saul (c. 1025–1000 B.C.E.*)*

do many things and will succeed in them" (1 Sam. 26:21, 25). Saul also grants that David will supplant him:

> You are more righteous than I; for you have repaid me good, whereas I have repaid you evil. . . . And now, behold, I know that you shall surely be king, and that the kingdom of Israel shall be established in your hand. (1 Sam. 24:17, 20)

David

David's good fortune in being dismissed by suspicious Philistines from fighting against Saul and Jonathan did not last, for special-interest groups persuaded him to hand over Saul's seven sons for execution. Only Merib-baal* escaped Gibeonite revenge, thanks to a crippling illness that rendered him unfit for kingship in the view of the ancient Israelites. David's attitude toward this lone survivor in Saul's family is described as ambiguous, initially favorable but eventually neutral. It is said that Ziba, who administered Merib-baal's estate for him, accused his lord of supporting Absalom, a charge Merib-baal later denied. Unable to decide who spoke the truth, David divided the property. It is left unclear how David expected Saul's son to tend the land. There were some people who remembered Saul with great appreciation—the people of Jabesh-gilead who retrieved the bodies of Saul and Jonathan from the walls of Beth-shan and gave them a proper burial, and Saul's concubine, Rizpah, who guarded the corpses of Saul's seven sons from birds and wild beasts until she gained public support that prompted royal action to give the corpses a proper burial.

The depiction of David contrasts markedly with that of Saul, although not all his weaknesses are concealed. His emergence to power is described both realistically and in terms of popular legend. According to the former view, he earned a reputation for courage as a leader of a band of malcontents, spending considerable time in questionable relationships with the Philistines. The number of foreigners in his special militia is astonishing, because he entrusted his life to these men rather than to Israelites. This mighty soldier is described as a ruthless plunderer who took what he wanted regardless of the consequences. The irony is that Samuel's warning against the abuse of power that the people could expect from kings (1 Sam. 8:10–18) is associated with Saul, whereas in reality the excesses of David and especially of Solomon gave birth to this anti-monarchical feeling. The other explanation for his rise to power is not unrelated to this one, but it credits David with the defeat of Goliath, although elsewhere that feat is attributed to an otherwise unknown El-hanan. The exact circumstances that brought David to Saul's court are unclear; competing traditions about him as a fighter and as a musician have not been reconciled in the final narrative of those early years.

---

*Merib-baal is the name of Saul's son, although in some cases the offensive *baal* ending has been removed and in its place *bosheth* (shame) has been written.

The oasis of Ein Gedi, on the western side of the Dead Sea. David is said to have taken refuge at this oasis while fleeing from Saul.

The story of David sings his praises as a leader of men. Two incidents demonstrate his ability to instill loyalty in others. When an Ammonite ruler indirectly insulted him to provoke war, David did what was necessary to prevent his emissaries from suffering shame over the way Hanun had treated them. On another occasion David was so moved by an act of devotion by some of his soldiers who brought water from a well at Bethlehem that he poured it out to the Deity. Into this category also goes the incident that explains the origin of a custom permitting soldiers who guard equipment to share equally in the spoil acquired in battle. A raid on David's camp in his absence prompted him to follow the attackers and to retrieve everything that had been taken, including his wives. On returning, David insisted that those persons who had remained to guard the baggage should share equally in what was brought back from the battlefield. It is consonant with such a picture of David that foreigners like Ittai and the aged Barzillai demonstrate unbroken friendship for him.

Rebellious Children

Nevertheless, the impression is left that David lacked the ability to handle his children. Two palace revolts marked his rule, as Absalom and Adonijah vied to replace their aging father. In all other circumstances David is portrayed as cunning and ruthless, whether pretending madness before

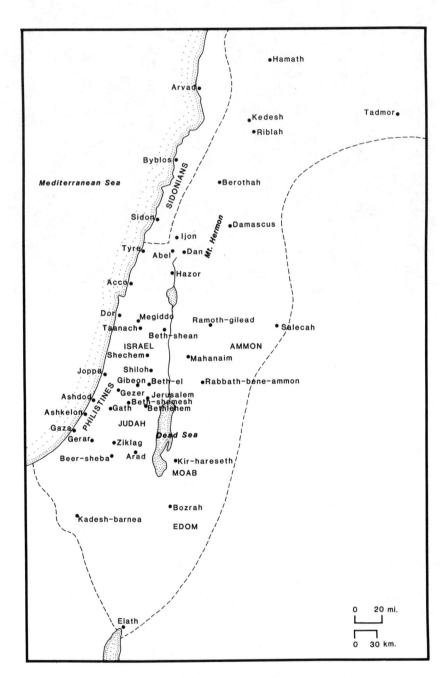

The Kingdom of David (c. 1000–960 B.C.E.*)*

a Philistine ruler or killing every man, woman, and child in the villages that he raided lest a survivor identify him or his men as the attackers. But David is described as unable to act decisively in curbing the excesses of his children, who threatened his rule more effectively than any external enemy. Joab's rebuke of his king on this matter after Absalom's death indicates the gravity of the situation, and this faithful commander of the army must surely have known that he spoke at great risk. The story reports that David was unwilling to permit anyone to talk so freely with him, and Joab paid the ultimate price for his loyalty.

A strong religious sentiment has found its way into the descriptions of David and Saul, and this perspective actually gives the stories their final appearance. Even here a prominent tension exists; although the Deity tells a disappointed Samuel that external appearance is insignificant in choosing a king (Saul was earlier described as exceptionally handsome and tall), still David's appearance as ruddy and handsome is specifically mentioned. Similarly, it is said that God does not repent, but also that God repented for having chosen Saul to be king. Apart from the general attempt to assert that the Deity had rejected Saul and chosen David, there is one obscure story about a plague that struck the country. The blame is placed on David, presumably for taking a census as preparation for calling young men into a standing army. The prophet Gad offers David three choices: three years of famine, three months of attack by enemies, or three days of pestilence. David's response is entirely out of character with the soldier who appears elsewhere. "I am in great distress; let us fall into the hand of the Lord, for his mercy is great; but let me not fall into the hand of man" (2 Sam. 24:14). The story proceeds to give an explanation for the selection of the threshing floor of Araunah as a sacred altar, which later became the site of the Solomonic Temple. Perhaps this is an appropriate ending to the books of Samuel, because the episode exalts the religious dimension at the expense of the historical, a tendency we have observed throughout the stories about Samuel, Saul, and David.

◆ 9 ◆

Kings

THE Book of Kings tells the story of the monarchy in Israel from the death of David until its cessation, signaled by the death of Jehoiachin in exile at some time after 561 B.C.E. From the time Jeroboam established a rival kingdom in the north until its collapse in 722 before an Assyrian army, the account shifts back and forth from one kingdom to the other. Using an abundance of sources, the author has compiled a unified story to illustrate a religious conviction that the fate of the monarchy and its human subjects was determined by its refusal to obey the preaching of the prophets and to heed their frequent warnings. Specifically, the kings are judged with regard to their attitude toward the Deuteronomic demand for exclusive worship of Yahweh at Jerusalem. The intention was not only to explain the defeat of Israel and Judah, which implied to many the superiority of the Assyrian and Babylonian deities, but also to present a lesson from history for the surviving generation, who faced a decision that would fix their own destiny.

SELECTIVE HISTORY

This selective rendering of historical facts pertaining to the Israelite monarchy has prompted phrases like "philosophy of history," "theology of history," and "prophetic history." Each one of these expressions attempts to capture the unusual way in which history lays the foundation for a theological edifice. The historical dimension is clearly present, for the particularity of the events is noteworthy. Many of the episodes derive from state archives, and therefore they reflect special events in a given place and time. The incidents are not endowed with representative capacity, nor are they universalized. Furthermore, the author often referred to sources in which a fuller narrative could be found. This admission of selectivity implies that the author did not try to deceive readers, but

144

rather that the story being told was interpreted history. Economic and political factors hardly come into play here, for their only significance to the author is to confirm a theological perspective. The controlling factor, therefore, is dogma rather than history, and consequently the expressions at the beginning of this paragraph are to some extent misleading.

The whole course of the monarchy is assessed from a perspective that emerged in the late seventh century with King Josiah's innovative reform. The motto for this reform, exclusive worship of Yahweh at the Jerusalem Temple, was imposed in assessing all Josiah's predecessors, both in Judah and in the northern kingdom. To be sure, the basis for the reform was found in Deuteronomy, a book that reportedly was discovered during repairs on the Temple, and ultimately on the blessings and curses within that book. Nevertheless, the criterion by which previous kings were judged is anachronistic, and the resulting account is, from one perspective, a travesty. Without exception, all kings who ruled in the north are condemned because they encouraged worship at rival sanctuaries, Bethel and Dan, despite the original orthodox claim to worship an invisible Yahweh astride a golden bull. Among Judean kings only Hezekiah and Josiah receive absolute approval, because of the reforms they instigated. In the judgment of the author who compiled this account, virtually every achievement of the other kings counts for naught, whether a humanitarian advance or victory in the international struggle for power.

PROPHETIC WORD

This biased presentation of the monarchy exhibits at least three discernible strands of thought, the basic story line and two editorial revisions from circles where prophecy and law shaped the manner of thinking. The prophetic redaction takes pains to show how again and again the prophetic word worked itself out in actual historical events; for example, the prediction in 1 Kings 13 by an anonymous man of God that the altar at Bethel would be desecrated is said to have been fulfilled to the letter in Josiah's day. Within the larger history of Samuel through Kings, this scheme of prediction and fulfillment occurs twelve times, thus leaving the impression that prophecy was a force to be reckoned with in the ancient world. The alternative strand is characterized by a legal understanding of events, particularly as that phenomenon occurs in Deuteronomy. It is difficult to determine the date of the three strands, although some assistance is provided by Huldah's prophecy in 2 Kings 22:20, which must surely antedate Josiah's violent death in 609. However, this note may derive from an earlier prophetic source and may not have been altered when taken over into the larger story. In any event, the final account was not completed before 561, unless the observation about Jehoiachin's changed status in exile was subsequently added to the narrative.

The ruins of ancient Megiddo, near which King Josiah met his death in battle with Pharaoh Necho.

Framework

The fundamental thesis of the story manifests itself in two distinct forms: a framework consisting of introductory and concluding formulas, and discrete blocks of sermonic material. The framework first appears in 1 Kings 14:21 and continues to the end of the account of the monarchy, although it is missing from the stories about the kings who were deported by Assyrian and Babylonian armies. The introductory formula normally gives the age of the king of Judah at accession, the length of his reign, his mother's name, and a verdict on his piety (that is, whether or not he measured up to Josiah in respect to exclusive worship of Yahweh at the Jerusalem Temple). The details for the northern kings are slightly different, for the narrative does not list their age on coming to the throne or their mother's name. The concluding formula refers to fuller sources and mentions any interesting achievements, gives an account of the king's death (and burial, for the kings of Judah), and names his successor. This framework is slightly altered in places where fuller details occur in the story itself. The entire framework is missing from the account of Athaliah's brief reign in Judah, and this interregnum is not even counted in the history of the Davidic dynasty.

The sermonic blocks are confined to Solomon's prayer on the occasion of the dedication of the Temple and extensive reflections on the reasons for divine punishment in 2 Kings 17. Two additional minor reflections of this nature appear in 2 Kings 23:26–27 and 24:2–4, where the Deity is portrayed as determined to cast off Judah because of Manasseh's evil deeds and where foreign invaders are explicitly said to have acted at Yahweh's bidding to bring about Judah's collapse. Solomon's prayer assumes a representative character, offering divine help to repentant people in various circumstances, specifically during famine, warfare, and exile. The point is clearly that an exiled community can still affect its destiny if the leaders make the right choice, for they can heed the prophetic word that most of their kings ignored. The other sermonic exposition is offered as an explanation for Assyrian victory over Israel, which came despite frequent warnings by prophets.

> But they would not listen, but were stubborn, as their fathers had been, who did not believe in the Lord their God. They despised his statutes, and his covenant that he made with their fathers, and the warnings which he gave them. (2 Kings 17:14–15a)

The text proceeds to accuse Israel of worshipping idols and fashioning two golden calves, paying homage to Baal, and making the supreme offering, their children, to alien gods. However, an accusing finger also points to Judah, which is described as walking in customs introduced by the northern counterpart.

These introductory and concluding formulas and sermonic blocks enabled the author to communicate a particular message without fundamentally altering the sources underlying the account. It appears that a rich treasury of sources contributed to the final story: (1) the Book of the Acts of Solomon; (2) the Chronicles of the Kings of Judah; (3) the Chronicles of the Kings of Israel; (4) the Book of the Upright (or Song); (5) the story of David's last days; (6) prophetic traditions about Elijah; (7) prophetic traditions about Elisha; (8) material about Ahab's wars against the Aramaeans; (9) prophetic traditions about Isaiah; and (10) stories about various other prophets. Essentially, these sources comprise written archival materials from both kingdoms and prophetic traditions, perhaps oral. The latter are filled with popular sentiment that placed a premium on the miraculous event as opposed to ordinary happenings. Because the author's sources contained "sober" history and legend, the finished story should occasion little surprise.

Alternating Kingdoms

The author's practice of jumping back and forth from one kingdom to the other has a tendency to confuse readers, and the resulting chronological system baffles the experts. One source of confusion is the way the author uses different reckonings, a synchronization based on accession years and absolute chronology referring to regnal years, which cannot be reconciled with one another. In addition, coregencies seem to have been calculated into the total system, but there may actually have been more

than the one that is mentioned (Azariah, also called Uzziah, and Jotham).
Perhaps different calendars were also used, as some interpreters believe.
The chronology in the septuagint suggests that errors of various kinds
have occurred in transmission. The chronological confusion is eased
somewhat by foreign records, particularly Assyrian but also Babylonian.
In those instances where allusions to earthquakes and eclipses occur,
fixed dates can be ascertained on the basis of astronomy. Beyond that
clarification of a few dates by reliable means, there are several different
schemes by which interpreters attempt to explain the chronology in
Kings: (1) the appeal to ancient Near Eastern records as normative, to
which biblical dates are subjected and corrected; (2) the acceptance of
biblical dates as normative and attempting by various means to clarify
any difficulties; (3) the assumption that the biblical chronology is correct
and can be harmonized; and (4) the belief that the biblical chronology
is fiction. The first two approaches are less tied to confessional positions,
conservative or liberal, and therefore offer better alternatives toward resolving this complex problem of chronology.

The division of Kings into two books, and indeed the separation from
the books of Samuel, which did not become fixed until the fifteenth century C.E., do not come at convenient breaks within the narrative. The
story about David's difficulties with his children, the so-called succession
document, continues into the first two chapters of Kings. Furthermore,
the account of Ahaziah and the prophets Elijah and Elisha is broken by
the division between First and Second Kings. One explanation for the
unnatural break is purely mechanical, the wish to have two scrolls of
comparatively equal length. Another suggestion takes its cue from the
formula that opens three other books in the Deuteronomistic history,
"after the death of . . ." (Josh. 1:1; Judg. 1:1; 2 Sam. 1:1). The contents
of Kings are easily outlined in terms of distinct epochs: the conclusion
to the story about David (1 Kings 1–2); the era of Solomon (1 Kings 3–
11); the divided kingdoms, from the beginning until the fall of the north
(1 Kings 12 thorough 2 Kings 17); and the kingdom of Judah, from 722
until the deportation in 587 and subsequent events reaching to about
560 (2 Kings 18–25).

Elijah and Elisha

Some of the stories from the ninth and eighth centuries represent the
golden age of Hebrew narrative. The Elijah episodes reflect a high level
of religious sophistication that came only after long reflection on the customary language associated with divine manifestation. The exquisite
narrative about the encounter with the Deity on Mount Horeb serves as
a corrective to excessive emphasis on external phenomena such as earthquake, fire, and strong winds in describing the Deity's self-revelation.
In this story the Lord appeared in a muted voice, the stillness following
the display of wonders. Furthermore, the Deity assured the tired prophet

The distant mountain is Carmel, where the contest between the prophet Elijah and eight hundred and fifty prophets of Baal and Asherah was held.

that the success of the divine enterprise did not rest on his shoulders alone, for faithfulness was not always evident to the naked eye. Elijah's rebuke of Ahab for his part in murdering Naboth and seizing his choice vineyard also deals responsibly with the complicated problem of relationships between the individual and the state, although the issue is made all the more complex by competing views of the crown. Jezebel, Ahab's queen, acted in conformity with Phoenician concepts of land and royal prerogative, whereas Elijah criticized them both on the basis of ancient Yahwistic belief that land should not be sold outside one's family group. The contest on Mount Carmel alludes to the restoration of an altar to Yahweh, which the wondrous element in the story nearly suppresses, but the account can only have arisen in circles where monotheism had taken firm hold over the imagination. Hence Elijah's mockery of the god Baal became almost as brutal as the purported slaughter of his prophets. Such a story exudes utter confidence in the Deity being exalted as the true God.

A single episode in the Elisha narrative takes up the problem of personal conviction as opposed to official responsibility and concludes on a remarkably tolerant note. Naaman, the Syrian soldier who came to Elisha seeking a cure for leprosy, acknowledged that his official duties as a high-ranking officer might compromise his newfound faith. His mind was quickly set at ease when a remarkably tolerant and pastoral Elisha

The Jordan River, in which the Syrian captain, Naaman, washed at Elisha's instruction and was reportedly cleansed from leprosy.

encouraged Naaman to transport some dirt from Israel to Syria (thereby assuring Yahweh's presence in an alien land) and to carry out his responsibilities to the Syrian state without anxiety.*

Micaiah ben Imlah

The relationship between a prophet and the state, especially as national causes were embodied in a leader, is the subject of the story about Micaiah ben Imlah. The issue is complicated by the fact that two kings are treated here, one of whom (Jehoshaphat) seems to have been a vassal to the other (Ahab), if one can draw such a conclusion from his readiness

---

*The implication is that govermental officers were required to endorse official religious policy; hence Naaman would have to worship Syrian deities. The prophet opened the door to a practice of mental reservation, one which at a later time Daniel refused to enter even to save his life.

Ashurnasirpal II (883–858), whose name, titles, and heroic deeds are inscribed on the chest of the statue.

to expose himself to physical danger so that Ahab might escape harm. The problem is further complicated by dissension among prophets themselves over their proper role in government. Ahab believed that inquiry about the Deity's wishes with respect to a planned military venture should restrict itself to official cult prophets, whereas Jehoshaphat expressed reservations about their objectivity. When an outsider was summoned, a representative of the prophets advised him to concur in their recommendation to avoid dampening the king's morale, and perhaps also to add another prophet's weight in bringing about a favorable message. Micaiah refused to accept this counsel, for he recognized a higher obligation than the one to the king. The resulting confrontation between one prophet and the heads of state, and between Micaiah and a host of prophets, was inevitable, as was imprisonment of one who dared to challenge a king who had seized supreme authority for himself. However, the intention of the story was not to portray the vicissitudes of a courageous prophet, for his ultimate fate is undisclosed, whereas the Deity's control of human events is asserted with great poignancy. Ahab's clever effort to conceal his true identity during the fateful battle was frustrated when an arrow, shot at random, found its royal target. The king whose language had copied the divine messenger formula, "Thus says the king," succumbed to the power of a Deity who guided the path of that arrow, and in so doing left the people scattered like sheep without a shepherd.

Micaiah's struggle to gain a hearing for an unpopular word illustrates a peculiar problem that plagued biblical prophecy more and more. The failure of prophets to speak with one voice produced strife within their ranks, represented in this story by Zedekiah's physical abuse of Micaiah and his verbal retort that promised future shame for the king's loyal supporter. Here the actual source of disagreement among prophets is attributed to the Deity, who achieved the divine plan for human events by deceiving cult prophets and consequently by leading Ahab to his death. Once this sort of thinking took root, it created havoc in those circles where competing prophetic words had to be adjudicated, for it was impractical to postpone action until unanimity among the prophets was achieved.

The Man of God and the Prophet at Bethel

This issue gave rise to the prophetic legend in 1 Kings 13, which tells of an anonymous man of God who went to Bethel and denounced the sanctuary, coming into direct conflict with King Jeroboam I and eventually with an old prophet from Bethel. The narrative recognized the possibility that authentic prophets might betray their commission, especially when confronted with deceitful words from others who claimed to possess a more recent word from the Deity. However, the fluidity of prophetic witness also moves in the other direction: a lying prophet may later utter an authentic message form the transcendent one. Perhaps the violent death of the man of God points to the serious repercussions brought about by this unresolved conflict. Nevertheless, the story refrains from depicting either prophetic figure as the villain (assuming that the phrase, "he lied to him," is a gloss), and indicates that even the prophet from Bethel had profound respect for the disobedient man of God. Given the central position of prophetic warning in the larger narrative, it is a testimony to the author's fidelity to sources that this episode focusing on the problematic nature of the phenomenon of prophecy has been preserved.

The remains of a storage building at Hazor (ninth century B.C.E.*).*

The Heightening of the Miraculous

Not every episode in which prophets play a prominent role achieves such heights of ethical and spiritual perception as the preceding ones. In some ways the Elisha stories generally represent a level of piety that seems considerably less developed than the views within the narratives about Elijah and Micaiah. Precisely for this reason some critics have proposed to place Elisha before Elijah chronologically,* although a better response to the difficulty is to attribute the two traditions to distinct groups. Several features of the Elisha stories suggest that his followers experienced severe economic conditions—the borrowed ax, the threat of having to sell children into slavery to repay a debt, the inadequate supply of food. In desperate circumstances religious groups are often inclined to give fantasy free reign, if only to relieve the misery. The

---

*It is well known, however, that religions do not develop in an unbroken line from primitive to more sophisticated expression, for certain pockets of less developed religious expression persist alongside highly refined religion. This observation is also true of the modern religious situation.

A fragment of a stela, the famous Rosetta Stone, that provided the key to deciphering Egyptian hieroglyphics. The inscription is in two languages, Egyptian (demotic, a late cursive script, and earlier hieroglyphics) and Greek.

frequency of miracle in the Elisha stories is therefore understandable, although they occasionally offend modern readers—for example, when the prophet severely punishes children for mocking his baldness. Being torn limb from limb by a bear seems severe punishment for their offense. The stories also approach the ludicrous at times—for instance, the report that a corpse thrown into Elisha's grave in haste promptly came to life. The duplicate story about reviving a small child, which occurs in the Elijah and the Elisha cycles, did not seem sufficient glorification of these prophets, at least to the author of this tale about the miraculous powers of Elisha's dead body.

A similar desire to emphasize the wondrous power of the Deity has resulted in the inclusion of a story about the prophet Isaiah, who announced that a frightened King Ahaz had no cause for fear before Sennacherib's mighty army. Accordingly, the death angel slew 185,000 enemy soldiers, who "melted like snow at a single glance of the Lord"; consequently Jerusalem was spared. So far, there is agreement with the same story in Isaiah. However, a variant tradition appears here as well, the concession that Sennacherib's army devastated Judah and imposed a heavy burden on the royal treasury, a historical fact that sources outside the Bible have documented.

The willingness to present another side of the story, even when it may have been risky to do so, has resulted in a portrait of David's last days that greatly tarnishes his reputation. The purpose of the anecdote about the search for a lovely young woman to keep the old king warm relates to the ancient notion that an impotent king was no longer fit to govern a nation. The episode makes this point in subtle fashion. Therefore, a successor had to be acclaimed, and to do so required prompt action. Although Adonijah seized the initiative, supported by the priest Abiathar and Joab, the commander of the army, it was to no avail, for Nathan the prophet and Zadok the priest used Bathsheba to manipulate the old king into naming Solomon as his successor. The final chapter in David's life is not pretty: he is pictured as instructing Solomon to extinguish various people who had wronged the king in times past. A ruthless Solomon carried out the bloodbath and thereby established his kingdom.

Solomon

The depiction of Solomon likewise combines competing appraisals of him as a ruler. The early narratives are entirely favorable toward this monarch whose piety and wisdom are nicely illustrated in the account of a dream vision at Gibeon and the story about two harlots who seek a judgment from the king. The language of the dream vision at the great high place resembles Egyptian royal accounts (the king describes himself as a little child who does not know how to go out or come in and asks for a hearing heart); because Solomon tried to model his rule on the

The south gate of Gezer, the city given to King Solomon as a dowry by Pharaoh Siamun in the tenth century B.C.E. *As part of his reconstruction of the city, Solomon built this three-chambered gate in a style that is also found at Hazor and Megiddo.*

Egyptian pattern, such imagery is appropriate. The folktale about the two harlots arguing over who was the actual mother of a surviving infant demonstrates the king's superior wisdom. Assuming that the genuine mother would express compassion for the infant and give it up rather than see it cut in half by a sword, Solomon thus put the two women to a test and awarded the infant to the compassionate one. Variants of this story have shown up in more than a score of different cultures, suggesting that it was a common motif in the ancient world. The last part of the narrative about Solomon, however, no longer celebrates his piety or his wisdom, for which the queen of Sheba is reputed to have made a long journey, but adopts a sharply critical stance. The king's fatal weakness was the same one that overcame the great Samson—foreign women. Solomon is said to have constructed places of worship for his many foreign wives, who continued the veneration of their respective deities in Jerusalem.

> He had seven hundred wives, princesses, and three hundred concubines; and his wives turned away his heart. For when Solomon was old his wives turned away his heart after other gods; and his heart was not wholly true to the Lord his God, as was the heart of David his father. For Solomon went after Ashtoreth the goddess of the Sidonians, and after Milcom the

The southern part of a Solomonic city gate at Hazor. Running along the left side of the three-chambered gate is a casemate wall, especially designed to withstand attackers.

abomination of the Ammonites. So Solomon did what was evil in the sight of the Lord, and did not wholly follow the Lord, as David his father had done. (1 Kings 11:3–6)

For this reason, the text continues, the Deity will bring about a rupture in the kingdom, leaving only one tribe, Judah, to Solomon's successor,* and that concession is due to David's faithfulness. The occasion for this division of Solomon's empire is described in crude language, when an arrogant Rehoboam spurns advice from older and wiser heads in favor of suggestions from young supporters to increase the burden on the subjects. Rehoboam boasted that his little finger, a euphemism, was thicker than his father's loins. "My father chastised you with whips, but I will chastise you with scorpions" (1 Kings 12:11). Who could blame Jeroboam and all Israel for their seditious shout:

> *What portion have we in David?*
>   *We have no inheritance in the son of Jesse.*
> *To your tents, O Israel!*
>   *Look now to your own house, David. (1 Kings 12:16)*

---

*In actual fact, part of the tribe of Benjamin also aligned with Judah. Hence it is customary to speak of the ten lost tribes of Israel, assuming that tribal groups survived in the kingdom to the south.

With this cry the people began to journey on separate paths toward a common end, defeat at the hands of enemy soldiers and deportation to a foreign land. That dark story is chronicled in some detail, always with a single thought in mind: the collapse of the two kingdoms came because the people refused to listen to prophetic warnings and thus kept alive syncretistic worship rather than obeying Deuteronomy's demand for exclusive worship of Yahweh at the sanctuary in Jerusalem.

The Latter Prophets

PROPHECY was by no means limited to ancient Israel. Although its existence in Egypt is contested, there can be no doubt about its presence in Syria and in Mesopotamia. The earliest widespread example of the prophetic phenomenon occurred in Mari during the eighteenth and seventeenth centuries B.C.E. Prophets were also associated with the worship of Ishtar of Arbela, a fertility goddess in Assyria, and the Zakir stele from Hamath in Syria (c. 800 B.C.E.) mentions the practice of consulting the Deity before embarking on a military endeavor, and receiving a message by means of seers. Furthermore, the Egyptian *Tale of Wen Amun* provides indirect evidence for Canaanite prophecy, for it refers to an ecstatic who proclaimed an oracle while seized by the spirit.

✳ PROPHECY AT MARI AND IN ISRAEL

The similarities between Israelite prophecy and the earlier phenomenon in Mari are so striking that its origins must be sought there. About thirty letters in the extensive documents that have survived from King Zimri-Lim's correspondence refer to prophets, both male and female. The affinities between these prophets and their Israelite counterpart are formal and substantive. In both areas, Mari and Israel, the prophets used a messenger formula, "Thus hath the god spoken," and interpreted their action as the result of having been sent. Moreover, they threatened the king in the Deity's name or promised deliverance to the one whom the Deity loved. Even the same language often occurs, such as the reassuring words, "Fear not, for I am with you," or the threat that the Deity will catch the enemy in a net. Concern for the dynasty and temple also find expression in both localities. Perhaps more surprising is the existence of the same kinds of prophets, with different words to describe each type. In Mari

159

there were ecstatic prophets and seers (answerers); in addition, certain members of the laity seem also to have functioned as spokespersons for the Deity. In Israel, too, there were seers, ecstatics, and individuals who denied their membership in the first two groups but who uttered words in behalf of the Deity. Both men and women acted as prophets in Mari and in Israel.

At Mari the prophets sometimes made use of visionary language, particularly dreams, and omens. The latter category of revelation was developed into a "science" by which cultic functionaries could predict the future. Thousands of clay livers have been discovered, witnessing to the importance of this means of coping with life in ancient Mesopotamia. Priests were trained to read the entrails of sacrificial animals and thus to determine whether the day was auspicious or not. All kinds of things possessed potential as omens, and priests became masters at reading them. In some instances cultic prophets performed a similar function, answering questions that were asked at the temple where they officiated. In Israel occasional examples of using technical means for predicting the future actually occurred, although they were probably rare. Into this category must fall the use of musical instruments to induce a prophetic vision and reading the future on the basis of the number of arrows a king shoots. Within priestly circles the casting of the sacred lots (Urim and Thummim) belongs to the same class of divination.

Ecstatic experience characterized one group of prophets at Mari, and a similar abandon occurred in Israelite prophecy during its early stages. There are stories about bands of prophets whose ecstasy overwhelmed the young Saul, leading him to join them in the strange conduct. A similar behavior is attributed to the prophets of Baal in the contest between them and Elijah on Mount Carmel, but the narrator has Elijah mock them for excessive self-lacerations. A late text in Zechariah 13 seems to imply that Israel's prophets also went to such extremes, or else that they marked their bodies in some manner as a sign of membership in the prophetic guild, for the passage states that prophets will become ashamed of their wounds and try to conceal them. Nevertheless, Israel's prophecy was generally characterized by self-consciousness, so that a distinction should be made between ecstasy of absorption and ecstasy of concentration. The latter form applies to prophets like Isaiah, Jeremiah, Amos, and Hosea.

Because the prophets at Mari sometimes publicly announced things that did not please the king, certain measures were taken to prevent irresponsible criticism of royal policy that might have fostered revolt among the populace. The letters mention a piece of a garment and lock of hair as having been sent along with the report of prophetic activity. It has been conjectured that this represents a means of controlling prophecy, for the prophets were held responsbile for the effects of their public words. In Israel, too, prophets often came into direct conflict with kings, although in many cases the two seem to have worked together amicably.

Cooperation generally took place when prophets functioned as officials of the royal cult. It appears that prophecy at Mari was a peripheral phenomenon, inasmuch as the prophets were associated with minor deities.

STAGES OF PROPHECY IN ISRAEL

Israelite prophecy began during the earliest stages of the monarchy and passed from the scene shortly after the fall of Judah, with rare exceptions. Three distinct stages are discernible: (1) preclassical, (2) classical, and (3) postclassical. The first, preclassical, covers the period until Amos (c. 760 B.C.E.). This type of prophecy is associated with groups who belonged to a particular cult and were characterized by contagious ecstasy. Often an individual stands apart from the group, showing greater kinship with classical prophets (for instance, Elijah and Micaiah ben Imlah). These ecstatic prophets are called men of the spirit or men of God, perhaps also seers. Classical prophecy refers to the period from Amos to Second Isaiah, the unknown prophet of the exile who composed Isaiah 40–55. In classical prophecy, threat or promise dominates, and the prophetic word comes to the fore rather than prophetic legend. In postclassical prophecy, the emphasis falls on eschatology (reflection on the last days), and inspiration seems to derive from the study of earlier prophetic words. Furthermore, the Temple cult tends to dominate the discussion in this period, along with questions pertaining to ritual purity. It is possible that at a late date prophecy was absorbed into the Levitical singers within the precincts of the Temple.

Two different forms of prophecy seem to have merged in ancient Israel, the seer and the ecstatic. Two terms for the prophet refer to the element of divination (ro'eh and chozeh); both of these can be translated "seer," although the former implies normal sight and the latter suggests an ability to see beyond the physical manifestation. A third term for prophet calls attention to the fact that the Deity has laid hold of an individual (nabi', from an Akkadian word meaning "called"). According to 1 Sam. 9:9 the older term for seer later gave way to the expression for one who has been called, and continuity between the two types of prophecy is claimed. That view is represented in quite a different way in prophetic collections; for instance, the superscription to Amos (1:1) refers to words that he saw, and the book combines words and visions.

THE PROPHETIC EXPERIENCE

In all probability prophetic experience consisted of four distinct stages. Naturally a divine call preceded everything else. The prophet sensed divine constraint, a summons that was completely irresistible. In a num-

ber of instances prophets record this summons, perhaps to legitimate
their prophetic ministry. The prophetic phenomenon itself consisted of
(1) the secret experience by which a divine word was received, (2) the
interpretation of this enigmatic word in terms of the prophet's own religious views, (3) the formulation of this word with its accompanying
threats or promises, and (4) the artistic development of the word so that
it communicated with ordinary people. If this description of the prophetic
experience is accurate, it means that an ecstasy of concentration characterizes the first stage only. During the other three stages, the prophet
exercised full control of mental capacities.

Israelite prophecy was oral, with the possible exception of a few liturgical compositions. The prophets were speakers, not writers; this fact
played a significant role in shaping the form of prophetic words. They
are sprinkled with refrains, thematic expressions, and words that aided
the memory. In addition, these prophetic speeches frequently use the
language of direct address, indicating that hearing rather than reading
is the mode of receiving the words. One special feature of prophetic
communication is notewothy: prophets frequently acted out their message
by means of unusual conduct. Such symbolic action dramatized the
prophetic announcement and, in the eyes of some interpreters at least,
set into motion the events that were being proclaimed in this forceful
manner.

Preachers of Repentance?

It is not clear whether Israelite prophets preached repentance or not.
While some interpreters think the prophetic message consisted of an unconditional threat or promise, others believe that the word was always
contingent. Without doubt, the Deuteronomistic author understood
prophets as preachers of repentance. In this view the response to the
prophetic message shaped the nation's destiny, and with it, that of individuals. For some scholars the prophets simply announced the Deity's
determination to destroy or to save, and nothing that the people did made
any difference. But such a view seems to take prophetic language too
literally. In any case, the literary theory on which this understanding
rests is hardly compelling, for it assumes that appeals to repentance within
the prophetic literature are secondary. In one area, to be sure, there was
little opportunity for conversion. Israel's prophets frequently announced
oracles against foreign nations, and because these were heard only by
Israelites one can reasonably assume that their intention was something
other than to provoke moral conversion. The story of Jonah is, of course,
quite different.

These considerations lead to an observation about the ethical character
of Israelite prophecy. The nations surrounding Israel were not wholly
lacking in moral attributes, despite the harsh prophetic indictment of

Canaanites in particular. Examples of ethical concern for the well-being of widows and orphans are well documented in Canaan and Egypt. Nevertheless, Israelite prophecy has a high concentration of ethical concern for justice and right dealing within society, and the moral imperative is addressed to kings and high officials, as well as to ordinary citizens. Israel's prophets have been rightly called the voice that the Deity lent to the oppressed poor, hence a shriek in the night. Precisely because the prophets experienced divine pathos (suffering), they gave voice to that agony and summoned the people to alter their ways so that social justice might run down like a mighty stream.

Antagonism toward Religious Syncretism

One other feature of classical prophecy was its antagonism toward religious syncretism. Residence in Canaan easily promoted tolerance insofar as other religions were concerned, for Israelites freely intermarried with the local peoples. Furthermore, Israel, once it had adopted agricultural life, needed to assure fertility; it therefore seemed logical to pay homage to those Canaanite deities whose power over vegetation was thought to be incontestable. Later, when other deities demonstrated their superiority on the battlefield, it was only natural that Israelites adopted various aspects of their conqueror's religion. The prophets did battle against every infringement on Yahwism by alien worship, and it appears that they succeeded more in the official sanctuary than among the populace at large. At any rate, foreign influence made its presence felt at various periods of Israel's history.

☀ False Prophecy

No analysis of Israelite prophecy would be complete without a discussion of the phenomenon called false prophecy. It happened that prophecy covered a wide spectrum in ancient Israel, and diversity of viewpoint eventually produced prophetic conflict. Competing voices spoke on behalf of the same Deity, and the people were confronted with a situation in which they had to choose between rival messengers, each of whom claimed divine inspiration. At times the prophets themselves came into direct confrontation, and then one person had to accuse the other of dissimulation. The situation became so acute that various criteria arose to assist in the decision about authentic as opposed to bogus prophecy, but no adequate means of settling this difficult matter was ever devised. Even as late as the New Testament era, new criteria had to be put forth to prevent abuse by traveling evangelists. The failure to settle this problem in ancient Israel was a major factor in the decline of prophecy, for it became increasingly difficult to decide which prophet to heed.

This disagreement among prophets arose from something far more

basic than individual temperament or desire to please certain factions
of society. At the root of the problem was an understanding of the Deity's
purpose where Israel was concerned. For some prophets the special bond
between God and Israel meant that nothing, not even sin, could alter
divine intentions. Accordingly, these prophets emphasized the promise
of well-being, often associating it with David and the Jerusalem cult,
and proclaiming the ruin of foreign nations. Other prophets insisted that
Israel's sin had canceled her special status, or at the very least had introduced the necessity for punishment before the promises of peace and
tranquillity could materialize. Thus the concept of election lay at the
heart of the controversy, and various prophets understood this concept
differently. The issue was further complicated by the course of Israel's
history, for the same prophet sometimes changed his message radically
because of the different historical context. Ezekiel, for example, changed
from a prophet of judgment to a messenger of salvation once Jerusalem
was defeated. From this specific instance it is obvious that prophets endeavored to proclaim a word that was appropriate to the context. Naturally, not all prophets understood the situation in the same way.

Radical Proclamation

The message of Israelite prophecy was radical in more ways than one.
In one sense a prophet such as Amos announced a radical "no" against
everything that the royal cult stood for, from religious excess to oppression
of the poor by the new class of rich landowners. Such prophets dared to
reverse the dominant concepts of their day, for they firmly believed that
the Deity authorized them to speak in this bold fashion. But the prophets
were radical in another sense, for they tried to return to the roots of their
faith. A theological conservatism therefore expressed itself in prophets,
who sought to preserve the spiritual legacy from past generations. This
glance toward the past for inspiration has led some critics to designate Israel's prophets as interpreters of the law, although there is very
little conscious allusion within the prophetic literature to the Mosaic
legislation.

Prediction of the Future?

The Greek word for prophet (*prophetes*) has a prefix which has come to
occupy a prominent position in the modern concept of prophecy, despite
its ambiguity. Prediction of the future was not the essential aspect of
ancient prophecy, even if it did occur on occasion. In Israel most predictions were general ones, and those that expressed specific forecasts
about the future usually failed to come true. The numerous unfulfilled
prophecies need not trouble anyone because all prophecy is contingent
on human response and divine decision. If humans repent, the Deity

may alter the word directed toward Israel; indeed, the freedom of the Deity may exercise itself irrespective of human response.

The futility of ascertaining the future was demonstrated by prophetic successors, the apocalyptists. It appears that prophecy became so obsessed with the future that it began to distinguish between this age and the next. In this way present suffering could be endured because of the hope for better things in the messianic age. While messianic prophecy did not produce very lavish descriptions within prophetic literature, there are important passages in Amos, Micah, and Isaiah that speak about an age of peace when everyone will be able to rest without fear of harm. Central to the last of these texts is a royal figure who is patterned after David, God's anointed one. This kind of expectation flourished in late prophecy and was endorsed by apocalyptic writers, who envisioned a decisive act on the Deity's part that would inaugurate the age of the Messiah and overcome all wickedness. Since Elijah was believed to have ascended into heaven without dying, he was expected to return before the messianic age could dawn. A note of expectancy therefore entered prophecy in its new manifestation, and with it the sense of urgency about ritual purity lest the Holy One appear and bring destruction to those who had defiled themselves.

◆ 10 ◆

Isaiah

T HE prophet Isaiah appeared somewhat later than Amos and Micah, and although he mentions neither Amos, whose ministry was directed to the northern kingdom, nor Micah, who, like him, addressed Judah and especially its capital, Jerusalem, Isaiah shares certain features with each of these prophets. The most obvious link with Micah is the small block of material announcing an era of universal peace when the house of the Lord will be exalted on the highest mountain and nations will gravitate to this center of learning and justice (Isa. 2:2–4; Mic. 4:1–4). The vision concludes with one of the most memorable expressions of hope within the Hebrew Bible:

> and they shall beat their swords into plowshares,
>   and their spears into pruning hooks;
> nation shall not lift up sword against nation,
>   neither shall they learn war any more. (Isa. 2:4; Mic. 4:3)

To this Micah adds:

> but they shall sit every man under his vine and under his fig tree,
>   and none shall make them afraid;
> for the mouth of the Lord of hosts has spoken (Mic. 4:4).

Isaiah's affinities with Amos, if less striking, are nonetheless real, appearing most clearly in Isaiah's denunciation of persons who devote their waking hours to drunken revelry accompanied by music but who cannot recognize the Deity's hand in every day life. As punishment for their stupor the guilty nation will be taken into exile (Isa. 5:11–13; Amos 6:1–7). Similarities between these two prophets extend beyond this, however, in the use of prophetic speech forms and themes: for example, laments, attitude toward cultic ritual, and the understanding of righteousness and justice. Isaiah also remains silent about his older contemporary Hosea.

166

Assyrian soldiers of Tiglath-pileser III (745–728) are depicted leading away the booty after defeating a town, possibly Astaroth.

THE TIMES

As we have already seen, these were troubled times throughout the Fertile Crescent,* largely because of ambitious efforts by various Assyrian rulers to extend their empire as far west as Egypt. That resurgence of Assyria received new impetus from Tiglath-pileser, who came to power in 745 B.C.E., roughly the time of Isaiah's appearance on the scene as a prophet in Jerusalem. By 701, the time of Isaiah's last recorded oracles, Sennacherib had marched against Judah with devastating force, destroying forty-six cities and shutting up King Hezekiah like a bird in a cage,

---

*The Egyptologist James Breasted described the region of the Mesopotamian valley, Syria, Palestine, and Egypt as the Fertile Crescent. Although the term is not exactly accurate, scholars have continued to use it.

Excavation of the Philistine city of Ashdod, one of the five major cities of Philistia.

to use the language of the account preserved by the victorious Assyrian ruler. Midway between these two dates, 745 and 701, the city of Samaria was besieged and after three years fell either to Shalmaneser or to Sargon II. Assyrian presence was felt at still other times, particularly as a result of local revolts and the withholding of tribute often associated with the death of a king. The Israelites suffered from heavy tax burdens in 742 and 732 because of bold decisions to withstand Assyria, and the southern kingdom under Hezekiah barely escaped the fate of other collaborators in a rebellion that occurred about 713. In this instance the city of Ashdod bore the brunt of Assyrian anger, and the countries of Moab and Edom also paid dearly. During the last fifty years of the eighth century, the Assyrian empire extended its boundary to include Syria, Philistia, Ammon, Moab, Edom, Judah, and Sidon. Even Tirhakah of Egypt was defeated in a skirmish at Eltekeh, but the Assyrians were unable to take full advantage of this victory because of the unstable situation in Nineveh. The prophet Isaiah endeavored to interpret the religious significance of these momentous events, especially as they related to the land of Judah. As a consequence, most of his recorded oracles relate to three political crises: the so-called Syro-Ephraimite war in 734–732, the rebellion by Ashdod and a small coalition of neighboring powers in 713, and the invasion by Sennacherib in 701. The remainder of the sayings that actually derive from Isaiah represent his criticism of Jerusalemite society, a criticism that seems to have encountered stiff resistance.

The superscription in Isa. 1:1 identifies Isaiah as the son of an otherwise unknown Amoz and states that he prophesied under four Judean kings: Uzziah, Jotham, Ahaz, and Hezekiah. Little more is known about the prophet's personal affairs; he had two sons, to whom he gave the symbolic names Shear-jashub (a remnant will return) and Maher-shalal-hashbaz (the spoil speeds, the prey hastes). The second son was born to a woman who is specifically called a prophetess; she is not identified as Isaiah's wife, although such a relationship may be assumed. In any case, the obtaining of witnesses for this act of conception sets it out of the ordinary and therefore may suggest that this prophetess was not his wife. Since Isaiah had easy access to royalty, many scholars have concluded that he belonged to an aristocratic family, but the argument is not conclusive. Uncertainty also surrounds the exact nature of the extraordinary vision in chapter 6, which until quite recently has generally been regarded as the prophet's call to divine service.

A VISION OF THE ENTHRONED DEITY

The exquisite description in Isaiah of a momentary prophetic glimpse beyond the earthly temple to the heavenly one is rich in theological expression, and it has often provided the decisive clue for understanding the idea of the holy.* The earthly ruler, Uzziah, had died, but the prophet became conscious of a greater reality, the enthroned Lord of the universe. Nonhuman creatures attended this heavenly king, and these six-winged seraphim sang appropriate praise: "Holy, holy, holy is the Lord of hosts; the whole earth is full of his glory" (6:3).† Aware of his own sinfulness and terrified by the reverberations of this singing, Isaiah acknowledges his unclean state and expects the worst, until a seraph communicates forgiveness to him in a tangible gesture, the touching of his lips with a live coal from the altar. At this point Isaiah's attention shifts again to the enthroned one, who asks a question that evokes immediate response from him: "Whom shall I send, and who will go for us?" . . . "Here I am, send me" (6:8). What follows is an astonishing commission. Isaiah is told to increase the resistance of the people so that they will refuse healing and subject themselves to eventual destruction.

> Make the heart of this people fat,
> and their ears heavy,
> and shut their eyes;
> lest they see with their eyes,
> and hear with their ears,

*Rudolph Otto, *The Idea of the Holy*, 2nd ed. (London: Oxford University Press, 1950).
†The technical expression *Trishagion* derives from the threefold repetition of the word holy.

and understand with their hearts,
and turn and be healed. (Isa. 6:10)*

The present position of this commission serves to relate it to the social criticism that precedes it and to the prophetic oracles that immediately follow. The strange wording of the commission sums up Isaiah's disappointment over the people's rejection of his criticism. The effect of his ministry has been entirely negative, a hardening of hearts and a stiffening of resistance to the Deity's word as proclaimed by the prophet. The extent of that stubbornness is given concrete expression in King Ahaz's refusal to exericise faith at a decisive moment. The vision therefore equips Isaiah for a confrontation that is fraught with consequence for himself and for the nation.

THE SYRO-EPHRAIMITE WAR

The political context for confrontation was explosive. Rezin, the king of Syria, and Pekah of Israel planned to rebel against Assyria but failed to persuade Judah's ruler, Ahaz, to join them in this act. They therefore attacked Jerusalem in an effort to replace him with the son of a certain Tabe-el† who would cooperate with them. Terror gripped the Judean king and his subjects; in the words of the narrative their hearts "shook as the trees of the forest shake before the wind" (Isa. 7:2). Accompanied by his son Shear-jashub, Isaiah approached Ahaz and assured him that he had nothing to fear from these two smoldering stumps of firebrands. However, the prophet insisted that faith was a requirement for a secure government: "If you will not believe, / surely you shall not be established" (7:9). The king was unable to meet the requirement, as the sequel to this story reveals. The Deity invites Ahaz to pose a test, one that has no limits, but he piously responds that he will not inquire of the Lord or put the Deity to a test. Now the king who has wearied the prophet and his God must listen to an ominous sign: "Behold, a young woman shall conceive and bear a son, and shall call his name Immanu-el. . . . The Lord will bring upon you . . . the King of Assyria" (7:14–17). Like the name of Shear-jashub, this one is ambiguous; it may conceal a promise or a threat. "A remnant will return" implies that the calamity will not

---

*The same sort of thing occurs in the Gospel of Mark, which depicts Jesus as determined to conceal knowledge lest the people repent. The explanation for such strange language begins with an assumption of divine sovereignty, and concludes that if something happened the Deity must have willed it. The obvious conclusion is that the Deity actually intended for the people to perish. Naturally, this was the ancient author's way of dealing with the people's incorrigibility. It therefore says more about human nature than about transcendence.
†Presumably, the individual's name was Tabe-el (God is good), as given in the Revised Standard Version, but the Hebrew has been changed to read Tabeal (not good), hence a nobody.

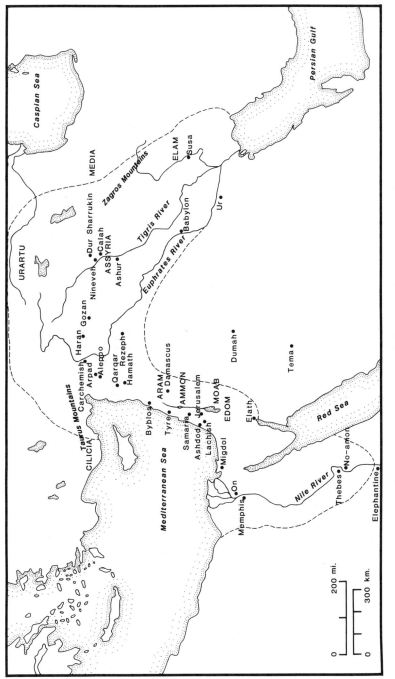

The Assyrian Empire (eighth–seventh centuries B.C.E.)

be complete; on the other hand, the emphasis may have been on the extent of destruction from which only a few people will escape. Likewise, the name Immanu-el suggests God's presence with the people, but here it bodes evil. It is impossible to determine who the young woman was, although the likely mother-to-be was the king's wife. However, some interpreters believe Isaiah was thinking about his own wife. In all likelihood, he draws on traditional hopes about a wondrous birth that will usher in an era of peace and prosperity, but he uses the familiar material in a wholly unexpected manner. A certain degree of tension therefore exists within the narrative, which juxtaposes a potentially promising birth and name, as well as language reminiscent of food for the gods, with explicit threatening words.

TRUST

A single prophetic statement stands out in this episode, both in style and in content. That memorable word is Isaiah's play on the word faith, which cannot easily be rendered in felicitous English (7:9). In the prophet's view, Ahaz must place absolute trust in the Holy One of Israel if his kingdom is to stand a chance of being firm, the essential meaning of the verb 'amen, usually translated as to believe. The path to security did not lie along alliances with alleged superpowers, whether Egypt or Assyria, but in firm resolve to rely wholly on the Deity. This was the unbending position that Isaiah took, and he insisted that Judah's kings subscribe to it as well. From their perspective, it must have appeared as the road to annihilation. Both prophet and king were surely convinced that the other had divorced himself from reality. For Isaiah the only sure thing was the divine intention for the nations of the world, whereas Ahaz and his successors believed that power rested in the military.

PRIDE

It seemed to Isaiah that a single factor stood in the way of complete trust in the Holy One of Israel, and that obstacle, pride, characterized royalty and subjects alike. The prophet recognized the audacity of humans dictating what is right and proper to Deity. The ludicrousness of such presumption is captured in a rhetorical question: "Shall the ax vaunt itself over him who hews with it, / or the saw magnify itself against him who wields it?" (10:15). The idea is pressed further to include the absurd reversal of things, a rod wielding the one who lifts it or a staff lifting the person who is flesh and blood, not wood. It was Isaiah's belief that the Deity wielded the rod as an instrument of punishment, and the Assyrian sovereignty sprang from this reality rather than from Yahweh's weakness in the struggle with the deities in whose names Assyrian kings waged war. Isaiah interpreted the Assyrian advance as entirely orchestrated by the Holy One of Israel, for Assyria was the rod that the Deity used to punish a proud nation. These inhabitants of Judah had grown up under divine solicitude, but they had rebelled against their loving parent. Isaiah could only characterize such conduct as stupidity, worse than the behavior of dumb animals.

> The ox knows its owner,
>   and the ass its master's crib;
> but Israel does not know,
>   my people does not understand. (Isa. 1:3)

The prophet was convinced that such pride and its consequence, rebellion, could not stand, for the Deity would abase the proud and exalt the humble.

This exaggerated view of one's importance resulted in a reversal of values in society, a tendency against which Isaiah spoke harsh words.

> Woe to those who call evil good
>   and good evil,
> who put darkness for light
>   and light for darkness,
> who put bitter for sweet
>   and sweet for bitter!
> Woe to those who are wise in their own eyes,
>   and shrewd in their own sight! (Isa. 5:20–21)

The context implies that these individuals thought they could discern the hidden activity of the Deity, or perhaps that they had abandoned all hope that the Lord would act one way or another. The result was an exalting of their own selfish desires, along with a rationalization of their conduct that accomplished a complete reversal of morality. This pride allowed power-hungry possessors of capital to purchase huge estates, disenfranchising the poor and robbing them of their ancestral heritage.

MESSIANIC TEXTS

Proud and selfish conduct threatened the well-being of society and, at least indirectly, reflected badly on the king, whose responsibility was to promote justice. Nevertheless, visions of a better day were nurtured despite this actual disappointment in the Davidic rulers. The origin and date of these two "messianic" texts is uncertain, but they may have been proclaimed in connection with the birth of a royal child, perhaps Hezekiah. The first text, 9:1–7, promises victory over the oppressor, presumably achieved by the Deity, and a consequent birth of a prince who will rule justly. The text recalls the day of Midian, a glorious victory for the Israelites, and dreams about a time when all clothing worn by soldiers will be put to the torch. It rejoices over the birth of a son who will receive throne names: "Wonderful Counselor, Mighty God, / Everlasting Father, Prince of Peace." The other text, 11:1–9, emphasizes the young king's wisdom in executing justice throughout the land and describes an era when peace will reign among humans and animals. This idyllic return to Eden concludes with a promise:

> They shall not hurt or destroy
> in all my holy mountain;
> for the earth shall be full of the knowledge of the Lord
> as the waters cover the sea. (Isa. 11:9)

SINFUL JUDAH

The sharp contrast between these hopes and actual reality cannot escape the reader of the book of Isaiah. Perhaps that contrast appears best in the prophet's caricature of Jerusalemite women, haughty daughters of Zion who

> walk with outstretched necks,
> glancing wantonly with their eyes,
> mincing along as they go,
> tinkling with their feet. (Isa. 3:16)

Isaiah's painstaking description of the lavish adornments these women wore to enhance their beauty serves to demonstrate their complete disregard for the poor, a crushing of the Lord's people. This disparity between abject poverty and tasteless display of wealth prompted Isaiah to announce that these rich women would soon lose everything, including their honor. The prophet's final words about these women must have sent a shudder through all who put any stock in his word: a day is coming when seven women will beg one man to marry them, promising to pay for their own food and clothing.

That is the kind of fall envisioned in chapter 14, which uses traditional imagery to describe the emergence and decline of a mighty power. Here the language applies to Babylon and ushers in the restoration of an exiled people, so, of course, it cannot be from Isaiah in its present form. Nevertheless, it conveys an attitude toward pride that he certainly shared, a conviction that the Deity would overthrow arrogance wherever it appeared. Here Canaanite language associated with deities sets the poetry apart from ordinary affairs. The Day Star, son of Dawn, has fallen, for he aspired to deity. The imagery is that of the mythic mountain of the gods in the north, where this earthly king thought he would sit enthroned like the Most High. The former victims of his might have difficulty imagining that this one who now lies amid the corpses thrown in a pit rather than in an expensive sepulcher can actually have sent terror wherever he appeared. They ask themselves who could have believed that the king before whom nations trembled would receive a burial like that of an untimely birth?

Such reversal of fortune also struck lesser figures, most notably the steward Shebna, whose pride prompted him to carve out an impressive niche for himself in a rock sepulcher. For this high estimate of his worth, Shebna earned Isaiah's scorn, along with a prediction that he would be replaced in office by Eliakim and cast out to die in a foreign land where his splendid chariots would lie in dust. Likewise, even Hezekiah, whose engineers accomplished the remarkable feat of digging a tunnel for more than 1,700 feet in solid rock from the Gihon spring to the inner city of Jerusalem, heard Isaiah announce the king's approaching death, but in this instance Hezekiah's ardent prayers moved the Deity to compassion. According to the devotional legend that is attached to the collection of Isaiah's oracles, the king was granted an additional fifteen years. His response is far from flattering, in that it presents Hezekiah as a ruler whose primary concern was his own well-being, let come what may to his children and the royal treasury. Isaiah's attitude toward this king seems to have been ambiguous. On the one hand, he acted to assist in restoring Hezekiah's health, even prescribing medical treatment for him. On the other hand, Isaiah rebuked the ruler for displaying the royal wealth to envoys from the Babylonian Merodach-baladan, presumably because the prophet suspected that Hezekiah intended to join this king in rebelling against Assyria.

SENNACHERIB'S INVASION

It appears that Isaiah became convinced that Assyria overstepped its bounds in acting as the agent of divine punishment. He therefore resisted the invasion by Sennacherib in 701, promising Hezekiah that Jerusalem would be spared the slightest danger. The story is an extraordinary example of narrative art, rich in rhetoric. The spokesman for Sennacherib, the Rabshakeh, begins his public appeal for surrender by discounting Egyptian assistance. In his words, the pharaoh is a "broken reed of a staff, which will pierce the hand of any man who leans on it" (36:6). He then proceeds to demolish any claim of aid from the Lord; after all, he reasoned, Hezekiah has removed all the high places and altars, a reference to the reform this king carried out similar to that in Josiah's day. The hidden argument was that the Deity was displeased over these innovations, and the assumption was that many people in the audience shared this belief. The Rabshakeh now resorts to calculated terror; he proposes a wager that if he gave the people two thousand horses they would be unable to provide enough riders for them. The point is obvious: how

The Siloam tunnel. An inscription discovered here tells how King Hezekiah's engineers achieved the remarkable feat of providing a hidden channel to bring water into the city of Jerusalem.

then can you resist the mighty Assyrian army? Having gained the people's attention, he immediately presses for a decision by claiming the Lord's blessing on his invasion, a claim that could appeal to Isaiah's earlier conviction that Assyria was the rod of the Deity's anger. At this point Judah's officials urge the Rabshakeh to negotiate in Aramaic, the diplomatic language of the time, so that the people will not be terrified, but he refuses to give up his advantage. Now he warns these people that they are doomed "to eat their own dung and drink their own urine" (36:12), and offers them a better alternative. If they will surrender, they can eat their grain and drink their wine in peace until he comes to take

Sennacherib (704–681) receives prisoners and spoil from the capture of Lachish.

them away to a land like theirs, one with grain and wine, bread and vineyards. The Rabshakeh's parting word is a reminder that the gods of other cities, Hamath and Samaria, for example, have been unable to withstand Assyria's might.

Isaiah's participation comes later, after his advice has been urgently sought. He tells the Judean king to take heart, for the Lord will spread a rumor that will turn Sennacherib's attention away, and he will be slain in his own land. Isaiah promises that Sennacherib will not come to Jerusalem, "or shoot an arrow there, or come before it with a shield, or cast up a siege-mound against it" (37:33). This promise did not hold true, of course, for Sennacherib did indeed ravish the country and besiege Jerusalem, requiring an immense sum in tribute from Hezekiah. However, the city was remarkably spared, and perhaps this reprieve at the last minute generated the legend about the destruction of 185,000 Assyrian soldiers in a single glance of the Lord. This is a rare instance in which three accounts of the incident have survived (four, if one counts the version in Chronicles): competing stories in the Book of Kings, reproduced in Isaiah 36–39, where the legendary account prevails, and the

The Taylor Prism, which mentions Sennacherib's victory over Hezekiah, together with the defeat of forty-six cities of Judah.

official Assyrian record. Some interpreters have gone to great lengths to defend the historical accuracy of the depletion of Sennacherib's army; older attempts to explain the event as a plague, which were based on an obscure allusion in Herodotus, have largely been abandoned in favor of a claim that the biblical story combines two attacks on the city into a single invasion, but the evidence for two campaigns by Sennacherib against Jerusalem is not compelling.

Faced with such a powerful enemy as the Assyrians, Judah's kings naturally turned to Egypt for help. During the revolt against Assyria concentrated in Ashdod, the prophet Isaiah stripped and walked naked and barefoot for three years, dramatically warning the rebels that even those on whom they relied, Egypt and Ethiopia, would be carried off into exile. For a man to expose his nakedness was scandalous even beyond the same conduct in a woman, so this bold symbolic act seems to have achieved its purpose, for Hezekiah withdrew from the coalition of revolutionaries in time to escape Assyrian retaliation. Elsewhere Isaiah attacks head-on Egypt's reputation for wisdom, insisting that the Holy One of Israel is also wise. The prophet thinks those who put their trust in horses and chariots will encounter soldiers on swifter steeds; therefore, Isaiah urges a different attitude, faith in the Deity. "In returning and rest you shall be saved;/in quietness and in trust shall be your strength" (30:15). This sort of trust had nothing in common with a despairing attitude that seems to have seized some of the inhabitants of Jerusalem, who sang to forget their immediate danger: "Let us eat and drink,/for tomorrow we die" (22:13).

DESPAIR

This feeling of utter hopelessness is expressed elsewhere as a drunken stupor, a deep sleep poured out on the prophets and all those learned individuals whose advice sustains society and its government. Isaiah seems drawn to vocabulary about knowledge and instruction, and this feature of his style has led to theories associating him in some direct way with Israel's wisdom tradition. Much of this material focuses on teaching and reading, but its value for clarifying ancient Israelite education is limited. In one case the people mock Isaiah by quoting what appears to be infant's babble (28:9–13), and in another they are subjected to a description of appropriate agricultural activity, the point being that the Lord also understands when to do a given thing for best results (28:23–29). Another passage, which resembles late prose texts, presents a situation that describes the effect of deep sleep. When given a book, those who can read complain that it is sealed, and those who are illiterate confess that they cannot read. In this context the major themes in Isaiah's prophecies almost explode:

> *Woe to those who hide deep from the Lord their counsel,*
>   *whose deeds are in the dark,*
>   *and who say, "Who sees us? Who knows us?"*
> *You turn things upside down!*
>   *Shall the potter be regarded as the clay;*
> *that the thing made should say of its maker,*
>   *"He did not make me";*
> *or the thing formed say of him who formed it,*
>   *"He has no understanding"? (Isa. 29:15–16)*

It is almost as if Isaiah summed up his social criticism in these words, just as he sought by dramatic action to record his prophetic utterances (8:16). There Isaiah decided to write down the oracles and to seal them in the presence of those who had been instructed in appreciating such disclosures. They therefore became an enduring testimony to his faithfulness that later generations could judge against the actual course of history, and in so doing these students of the prophetic word could recognize the wisdom in consulting the Lord rather than resorting to specialists in divination.

UNFULFILLED PROPHECY

In some cases, oracles that purport to derive from Isaiah hardly convey the notion that he accurately predicted the future. That statement is particularly true of the announcement that Israel was destined to take her place alongside the two other major powers of the time, Egypt and Assyria.

> In that day Israel will be the third with Egypt and Assyria, a blessing in the midst of the earth, whom the Lord of hosts has blessed, saying, "Blessed be Egypt my people, and Assyria the work of my hands, and Israel my heritage." (Isa. 19:24–25)

It is also true of such grand promises as those which declare that the desert will be transformed and a holy highway will appear when God comes to save. But here one notices a style and theme that belong to the unknown author of chapters 40–55.

> *Then the eyes of the blind shall be opened,*
>   *and the ears of the deaf unstopped;*
> *then shall the lame man leap like a hart,*
>   *and the tongue of the dumb sing for joy.*
> *For waters shall break forth in the wilderness,*
>   *and streams in the desert.... (Isa. 35:5–6)*

One feature of this text recalls another suspect passage, chapters 24–27, often labeled the Isaiah apocalypse because of its kinship with later texts like Zechariah 9–14 and Daniel. That common link between chapters

35 and 24–27 is the dream that sorrow and sighing will vanish, which can only signify divine resolve to banish death and to dry every tear that forms in the eyes of humans, but that happy time must first be preceded by a shaking of heaven and earth.

SECOND ISAIAH

Since the first thirty-nine chapters of the book contain some texts that represent later literary and theological characteristics, why should chapters 40–55 be treated separately? The reasons are numerous, but the most compelling of them seem to be:

1. The historical context is different.
2. The literary style is distinctive.
3. The religious ideas are different.
4. Prophecies in chapters 1–39 are understood in chapters 40–55 as having been fulfilled long ago.

The author of chapters 40–55 addresses exiled Judeans of the sixth century who live under Babylonian tyranny, and he views Cyrus as their emancipator. The Temple lies in ruins, and the fulfillment of prophecies concerning Babylon is judged to have taken place. The style is lyrical, argumentative, and rich, and the language is appropriate to the sixth century. Monotheism has emerged on the historical scene, and various arguments for the incomparability of the Lord are put forth. Accompanying this new understanding of deity is a revolutionary interpretation of suffering as vicarious, that is, for the sake of others. This idea comes to light in passages about a servant of the Deity, and a new understanding of history as human events completely determined by divine plan. For convenience, scholars have dubbed this unknown author Second Isaiah (often written as Deutero-Isaiah).

Date

It may be possible to date these chapters precisely, if the reference to the completion of servitude really refers to the forty-year requirement for military service. Because the fall of Jerusalem is the point of reference, the date of this composition would be about 547, the year the Persian king Cyrus conquered Croesus of Lydia, the king whose legendary wealth is widely extolled. This date accords with the fact that Babylon had not yet fallen, although that drama was beginning to unfold. This anticipation of deliverance explains the celebrative mood that characterizes the poetry in chapters 40–55. The author thinks of Cyrus as the anointed one chosen by Israel's God to set her people free. Here is a remarkable attitude toward a foreigner, but it is one that seems justified by the language of the

Cyrus Cylinder, which shows astonishing similarities with the style and expressions in these chapters. The conquering Persian ruler set the captives free in 539, when he entered Babylon without resistance and issued a decree that demonstrated considerable tolerance of religious differences. This king's attitude toward subject peoples represented a fundamental change from that of Babylonian rulers, for Cyrus believed that people would be better citizens if they were permitted to live in their own homeland and to worship their god freely.

Although the poetry in these chapters is highly lyrical, often excelling in exquisite descriptions of transformations in nature, the message is nonetheless quite concrete. The author makes three points, and repeats them again and again: (1) the Creator has redeemed the people Israel and has brought about a new exodus; (2) this deliverer alone is God, for idols are nonentities; and (3) a servant of the Lord will bring into being a new relationship between Deity and people. The rhetoric is the hyperbole typical of lament, and the mood is one of absolute certainty. This assurance that the day of salvation has dawned issues in comforting words for some people but merciless ridicule for all who worship other deities.

Creation

With Second Isaiah the theme of creation comes to the center of theological reflection, and that event is closely related to another one, the deliverance of subject peoples. The mythological understanding of the origin of the universe as the result of conflict is here applied to the redeemer's struggle to rescue an oppressed group. The Exodus is therefore interpreted as a battle between order and chaos, and the Lord is represented as the victor over the rebellious sea. This same one who conquered evil's minions centuries earlier has recently engaged in combat once more and has done something so marvelous that the former things pale in comparison. Therefore, the poet urges the ransomed people to forget those memorable past events in anticipation of new things of grand proportions.

This emphasis on creation heightened an old problem, the existence of what humans perceive to be evil. If the Lord is really as powerful as the poet suggests, why is life beset with evil on every hand? The author insists that the Creator is responsible for both misfortune and blessing.

> *I form light and create darkness,*
> *I make weal and create woe,*
> *I am the Lord, who do all these things. (Isa. 45:7)*

At the same time, the poet denies that chaos is an operative word, for the Lord formed the universe to be inhabited. Like many others who find this problem to be beyond human ken, the poet borrows an idea from Isaiah of Jerusalem to silence doubters.

Woe to him who strives with his Maker,
   an earthen vessel with the potter!
Does the clay say to him who fashions it, "What are you making"?
   or "Your work has no handles"? (Isa. 45:9)

In doing so, the author acknowledges that there are limits to human knowledge, and concedes further the essential nature of deity as hidden: "Truly, thou art a God who hidest thyself, / O God of Israel, the Savior" (45:15).

The centrality of the creation story in the Babylonian Akitu festival* may throw light on this theme in Second Isaiah, who seems to have witnessed this dramatized event and to have reacted strongly against its implications. The Lord did not need to consult the other gods before creating the world; indeed, there were no other deities to be consulted, for the idols that were paraded through the streets during the festival are weaker than the people carrying them. The poet never tires of asserting that the Lord controls past and future: "I, the Lord, the first, / and with the last; I am He" (41:4). No deity preceded the Lord, and none will outlast the only savior. By contrast, the idols are fashioned from wood and overlaid with gold; that is, humans brought them into existence, and the resulting idols are incapable of moving. This point is pressed by a later prose text that mocks the entire procedure by which idols were made and ridicules those who pray to the works of human hands for deliverance (44:9–20). Here, too, a link occurs with an idea that we have already mentioned, the stupor that overtakes those who turn away from the Deity.

Prediction

The point of consulting deities was to discover what the coming year held for the worshipper. Second Isaiah denies that such information can come from any source but the Creator. This denial carries in its train an affirmation that the redeemer is unique precisely because the future is open to Israel's God. The poet claims that the Lord announced beforehand the events that are unfolding before the eyes of the exiled peoples at that very moment. In this connection, the fulfillment of Isaiah's prophecies about Babylon is singled out as decisive proof that the God of Israel controls the future and therefore can predict coming events with complete accuracy. Accordingly, Second Isaiah challenges the foreign deities to set forth their case and to "Tell us what is to come hereafter, / that we may know that you are gods" (41:23).

The practical value of this comforting knowledge about the one who

---

*Akitu was a New Year's celebration that seems to have lasted seven days, on the third of which the creation story was recited. The exact nature of this festival remains unclear, however.

controls the future can hardly be exaggerated, for it enabled subject peoples the more readily to resist every temptation to worship the deities of those who defeated them on the battlefield. The repeated exhortation, "Fear not, for I am with you," served to encourage bold resistance to these deities. The poet's adoption of boasting formulas often used by Mesopotamian kings may sound strange on the lips of one who desires humility in humans, but these declarations that "I am the greatest" succeed in exalting the Lord, who, in the eyes of many, had bowed in defeat before Babylonian deities. The boasts also focus attention on the vast gulf that separates humans and their Creator, whose ways and thoughts are higher and whose intentions never meet frustration. It naturally follows that the divine word will inevitably succeed in its goal, in the same way that rain and snow enable the earth to produce those things that make life possible as well as pleasant. Heaven and earth may vanish in smoke, but the Lord's redeeming hand will endure.

By stressing the uniqueness of the Creator, Second Isaiah runs a serious risk, the withdrawal of the high God from the human arena. The addition of redeemer as an attribute of the Deity guards against this danger. The only Creator is also the savior who manifests an active interest in the exiled people, but that compassion is not reserved exclusively for them. Exactly how far in the direction of universalism this poet goes is a matter of considerable debate, and these two categories, creator and redeemer, add to the difficulty of settling that argument. The former tends toward universalism, inasmuch as the Creator of the universe would hardly despise the results of divine intention. The latter accords better with a narrower understanding of things, since the form in which it occurs in chapters 40–55 singles out one group as special recipients of divine favor. It seems that the poet thinks foreign peoples will benefit indirectly from Israel, who will function as a light to the nations. Nevertheless, the foreign king Cyrus receives the exalted title "messiah"; here alone in the Hebrew Bible is this word applied to a non-Israelite.

The Servant

Just as one foreigner, Cyrus, stands out in the poet's mind, so does a single Israelite. This individual seems to possess an unusual quality that is attributed to Abraham and Jacob, the ability to stand on his own as one person and at the same time to represent a whole people. For this reason, which seems to explain a similar fluidity within the description of the servant figure, many interpreters believe that the poet spoke of both—Israel and one individual within the larger entity. Modern readers may be led astray by the term servant, which seems to suggest a lowly estate. In the ancient world the word "servant" is often used of royalty, and this may be true here. That suspicion is further strengthened by the use of first person in the biographical narrative, for only royal inscriptions in the ancient Near East did so. Nevertheless, some notables other than kings also bear the exalted title "servant," and that fact has led interpreters to identify the servant of the Lord with Moses, as well as with kings such as Jehoiachin and high officials like Zerubbabel. Four texts are usually isolated for discussion of the servant (42:1–4; 49:1–6; 50:4–11; and 52:13–53:12), but many critics think the fourth one was written by the servant's admirers, whereas the other three are taken to be the work of a single poet. The first poem announces that the servant will inaugurate an era of justice under the power of the spirit, one characterized by gentle firmness. In the second poem the servant is identified as Israel, but his mission is to bring back the tribes of Jacob. As if to correct such self-centeredness, the Deity lays an even heavier burden on his shoulders, to function as a light to the nations. Presumably, Israel's entire existence as a favored one will evoke a single response in all who behold it: let us also go up to the mountain of the God of Israel so that we may participate in the divine blessing. The third poem introduces a hint of suffering that the servant must undergo, a theme that dominates the last poem. In this initial exposure of this notion, the servant is described as one who has been taught by the heavenly teacher, and he therefore endures affliction without flinching, for he is confident that his tormentors will disappear. The final poem tells about the servant's extreme suffering at the hands of violent persons and reflects on the implications of that event. Initial impressions that the servant was guilty of some unknown crime that brought on his punishment gave way to deeper thoughts that the suffering he endured had significance beyond his own personal situation. The author boldly interprets the servant's suffering as an act of selfless love, a gift that benefited many. To make this point, sacrificial terminology seems most helpful, and the servant is likened to a lamb that was offered as an atonement for sin. This imagery and the hyperbole typical of individual laments make the fourth poem difficult to understand; in the eyes of some, the latter feature even casts doubt on the prevailing assumptions that the servant was actually put to death. If that view should prevail, it would make unnecessary the thesis that this fourth poem came from a hand other than that composing the first three.

These themes that characterize chapters 40–55 are set within a larger framework, which consists of an electrifying emotion of expectancy. From the opening divine commission that the unknown prophet is to comfort the people of God to the closing announcement that they will go out in joy, the intensity of an unfolding drama fills the air. Even nature itself joins the human population in lively celebration.

> the mountains and the hills before you
>   shall break forth into singing,
>   and all the trees of the field shall clap their hands. (Isa. 55:12)

The occasion for such joy is the coming of the divine Shepherd who will

> gather the lambs in his arms,
> he will carry them in his bosom,
> and gently lead those that are with young. (Isa. 40:11)

The brief moment during which the Lord forsook Israel is past, and everyone will compete to be known as the special heritage of that Deity.

THIRD ISAIAH

The final chapters in the book of Isaiah, 56–66, seem to comprise independent texts that have been brought together as a kind of anthology, although certain themes that persist in much of the material lead some critics to think of a single author for the bulk of the chapters. Because these texts represent a different perspective from those dominating the first two "Isaiahs," scholars use the convenient label Third Isaiah (or Trito-Isaiah) for chapters 56–66. The texts also seem to reflect a slightly later historical situation, perhaps the last two decades of the sixth century to the middle of the fifth century. A noticeable feature of the texts is the tendency toward exposition of earlier sacred traditions; here the transition from prophecy to exegesis has begun,* for the aim is to interpret the full import of a written word that has come to be understood as divine disclosure for the present people of God.

Religion without a Cult

During the exilic period the captives had been required to get along without the Temple cult, and for more than seventy years they had to worship the Deity in some fashion other than by animal and cereal offerings. Expediency had forced many residents in an alien land to take a hard look at the entire sacrificial cult and to evaluate its contribution to society in the light of consistent prophetic criticism. To be sure, this attack on the cult was directed at its abuse, but the extreme language to which the prophets sometimes resorted may have convinced some people that the destruction of Jerusalem's holy place was a service to religious life. In any event, a strong protest against the necessity for a Temple surfaces in Third Isaiah, and the polemic is usually thought to have arisen when the prophets Haggai and Zechariah burst on the political scene and strongly urged the rebuilding of the Temple. Within five years after their first dated oracle, 521, the community dedicated a newly constructed Temple. A few older persons who recalled the grandeur of Solomon's

---

*The Greek noun *exegesis* (a leading out) has become a standard term for the interpretation of a text.

A model liver, made of clay, used by diviners in Mesopotamia to ascertain the future. After sacrificing an animal, diviners studied its liver for indications of coming events.

Temple wept because of the difference between the two structures, but such remorse is quite different from the view expressed in Isaiah 66:

> Thus says the Lord:
> "Heaven is my throne
>   and the earth is my footstool;
> what is this house which you would build for me,
>   and what is the place of my rest"? (Isa. 66:1)

> "He who slaughters an ox is like him who kills a man;
>   he who sacrifices a lamb, like him who breaks a dog's neck;
> he who presents a cereal offering, like him who offers swine's blood;
>   he who makes a memorial offering of frankincense, like him who
>   blesses an idol." (Isa. 66:3)

That radical position with regard to the Temple cult has been blunted by a prosaic promise that the Deity intends to bring back exiled Israelites who remain in foreign lands, and some of these will even be chosen to officiate in the cult. So priestly is this passage that it likens the people's return to a cereal offering in a clean vessel; nevertheless, the openness toward exiled brothers who will swell the ranks of priests and Levites suggests that this select group within Israelite society had come on hard times.

Universalism

Another revolutionary idea in these texts concerns the status of some persons who had remained on the fringes of Israelite society insofar as their active participation in and benefit from the law were concerned. According to 56:3–5, resident aliens and eunuchs will have full benefits from worshipping the Lord. Eunuchs will have no reason to suspect that they are cursed because they are unable to reproduce. To them will be given a memorial that outlasts sons and daughters, for a permanent name will be theirs within the house of God. Resident aliens also will take comfort in the knowledge that they belong to the Deity, who will not turn away from them. Here, too, an attitude toward the Temple that is different from the one discussed previously comes to expression, and sabbath observance stands out as well. However, the openness toward foreigners who abide by the Jewish law is noteworthy:

> their burnt offerings and their sacrifices
>   will be accepted on my altar;
> for my house shall be called a house of prayer
>   for all peoples. (Isa. 56:7)

Elsewhere in Third Isaiah a poet addresses the heavenly parent in wholly submissive sentiments: we are clay, you are the potter, so have compassion on the work of your hands. In this context the worshipper chooses to linger on only one occasion of sorrow, the burning of the holy and beautiful house "where our fathers praised thee" (64:11).

Spiritualization

By far the most radical teaching in Third Isaiah involves the correct understanding of fasting. Denying that a proper fast has anything to do with bowing in humility and spreading sackcloth and ashes, the poet urges actions that will benefit society.

> Is not this the fast that I choose:
>   to loose the bonds of wickedness,
>   to undo the thongs of the yoke,
> to let the oppressed go free,
>   and to break every yoke?

> *Is it not to share your bread with the hungry,*
>   *and bring the homeless poor into your house;*
> *when you see the naked, to cover him,*
>   *and not to hide yourself from your own flesh? (Isa. 58:6–7)*

It is in complete harmony with this viewpoint that the poet declares in 61:1–4 that the one empowered by the spirit searches out a special clientele: the afflicted, the brokenhearted, the prisoner, the person in mourning. Bringing relief, healing, freedom, and joy is the ministry of the anointed one. Such is the answer this poet gives to the perennial question: why has the Deity ignored our fasting and prayers?

These texts indicate that the people were not tempted to despair because of their hopeless situation, but rather that some of them resorted to religious practices that were not sanctioned by the officials in Jerusalem. The worship of Molech receives special notice here, and the author provides considerable detail about the extremes to which such devotees went, including human sacrifice and sexual abandon. It seems that the Deity's patience has been interpreted as weakness, and the people have resorted to their idols once again.

Idolatry

The radical attitude toward foreigners did not carry with it a tolerance toward their deities. As a matter of fact, even the aforementioned positive appreciation for resident aliens was limited to those who later came to be known as God-fearers. The foreigners who did not keep the sabbath and abide by the law will contribute to the happiness of their former subjects in very concrete ways.

> *Aliens shall stand and feed your flocks,*
>   *foreigners shall be your plowmen and vine-dressers;*
> *but you shall be called the priests of the Lord,*
>   *men shall speak of you as the ministers of our God;*
> *you shall eat the wealth of the nations,*
>   *and in their riches you shall glory. (Isa. 61:5–6)*

This idea is so overwhelming that it prompts the poet to envision a city with its doors forever open so that foreign wealth can flow through them unhindered, with kings bearing tribute at the head of the procession (60:11).

Earlier visions of an era of peace capture the imagination once more, now with cosmic dimensions. These include a new heaven and a new earth, along with the total eradication of sorrow. The supreme enemy, death, will have been tamed, although not entirely banished, and long life will become a reality for one and all. The horrible futility curses have suddenly lost their power, for those who build houses will actually live in them and those who plant vineyards will eat their fruit.

> *The wolf and the lamb shall feed together,*
> *the lion shall eat straw like the ox;*
> *and dust shall be the serpent's food.*
> *They shall not hurt or destroy*
> *in all my holy mountain,*
>   *says the Lord. (Isa. 65:25)*

This era of peace will be inaugurated by one who is mighty to save.

Ancient Canaanite imagery lies behind the terrifying picture of the avenging Deity who is bloodstained from walking in the gore of vanquished victims.* Like one who treads on grapes, the Lord is portrayed as stamping out the grapes of wrath on a day of vengeance. This portrayal of an avenging Deity places in perspective the following description of Israel's waywardness despite divine guidance through Moses and Abraham. Here the poet endeavors to appropriate sacred tradition in a way that will bring comfort to a later community that had great difficulty recognizing signs of the Deity's favor. When the new day dawns, however, that will not be a problem because the Deity will replace the sun, and that new source of warmth and vision will never set, "for the Lord will be your everlasting light, / and your days of mourning shall be ended" (60:20). Renewed hope within the book of Hosea had expressed itself in a renaming of Israel; that old notion comes to light once more in Third Isaiah:

> *You shall no more be termed Forsaken,*
> *and your land shall no more be termed Desolate;*
> *but you shall be called My delight is in her,*
> *and your land Married. . . . (Isa. 62:4)*

---

*This is an allusion to Anat, the warrior goddess. There is also a story from ancient Egypt in which divine wrath is neutralized by making the land appear to be bloodstained from carnage.

◆ 11 ◆

Jeremiah

THE book of Jeremiah reflects the tumultuous events of the age during which it came into existence. About the time of Jeremiah's call (626 B.C.E.), Nabopolassar was successful in taking the city of Babylon. Four years later the Judean king Josiah launched a religious reform that had far-reaching consequences. In 612, Nineveh, the capital of the Assyrian empire, succumbed to the overwhelming might of the combined forces of Babylonians and Medes under Nabopolassar. Although the Assyrian kingdom survived for three more years, it finally fell to the great Nebuchadnezzar, the son of Nabopolassar, who also dealt Egypt a crushing blow at Carchemish in 605. These years were significant ones for the little kingdom of Judah, for Josiah made the fatal mistake of opposing the Egyptian army that was moving toward Carchemish to assist the beleaguered Assyrians. That brief interlude took place in 609 and resulted in Josiah's death at the hands of Pharaoh Necho. In 597 Nebuchadnezzar besieged Judah, taking captive a large number of citizens from the upper levels of society. The final blow came ten years later, when Jerusalem was reduced to rubble, and the entire country was devastated by Babylonian soldiers.

BABYLON OR EGYPT?

These tense political maneuverings affected the attitudes of Judean citizens in significant ways, for the people had to choose sides between Babylon and Egypt, the two powers to be reckoned with once Assyria went down in defeat. In Jerusalem two factions vied for popular support, a pro-Egyptian and a pro-Babylonian party. The prophet Jeremiah chose to support Babylon because he was convinced that the Deity had appointed this powerful nation to maintain order in the created world. Judah's kings leaned in the opposite direction, perhaps mindful of Josiah's

191

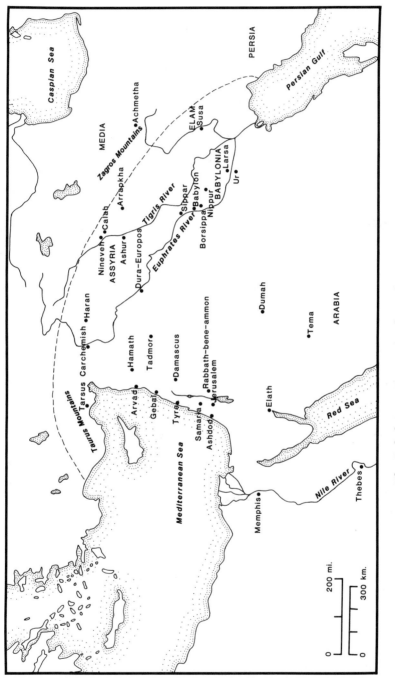

The Babylonian Empire (early sixth century B.C.E.*)*

fate. Egypt's nearness to the Judean borders seemed sufficient cause for allegiance to the pharaohs, and their promise of military support against Babylon must have been immensely reassuring. In such a political climate, Jeremiah's outspoken endorsement of Babylonian power inevitably led to charges of treason. Only the friendship of certain high officials in the royal court prevented his death at the hands of those who viewed his conduct as dangerous to the citizenry.

The Egyptian party did not lack prophetic spokesmen, and the presence of oracles condemning Babylon, in contrast to Jeremiah's lofty vision for that nation, created a highly volatile situation. In this difficult setting Jeremiah often became the object of persecution and public ridicule, particularly from religious officials associated with the Temple in Jerusalem. His own scorn for the magical function of that sacred place in the minds of many worshippers did nothing to alleviate their suspicion that he was not only their enemy but an enemy of their Deity as well. As if such opposition from fellow prophets and priests were not enough, Jeremiah also believed that the Deity dealt unjustly with him. For years the obedient prophet proclaimed the word that he thought came from God, a message of utter destruction for Judah. During all these years relative prosperity had prevailed, and even brief invasions by Babylonian soldiers had not eventuated in the complete destruction of Jerusalem that Jeremiah had predicted. It therefore seemed to him that the Deity had both misled and overpowered an obedient servant. Courageously, Jeremiah said so, and the intensity of that inner struggle matched the outer conflict that he encountered on every side. Even after the fall of Jerusalem in 587, when Jeremiah's prophetic word was finally confirmed by irrefutable evidence, the prophet did not receive popular approval. His last years of forced exile in Egypt merely shifted the scene of conflict, for he continued to oppose the religious practices of his fellow exiles.

Jeremiah's long prophetic activity covered four distinct periods. The first coincided with the reign of Josiah, the second took place under King Jehoiakim, the third occurred during Zedekiah's troubled rule, and the fourth was in the immediate aftermath of Jerusalem's fall. A considerable lapse of time seems to have separated the first and second periods of activity, and a comparable silence followed the second period of his prophecy. In all, his public ministry spans more than forty years, from 626 to about 585.

A SHORTER MINISTRY

This understanding of Jeremiah's prophetic activity has been challenged, largely because nothing in the tradition that has survived seems to come from the reign of Josiah. This silence is astonishing because that king championed a religious reform based on the supposed discovery of the book of Deuteronomy during repairs on the Temple in Jerusalem. Perhaps the consultation of the prophetess Huldah, rather than Jeremiah, over the authenticity of the book on which Josiah's reform was based is understandable, for at that time Jeremiah was still quite young. Nevertheless, one is hard pressed to explain why he is not credited with taking a position for or against these revolutionary events. At best a couple of references have seemed, to some, to echo this reform and to indicate Jeremiah's initial support but subsequent disillusionment with the direction in which it was moving. On one occasion, he spoke of the false pen of scribes who have distorted the teaching, a statement that could imply that Deuteronomy had been wrongly applied, at least from Jeremiah's perspective. Elsewhere the prophet complains about animosity toward him on the part of his own family; some interpreters have explained this complaint as a reaction against the loss of priestly employment resulting from centralization of worship in Jerusalem. Naturally, this understanding of the text assumes that Jeremiah belonged to the priestly family descending from Abiathar, whom Solomon banished to the little village of Anathoth, about five miles northeast of Jerusalem. Jeremiah's father may very well have been a priest, but the evidence is far from persuasive. Priests were not the only residents of Anathoth, and access to the Temple precincts may have come to Jeremiah because of his prophetic vocation.

According to the superscription in Jer. 1:1–2, that call came to him in the year 626, at which time he protested that he was just a lad (na'ar).* The word may not suggest extreme youth, because it has a wide range of usage, from a mere child to a seasoned soldier. His birth, then, may have occurred around 650, unless the reference to Jeremiah's call really implies that the Deity issued that summons on the occasion of the prophet's birth. The description of Jeremiah's call in chapter 1 makes that view impossible, for the prophet enters into dialogue with the Deity, answering questions that are addressed to him and openly protesting against the mission for which he has been set apart.

THE CALL

Jeremiah's call consists of two visions, an almond branch and a boiling pot. The first conveys the divine surveillance of human conduct and the impending punishment for gross misconduct on the part of those who lived in Judah. The second offers an enigmatic hint about the instrument of destruction, which appears here as a foe from the north. Just as the hot cauldron is about to boil over, so an enemy is poised to sweep down from the north, the mythical realm of the gods who were thought to dwell

*It should be noted that superscriptions within prophetic literature seem to have been added at a later time, and therefore they are less reliable than might be supposed.

on a mountain in the north. On the basis of a brief reference in Herodotus, some have believed that Jeremiah envisioned an invasion by the dreadful Scythians, although it seems more likely that he was purposely obscure. In time Jeremiah became certain that the destruction would result from an invasion by the mighty Babylonian army.

At least two features of Jeremiah's vocation stand out when one considers his prophetic ministry alongside that of Isaiah, Ezekiel, and Hosea. In their cases, each had a wife, and they all used their relationship with their spouses to communicate different messages to the people. Jeremiah thought such domestic pleasure was forbidden him by divine decree, for the troubled times in which he lived did not encourage marital happiness. Such shunning of marriage was unusual in the ancient world, and it points to the extent to which Jeremiah's whole life was absorbed by his vocation. The other noteworthy feature of his ministry was Jeremiah's conviction that the Deity did not want him to intercede for the doomed nation. The implication was that a decision had already been made with regard to the fate of a guilty people, and nothing could reverse that verdict. The prophet whose global mission is described as planting and uprooting, building and destroying nations, is reduced to impotence in the interval between the announcement of calamity and its eventual arrival.

INTERNALIZATION OF THE OFFICE

The virtual absorption of Jeremiah's personality into the prophetic office makes it notoriously difficult to distinguish between historical fact and literary fiction. The form in which the book survived does not ease the difficulty, for at least four distinct literary strata appear. First, there are brief poetic oracles in the first person; these occur largely in chapters 1–25. Then there are narratives in the third person (19:1–20:6; chapters 26–29 and 37–44), first-person sermons in prose with headings in the third person (1:4–10; chapters 7, 11, 18, 21, 25, 32, and 34), and oracles against foreign nations (chapters 45–51). The final chapter (52) is a historical appendix, one that largely reproduces the account in 2 Kings 24:18–25:30. The matter is complicated by the fact that about one eighth of the Hebrew text is missing from the Greek translation, and the oracles against the nations follow 23:13 rather than 45:5, where they begin in the Hebrew text.

The prominence of nations other than Judah in Jeremiah's thought reflects the extraordinary influence Babylon and Egypt wielded at the time, for political vassalage carried in its train religious loyalties as well. The total capitulation to Assyrian worship during Manasseh's reign introduced all kinds of foreign practices into the cult at Jerusalem. His grandson's sharp break with these practices accompanied a political rebellion against distant Assyria, more and more troubled by revolts throughout its vast empire. The measures set into motion by Josiah's reform, however thorough and in some respects ruthless, lasted little more than a decade, and Jehoiakim seems to have encouraged a resurgence of foreign religious sentiment, with its accompanying ritual.

To judge from Jeremiah's allusions to the religious practices in Judah, it is probable that the Assyrian astral cult had made substantial progress there toward capturing the imagination of the people. Although the frequent reference to passing sons and daughters through fire, a ritual in the worship of the deity Molech, is not altogether clear, it seems to imply human sacrifice. Because fire was thought to be the purest of all elements, children were set apart for sacred purification by it; naturally, this constituted an act of ultimate devotion on the part of their parents. Worship of the Queen of Heaven also characterized these people, who insisted on submitting the Deity to a simple test to determine whether worship was rewarded or not. In one confrontation with the prophet Jeremiah, the people are portrayed as motivated solely by pragmatic considerations; when rebuked by Jeremiah for abandoning the Deity whom Moses and subsequent generations had worshipped, they insisted that it had not profited them to serve Yahweh. To the contrary, they claimed, worship of the Queen of Heaven had yielded rich dividends. Consequently, these people remained impervious to appeals grounded in morality or loyalty to the past, and they elevated pragmatism above all else.

A sexual dimension of this worship appalled Jeremiah, who echoes earlier views expressed by the prophet Hosea and sentiments that Jeremiah's contemporary Ezekiel uttered in exile. Briefly put, Judah refused to profit from the lessons provided by her older sister Israel, whose harlotry was so pervasive that it brought about the collapse of a kingdom. This inclination toward sexual license was all the more regrettable since Judah came from pure stock. Jeremiah communicated this idea two different ways; one of them came from the realm of nature, the other from the family context. He asserted that Yahweh chose a choice vine and planted a pure seed. Like Hosea, the prophet Jeremiah imagined an initial period when the people of God expressed their devotion in appropriate ways, which did not include sacrifice. The family image is also two-dimensional; the people's initial love is compared to the devotion of youth and to the purity of a bride.

SELF-DECEPTION

Jeremiah's term for the religious mentality that held the people in its grip was self-deception (*sheqer*). He used this word often, for it called attention to the insubstantiality of popular belief. In his judgment the bond uniting people and Deity was a fragile one, inasmuch as it consisted of mutual back scratching. It seemed to him that everyone had fallen victim to unjust conduct, and a search of the entire holy city turned up no one who possessed virtue. The sovereignty of wickedness among the lower classes was just what Jeremiah expected, but the discovery of a similar situation among the nobility came as a shock to him. The ancient concept that ruling officials were responsible for maintaining the well-being of impoverished citizens—widows, orphans, the landless poor— had been abandoned by people who thought only of their own welfare.

BROKEN CISTERNS

Nothing communicated the emptiness of popular religion quite so effectively as a single metaphor, the Deity as a water source. Jeremiah accused the people of abandoning the fountain of living water and of replacing it with cracked cisterns:

> *for my people have committed two evils:*
> *they have forsaken me,*
> *the fountain of living waters,*
> *and hewed out cisterns for themselves,*
> *broken cisterns,*
> *that can hold no water. (Jer. 2:13)*

The offense was therefore a double one, stupidity in the first instance and delusion in the second. Ignoring evidence from the past that Yahweh was a reliable source of life, these hapless people turned to others without recognizing the futility of their effort. Jeremiah's compassion for these deluded citizens gave birth to an appropriate image, the eyes as springs from which flowed a constant stream of water.

> *O that my head were waters,*
> *and my eyes a fountain of tears,*
> *that I might weep day and night*
> *for the slain of the daughter of my people!*
> *(Jer. 9:1; 8:23 in the Hebrew text)*

Tradition became so enamored of this image that the complaints making up the little book of Lamentations that describe the situation resulting from the fall of Jerusalem were associated with Jeremiah's name. The resulting description of him as the weeping prophet has a textual basis other than Lamentations, but it is nevertheless a distorted view of Jeremiah. He may have wept at Judah's fate, but he courageously proclaimed the unpleasant prospect in the face of overwhelming opposition. This resolve to state the truth as he saw it, regardless of the consequences, prompted Jeremiah to assert that the people kept their wickedness fresh just as a well maintains a permanent source of pure water. The irony of this statement approaches bitter sarcasm; it implies that those who scorned the well of living waters in favor of cracked cisterns have constructed special repositories for their own evil deeds.

SYMBOLIC ACTS

On a number of occasions Jeremiah boldly confronted the masses with their questionable conduct by engaging in symbolic acts, a practice that played a minor role in Isaiah's ministry but assumed signal prominence for Ezekiel. Perhaps the most controversial acts on Jeremiah's part involved pottery. In one instance he observed a potter at work, and from this experience the prophet discovered a message from the Deity. While shaping a vessel, the potter noted that it had become spoiled; he therefore reshaped the pot according to his original intention. From this object lesson Jeremiah concluded that God would refashion the people, whose misdeeds had rendered them unfit for their original destiny. On another occasion Jeremiah took a potter's flask and broke it at the entrance of the Potsherd Gate in the presence of representative elders and priests. This symbolic act was dutifully explained, lest its ominous meaning escape anyone. The valley of Topheth, which had become a sacred place for human sacrifice, will shortly be desecrated by human corpses, for the available cemeteries will not suffice for all those who die in Jerusalem's fall. In this verbal assault on the worship of Baal and its accompanying human sacrifice, Jeremiah makes an astonishing claim, that this abominable practice never entered the Deity's mind. An alternative view has survived, however, in the ancient law requiring firstborn sons, oxen, and sheep (Exod. 22:29–30), as well as in the story about Abraham's supreme test, the divine command that he sacrifice Isaac on a distant mountain. The prophet's lofty view of Deity closes the door to such extreme measures of achieving divine favor. In this respect, Jeremiah advances beyond the position held by his predecessor Micah, who asked the rhetorical question whether God required the fruit of the body as payment for one's sin.

These two prophets concurred on one important detail, the fate of Jerusalem; the active memory of Micah's prediction became a factor in sparing Jeremiah's life. Standing in the gate of the Temple at Jerusalem, Jeremiah scolded the worshippers for conduct that gave little indication that they prayed to one who demanded morality. In his view they broke five of the ten commandments: stealing, murdering, commiting adultery, swearing falsely, and going after alien deities. Then, oblivious to the seriousness of their deeds and callously indifferent to the suffering their conduct inflicted on orphans, widows, and resident aliens, these pious people took refuge in the Jerusalemite Temple. Their esteem for this sacred edifice is understandable in the wake of Josiah's reform measures, which elevated the Temple at Jerusalem as the only governmentally sanctioned place for Yahweh worship. The prophet insists that divine favor is indeed an option for the people, provided that they change their ways and thereby establish justice in their dealings with others. Failing this total conversion in mind and deed, the people will witness the complete destruction of the Temple in Jerusalem just as their ancestors had beheld the annihilation of the earlier sanctuary at Shiloh.

This denunciation of the holy place offended many people, who demanded that such blasphemy be punished immediately. In the discussion that determined the prophet's fate, according to one of the two accounts that have survived, precedent was discovered for allowing Jeremiah to go free, as well as for executing him. Micah had predicted that the city would be plowed as a field and the mountain on which the Temple rested would become a wooded height, but this prophecy went unpunished. On the other hand, a certain Uriah had not fared so well after a similar prophecy about the city. An angry king sought his life, and refused to be deterred by Uriah's flight to Egypt, whence Jehoiakim's servants brought him for execution, which was speedily carried out. While it is difficult to assess this account, the final verse in chapter 26 leaves the impression that the chief factor in Jeremiah's survival was the support provided by a prominent official, Ahikam.

Conflict with Hananiah

Another symbolic act that Jeremiah performed resulted in bold counteraction on the part of a certain prophet named Hananiah, who believed that Jerusalem would experience divine favor rather than the dark prospect announced by Jeremiah. Wearing an ox yoke on his shoulders, Jeremiah openly portrayed a life of bondage for Judah and its inhabitants, whereupon Hananiah broke the wooden yoke and proclaimed his positive message in place of Jeremiah's bleak one. In this situation Jeremiah's inner wishes prompted him to harbor hope for divine favor, and this ambiguity between conviction and hope expressed itself in full view of the populace. Like Hananiah, who insisted that Nebuchadnezzar's strong grip on Judah would be eased within two years, the prophet Jeremiah wished that it would come true. However, he reminded an overly optimistic Hananiah that genuine prophets had consistently proclaimed ill tidings from the very beginning, so that the burden of proof fell on one who dared to break away from that tradition. This time Jeremiah went away, leaving the impression that he had been silenced by his opponent; some time later Jeremiah came to reaffirm his former conviction, and, putting on a yoke of iron, dared Hananiah to break it. Now Jeremiah seems to have overcome whatever doubts he may have nursed, for he withstood Hananiah to his face, denouncing him as a fake. In Jeremiah's opinion, Hananiah had deceived the people and had not been sent by the Deity. For that grave offense, Hananiah would die that very year; a final note reports that Jeremiah did not have to wait very long to see this prediction come to pass, for the optimistic prophet died two months later.

One further symbolic act involved intimate apparel, the equivalent of an athletic supporter. Jeremiah purchased a linen waistcloth and put it on for a time, later depositing the garment in a crevice of a rock on the Euphrates, presumably a tiny tributary nearby rather than the great river far away. After a while he retrieved the garment only to discover that it had disintegrated, and the fate of the cloth symbolized for him the ruin of Israel and Judah, who had clung to the Deity at first but had subsequently turned away.

Celibacy

No symbolic act mentioned so far had such far-reaching personal consequences as Jeremiah's decision to remain unmarried. In his mind the times called for drastic measures, and his refusal to take a wife and to have children focused attention on the disjointed times. Others went about their daily routines without pausing to think about the impending calamity, but Jeremiah's very loneliness proclaimed that approaching ruin to one and all. No children played about his feet, their happy laughter bringing joy to his heart, and no beloved spouse awaited his return after a long day of fruitless appeal to stubborn sinners. Lacking a wife with whom to discuss his inner turmoil, the prophet turned more and more to the one whose word had closed the door of matrimony in his face. The resulting complaints reveal the innermost feelings in a manner and to a degree that was never matched in the literature that has survived from ancient Israel.

CONFESSIONS

The deeply personal quality that resonates throughout Jeremiah's special laments made many scholars assume that he had bared his very soul in them. Accordingly, they were thought to contain a painful story of the prophet's struggle against his Deity, a conflict that ended in utter despair. This autobiographical understanding of the so-called confessions has recently encountered strong opposition, largely on the grounds that their language is highly reminiscent of laments within the Book of Psalms. This stylistic affinity has given rise to the claim that Jeremiah speaks for the worshipping community in these laments. It follows that the singular pronoun, according to this interpretation, stands for the plural, and the texts provide no historical evidence about Jeremiah. Not everyone has found this argument compelling, for it is certainly possible that the prophet chose to express personal feelings in language that had already demonstrated a capacity to cover a broad range of strongly felt piety. If the laments in the Book of Psalms gave voice to the individual and collective yearnings for divine presence to overcome various enemies, personal or otherwise, then Jeremiah could have chosen to express his own inner struggle in such familiar language.

Dialogue

The texts of the laments are Jer. 11:18–12:6; 15:10–21; 17:14–18; 18:18–23; and 20:7–18. The first and second laments constitute a dialogue between the prophet and the Deity, whereas the last three comprise monologues, with the divine response no longer promising relief. As a matter of fact, even the two answers that are attributed to God scarcely offer any comfort to Jeremiah, for they inform him that things will become worse, and they urge repentance on his part lest he forfeit his calling. The three laments that have no response become increasingly bitter, particularly in their open desire for revenge against those who sought to harm Jeremiah, but also with respect to the Deity. The final note, at least in the order in which they now appear, is one of dark despair, a cursing of life itself.

The initial lament wrestles with the vexing problem for which modern interpreters have coined the word *theodicy,* which means the justice of God. Jeremiah begins by affirming such justice, but then he proceeds to mention powerful evidence that renders the notion problematic. The central thrust of his complaint points to the impression that evil thrives on earth precisely because of a negligent or capricious Deity. The prophet, however, cannot abandon his conviction that God has full knowledge about what transpires on earth, and this perception causes him great consternation. In his view, it takes no special gift to recognize the people's hypocrisy, their contemptible behavior despite confessions of devotion to Yahweh. These men were plotting to destroy Jeremiah, who resembled an innocent lamb that has been set apart for slaughter. The divine promise that those who plot to kill him will die is coupled with a more somber one, a challenge that he gird up his loins for an even greater test.

The second lament entertains an unthinkable possibility, that the fountain of living waters has actually become a deceitful brook. Jeremiah has placed his trust in the Lord, who seems to have failed him in the last resort. The language with which the prophet describes the bond between him and Deity emphasizes the carnal pleasure Jeremiah found in such intimacy. The prophetic word, distasteful as it was because of its ominous content, has been internalized, and Jeremiah has come to feel immense delight over his vocation. Even his enforced loneliness became a positive aspect of his ministry because it required him to seek companionship with the Deity rather than associating with persons whose every thought was selfish. Nevertheless, Jeremiah suffered from an incurable sickness, an inability to believe that the Deity was at the helm of the ship when the sea threatened to swallow a faithful messenger. An accused Deity goes on the attack, issuing a sharp warning to the prophet that he is in danger of betraying his profession. If Jeremiah will repent and utter appropriate words, he can continue to be a prophet, and divine protection will follow.

Monologue

The image of sickness continues in the third complaint, which expresses Jeremiah's dismay over the long delay between his announcement that destruction was imminent and the actual fulfillment of that prophecy. Seizing the opportunity to discredit Jeremiah, his enemies taunted him without mercy: "Where is the word of the Lord?/Let it come!" (17:15). According to a comment in the story about Jeremiah's altercation with Hananiah, twenty-three years had passed since the original prophecy fell from Jeremiah's lips. The interval between the prediction and its occurrence naturally invited such mockery. Jeremiah's only recourse was to remind the Deity that he had maintained a patient stance, refusing to press for hasty fulfillment of the threatening word. Not quite content with this option, the unhappy prophet renewed his earlier plea that the Deity vindicate him at the expense of his enemies.

The desire for revenge becomes the essential feature of the fourth lament, and it enjoys free expression. Verbal attacks on the prophet have hurt so deeply that Jeremiah prays for the death of his accusers and everyone who was in any way associated with them, including wives and children, whose deaths Jeremiah earnestly desires. There is a certain irony here that seems to escape the prophet. The basis for his complaint is that he has prayed for their well-being, but they have returned evil for good. Now he decides to move closer to their standard of conduct; in return for evil, he will give even greater evil. It is little surprise that the Deity does not dignify Jeremiah's prayer by responding, for the word had actually perished from the prophet, despite the opening assurance that Torah would not perish from priests, nor counsel from the wise, nor the word from prophets. Embedded in this lament is an item that seems to offer valuable sociological information concerning three distinct institutions and their essential pedagogic tool. Priests instructed others in matters of the Law, the wise offered counsel, and prophets spoke the divine word.

The last lament borders on blasphemy and ends in a curse; between the two, an invitation to sing the Deity's praises has been inserted by someone who found Jeremiah's language to be excessive. The prophet accuses God of seduction and rape; like an innocent young woman, Jeremiah had yielded to persuasive talk and overwhelming strength. Having become an object of ridicule, he determines to shut up the divine word in his body, thereby removing the occasion for mockery. Like its author, the word proved too powerful for Jeremiah, and he became weary from holding it within. The image of fire suggests the devastating force with which the prophet struggled, and against which he was no match. Still, Jeremiah believed that a deceiving Deity knew the difference between his heart and those of his enemies, and would necessarily come to his aid. The final curse shares no such optimism and ends with the grotesque thought that Jeremiah's mother should have remained permanently pregnant rather than giving birth to one who must experience shame and sorrow. Only the memory of the awful destruction of Sodom and Gomorrah is deemed suitable in describing Jeremiah's troubled lot.

Even those scholars who view these laments as expressions of communal concerns must acknowledge that Jeremiah suffered grievously because of the prophetic word that he directed against the inhabitants of Judah. To be sure, the narratives that provide such information have been shaped by the concerns of the community in exile, and they therefore may reveal more about their own experiences than about actual events in Jeremiah's life. If the religious circumstances in Babylon were not totally different from those in Judah before the fall of Jerusalem, it may be permissible to draw historical conclusions from the stories, but it must never be forgotten that we are dealing with a living tradition. In any event, the tradition certainly depicts Jeremiah as one who was much sinned against.

Persecution

Although the sermon in which he attacked the role the Temple had come to play in the lives of callous persons did not eventuate in a sentence of death, Jeremiah's symbolic act involving a potter's flask and the accompanying denunciation of religious ritual must have aroused the ire of a certain Pashhur, who was responsible for keeping order in the Temple. It may be that this story has been attached to the wrong text, for it would be more appropriate coming after Jeremiah's Temple sermon. However, Pashhur may have found Jeremiah's prophecy about the city's destruction sufficiently offensive to justify intervention, especially because that utterance took place in the court of the sacred precinct, bringing Jeremiah directly under his jurisdiction and giving Pashhur the pretext for administering a sound thrashing. After beating Jeremiah, the chief officer in the Temple put him in the stocks for a day of humiliation. Once Jeremiah was freed, his tongue became equally free in announcing Pashhur's imminent captivity and eventual death in a foreign land. Nevertheless, Jeremiah seems to have been ordered to stay away from the Temple.

This banishment from the place where the religious imaginations assumed tangible expression required Jeremiah to take drastic measures. Because he could not appear in public, he chose to do the next best

The excavated remains of Ramat Rachel. Jeremiah rebuked King Jehoiakim for expending large sums of money to construct a palace here.

thing, to send a written message that his faithful friend Baruch could read aloud. So Jeremiah dictated from memory all his previous oracles against Israel and Judah, reaching all the way back into Josiah's reign, and Baruch wrote them on a scroll. Then he took that scroll to the Temple on a day set aside for fasting and read it to the assembled congregation, one of whom was so impressed that he asked Baruch to read it again, this time in the presence of a group of princes. Having determined that Jeremiah was the source of these words, Micaiah and the nobles warned Baruch to find a suitable hiding place for himself and Jeremiah. The princes then proceeded to read the scroll to King Jehoiakim, who showed his disdain for the prophet and his message by cutting the scroll into pieces and throwing them into the fire, a gesture that is often thought to have as its purpose the nullification of a powerful word, although contempt for a prophetic word is an adequate reason for the action. When a hiding Jeremiah learned of the king's deed, he dictated the entire scroll again, and Baruch put the message in writing. This story concludes with the statement that the original content of the scroll became greatly enlarged with similar words, which may be the author's concession that tradition was at work.

Jehoiakim's contempt for Jeremiah did not ingratiate him to the prophet, who condemned the king to the burial of an ass. The prophet predicted that, instead of the customary mourning rites, the event would be an unceremonious dragging of the royal corpse outside the city, where the dead king would be hurled into a common grave. Jeremiah was especially moved by the gulf between father and son in the area of common decency. In his opinion King Josiah championed the cause of the poor, whereas his son Jehoiakim thought only of personal profit, competing in building an elaborate cedar palace at taxpayers' expense. This text contains a remarkable statement that sums up Jeremiah's understanding of what it means to know Yahweh. In a word, one who practices just dealings and right actions by defending the cause of those unfortunate persons in society who cannot fend for themselves—this individual truly knows the Deity.

Suspicion of Treason

When the Babylonians besieged Jerusalem and the frightened citizens endeavored to keep their morale high, Jeremiah's message bordered on treason. The suspicion that Jeremiah had betrayed his country seemed to be confirmed when he left the city while it was under attack, although the siege had been temporarily lifted because of the approach of an Egyptian army. His arrest on charges of desertion under fire must have been difficult to refute, and the apparent flimsy excuse that Jeremiah offered for his journey did little to further his cause. A plot of land in his family's possession had gone on the market, and Jeremiah had pur-

The remains of ancient Lachish, one of the last cities in Judah to fall prior to the capture of Jerusalem in 587 B.C.E. Some letters discovered at Lachish reflect the political situation during the last days under Babylonian siege and report that signals are no longer visible from a nearby city, Azekah.

chased it through intermediaries; now he wanted to inspect the property. The ancient notion that land should stay in the family motivated the prophet, but that tradition was not the real reason for his action. Actually, he understood the purchase as an object lesson; by buying land in such adverse circumstances Jeremiah offered hope that after the invading army had punished the nation for its evil ways life would return to normal once more, with people buying and selling land as before. His imprisonment is therefore a logical action on the part of a ruler who seems to have lacked the ability to face the heavy demands of his day. King Zedekiah did not know what to do about this troublesome prophet, if tradition accurately reflects these events. He seems to have consulted Jeremiah secretly in a desperate search for knowledge about future events, and to have feared lest powerful court officials discover that he had resorted to such measures. When a different kind of court official came to him with a compassionate request that Jeremiah be rescued from a cistern into which Zedekiah had allowed him to be thrown, the king gave permission for Ebed-melech, an Ethiopian, to remove the prophet from the dungeon and to place him in the hands of the court guard.

The Fall of Jerusalem

The fall of Jerusalem confirmed the accuracy of Jeremiah's consistent message, but the changed situation did not bring him much honor. To be sure, the grateful Babylonians gave him a choice between staying with the few people who were left in the devastated country and accompanying the captives to Babylonia. Jeremiah chose to remain in the homeland and was allowed to join Gedaliah, the governor whom the Babylonians appointed over the land, at the little town of Mizpah. This brief interlude was hardly one in which the old prophet could find rest, for discontent among the people soon erupted into violence, specifically the murder of Gedaliah and the senseless killing of many religious pilgrims who had come from Samaria, Shiloh, and Shechem, cult centers of the earlier northern kingdom. Fearing retaliation from Babylonian authorities, the people sought counsel from Jeremiah, who advised them to take their chances by remaining at Mizpah and explaining the events that had brought about the death of the governor. This advice did not seem practical to the ones who had responsibility for acting, and they promptly set out for Egypt, taking Jeremiah along with them.

Conflict among Prophets

Those persons who compiled the traditions about Jeremiah presented him as one who was at odds with kings, court officials, the people, and other prophets. The last of these is somewhat surprising, for we expect those who speak for Deity to concur in what they say. Unfortunately,

This cuneiform (wedge-shaped writing) tablet, the Babylonian Chronicle, records the taking of Jerusalem ("the city of Judah") by Nebuchadnezzar II in 587.

that seems never to have been the case, for conflict among the prophets is acknowledged almost from the earliest stages of the phenomenon in Israel. Nowhere, however, did that strife become so open and persistent as it did in the Jeremianic tradition. Voices competed for attention, and each sentiment—punishment for sin and divine compassion—was rooted in ancient tradition. How was society able to distinguish authentic prophecy from bogus messages? There was no simple rule that could be applied in every circumstance, although Jeremiah tried to lay down certain criteria by which one could determine who spoke a word from Yahweh. Some of these criteria probably received lip service, at least, from everyone: authentic prophets do not commit adultery, speak in the name of Baal, or steal their words from others; true prophets have stood in the divine council—that is, they have received the oracles from the Deity. Other criteria that Jeremiah advocated would have found dissenters—for example, the dismissal of dreams and visions as reliable channels of inspiration. Even Jeremiah concedes the accuracy of visions on occasion, and earlier prophets like Amos and Isaiah held them in high regard. Another debatable criterion was the insistence that true prophets proclaimed ill tidings, a useful measuring rod in Jeremiah's encounter with Hananiah, but an indefensible criterion when applied universally, for that would restrict prophecy to a condemning function. The same weakness attends Jeremiah's belief that fulfillment confirms the authenticity of a messenger, a criterion that even the author of Deuteronomy had difficulty accepting. One of Jeremiah's latest predictions suffers badly on this very point, for the prophecy that Nebuchadnezzar would conquer Egypt did not come true, despite Jeremiah's symbolic act of hiding rocks in the mortar at the entrance of Pharaoh's palace.

In the opinion of the traditionists responsible for 23:33–40, the prophets had become a burden to the Deity, for they proclaimed their own desires rather than the divine will. In this text that has affinities with late midrashic interpretation,* there is an elaborate pun on the Hebrew word for oracle (massa'), which also meant a literal burden that one carries. Here the prophets are warned against using this technical term for the divine oracle and are advised to use simple language such as, "What has the Lord spoken or answered?" From such restriction on the vocabulary that is deemed acceptable in prophetic circles and from the accompanying threat to offenders, it is a short step to complete silencing of prophets. The inability to establish reliable criteria for distinguishing authentic prophets from bogus ones led some circles at least to reach a drastic decision that everyone who embarks on a prophetic ministry must be executed, and parents were charged with this grim task.

The problem posed by prophets who disagreed with Jeremiah extended beyond the borders of Judah, for messengers of God arose among the Jewish exiles with assurances that a return to the homeland would take place shortly. Because their promises coincided with popular hopes, which were fed by convictions that Yahweh intended good for the chosen people, they gladly listened to these prophets of deliverance. Jeremiah sent a letter to the exiles, urging them to abandon such foolish hopes. As he saw things, the best option for them was to establish permanent residence in foreign territory, and his recommendation included such simple joys as building houses and entering into marriages with the intention of having children. Jeremiah's sober implication that few, if any, of them would live long enough to join returning exiles must have dashed

---

*The term midrash derives from a Hebrew verb "to seek or search out." Its sense in later usage became highly technical (the Babylonian Midrash), but here the word is used to connote ancient attempts to illuminate the meaning of a sacred text.

the revived hopes of numerous captives, if they believed him rather than the opposing prophets.

The Exiled People: Good Figs

Whatever these exiled peoples thought about Jeremiah, he undoubtedly considered them to be far better than those who remained in Judah after Nebuchadnezzar defeated Jehoiachin and took him as a permanent prisoner in his imperial city. After all, these captives were the skilled craftsmen and smiths, and their king and his princes had merely inherited the folly that Jehoiakim set into motion. To describe these people Jeremiah used the image of good figs, whereas he characterized those who were left in Judah as spoiled figs unfit for human consumption. There was one group in Judah that earned Jeremiah's lasting respect; these were the Rechabites, who attempted to preserve the ways of life from the earliest times. Accordingly, they refused to live in houses or to drink the product of cultivated vines. When the Babylonian army threatened their survival, these Rechabites took up temporary residence within the protective walls of Jerusalem. Jeremiah chose to subject these visitors to a test, so he placed wine before them and urged them to drink. For their refusal to do so, he complimented the Rechabites who had been unwilling to compromise their principles regardless of the circumstances.

Since Jeremiah believed that the exiled populace stood a better chance than the inhabitants of Judah where divine favor was concerned, he recognized Yahweh's sovereignty beyond local borders. In fact, Jeremiah associated that rule with the creation of the universe, and in a poem of exceptional power he described the return of chaos throughout the land.

> I looked on the earth, and lo, it was waste and void;
>   and to the heavens, and they had no light.
> I looked on the mountains, and lo, they were quaking,
>   and all the hills moved to and fro.
> I looked, and lo, there was no man,
>   and all the birds of the air had fled.
> I looked, and lo, the fruitful land was a desert,
>   and all its cities were laid in ruins
>   before the Lord, before his fierce anger. (Jer. 4:23–26)

The one who orchestrated such catastrophe filled heaven and earth, so that it would not do to describe Yahweh as a God at hand without adding that the Deity was also far off (23:23–24). Such conviction about Yahweh's universal sway explains the strange symbolic act in which Jeremiah is required to take a cup of wine, which symbolized divine wrath, and to make foreign rulers drink it. Of course, it is impossible to determine how this command was carried out, whether by representatives who stood in for the kings of the affected nations, or merely by verbal proclamation. In any event, the oracles against the nations that have been included in the book of Jeremiah arose from a similar belief about Yahweh's sovereignty, although they reflect the changing historical circumstances of their composition.

A Book of Consolation

Uncertainty also surrounds the authorship of the little book of consolation in chapters 30–31. One brief section may very well represent Jeremiah's views about a restoration of the fallen northern kingdom (30:18–21). Although some scholars attribute the well-known promise of a new covenant to Jeremiah, others are persuaded that the Deuteronomistic language and style that permeates the text make that claim highly unlikely. The text concedes the failure of the original covenant between Yahweh and Israel, chiefly because the tablets of the Law were external, and promises a new covenant that will be internalized. The result will be immediate knowledge of the Deity, thus rendering obsolete all instruction in Torah. According to 32:36–41, the Deity intends to bring the captives back to their homeland and to make with them an everlasting covenant. This remarkably restrained picture of future security may represent Jeremiah's true feelings, for he believed that genuine conversion would bring divine forgiveness. This theme was so important to him that the word for returning (shub) occurs more than one hundred times in the book.

Jeremiah's personal misfortunes may have pushed him perilously close to uttering worthlessness, but his eyes must have met those of suffering individuals throughout the city. He bristled when opportunistic individuals released their slaves during the Babylonian siege of Jerusalem but enslaved them again when the soldiers withdrew temporarily at the approach of an Egyptian army. Even his language often betrays an observer of human nature who keeps an ear to the ground, eager to discover popular sentiment. Thus he quotes a proverb that "fathers have eaten sour grapes but the children's teeth are set on edge"; he alludes to the mythical belief that death climbs in the window; he utters a proverbial saying that he has neither lent nor borrowed but everyone hates him; and he characterizes sinners as persons who like the leopard cannot change their spots or like the Ethiopian cannot change their skin, for these stubborn individuals have eyes but do not see and ears but do not hear.

✦ 12 ✦

Ezekiel

EZEKIEL'S membership in the select group of priests is beyond doubt. Even if the text had not specifically identified him as a priest, his language and major concerns would have suggested that he shared the world view of fellow priests. That observation is true despite the prophetic layer that has formed over the inner core of his thought, and this new feature of prophecy makes Ezekiel stand out from the others who preceded him. Futhermore, he is the first prophet of the exile, and that, too, makes him different from his predecessors, for the historical circumstances in which he proclaimed the divine word were entirely new. For the first time a canonical prophet addressed a subject people who lived in a foreign land and who were in immediate danger of losing their identity and of abandoning the faith that had sustained their ancestors. To some degree, at least, his extravagant language and behavior may have arisen as much from these circumstances as from his own personality.

EXTREME FORMS OF COMMUNICATION

A remarkable feature of Ezekiel's prophetic commission offers a clue along these lines, for it represents the Deity as acknowledging the need for extraordinary forms of communication if these rebellious people are to be reached. The comparison with those who speak a difficult foreign language is not particularly flattering to the exiles, for it affirms that such foreigners would listen to a prophetic word, whereas the hardened exiles will refuse to hear. Like Isaiah, whose commission warned of fruitless ministry, Ezekiel too is faced with the prospects of speaking to unreceptive hearts, but he is assured that such indifference will not dismay him. Perhaps his resort to shocking language that seems coarse by modern

211

standards, together with his use of bizarre imagery, was largely an effort to capture the attention and imagination of his audience, persons who had eyes to see but saw not and ears to hear but heard not (Ezek. 12:2).

THE STRUCTURE OF THE BOOK

In contrast to the imagery within the book, which is often confused and at times even weird, the book's structure is clear and simple. It consists of three parts: (1) prophetic words of judgment against the exiles (and Jews in Jerusalem, chapters 1–24); (2) oracles against foreign nations (chapters 25–32); and (3) words of hope (chapters 33–48). The last section actually comprises two distinct units, the divine promises of new life (chapters 33–39) and the specific description of a restored religious community in Jerusalem (chapters 40–48). Moreover, a detailed system of dating that runs throughout the book gives the impression of unitary authorship and careful planning, although the dates are confused and out of sequence in a few places, and they apply in every instance only to the specific unit rather than to the broader context. In at least one instance the date is puzzling; precisely what is meant by the thirtieth year in 1:1 cannot be ascertained, for the same verse clearly gives the further date of 593 B.C.E. as the occasion of Ezekiel's call. Some scholars have thought that the verse alludes to Ezekiel's age, although this is not the usual way of giving someone's age. Others have suggested that the reference is to the reform that Josiah instituted in 622, but that would be a highly irregular way of alluding to an event of such importance. The dates within the book supply the information that Ezekiel's ministry lasted from 593 to 571, roughly twenty-five years.

Incidental observations within the book reveal a few minor details about Ezekiel's life, specifically that he owned a house and that elders assembled in it on occasion. An account of a symbolic action mentions the death of his wife, the delight of his eyes, and another incidental remark suggests that he may have chanted his oracles. According to this text, the people viewed him as a good entertainer; he was like one who sings love songs with a pleasing voice and plays an instrument well. It is not clear whether this reference should be taken literally or whether it is merely comparing him with an entertainer. Elsewhere, when describing the Deity, Ezekiel uses simile almost to the point of overworking expressions such as "like," "likeness of," and so forth. From such scattered observations, then, little can be known about Ezekiel the priest, the son of Buzi. The opening verse locates him among the exiles who lived by the river Chebar, presumably a canal that flowed from the Euphrates and irrigated crops that were essential for the survival of the exiled Judeans.

THE PLACE OF EZEKIEL'S ACTIVITY

Where did Ezekiel carry out his prophetic ministry? Answering this question is extremely difficult, if not impossible. Two theories have attracted various followers: (1) he prophesied solely among the exiles; (2) he addressed both the exiles and the inhabitants of Jerusalem in person. It seems that a stronger case can be made for the first of these alternatives, especially when the visionary character of Ezekiel's language is taken seriously. In other words, what the prophet saw within the secret chambers of the Temple did not require his physical presence in Jerusalem, any more than his denunciations of foreign nations necessitated his presence there. The visions were the result of extraordinary clairvoyant powers, and their substance was formed from the combined information acquired through human and divine mediation. The death of Pelatiah while Ezekiel was prophesying does not necessarily imply that this event was triggered by his having heard threatening words. Moreover, this episode shows signs of editorial activity, in this instance a midrashic use of an ancient prayer of intercession.

From the book of Jeremiah comes confirmation that the exiles harbored great expectations for an early return to Judah and that this hope was nourished by prophetic spokesmen. Ezekiel thinks that his task is to dash such dreams and thus to force the exiles to assume responsibility for their future. His was no easy task, for he had to destroy false hopes without killing the spirit of the exiles who already thought that they suffered in an alien land because of their parents' sins. His means of achieving this goal was to issue unrelenting attacks on apostasy and to paint the picture in dark hues, for he was convinced that judgment would soon fall on Jerusalem. Once that calamity struck, however, he shifted the emphasis from judgment to comfort, so that one correctly speaks of a pastoral ministry after 587. From that date forward his primary concern was to combat despair, a sense of drifting in a sea that had swept all cherished values aside. To do that, Ezekiel shared his own vision of a revived nation and a restored community in Jerusalem with Yahweh securely on the throne.

PRIESTLY VIEWS

Priestly sentiment pervades Ezekiel's program for a restored community, from the actual laws for the Zadokite priestly hierarchy to the subjection of the ruling prince, so that he played only a minor role—namely, allocating land and providing supplies for the smooth operation of the Temple ritual. Rivalries within the priesthood persist, at least in their effect, for Levites are relegated to service functions, and this subservient status is specifically described as punishment for sin. On this matter Jeremiah differed, for he did not think the Zadokite priests were blameless. Even the final shout, "Yahweh is there," may represent an attack on the Deuteronomic refrain that promises the presence of Yahweh's name, for now the glory, once besmirched and driven from the inner sanctuary to the Mount of Olives, has taken up permanent residence in the restored Temple. The language of the Yahwistic creation account has contributed to this idyllic picture, for a river flows from the holy place as far as the Dead Sea, spreading life and abundance of growth wherever it reaches. The picture is surprisingly sober in some respects, for tribal allotments are chosen on an equitable basis, and actual political situations are dutifully acknowledged, with the exception of Philistine territory, which is swallowed up by the people of God.

Ezekiel's priestly background is discernible in texts other than the final picture of a restored community. Sometimes it surfaces in strange ways, for example, when he objects to cooking food over human dung and receives a special dispensation—he can use animal manure instead. Here he reminds the Deity that he has never allowed himself to become ritually unclean, for such is abhorrent to him. To depict the utter deprivation that awaits the people in Judah when the Babylonians attack, he is perfectly willing to act out the difficult situation envisioned by this symbolic act, but he cannot abide anything that would go against his priestly convictions about purity and impurity.

This priestly predilection is so noteworthy that it has colored the way in which the prophet denounced the apostasy that he saw in the secret chambers of the Temple. Here and elsewhere there is a pronounced affinity with certain sections of the Holiness Code in the priestly narrative, particularly Lev. 26:14–45. Ancient sacred language is being revived in Ezekiel, so much so that some interpreters think a redactor has consciously shaped large portions of the book, chiefly in chapters 5, 11, 12, 13, 16, 20, 21, 23, and 34. Duplications within the book and internal linkages of certain chapters—for instance, chapters 18 and 33—seem to confirm the suspicion that Ezekiel's original composition has attracted considerable updating. At times this modification of an earlier oracle has resulted in confused images, as in the application of Ezekiel's symbolic escape through a hole in the wall to King Zedekiah. Here, too, Ezekiel departed sharply from Jeremiah's sympathetic attitude toward this monarch, for Ezekiel has nothing but rebuke for him. In one harsh denunciation of this unfortunate ruler, Ezekiel recalls very old mythic imagery associated with the early sanctuary at Shiloh.

> Remove the turban, and take off the crown; things shall not remain as they are; exalt that which is low, and abase that which is high. A ruin, ruin, ruin I will make it; there shall not be even a trace of it *until he comes whose right it is;* and to him I will give it. (Ezek. 21:26–27; emphasis added)

Zedekiah did not have long to wait before he suffered unbearable agony, the slaughter of his children and the blinding of his own eyes.

Just as the Temple cult is central to the description in chapters 40–48 and aberrations in that worship constitute the crime in the visions of chapters 8–11, so external observance of the sabbath comes to prominence in Ezekiel's thought. A precedent appears in Jer. 17:21–27, a probable later gloss that makes divine favor depend on faithful adherence to the laws governing sabbath observance, but Ezekiel advances far beyond this text, at least in the number of references, twelve, to the Deity's sabbaths. At times it is impossible to determine whether impurity is the fundamental issue, or whether Ezekiel has another thing in mind. That problem arises with the allegory about a boiling pot, which is filled with meat and rust, for the emphasis on filthy lewdness is only part of the story depicted here. Nevertheless, the priestly influence on Ezekiel's thought has left an indelible mark.

The mixing of ethical and ritual matters reveals just how important Ezekiel took his priestly ties to be. For him, morality included both dimensions of life, and anyone who wished to honor the Deity would attend to each with equal care. When the prophet gives specific instructions about private conduct, he sets the ritual side by side with the ethical.

> If a man is righteous and does what is lawful and right—if he does not eat upon the mountains or lift up his eyes to the idols of the house of Israel, does not defile his neighbor's wife or approach a woman in her time of impurity.... (Ezek. 18:5–6)

This priestly predilection has struck many readers as somewhat odd in its consequences: an impersonal style, a distant tone, an abstract stance, and casuistic argument that has a timeless quality and therefore does not seem at home in any precise historical setting.

NEW FORMS

The customary literary forms within prophetic literature do not make their appearance in the Book of Ezekiel; instead of threat, invective, and disputation, long prose visions and allegories carry the burden of the prophetic message. Brief poetic oracles rarely occur, but when the prophet does resort to poetry he shows remarkable skill, both in his use of mythic imagery and in his language. The exquisite description of Tyre's splendor and its loss demonstrates rare poetic artistry and vast erudition; this poem stands as a powerful tribute to a neighboring state whose mercantile fleet enriched the lives of many while filling the city treasury at the same time. It is a testimony to Tyre's greatness that even Alexander the Great's army needed more than seven months to conquer it.

The emphasis on the enemy from the north is Ezekiel's way of bringing

One of two colossal winged figures that guarded the doorway to the palace of Ashurnasirpal II at Nimrud (883–859).

old fears into the open so that they may be dealt with responsibly rather than nestling undisturbed in the dark recesses of the nation's subconscious. Jeremiah had threatened Judah with this awful prospect of an enemy from the north, and now Ezekiel implies that this awesome force is no longer poised to strike Judeans but will concentrate on the most formidable of her immediate neighbors. Some of the traditions in chapter 28 seem to be Ugaritic, for example the wise Dan'el* and the mountain

---

*The hero of the narrative *Dan'el and Aqhat* was a king whose reputation for justice was widely acknowledged.

of the gods, but these traditions have been combined with Israel's story of paradise and other mythical ideas from unknown sources. In this case the similarity with Isaiah's poem about the fall of the Day Star is noticeable, particularly the overweening pride of the respective victims.

Like many of his predecessors, Ezekiel believed that the Deity issued a call that launched him on a course marked by immense torment, for he carried out his daily responsibilities under divine constraint. However, Ezekiel's description of the vision in which he received his commission has little, if anything, in common with previous accounts in the Books of Amos, Isaiah, or Jeremiah. In essence, Ezekiel describes a divine manifestation, but the accompanying weather phenomena have been greatly altered, and restraint characterizes the references to the Deity and its mode of transportation. Although the vehicle resembled wheels within wheels and the four living creatures resembled humans, Ezekiel leaves no doubt about the inadequacy of such language. The same humility occurs when he attempts to describe the firmament, the throne, and its occupant. Ezekiel dares say no more than, "Such was the appearance of the likeness of the glory of the Lord" (1:28). To be sure, he has allowed his imagination to dwell on objects from his new historical setting; the four creatures who had human faces and bodies, wings, and faces of a lion, an ox, and an eagle are familiar from Mesopotamian architecture. When all this symbolism is stripped bare, the message is simply that the divine glory possessed mobility and transcended spatial barriers. The cherubs, the sun god seated on the heavenly disc, the chariot of the gods—all this and more has been turned into something surrealistic.

SON OF MAN

Ezekiel thinks that he hears himself addressed by this enthroned one, and the title to which he answers, "son of man," becomes a familiar mode of expression. In this book it simply means "human being," and the interesting thing is that the Deity does not use "son of Israel." Nowhere in the book of Ezekiel does the title "son of man" have the technical meaning that it came to possess in Daniel and in the New Testament. Once the Deity has obtained Ezekiel's attention, a wholly uncomplimentary characterization of Israel as a rebellious house follows, and the newly commissioned prophet is fed a strange meal. He is asked to eat a scroll, which tastes like honey to him. The symbolism echoes a similar passage in the confessions of Jeremiah, although for Ezekiel it suggests that the prophetic word was written from the outset. Just as Jeremiah was like a bronze wall when the people turned against him, so Ezekiel is told to set his face against them, a phrase that occurs nine different times.

The description of Ezekiel's call uses the image of a watchman over Israel, and subsequent reflection about this understanding of prophecy takes place in a later context. The responsibility of a watchman cannot be exaggerated, for on his faithfulness and alertness the lives of countless people depended. In Ezekiel's view he was entrusted with the destiny of the exiled peoples, and failure to warn them placed his own neck in jeopardy as well as theirs. The prophet was only responsible for issuing a warning, not for the people's response to this warning. As long as he alerted the populace to approaching danger, he had faithfully carried out his task. This attitude may sound like a heartless one for a prophet to adopt, but it should be placed alongside Ezekiel's carefully articulated appeals on the Deity's behalf that the people turn and live. Here the attachment of a divine promise is particularly significant, and it seems to mark a new departure within prophecy.

SYMBOLIC ACTIONS

There is little doubt that Ezekiel's symbolic actions represent something new, at least in frequency and in character. The earlier notion that the spirit controlled prophetic inspiration, which had receded for a time in favor of the word, comes to expression once more, and Ezekiel even introduces the idea that the spirit transports prophetic individuals by the hair, a concept that occurs later in apocalyptic texts such as Daniel.* The general notion may be very old, however, for the Elijah narrative assumes that the spirit transports prophets from one place to another with ease. Nevertheless, Ezekiel argues his case with complete awareness of the self and the physical circumstances in which he finds himself, so that it is a mistake to emphasize the ecstatic features of his behavior. The symbolic actions appear strange to modern readers, but they were not entirely beyond the realm of ancient expectations. He allowed himself to be bound with cords, remaining dumb for a specific time, and thus portrayed the coming captivity; he lay on his left side for 390 days and on his right side for 40 days, announcing the duration of the exile, as he saw it, 430 years from the time of Solomon's Temple; he built mock siege works on a brick, indicating the attack against Jerusalem; he ate measured portions of bread that had been cooked over cow's dung, suggesting that the Judeans would have little to eat when Babylon finally attacked; he scattered his hair in three different ways, proclaiming by this means the disbursement of the Judeans throughout the land; he dug a hole through a wall and escaped with his few belongings, just as native Jerusalemites would

---

*The anecdote in question appears only in the Greek text. Here the spirit transports Habakkuk to Babylon, where Daniel waits in a lion's den to receive the food brought to him by the Judean prophet.

soon do; he ate his food while trembling with fear, a terrifying prediction of what awaited the stubborn Judeans; he marked two routes for the Babylonian king to take on his march toward Jerusalem; he shed no tears when his wife died, and thereby portrayed the coming loss of the Deity's delight, the Temple, with none to mourn this great loss. In all these actions Ezekiel actively portrayed coming events that were already real in his mind, and in one instance he asked that a record be kept, for, he said, on that very day the siege of Jerusalem had begun.

VISIONS AND ALLEGORIES

New, also, is the literary form in which Ezekiel clothed the prophetic word, at least in the preponderance of bizarre visionary descriptions and allegories. The vision in which Ezekiel sees secret worship within the inner chambers of the Jerusalem Temple is an amazing example of clairvoyance, leading some scholars to argue that Ezekiel must actually have been present or that spies in the faraway city passed along this information to him. Ezekiel saw seventy elders as they worshipped various images in animal forms, a legacy that he thinks had been transmitted in secret from as far back as Israel's stay in Egypt and that had persisted despite concerted efforts to eradicate idol worship. The popular sentiment, here attributed to these apostate elders, that, "The Lord does not see us, the Lord has forsaken the land" (Ezek. 8:12), suggests that such worship was viewed as a sort of emergency parachute to be used when everything else failed. According to this vision, the women are equally guilty, for the prophet sees women weeping for Tammuz, the Mesopotamian dying and rising vegetation god. In addition, Ezekiel beheld twenty-five men who had boldly turned their backs to the Temple and were facing the east so as to worship the rising sun. The next vision implicitly condemns all those who are guilty of such worship, for it describes an individual whose responsibility was to place a mark on the foreheads of everyone who resists this idolatry, even by so much as a sigh or a groan. Those receiving this mark will escape when the six heavily armed men carry out the Deity's command to slaughter everyone in the city whose heart has strayed from the pure faith.

Whereas the content of the visions is intelligible in almost all instances, the same cannot be said of the allegories, which often are confused and completely illogical. Perhaps the worst offender is the allegory of the eagle that snatched the tip of a cedar of Lebanon and transplanted it in another land, and of still another eagle that was attracted to a healthy seedling, transplanting it in a fertile place. To the question, "Will the second vine thrive?" Ezekiel offers an astonishing response, introducing a menacing east wind that will dry up the ground where the young plant rests. Although the horticulture is certainly strange, the point, which the prophet proceeds to belabor, is altogether convincing: Nebuchadnezzar took the young Judean king, Jehoiachin, to Babylon, but his successor, Zedekiah, turned to Psammetichus II of Egypt for protection, which will be inadequate when King Nebuchadnezzar sets his sights on Jerusalem.

AN ALLEGORY ABOUT TWO HARLOTS

The allegory about two sisters, Oholah and Oholibah, may be indebted to Hosea for its general content, but the treatment is unique to Ezekiel. This description of Israelite and Judean history, as enacted by their capital cities, Samaria and Jerusalem, is undoubtedly the most negative self-history that any ancient country has produced. The first sister set an example of harlotry and paid dearly for her behavior, but her younger sister refused to profit from this negative example, and actually exceeded the lewd excesses of her older sister. A similar allegory refers to Judah's origins, and uses some of the coarsest language in the Hebrew Bible. According to this account, she was born to an Amorite father and a Hittite mother who cast her in an open field to die, an ancient custom resulting from the perception of a daughter as a financial burden, but the Lord discovered the infant and took pity on her. Then the Deity performed midwife service, cutting the navel cord and washing off the blood, and subsequently reared the girl. In due time she blossomed and became sexually desirable, so the Lord married her; but in return for the fine clothing and rich food lavished on her, she sought other lovers and betrayed her covenant partner. In total disregard for convention, this harlot actually paid her lovers for their services. Now she must undergo the shame of exposure and agony of stoning. Here, too, Ezekiel cannot resist the temptation to accuse wayward Judah of ignoring negative examples provided by older and younger sisters, Samaria and Sodom. It appears that the people had resigned themselves to such lewdness, citing a proverb, "Like mother, like daughter." Admittedly, the language of these two allegories is offensive to modern ears, but the symbolism is a poignant reminder that religious unfaithfulness and its accompanying lewdness constituted a breach of personal trust, and therefore they were all the more heinous.

There are other poetic enigmas in which Ezekiel attempted to convey the contents of his inner vision. One thinks of the powerful song about a sword that was sharpened and polished for slaughter (21:9–10); the lament about a lioness whose young whelps were taken to Egypt and Babylon, an allusion to King Jehoahaz and to Jehoiachin; the poem about a pot into which meat is placed, but rust spoils the food, just as Judah's apostasy has ruined its people; and the description of a vineyard that had a mighty stem, until it was destroyed, an obscure reference to Zedekiah's unfortunate end in enforced darkness.

FAITHLESS PROPHETS

Like the prophet Jeremiah, Ezekiel encountered individuals in his own profession who had betrayed their calling and who provoked his open rebuke. Some of Ezekiel's argument in this situation echoes that used by Jeremiah hundreds of miles away: these prophets are proclaiming lies, their own wishes, rather than the Deity's; they announce peace although calamity is surely present; they do not have access to the divine council. The dominant image, however, is that of whitewash, a thin veneer on a wall to give the illusion of stability. Ezekiel thinks the prophets encourage the people in their delusions of security and that the wall on which they place their trust will crumble at the impact of the impending torrent. Female prophets are also targeted for Ezekiel's scorn because they practice sorcery for gain. Ezekiel mentions wristbands and head veils, which they use in some unknown manner to hunt for victims, and he apparently thinks these prophetesses encourage perfidy and discourage honest dealings.

In his judgment, the Deity will frustrate the actions of such prophets and thus cause them to know that Yahweh is Lord. Here is one of more than seventy occurrences of this formula of self-declaration in the book of Ezekiel. The formula may reach back to Israel's earliest sacred tradition, and for Ezekiel it seems to point to a decisive action on the Deity's part that will impart reliable knowledge about Yahweh, the unknowable one who freely removes part of the veil for the good of humans. What the prophets claimed to be authentic words of the Deity will at last be revealed as false, and the people will recognize the delusion on which they have staked their lives. For Ezekiel, the prophetic word plays somewhat less of a role than vision and spirit, for divination has become a significant means of discovering the divine will. According to the narrative in 21:18–23, Ezekiel realized that the practice extended beyond Israel's borders, for he pictures the King of Babylon as consulting teraphim, shaking arrows, inspecting livers of sacrificial victims, and casting lots in an attempt to determine whether to attack Ammon or Judah first.

DECEPTION BY THE DEITY

One of the most amazing features of Ezekiel's thought surfaces in another passage in which prophets come under close scrutiny. Here the Deity boasts of having deceived the prophets, and, without any apparent sense of the injustice of the decision, vows to obliterate the unfortunate prophets. In another place Ezekiel even represents the Deity as saying:

> Moreover I gave them statutes that were not good and ordinances by which they could not have life; and I defiled them through their very gifts in

making them offer by fire all their first-born, that I might horrify them; I did it that they might know that I am the Lord. (Ezek. 20:25–26)

Jeremiah had taken quite another approach where human sacrifice was concerned, claiming that such a thought never entered the Deity's mind; but Ezekiel concedes that Yahweh was indeed responsible for such horrible practices as these. To soften the blow that inevitably follows such an admission, the prophet affirmed a noble purpose behind the Deity's questionable laws, specifically illuminating the unspeakable horror in such conduct. Jeremiah's approach to this problem amounted to shutting his eyes in the face of evidence to the contrary, and Ezekiel's represents a theological position that can scarcely command respect because it depicts the Deity as immoral. Nevertheless, his is the response that has found frequent advocacy within the Hebrew Bible, at least with regard to the belief that Yahweh deceived worthy opponents like the pharaoh of the Exodus, King Ahab, David, and others.

INDIVIDUAL RESPONSIBILITY FOR EVIL

Just as Jeremiah was forced to combat popular sentiment that had a crippling effect on society, so Ezekiel encountered the same proverb: "The fathers have eaten sour grapes, and the children's teeth are set on edge" (18:2). One can readily grasp the persuasiveness of this half-truth, for the children in exile were indeed suffering for something their parents had done. However, the mistake lay in their assumption that nothing could alter their destiny now that their elders had acted. Ezekiel tried to nip this undesirable growth in the bud by forceful assertions that individual initiative counted for something. In chapters 18 and 33, both of which treat this subject, Ezekiel's language is strongly individualistic, giving rise to frequent claims that here and in Jeremiah's similar remarks one witnesses the birth of individualism. Such assertions lose sight of the highly personal nature of Yahwism from ancient times, both with regard to responsibility for keeping statutes that were thought to represent the Deity's will and with respect to individual piety. To be sure, the emphasis shifts in Ezekiel's time, but it does so in response to a specific situation.

The presuppositions of collective reward and retribution were endangered by the collapse of statehood, and Ezekiel desperately struggled to keep a nation alive. To do so, he insisted that God acted fairly, for that was the unspoken issue that required prior attention. The prophet's efforts in this regard are hardly adequate, for he does little more than state his opinion in contrast to an opposing view that seemed terribly attractive. On the one hand, the people denied the justice of the Lord's dealings with them, and on the other hand, Ezekiel affirmed the rightness of those divine workings. Who was correct, and how was the truth going to be revealed? Not by mere counterclaim, to be sure. It is suggestive that precisely in this context Ezekiel begins to overcome some of the icy coldness that scholars have observed in the prophet. Conscious that no convincing proof of the Deity's justice was forthcoming, Ezekiel dared to meditate on the very heart of God, and the resulting affirmations are revolutionary, at least in their setting amid unrelenting threats of divine wrath. This reflection on Yahweh's inner desires convinces Ezekiel that the Deity eagerly longs to bestow life rather than death, a theme that had somehow receded into the background temporarily. Now Ezekiel pleads with a despairing people, urging them to turn and thus bring joy to the Deity and well-being for themselves.

> As I live, says the Lord God, I have no pleasure in the death of the wicked, but that the wicked turn from his way and live; turn back, turn back from your evil ways; for why will you die, O house of Israel? (Ezek. 33:11)

Here is an emotional appeal like the sermonic material attributed to Moses in the book of Deuteronomy, which reaches a climax with the following words: "I call heaven and earth to witness against you this day, that I have set before you life and death, blessing and curse; therefore choose life . . ." (Deut. 30:19).

Perhaps Ezekiel's extreme language carried him to excess in one important respect—the emphasis on the present direction of one's conduct. It seems that he thinks a lifetime of virtuous conduct can be nullified by one wicked or thoughtless act and that a long history of villainy can be atoned for by a single good deed. The cumulative effect of behavior, good or evil, is downplayed here, and that strategy is helpful when one considers what such thinking had done to Ezekiel's audience. However, the corrective that Ezekiel offered for the moment carries an even worse consequence, the subtle shift in ethical obligation from the sum total of one's conduct to the last moment of one's life. The fruit of this seed that Ezekiel planted in fertile soil will soon be eaten by thinkers such as Sirach (the author of Ecclesiasticus), a teacher who lived about 190 B.C.E. and who influenced many young minds.

NOAH, JOB, AND DAN'EL

To make his point about individual responsibility as emphatically as possible, Ezekiel called to memory the names of three ancient heroes who were noted for their intercessory powers: Noah, Daniel, and Job. In the prophet's view these three would be unable to save anyone but themselves if they were still alive. It is likely that Ezekiel had in mind the hero of Ugaritic legend, Dan'el, rather than the later biblical hero with the same name. Naturally, there is no place for intercessors in a society where one's conduct shapes destiny, unless the role of the mediators is that of influencing in some way the behavior, rather than merely

A portion of the Canaanite legend of Dan'el and Aqhat.

the fate, of those for whom they are praying. At this point in Ezekiel's
thinking—that is, prior to the fall of Jerusalem—nothing would suffice
to halt the destructive force let loose by the Deity's four agents: sword,
famine, evil beasts, and pestilence. The vine that has been charred on
both ends will be good for nothing when fire is renewed once again, and
even its wood will be worthless. Like Jeremiah, the prophet in exile
believed that there was no one who was righteous in all the land, surely
an exaggerated statement in light of the survival of Ezekiel's words, for
in some circles at least there must have been people who stood for the
right thing regardless of the cost.

USE OF ANCIENT TRADITIONS

A curious feature of Ezekiel's written legacy is the conscious use of earlier religious traditions, sometimes with extensive reflections about the texts. This is true of the many places where the Holiness Code lies behind Ezekiel's prose, but it goes beyond that to include intercessory prayers such as this one: "Ah Lord God! Wilt thou make a full end of the remnant of Israel?" (11:13). Moreover, Ezekiel's references to the end that has come on the earth, a day that is characterized by tumult rather than joyful shouting on the mountains, echo Amos's memorable attack on the optimistic hopes of his contemporaries. One can hardly avoid the suspicion that such phrases represent intentional adaptation of earlier prophecy. This section, which has several affinities with Amos, concludes with one observation that also occurs in the book of Jeremiah: "Disaster comes upon disaster, rumor follows rumor; they seek a vision from the prophet, but the law perishes from the priest, and counsel from the elders" (Ezek. 7:26). It is noteworthy that "vision" here replaces "word," which appeared in Jeremiah's formulation of this same point, for Ezekiel valued the visionary experience far more than his predecessor did; moreover, what the people in the Jeremianic text claimed would not happen is here represented as actually taking place.

APOCALYPTIC

Ezekiel's place in Israel's religious development does not come from his use of earlier traditions but from his influence on those which followed. That influence is usually captured in such an expression as, "Ezekiel is the father of Judaism, and the forerunner of apocalypticism." The first description arises from the strong priestly and legal features of his thought, essential characteristics of postexilic Judaism. For him, obedience to the Law and sabbath observance constituted right conduct, and the Temple cult as regulated by Zadokite priests was central to everyday life. The second feature of the description is equally significant, for the apocalyptic understanding of reality increasingly gained strength in the next five centuries, becoming a force to be reckoned with in the second and first centuries B.C.E. and the first two centuries of the Christian era. Ezekiel cannot rightly be called an apocalyptic book, but it does make use of imagery similar to that literary genre, especially in the allegory about Gog of Magog (chapters 38–39). The story line is simple: an enemy from the north will attack the people of God but will be thwarted in the effort, and for seven months the victorious residents of Israel will bury their victims. Of course, the language is far richer, inasmuch as Ezekiel describes the battle as if it were of cosmic proportions, exaggerates the scope of the victory, and gives the ending an ironic cultic twist. The Deity will rain fire and brimstone on the enemy who dared attack the mountains of Israel, and their weapons will supply adequate firewood for seven years. Furthermore, the birds and beasts will enjoy a sacrificial feast of the enemy's carcasses, and all the bones will be buried in a special valley called Hamon-gog (the multitude of Gog). Such hyperbole plays on the fears and dreams nurtured by Ezekiel's contemporaries, fears fueled by rumors of powerful kings in the north and hopes that those who aspire for nothing more than living securely on the mountains will one day be permitted to do so unmolested. Although most of the names are easily identified from the ancient world, they should not be pressed, for this kind of literature thrives on the use of stock expressions that apply to any number of historical circumstances. Indeed, the timelessness of such prophecies stands out all the more because of allusions to former prophets who spoke of the enemy from the north and because of frequent references to the present moment as falling within the latter days. The earlier reflection on a special event, the day of the Lord, here recurs again and again in the cryptic expression "on that day."

DEAD BONES WILL LIVE

The themes of restoration and security are not limited to protoapocalyptic texts within the Book of Ezekiel but occur in quite unrelated literary forms. Without a doubt the best known of such passages is chapter 37, the vision of the valley filled with dry bones. The prophet envisions a nation that has lost all hope, for it consists of nothing but dry bones. This nation represents the people of Israel, who lay scattered in an alien land and, from all appearances, devoid of hope. The Deity puts a question to Ezekiel: "Son of man, can these bones live?" to which he can manage no more than the answer, "O Lord God, thou knowest." As the prophet looks on in awe, the dry bones begin to take on flesh, sinews, and skin, until at last life-giving breath enters them once more. The vision is so clear that none could possibly misunderstand its import, but Ezekiel has the Deity explain it nonetheless, conceivably in order to call attention to the people's loss of hope: "Son of man, these bones are the whole house of Israel. Behold, they say, 'Our bones are dried up, and our hope is lost; we are clean cut off' " (37:11). If this amazing bit of national resuscitation seemed difficult to believe, the accompanying promise was equally wondrous. Ezekiel is told to take separate sticks on which he is to write the names Israel and Judah; then he must join the two sticks into one, explaining to the people that the Deity intends to reunite the northern and southern kingdoms under a single shepherd, David. The implication is that the one who revived a dead nation can surely bring its greatest king back to life.

PRINCE AND SHEPHERD

Although Ezekiel is unable to imagine a restored nation without a king at its head, he does qualify that office and restrict its power appreciably. One way he does this is by displaying a preference for titles other than king; two prominent ones in his vocabulary are prince and shepherd. The description of the rebuilt Temple restricts the use of the gate facing east to the Deity but permits the prince to enter by the vestibule of the gate for the purpose of eating bread before the Lord. This may appear to exalt the prince, and that impression seems to be confirmed by the active role he takes in providing appropriate offerings for the Temple cult, but certain other things give quite a different perspective. Possibly the most instructive of these negative attitudes toward the prince in the restored community is the warning that he must not appropriate any property belonging to the people and give it to his own children. Here the ancient ideal surfaces once again, the belief that land belongs to each family and should not be transferred to anyone outside the family unit. By far the harshest rebuke of royal abuse of authority involves the other image, the shepherd.

Chapter 34 consists of a prophetic attack on Israel's shepherds, who looked out for their own interests rather than for those of the sheep under their care, and a divine promise that the Deity will demonstrate what it means to be a good shepherd. There can scarcely be a more effective description of the corruption that power makes possible.

> Ho, shepherds of Israel who have been feeding yourselves! Should not shepherds feed the sheep? You eat the fat, you clothe yourselves with the wool, you slaughter the fatlings; but you do not feed the sheep. The weak you have not strengthened, the sick you have not healed, the crippled you have not bound up, the strayed you have not brought back, the lost you have not sought, and with force and harshness you have ruled them. So they were scattered, because there was no shepherd; and they became food for all the wild beasts. (Ezek. 34:2–5)

The vulnerability of the people to foreign soldiers is here attributed to the failure of kingship, and just as shepherds are responsible for the sheep they lose to wild animals, so these kings will pay for their neglect and abuse. The matter does not stop there, however, for the Deity then determines to search for all the stray sheep and to feed them in the manner appropriate to shepherding. Here the imagery becomes considerably more complex, for punishment and separation enter the picture. The enemy also exists within the flock, for there are bad sheep and goats that muddy the waters and trample the grass, making it difficult for the weaker sheep to survive. It will be necessary, therefore, to separate the good sheep from the bad, a task that the Deity as shepherd will undertake. This idyllic picture ends on a more traditional note, as if the harsh attack

*The Dead Sea, called the Sea of Salt in the Hebrew Bible. Ezekiel imagined a
time when its water would be purified so that the sea would teem with fish.*

on kingship had not occurred, for the Deity promises to set one shepherd,
David, over the sheep. Nevertheless, Ezekiel emphasizes the presence
of the Deity and designates David as prince. The final promise of a covenant of peace and banishment of wild beasts so that "none will make
them afraid" returns to the earlier image of the Deity as shepherd: "And
you are my sheep, the sheep of my pasture, and I am your God, says the
Lord God" (34:31). The powerful attraction of such symbolism gave rise
elsewhere to expressions of religious devotion like the well-known
Twenty-third Psalm, which praises the Lord as personal shepherd, and
this idea plays an important role in the New Testament and in early
Christian literature.

A NEW SPIRIT

Ezekiel did not think of the restored community as merely the old Israel
with a new lease of life. Rather, he insisted that they would undergo a

decisive transformation, which he described as a new spirit, a new heart, a new covenant. Jeremiah emphasized the last of these, which he thought would replace the written tablets of stone. For Ezekiel, the decisive issue is the spirit, which had become stubborn and idolatrous but which would be replaced by an obedient mind, one wholly responsive to the written Law. Whereas Jeremiah insisted that knowledge of the Deity's will would be innate, Ezekiel was less willing to give up the objective function of the Law and the subjective role of its priestly conservators. Both prophets envisioned a decisive change in heart, a turning to God, and a lasting covenant, as opposed to the previous one that had run its course. Like Jeremiah, the prophet Ezekiel denounced the elitist attitude of Judeans who remained in the homeland; they may possess the land temporarily, but the scattered exiles will return when the Deity decides that the time is right.

> And I will give them one heart, and put a new spirit within them; I will take the stony heart out of their flesh and give them a heart of flesh, that they may walk in my statutes and keep my ordinances and obey them, and they shall be my people, and I will be their God. (Ezek. 11:19–20)

◆ 13 ◆

The Book of the Twelve

HOSEA

THE name Hosea means "Delivering," but it seems singularly inappropriate for the individual who bore that name and endeavored to transform the people of Israel by bold action on his part. Hosea married a whore, who bore three children and somewhere along the way proved unfaithful to her husband. The prophet used this broken relationship as an object lesson, visibly enacting the Israelite experience with God. Hosea's purpose was to depict the suffering that the people had inflicted on the Deity and thus to shock them into repentance. Because the message of the prophet is intricately connected with the symbolic act, a clear understanding of that marriage is much desired.

Two Marriages

It is no easy task to understand Hosea's marriage and its implications, for the literary tradition is confused beyond comprehension. In the first place, we encounter two accounts of marriage with a wayward woman, the first in the third person and the other in autobiographical form. According to chapter 1, God told the prophet to take a wife of harlotry and have children of whoredom. An obedient Hosea married Gomer, the daughter of an otherwise unknown Diblaim, and she promptly gave birth to three children. To these three were assigned symbolic names.

The first child, a son, was called Jezreel, after a prominent town in which significant political events had shaped Israel's present destiny. Here, those actions by the prophet Elisha, which brought an end to the house of Omri and elevated Jehu to the throne, are condemned. Earlier traditionists described both persons as acting under divine command. The second child born to Gomer, a daughter, received the name "Not pitied," and the third, a son, was called "Not my people." The unmistakable message in these two names was that compassion was hidden from God's eyes where Israel was concerned, for its actions had demonstrated that it no longer gave allegiance to the Lord.

The third chapter is sufficiently different in details to lead interpreters to think in terms of two marriages. Hosea receives the divine command again to love a woman who is the object of another's attentions and who practices sacral sex. Having paid an appropriate price for her, the prophet isolates the newly acquired wife from her lovers and informs her that he will also refrain from touching her. It is not entirely clear whether this isolation is temporary or permanent, that is, whether its purpose is corrective or punitive. The second chapter deals with the destiny of Hosea's marriage partner, but its literary integrity is subject to doubt.

The allegorical interpretation of the marriage in chapter 2 shifts the focus from a prophet and his harlotrous wife to God and Israel. This change is so thorough that it affects the meaning of the pathetic father's plea that the children intercede on his behalf with the wayward mother. Consequently, we are not altogether certain that Hosea pronounces the equivalent of a divorce formula, the renunciation of a wife.

> Plead with your mother, plead—
> for she is not my wife,
> and I am not her husband. . . .
> (Hos. 2:2a; 2:4a in the Hebrew text)

As a matter of fact, the threat that follows seems to apply to Israel rather than to an individual, and the punishment is appropriate when wielded by God. Whereas the text mentions death by thirst, the human form of execution for adultery was stoning. If this interpretation is correct, it suggests that all of chapter 2 applies to the relationship between the people and God. It follows that we cannot speak of a divorce and remarriage where Hosea is concerned. How, then, must one understand the two accounts? Were there two different women, or do the two chapters report the same incident but from entirely different perspectives? Elsewhere a prophet did not hesitate to describe the Deity as a bigamist, for no stigma attached to this practice in ancient Israel. According to Ezekiel, God took two wives who competed with one another in adulterous behavior. These loose women represented the two kingdoms, Israel and Judah. In Hosea's case, emphasis falls solely on the northern kingdom, although occasional allusion to Judah may be genuinely Hoseanic.

Perhaps the two women in Hosea symbolize two divine responses to the people of Israel. The first wife suffers God's rejection; that fact is surely the import of the names pronounced over the last two children. The situation is less clear with regard to the woman in chapter 3. The indefinite time period ("You must dwell as mine for many days") may be interpreted in at least two ways. It could mean that the woman will eventually enjoy her husband's love, or it may imply complete rejection on Hosea s part. The same uncertainty surrounds those texts in the Book of Hosea that concern Israel's future.

Hosea's bold imagery presents problems for many readers who subscribe to modern concepts of morality. For this reason various attempts to defend the Deity's honor have arisen. For example, the allegorical understanding of the marriage arose as a means of lifting the story out of actual experience. In this view Hosea never really married a whore; instead, he used an allegory about himself and his wife to communicate a particular message to Israel. Naturally this approach crumbled for lack of evidence, or rather, it could not withstand the evidence in the text itself that real persons are the actors in chapters 1 and 3. Another means of protecting God's reputation begins with the peculiar phrase "woman of adulteries," which suggests a tendency toward a particular kind of behavior. In this view, Gomer was only potentially harlotrous when Hosea married her, and later that propensity manifested itself in full view. If this understanding of the phrase is correct, it means that the Deity did not actually command the prophet to marry a whore. While this approach technically absolves the Deity of conduct that is questionable (to some people), it fails to reckon with explicit statements in chapter 3 that the woman is wanton.

It seems best, therefore, to allow the text freedom to convey its message, rather than imposing modern standards of decency on it, but even this acknowledgement, important as it is, does not yet resolve all difficulties. What sort of prostitute was Hosea's wife in each chapter? In other words, did the women ply their trade on the street corners or in local sacred places? Although neither chapter uses the technical term for a cultic prostitute (q^edeshah, holy woman), that lack does not necessarily rule out such a meaning for the various expressions for sexual activity in chapters 1 and 3. Indeed, the allusion to raisin cakes suggests love offerings at religious sanctuaries, and the price that Hosea paid for the woman in chapter 3 may refer to payment for the loss of revenue to a high place. Certainly, the second chapter stresses the religious aspect of the woman's sexual behavior. In all probability the local high places served as the scene for the adultery that Hosea decries.

Should we proceed one step further and deny wrongdoing altogether on the physical level? Elsewhere Hosea uses the image of harlotry to refer to spiritual infidelity. Could that be the sense in chapters 1 and 3? It is unlikely, inasmuch as the very act of spiritual unfaithfulness carried in its train physical infidelity as well. Worship of Yahweh at the sanctuaries included the participation in sexual acts designed to encourage fertility in humans and in nature. Such conduct was the most natural thing in the world; the worshipper sacrificed what was most precious and received divine largess in kind.

Popular Religion

The popular religion in Israel that Hosea attacked with passion has usually been traced to the Canaanites, largely on the basis of religious apologetics within the Hebrew Bible. If we can take the biblical record at face value, it appears that the inhabitants of the land practiced a religion that emphasized natural powers. Crassly stated, the male Deity impregnated mother earth, who thus gave birth to all kinds of vegetation. The role of humans was to stimulate the Deity's erotic interests by engaging in sexual acts in holy places. By this means, they assured an abundance of food and children as well. Naturally, this kind of religion relied on a principle of sympathetic magic. Human beings controlled the Deity's actions by resorting to certain prescribed rituals, and this god existed largely if not exclusively for the sake of earthlings.

It should be noted that the surviving Canaanite texts lend virtually no support to this characterization of religion practiced by the indigenous population of Palestine. A text from Ugarit actually rejects the sexual use of women in religion, and one searches in vain for a single confirmation that prostitution lay at the center of Canaanite religion. The reader suspects that, as in Israel, popular forms of worship existed alongside official religion. For this reason it seems wise not to place much stress on the source of such worship. In all likelihood, a fertility dimension characterized Israel's religion from the very beginning. This assertion does not exclude the probability that contact with popular Canaanite religion encouraged the fertility element in worship and allowed it to thrive as never before.

Be that as it may, no one can legitimately question the claim that Israel worshipped Yahweh as giver of life and fertility. Perhaps this reality helps explain why Hosea found it so difficult to abandon the presuppositions of those he attacked. The prophet's vocabulary is so deeply embedded in the world view of the people that he adopts the marriage symbol as the appropriate one to depict God's relationship with Israel. No other symbol adequately expresses for him the intimate bond linking the people to their Deity. This conclusion seems to flow from the fact that Hosea dared to use marriage imagery even though such language was charged with potential danger. The risk was great that the people would envision Yahweh as a male giant who sprawled across mother earth each year and inseminated her for human good.

Knowledge of the Lord

The centrality of the marriage imagery is not limited to the first three chapters of the Book of Hosea. Nevertheless, in chapters 4–14 another theme rises to prominence alongside this one. One could even say that the opposite side of the coin labeled religious harlotry is an absence of knowledge about the Lord. Here, too, language of intimacy abounds; to know a person is so personal that it also functions to connote physical intimacy within marriage or outside it. Hosea uses these two themes over and over, as if by frequent repetition the message would be drummed into the minds of a heedless people. Some interpreters have

suggested that Hosea's essential point resides in the symbolic names
that God gave to the three children. In this view, the marriage is less
important than the actual names themselves. This assumption would
place Hosea alongside Isaiah, who also gave symbolic names to at least
two sons (Shear-jashub, "A remnant will return," and Maher-shalal-
hashbaz, "Spoil speeds, a prey hastes"). In Hosea's case, however, the
message is so closely tied up with the marriage that anyone who ignores
such imagery must surely err.

It therefore follows that an internal theme unites the entire Book of
Hosea, although chapters 1–3 are distinct from chapters 4–14. That theme
is religious infidelity and its impact in daily life. This prophet seems
particularly concerned about cultic offenses, whereas Amos emphasized
social injustice. Nevertheless, Hosea was not oblivious to human misery
resulting from official policy and abuse of power. As we try to understand
the prophet's overall message, we shall often confront a text and language
that defy comprehension. In fact, the text of chapters 4–14 is the worst
preserved in the Hebrew Bible, with a language and syntax all its own.
We must remember that this book is the only example of prophecy by
an Israelite that has been preserved, whereas the prophetic books from
the southern kingdom of Judah are numerous. We may be dealing with
a dialect that is quite different from the rest of the Bible. Alternatively,
the intense emotional involvement of the prophet Hosea may explain
the present state of the text, but this explanation is less likely.

Editorial Revision

Still another feature of the book complicates matters. It has been subjected to editorial activity, especially where the fate of the people was
deemed unacceptably harsh. This bold enterprise did not stop short of
reversing the names of the children. With one stroke of the pen Hosea's
message was blunted; the son whose name signified divine abandonment
will be called "My people," and the daughter whose name expressed
her outcast state will rejoice over a new appellation, "She has obtained
pity." As for the first son, his name will set into motion a natural chain
of events.

> And in that day, says the Lord,
>   I will answer the heavens
>   and they shall answer the earth;
> and the earth shall answer the grain, the wine, and the oil,
>   and they shall answer Jezreel;
>   And I will sow him for myself in the land.
> And I will have pity on Not pitied,
>   and I will say to Not my people, "You are my people,"
>   and he shall say, "Thou art my God." (Hos. 2:21–23)

A similar addition occurs at the end of chapter 1 (the beginning of the
second chapter in the Hebrew text). Here God reiterates the promise to

Abraham in Gen. 15:5 that the people will be as innumerable as the sand of the sea, and he adds that the two kingdoms of Judah and Israel will gather together and appoint a single ruler. No longer will they be considered illegitimate, for they will be known as children of the living God. On the basis of the sequence, Judah and Israel, scholars conjecture that the editor must have worked in the south, where the written account of Hosea's words must eventually have gone.

The extent of such redactional activity cannot be determined. In the final analysis, one's view of Hosea's word for the future of Israel is shaped by a prior decision about the integrity of the text. Nowhere does that fact appear with more clarity than in chapter 2, where one finds not only an extensive discussion of Israel's spiritual unfaithfulness, but also a powerful description of the transformation that the Deity will bring about through divine initiative.

Vivid Imagery

Neither the unusual syntax and grammar nor the editorial activity renders the Book of Hosea unintelligible, although they do pose problems in a number of instances. Perhaps the first thing that strikes readers of the book is the prophet's use of vivid images, the majority of which derive from the realm of nature. For example, he likens the Deity to a moth, dry rot, a lion, a leopard, a bear, a fowler, and possibly a vulture. In a similar vein, he characterizes Ephraim, the favorite designation for the northern kingdom, as a half-baked cake, a treacherous bow, an unwise infant refusing to be born, and grapes in the wilderness. The nation's fickleness is compared to four things that vanish in short order: the mist in early morning, dew, chaff in the wind, and smoke. Impending punishment is signified by lively images such as sowing the wind and reaping the whirlwind or being wrapped in the wings of the wind. The end result of such punishment is like the fate of a chip on the face of the waters, being washed hither and yon with absolutely no control over its own destiny. In the prophet's opinion, such a fate is entirely appropriate for a nation whose leaders feed on the sin of the people.

For the most part, such imagery functions within prophetic polemic against religious syncretism. Hosea seems to have been appalled by the official cult, at which an image of a golden bull enjoyed popular veneration. One can almost sense the prophet's revulsion in his brief declaration, "Men kiss calves!" (13:2). The same attitude pervades the account of Aaron's fashioning of a golden calf in Exodus 32. Such worship of a molten bull was viewed as wholly unacceptable to the Lord, for the sexual license that accompanied this religious devotion did not bring pleasure to the one who at the moment of this heinous sin was busily engaged in handing on the Ten Commandments to Moses. These negative attitudes must surely have arisen after the time of Jeroboam I, who set up the worship of golden bulls in Bethel and Dan as rival cults to Solomon's Temple. One can scarcely believe that the king would have chosen an offensive sacred image when his singular purpose was to unite the northern kingdom. It is therefore probable that this link with the past soon became an occasion for combining Israelite and Canaanite worship, or better still, for the flourishing of popular sexual worship.

Religious Syncretism and Rapacity

In any event, Hosea has nothing but contempt for the religious conduct of his compatriots. This rejection of cultic practice extends beyond veneration for golden bulls; indeed, the prophet also questions the use of wood in inquiring after the divine will. Once again the story of Israel's sojourn in the wilderness illuminates Hosea's allusion to the use of a wooden staff in ascertaining God's word. Apparently, priests set aside a small branch from a tree and waited to see whether it formed buds or withered away. In Hosea's time groves of trees were sacred sites, and, according to the prophet, such groves lured the masses to their shade. An enigmatic reference to men gashing themselves for grain and wine offers a faint echo of ecstatic behavior akin to that said to have been practiced by prophets of Baal in the contest on Mount Carmel that saw the prophet Elijah emerge victorious over a host of prophets. Hosea's immediate concern was more with sexual license than with bodily mutilation, and he deplored the fact that even brides commit adultery. Because the men had set an unworthy example, which the daughters readily followed, Hosea implied that the double standard where punishment was concerned should be rescinded. In other words, the brides and young women do not deserve death any more than fathers who behave in the same way their daughters do.

At one point Hosea describes the prophet as a fool, and the man of the spirit as a madman (9:7). It is not clear whether he refers to himself here or to some other members of the prophetic profession. The words may suggest that Hosea found himself doing objectionable things and uttering unaccustomed words because of the recalcitrant people. As a matter of fact, the reference could be a popular quotation that Hosea hurls in the face of his detractors, who characterize him as a fool and a madman. In any event, this verse does not seem to suggest dissent within the prophetic ranks as it manifested itself in the Books of Micah and Jeremiah. Nevertheless, the literary form of Hosea's oracles does lend itself to the supposition that the prophet enters into debate with detractors. The decisive difference is the identity of those discussion partners; for Hosea, they seem not to belong to the prophetic ranks.

The religious leaders do fall into the category of those who must endure Hosea's scorn, including both prophet and priest.

> Yet let no one contend,
>   and let none accuse,
>   for with you is my contention, O priest.

> *You shall stumble by day,*
> *the prophet also shall stumble with you by night;*
> *and I will destroy your mother. (Hos. 4:4–5)*

In such a situation where the leaders are no better than the people, Hosea thinks an inevitable leveling of society will take place when the harvest comes for both the leaders and their imitators. Like the prophet Amos, Hosea describes that divine judgment in terms of ancient futility curses.

> *They shall eat, but not be satisfied;*
> *they shall play the harlot, but not multiply;*
> *because they have forsaken the Lord*
> *to cherish harlotry. (Hos. 4:10)*

A similar attitude toward the political leaders suggests that the prophet Hosea was no more impressed with royalty than with priesthood. Indeed, he dates Ephraim's sinful ways from the time that it anointed a king. Once more Hosea preserves attitudes that differ from those that became operative in society, and here too the account that has survived within the Hebrew Bible reflects comparable negative views about kingship, although positive ones predominate.

Hosea's scathing indictment of royalty and the officials who were subject to them reaches its zenith in the following words: "By their wickedness they make the king glad,/and the princes by their treachery" (7:3). The irony of the situation is that such rapacity does not stop when it arrives at the palace gates. On the contrary, intrigue finally touches the king himself, resulting in regicide. That is, the king's failure to maintain justice in society—indeed, his actual promotion of villainy—has brought about his own murder. When royalty ceases to honor the canons of human decency, then those closest to the throne throw caution to the wind and aspire to higher position. Naturally, the threat posed by the Assyrian army exacerbated the situation, for the sense of imminent invasion encouraged lawlessness both for personal gain and for ideological reasons. On the one hand, payment of tribute to Assyria provoked anger among those who believed that they should rely on the Lord's mighty hand. On the other hand, stubborn resistance to Assyria in the face of overwhelming odds struck some as utterly foolish foreign policy. Hosea witnessed these difficult times and ridiculed the ruling authorities for going first to Egypt and then to Assyria, like a bird flitting from tree to tree. His words bristle with dismay, perhaps anger as well.

> *Ephraim is like a dove,*
> *silly and without sense,*
> *calling to Egypt, going to Assyria. (Hos. 7:11)*

> *For they have gone up to Assyria,*
> *a wild ass wandering alone;*
> *Ephraim has hired lovers. (Hos. 8:9; cf. 12:1)*

An Absence of Knowledge

The failure of leaders, both religious and political, to promote the divine will results in mass ignorance, according to the prophet Hosea. His favorite expression for this ignorance is that they lack knowledge of the Lord. If they had known the Lord, in the rich sense of that word, they would honor the divine revelation, the Torah. Like Amos, Hosea understands the knowledge of God as akin to the relationship of intimacy between a husband and wife, parent and child. In short, knowledge was not simply an intellectual category but was equally relational. Anyone whose actions betrayed a mutual relationship of trust demonstrated by those acts an appalling lack of knowledge. For Hosea, such was the case with Ephraim, and this disrespect extended to outright breach of the Ten Commandments, at least to the second tablet, which focused on human relationships.

> There is no faithfulness or kindness,
>   and no knowledge of God in the land;
> there is swearing, lying, killing, stealing, and committing adultery;
>   they break all bounds and murder follows murder. (Hos. 4:1b–2) ·

It is little wonder that Hosea believed Ephraim had sown the wind and was destined to reap the whirlwind. Precisely at this point of divine judgment things begin to get somewhat obscure. What did Hosea believe the future held for his contemporaries? One thing is clear beyond doubt: he expected the invading army to subject the people of God to horrible suffering. On one occasion Hosea even goes so far as to describe God as wholly without compassion, at least for the moment (13:14). As many interpreters have noticed, the punishment fits the crime.

> Give them, O Lord—
>   what wilt thou give?
> Give them a miscarrying womb
>   and dry breasts. (Hos. 9:14)

The prophet makes use of a standard threat, that of divine withdrawal, but in at least one instance Hosea implies that the Deity's purpose was to elicit genuine repentance (5:15–6:5). Here the goal of that divine absence seems not to have been achieved, for the liturgical text concludes with a divine soliloquy that accuses Ephraim of inconstancy and justifies God's heavy hand. Facile repentance and correct ritual count for less in the Deity's eyes than steadfast love and knowledge of God.

Divine Compassion

Hosea's God is hardly one-dimensional, especially where Ephraim's fate is concerned. After all, the Lord had at one time rejoiced over the discovery of these people, just as one is overcome by excitement when finding grapes in the wilderness. Stated another way, Yahweh had chosen Israel as a bride, and like a parent had lavished affection on the children. There is hardly a more poignant depiction of God anywhere.

> When Israel was a child, I loved him,
>   and out of Egypt I called my son.
> The more I called them,
>   the more they went from me;
>   they kept sacrificing to the Baals,
>   and burning incense to idols.
>
> Yet it was I who taught Ephraim to walk,
>   I took them up in my arms;
>   but they did not know that I healed them.
> I led them with cords of compassion,
>   with the bands of love,
> and I became to them as one
>   who eases the yoke on their jaws,
>   and I bent down to them and fed them. (Hos. 11:1–4)
>
> How can I give you up, O Ephraim!
>   How can I hand you over, O Israel!
> How can I make you like Admah!
>   How can I treat you like Zeboiim!
> My heart recoils within me,
>   my compassion grows warm and tender.
> I will not execute my fierce anger,
>   I will not again destroy Ephraim;
> for I am God and not man,
>   the Holy One in your midst,
>   and I will not come to destroy. (Hos. 11:8–9)

The translation above obscures the final ambiguity of this text, which seems to express the Deity's determination not to come into the city, either because divine absence will allow the people to survive or because the Lord will henceforth withdraw to allow the people's sins to fall on their heads. In one text, however, the promise of glorious things is undisturbed by threats of any kind. Here, too, a liturgy introduces the divine promise (as it does the soliloquy in chapter 6), but the final word here is a hopeful one:

> I will heal their faithlessness;
>   I will love them freely,
>   for my anger has turned from them.
> I will be as the dew to Israel;
>   he shall blossom as the lily,
>   he shall strike root as the poplar;
> his shoots shall spread out;
>   his beauty shall be like the olive,
>   and his fragrance like Lebanon.

> *They shall return and dwell beneath my shadow,*
>   *they shall flourish as a garden;*
> *they shall blossom as the vine,*
>   *their fragrance shall be like the wine of Lebanon.*
>   *(Hos. 14:4–7)*

Sin's terrible effects on nature, which 4:3 describes so tellingly, have at last been halted and even completely reversed.

To sum up, the message of Hosea had three themes: (1) the people have betrayed their favored relationship with the Lord; (2) they have therefore demonstrated a lack of knowledge by adopting religious practices that dishonor their maker; and (3) they will pay for these sins, but afterward God will smile upon Ephraim once more. In the view of many interpreters, the promise of divine favor derives from a time subsequent to Hosea. Hence, we shall not draw upon this aspect of the message in these concluding statements.

On the face of it, Hosea seems to stand in opposition to the religious practices of his day. It appears that the prophet offers an alternative way, one that sometimes is characterized as Yahwism versus Baalism. Nevertheless, the language of the prophet is thoroughly permeated by fertility concepts. Even the central metaphor, marriage, belongs to the world view of nature religions. If Hosea wanted to offer an alternative way, why did he adopt such language? Was the relationship between husband and wife the most apt imagery to describe the bond uniting the people with Yahweh?

Fertility Language

There is yet another reason for the prominence of such fertility language in Hosea's oracles. For him, Yahweh was the true giver of grain and oil, wine and fruits. In short, the authentic source of all fertility was also the Deity whom Israel revered as champion of enslaved people. It is no accident that a confession that orphans find mercy in the Lord precedes the beautiful promise about a future state of happiness in which things grow the way they did in paradise.

What, then, is the distinctive message in Hosea's oracles? His insistence on divine suffering brings humans and the Deity into intimate relationship, one that is every bit as vibrant as fertility religion. At the same time, Hosea removes the Deity from the natural realm of imitative magic. For the prophet, Yahweh's favor depended on loyalty and right dealings with one's fellows, not on proper sacrifices and sexual abandon at sacred sites. With Hosea there emerges the idea of a jealous God who is infinitely compassionate and who is transcendent as well. With the prophet there also begins the rupture between nature and cult; the result is belief in a coherent natural order.

JOEL

In prophetic religion natural catastrophes were understood as punishment for sin and occasions for repentance. The prophet Joel took that sort of reasoning one step further and interpreted a devastating locust plague and a drought as harbingers of the dreaded day of the Lord. The Book of Joel consists of two distinct units; the first two chapters use concrete descriptions of an actual calamity that struck the community, and the other two chapters (the Hebrew text has four chapters rather than the three in the English translations) have a vagueness that is typical of eschatological passages in the Persian and Greek periods.* Nevertheless, some interpreters have argued for a unity of the book, chiefly along one of two lines, either that it consists of a liturgy or that it comprises literary symmetry. Because liturgical texts draw upon material from various periods and contexts, an unevenness is to be expected. It is often difficult if not impossible to determine whether a liturgical text arose in its present form on a given occasion, or whether it came together segment by segment over a long period of time. As for the other argument, literary symmetry may result from editorial activity as well as from original authors; so that the presence of perfectly balanced units (lament and promise, announcement of catastrophe and promise of better days, summons to repentance and promise of spirit), if they really are such, does not necessarily prove that the entire book comes from one hand.

The exquisite description of a locust plague is one of the finest poems in the Hebrew Bible. In general, the language of the book is strongly influenced by that of eighth-century B.C.E. prophets, Amos, Hosea, Micah, and Isaiah. As a matter of fact, Joel appears to quote from several earlier prophets, especially Amos, Isaiah, Ezekiel, Zephaniah, and Obadiah. In addition, he uses older imagery from Canaanite literature so freely that an early date for the book during the struggle between Elijah and Baalism has been entertained by some critics. However, such ancient expressions have their counterpart in an impressive number of late features that seem to require that the book be dated between 400 and 350 B.C.E. Some arguments are based on silence, for example, the absence of references to traditional enemies (Egypt, Babylon, Assyria) and to kingship, especially in Joel 2:15–17. Others are more positive: the restored Temple and walls; the leading role played by priests in assembling the elders; the use of the word "Ionians";† the attitude to the nations; the use of "northerner" as a cliché; the understanding of the day of the Lord as a final judgment against foreign nations.

---

*The Greek word from which *eschatology* derives refers to the last things. It thus functions as a technical term for Israel's reflection about a decisive age when justice would prevail at last.

†*Ionians* is the term for Greeks, whose powerful presence in Palestine began in the late fourth century.

Merging Images

The first two chapters in the book comprise a lament that issues in a divine change of heart; the conversion arises from the nature of the Deity as compassionate rather than from the efficacy of correct ritual. Joel quotes a well-known confession that first occurs in Exod. 34:6–7, where the divine attributes of mercy and justice are celebrated, and carefully guards divine freedom with the expression, "Who knows whether he will not turn and repent . . . ?" (Joel 2:14). Nevertheless, the attitude toward the nations in the succeeding chapters resembles that characterizing earlier prophets of salvation, whom the classical prophets labeled charlatans because of their exclusive emphasis on Israel's chosen status regardless of its conduct. It may indeed be true that popular religion was championed by such prophets and that postexilic prophecy has its roots in these two groups, cult prophecy and popular religious feelings. In Joel's case, however, the people of God do not entirely escape criticism, for he urges them to rend their hearts and not their garments, so that their return to the Deity will be more than superficial ritual.

The imagery within the book, then, is not completely consistent, for the poet moves from locust plague to invading armies and to the effects of famine, and from an actual destruction of vegetation to description of the Deity's coming wrath against all the nations, who are summoned to judgment in the valley of Jehoshaphat. The thoroughness of the locusts' devastation is reinforced by a chainlike account of four kinds of insects.

> *What the cutting locust left,*
> *the swarming locust has eaten.*
> *What the swarming locust left,*
> *the hopping locust has eaten,*
> *and what the hopping locust left,*
> *the destroying locust has eaten. (Joel 1:4)*

The terrible impact of such destruction evokes a summons of various affected witnesses. The prophet first calls on old people, asking if their memory recalls anything so terrible, and then he turns to drunkards and priests, who will be adversely affected by the failure of the vines to yield grapes for wine and grain to produce cereal for sacrificial offerings. The invasion by locusts resembles the sound and fury of enemy soldiers. Joel enhances the comparison by conjuring up the image of an orderly army as the insects cover every inch of the land and turn lush growth like the garden of Eden into utter waste.

Promise

It seems that the people actually paid heed to the prophet's appeal for repentance, with the result that in the Deity's name the prophet promises rain and the resulting bounty. Along with this comforting word comes an allusion to divine victory over the dreaded foe from the north and a consequent outpouring of the spirit on everyone in Judah without discriminating between age, sex, or status.

> And it shall come to pass afterward,
>   that I will pour out my spirit on all
>   flesh;
> your sons and your daughters shall
>   prophesy,
>   your old men shall dream dreams,
>   and your young men shall see visions.
> Even upon the menservants and
>   maidservants,
>   in those days, I will pour out my
>   spirit. (Joel 2:28–29; 3:1–2 in the
>   Hebrew text)

The later Christian community understood their own day as the literal fulfillment of this prophecy, which is itself grounded in Moses' wish as articulated in Num. 11:29.

The Future

The eschatological sections of the Book of Joel (chapters 3–4 in the Hebrew, 2:28–3:21 in the English translations) shift an earlier prophecy about the day of the Lord as the Deity's judgment against Israel to the popular notion of that day as Israel's victory over its enemies. Even a portion of the majestic vision of universal peace that appears in Micah and Isaiah has been subjected to radical reversal: "Beat your plowshares into swords, and your pruning hooks into spears." The specific charge laid at the feet of the nations, here Tyre and Sidon, was trafficking in slaves to the Ionians, that is, the Greeks. For this offense, their own children will become slaves for the faraway Sabeans, and the Judeans will pocket the money from the sale. In this context Joel accuses the enemy nations of crimes similar to those specified by Amos against foreign peoples, the exchange of a boy for a harlot and a girl for wine. It is also noteworthy that the opening words of Amos occur in Joel too—"The Lord roars from Zion,/and utters his voice from Jerusalem" (Joel 3:16; Amos 1:2)—as does the reference to mountains dripping sweet wine and the hills overflowing (with milk, Joel 3:18; with wine, Amos 9:13). Like Amos, Joel spoke of the day of the Lord as one of darkness and gloom, but he shifted the wrath to foreign nations. His motive for this reversion to the message proclaimed by prophets of salvation has the Deity's reputation in mind rather than simply the well-being of the people of God. "Why should they say among the peoples, 'Where is their God?'" In short, the survival of God's people testifies to the Deity's might, whereas their defeat will convince outsiders that their God lacks the power to save.

AMOS

The first verse of the book attributed to the prophet Amos mentions words that he saw. The author of this superscription has thus offered a clue to a proper understanding of the book, and ultimately of the prophet Amos. We expect, therefore, to find oracles and visions within the book. In each case a series confronts the reader, and each series of oracles and visions is marked by similar expressions or refrains. Naturally, such literary features functioned initially to enhance the persuasive power of the spoken word, but they also contributed to the ease with which the prophetic tradition was remembered within the community.

Stylistic Features

The initial oracles against the nations (Amos 1:3–2:16) use the messenger formula that occurs with great frequency in prophetic literature ("Thus says the Lord") and a formulaic expression ("For three transgressions of X, and for four, I will not revoke the punishment"), which concludes with a specific cause for divine displeasure. Within those texts dealing with foreign powers (Syria, Philistia, Tyre, Edom, Ammon, Moab, and Judah), the Deity threatens to send a destructive fire against the guilty nation. Furthermore, in every instance except the last, a common feature links the powers together in reprehensible conduct: their crimes consist of atrocities toward a neighboring country during warfare. Unlike the others, Judah's offense is a religious one; that is, the nation has failed to abide by divine instruction. Both the language and the accusation against Judah reflect Deuteronomistic interest and activity.

The common stylistic feature of 3:3–8 is the rhetorical question flanked on each side by an emphatic statement. The argument depends upon a logical movement from cause to effect, and the examples signal calamity, with the exception of the first one. It may be that the allusion to two persons walking together cryptically refers to the prophetic mission, just as the final two verses offer the reason Amos felt constrained to utter this harsh proclamation.

> The Lion has roared;
>   who will not fear?
> The Lord God has spoken;
>   who can but prophesy? (Amos 3:8)

In a single verse emphatic declaration and rhetorical question alternate, and the question actually functions as an assertion (as is often true of rhetorical questions in the Hebrew Bible). In the present context Amos uses this device to heighten the certainty of the threatened punishment, which must surely have struck his listeners as a non sequitur.

> You only have I known*
> of all the families of the earth;
> therefore I will punish you
> for all your iniquities. (Amos 3:2)

Increasing the fear of punishment is also the literary function of the strong assertion in 3:7, which many scholars view as secondary because of the Deuteronomistic expression "his servants the prophets." Regardless of authorship, this verse reinforces the terror concealed in the threat of divine punishment.

A common refrain joins together the historical retrospect in 4:6–12, which seems to be a parody on ancient cultic recitations of divine solicitude. Whereas the people were accustomed to extolling the goodness of God in their daily lives, Amos probes a collective memory that normally enjoys no welcome in holy places. Not all of Israel's history had evidenced divine protection. As a matter of fact, a great deal of its experience was painful in the extreme. Precisely these experiences came on the people as a divine lesson. However, Amos concludes each description of disciplinary action from above with a sad observation (" 'yet you did not return to me,' says the Lord"). In the prophet's view, natural disasters such as famine, drought, blight, pestilence, and earthquake came for a specific reason. They represented the Deity's chastening rod, the purpose of which was to modify behavior. The same was true of warfare, whose ravages left death and stench. Such seems to be the impending threat with which Amos concluded this liturgy of wasted opportunity.

> Therefore thus I will do to you, O Israel;
> because I will do this to you,
> prepare to meet your God, O Israel! (Amos 4:12)

The following verse, in hymnic form, resembles 5:8–9 and 9:5–6. Three times the refrain, "The Lord (the God of hosts) is his name," sets this hymn apart from its context. It seems to function as a doxology of judgment,† thereby exonerating the Deity for destroying sinful people. The Creator uses nature itself as an instrument of punishment for those who ignore earlier warnings and persist in their evil deeds. Similar hymns occur in the Book of Job (5:9–14; 9:5–12), the first uttered by Job's friend Eliphaz and the second by the suffering victim himself. The Creator was

---

*The actual meaning of the Hebrew verb is "chosen."
†In Josh. 7:19 the condemned thief Achan is admonished to give glory to the Lord. Such voicing of a doxology on his part merely functioned to acknowledge the Deity's justice and did not cancel the sentence of death. This concern to give verbal assent to God's justice in cases of execution had far-reaching implications for later people, both Jewish and Christian.

awesome, whether wielding such power on behalf of humans or to their utter dismay.

The majority of oracles within the Book of Amos begin with one of two introductory expressions: "Woe to" and "Hear this word." In at least one instance, certain phrases recur as if to unite the literary unit further. That example is chapter 5, where the verb "seek" occurs with three distinct objects. One of those objects of human search is condemned, and the other two receive the prophet's commendation. The people are advised against seeking Bethel, by which is meant the consulting of divine oracles at the local sanctuary whose name signifies a house of the god El. Instead, they are urged to seek out the God Yahweh, and to practice justice as proof that they understand the significance of consulting the Lord. In short, seeking the Lord implies hatred for evil and love for good.

VISIONS

The visions within the book also have introductory expressions. Three of the five visions contain the words, "Thus the Lord God showed me," and a fourth says simply, "He showed me." The fifth emphasizes the active participation of the prophet, as opposed to passive viewing. Furthermore, the first and second visions evoke the same response in the compassionate prophet.

> *O Lord God, forgive [cease], I beseech thee!*
> *How can Jacob stand?*
> *He is so small! (Amos 7:2 [7:4])*

In both instances the divine response was the same, specifically a repentance and assurance that prophetic intercession had averted the disaster. Locusts would not devour the vital foodstuffs of the nation, and fire would not reach the underworld. The third, fourth, and the fifth visions elicited no comparable reprieve. The plumb line in the Deity's hand beside a wall implied corruption in the body politic; the basket of summer fruit signaled harvest time when the people would be cut down like grain;* and the smiting of the Temple foundations announced the Deity's displeasure over the religious life of the people itself. The movement within the five visions has powerful dramatic effect: from the entire universe to Jerusalem itself, and from nature's ravages to divine punishment.

LAMENT

We have by no means exhausted the discussion of stylistic features in the book. For example, Amos uses the lament form in chapter 5 with extraordinary effect.

---

*Prophets often used plays on words, in this instance the similarity in sound between the words for end *(qets)* and summer fruit *(qayits)*.

> *Fallen, no more to rise,*
> *is the virgin Israel;*
> *forsaken on her land,*
> *with none to raise her up. (Amos 5:2)*

The limping meter itself contributes to the power of this image; like the victim, the speaker seems overwhelmed, so that he can barely complete the line. It is even probable that the funeral lament was the original context for the expression "Woe to," which Amos used freely.

In ancient texts irony often eludes modern readers. Still, there are certain verses within the Book of Amos that exhibit unmistakable signs of irony. The clearest example is 6:1–7, in which the prophet describes the inflated self-esteem of his audience, only to acknowledge that the people will be accorded priority in being marched off as slaves. In addition, the sequence of the oracles against the nations is calculated to garner enthusiasm for the prophetic message, so that the final word against Israel must have fallen with unexpected force. Prophetic denunciation of foreign powers was essential to peoples of the ancient Near East, and Amos was merely fulfilling an office. The people must have thought that Amos's intent was limited in this way, until he actually included Israel in the list of guilty nations whose very existence stood in jeopardy at the moment.

Message

Niceties of expression were not an end in themselves. Instead, they served to reinforce the prophetic word, regardless of its origin in a vision or in an audition. Just what was Amos's message? Perhaps the most accurate account of the sum total of his visions and oracles is contained in a single word: "no." The divine negation of Israel's beliefs and practices was no idle word, but the prophet uttered it nonetheless. In the end he left only a faint hope that the fire would not consume everyone and that possible reprieve remained subject to divine freedom.

> *Hate evil, and love good,*
> *and establish justice in the gate;*
> *it may be that the Lord, the God of hosts,*
> *will be gracious to the remnant of Joseph. (Amos 5:15)*

In other words, there was no guarantee that changed behavior would effectively shield the people from harm, but continuing in evil would surely reap its harvest.

Indeed, the prophet Amos believed that all nations were subject to the Deity whom Israel worshipped. Although they imagined themselves as subjects of other gods, and in that understanding acted sometimes in such a manner as to do great harm to Israel, these foreign nations were in Amos's eyes culpable for behavior that had nothing to do with Israel or Judah. In every instance Amos threatens a foreign power for inhumane treatment of another foreign nation or its ruler: the Syrians tortured people of Gilead with iron instruments; the Philistines sold slaves to the Edomites; the Phoenicians did likewise; the Edomites hacked away relentlessly on a victim who actually belonged to the same larger family; the Ammonites ripped open pregnant women in order to expand the nation's borders; the Moabites burned the bones of the Edomite king.

Amos seems to think that in the atrocities an unwritten law has been violated, one that enjoys universal sway. Like the Geneva Convention governing conduct during modern warfare, this code of behavior specified what was acceptable in eighth-century international law. For such a message as Amos's to be effective, the people must have granted that such conduct was altogether reprehensible. That is, Amos argues from consensus, anticipating no objection with regard to actual charges leveled against the several countries. Perhaps he did encounter hostile reaction and even rejection of his fundamental premise, and scholars have strayed from the truth in emphasizing the cogency of Amos's argument. After all, he also placed the deliverance from Egyptian bondage alongside comparable events involving Israel's hated enemies, Syria and Philistia.

"Are you not like the Ethiopians to me,
    O people of Israel?" says the Lord.
"Did I not bring up Israel from the land of Egypt,
    and the Philistines from Caphtor and the Syrians from Kir?" (Amos 9:7)

One can scarcely imagine that those who listened to such harsh words concurred in this prophetic sentiment.

Elsewhere Amos seems wholly unconcerned about the possibility that his message would fall on deaf ears. Indeed, he seems to have gone out of his way to offend his audience, both in use of satire and in choice of expression. What else can explain the boldness with which Amos characterizes the women of Samaria as cows of Bashan, even if cows from this area were much in demand? Anyone who mocks the religious zeal of others scarcely intends to enter a popularity contest, and yet Amos rejects the people's scrupulous religious observance in no uncertain terms. He does so on the basis of conviction that compassion for other human beings ranks higher in the Deity's eyes than correct ritual performance. That emphasis on compassion includes cases where the Law was being circumvented by appeal to sacred obligation, for example, in 2:6–8. Here the people are accused of wanton disregard for the needs of the poor, so much so that they refuse to abide by the ancient law stipulating that an outer garment taken in pledge during the transaction of a loan must be returned by nightfall, inasmuch as the garment functioned as a blanket for the night hours. Their pious excuse was that they were sleeping on the garment at a holy place and hence seeking a divine oracle. Such a practice, called incubation, is familiar to us from the ancient world.

POPULAR RELIGION

The prophet's radical reversal of popular religious hopes leaves no room for compromise. Whereas the people believe the day of the Lord will dawn on them like a comforting light, Amos thinks in darker hues. The dread darkness will be so bleak that only death is an appropriate image. Two vignettes suffice to depict the horror such a day promises: fleeing from a lion one meets a bear, or leaning against a wall within the security of a house, one is bitten by a serpent.

A similar disregard for the feelings of his listeners characterizes Amos's attack on the people for mistreatment of the poor. Elsewhere Amos acknowledged the excessive zeal with which the people participated in the religious events of their day, but in 8:4–6 he suggests that their real interest lies outside the spiritual domain. For some at least, religious holidays were a nuisance because they reduced the amount of time when merchants could cheat defenseless customers. Amos insists that the Deity desires one thing above all else, the practice of right dealings in society.

> I hate, I despise your feasts,
>   and I take no delight in your solemn assemblies.
> Even though you offer me your burnt offerings and cereal offerings,
>   I will not accept them,
> and the peace offerings of your fatted beasts
>   I will not look upon.
> Take away from me the noise of your songs;
>   to the melody of your harps I will not listen.
> But let justice roll down like waters,
>   and righteousness like an ever-flowing stream. (Amos 5:21–24)

Unlike Hosea, the prophet Amos had little to say about worship of gods other than Yahweh. Both texts of this nature have been thought problematic, often on insufficient grounds. In 5:25–27 one finds a tradition about the forty years in the wilderness that is different from the one that survived in the Book of Numbers. Amos's question about sacrifice during the wilderness experience implies that it was not practiced at this time. Be that as it may, Amos announces that the people will transport their images of deities into a faraway land of captivity. An even worse fate is promised those who give allegiance to the gods of Samaria, Dan, and Beersheba (8:13–14).

The latter text comprises part of a prophetic oracle dealing with the remote future from Amos's perspective. Such reflections on days to come differ immensely from the eschatological ending to the Book of Amos, but the authenticity of both texts has been contested for different reasons. In the case of 8:11–14, the spiritual use of the concept of famine and thirst to represent hunger for the divine word seems to imply a later time when prophecy had fallen silent, a situation documented in Zech. 13:2–6. Things are quite different in Amos 9:11–15, for here a comforting word is attributed to Amos. While the reference to the fallen booth of David

Assyrian soldiers of Tiglath-pileser III carry statues of the gods of a captured town. The prophet Amos mentions this practice (5:26–27).

may signify the division of the kingdom after Solomon's death, it is more natural to assume that the unknown author had in mind the collapse of the northern kingdom in 722, or better yet the fall of Jerusalem in 587. The allusion to the remnant of Edom may indicate the later of these events, for at that time it seems that the people of Edom turned fleeing inhabitants of Judah over to the invading Babylonian army.

HOPE FOR THE FUTURE

The matter is complicated further by the restrained character of the hopes associated with the future restoration. The images are far less spectacular than many of those that typify later expectations. In the Book of Amos one finds quite simple aspirations: constant planting and harvesting, responsive mountain areas, rebuilt cities, verdant gardens, people dwelling in security. Nevertheless, the ravages of war linger in memory, as does deportation, making it unlikely that these marvelous descriptions of a happier day derive from the prophet Amos. His legacy more properly appears in the futility curses leveled against the individuals who perverted justice for a profit.

> *Therefore because you trample upon the poor*
> *and take from him exactions of wheat,*
> *you have built houses of hewn stone,*
> *but you shall not dwell in them;*
> *you have planted pleasant vineyards,*
> *but you shall not drink their wine. (Amos 5:11)*

This assessment of the situation with regard to the authenticity of the exquisite depiction of life in the future may be strengthened by taking 1:2 into consideration. This verse seems to function as the motto of the book, and hence it may be taken to indicate the nature of Amos's message. According to this verse, the Lord utters a destructive word from the holy mountain, Jerusalem. That menacing description agrees with the content of the final vision, which portrays wholesale destruction. According to Amos, there is absolutely no hiding place, for Yahweh's reach extends to Sheol itself. Naturally, that sovereignty goes all the way into other lands to which Israelite slaves might be taken.

To be sure, Amos does speak of a remnant, but its meaning is far from clear. The word seems to mean nothing more than "those who have survived," as for example, the remnant of the Philistines (1:8) and the remnant of Joseph (5:15). The imagery in 3:12, which recalls the law governing one's responsibility when sheep under his care fall prey to wild animals, cannot give support to the claim that the prophet believed that a righteous remnant would survive the calamity. The two legs and piece of an ear are insufficient to renew life. Entirely different are 5:3, which refers to the decimation of a city and an army, and 6:9, which describes the almost total destruction that some unknown lucky person escapes. Here the avoidance of the divine name is calculated to escape God's notice, thus assuring the survival of one person out of ten.

BIOGRAPHICAL INFORMATION

So far we have avoided two texts in the book that actually provide biographical information on Amos. By far the most difficult is 7:10–17, largely because the crucial sentence lacks a verb, but also because of a rare word used to describe Amos's occupation prior to his prophetic calling. Nevertheless, the passage as a whole is not obscure, and its meaning is for the most part easily grasped. The local priest took issue with Amos's threat against the reigning monarch and endeavored to silence the prophet, but to no avail. The priest, whose name was Amaziah, addressed Amos as a seer and advised him to earn his living by prophesying in the southern kingdom of Judah, for Bethel was a royal sanctuary. Amos answered that he was no prophet nor a member of a prophetic guild, but he was a herdsman and earned his living also as one who pinched sycamore fruit to make it ripen. Yahweh seized him and commanded Amos to prophesy against Israel. For attempting to frustrate the divine will, Amaziah must listen to a terrible condemnation: that his wife would be raped by enemy soldiers, his children would be slain, and he would be marched away to die in a ritually unclean land, where all Israel would also be taken.

Although this is the probable meaning of the passage, there are certain other possibilities that deserve consideration. First, the nominal sentence may be translated in the present tense, although doing so would have Amos deny that he is a prophet. Alternatively, Amos may reject the title *seer* and substitute the word *prophet,* but this conclusion assumes that a Canaanite particle rather than a negative preceded the word for prophet. One other word merits some explanation: the rare expression that scholars understand to mean one who does something to fruit. The problem is simple—there are no sycamore fruit trees in the region of Tekoa where Amos lived. For this reason some interpreters have sought to locate Amos in the vicinity of Galilee, where some evidence seems to indicate a town called Tekoa. A much better explanation is to think in terms of migrant work; that is, during the fruit season Amos went some distance away from home to work in the orchards.

The name of the town in which Amos lived is specified in another text that contains biographical information (1:1). Here Amos is identified as one of the shepherds at Tekoa, in all probability a small village south of Jerusalem. The word for shepherds is an unusual one, elsewhere used of king Mesha of Moab. At Ugarit a cultic official is referred to by this word. This fact has prompted some critics to propose that Amos was an important citizen who raised prize sheep for the royal cult, but it is highly unlikely that a small village would have had several such officials of the royal cult. The superscription to the Book of Amos also provides the date for his brief prophetic activity. It occurred during the reigns of Uzziah in Judah and Jeroboam II in Israel two years before the earthquake. The earthquake cannot be dated, although its destruction was sufficient to linger in the mind of one of Amos's successors. That vital bit of information appears in Zech. 14:5. Nevertheless, other clues within Amos's oracles have led interpreters to date the prophet somewhere around 760 B.C.E.

Two things are decisive in this regard, the economic prosperity of the residents of the northern kingdom and the weakened Aramaean state. The reign of Jeroboam was a long, prosperous one, marked by some victories over local cities. In 6:13 Amos characterizes the people as proud of the fact that they have overthrown the cities of Lo-debar and Karnaim, although the names may suggest mockery on his part. The first means "not a thing," and the second "horn." Elsewhere Amos showed himself capable of facile treatment of the names Gilgal and Bethel: ". . . for Gilgal shall surely go into exile *(haggilgal galoh yigleh),*/and Bethel shall come to nought" (5:5).

The disparity between rich and poor aroused Amos's ire, particularly because that difference came at the expense of the poor. The righteous were sold for silver, and the needy for a pair of shoes (2:6, cf. 8:6 where "the poor" replaces the word for righteous, as if the two were synonyms). With total disregard for the welfare of the needy, these newly rich people feasted on meat and drank wine in huge goblets. Furthermore they anointed themselves with the finest oils and lounged on couches inlaid with ivory in their winter as well as their summer homes. Naturally, such opulence led to merriment; like David, the people fashioned for themselves musical instruments and sang idle songs. It is little surprise that the people waxed confident that nothing could harm them. Amos took no stock in such assurance that "Evil shall not overtake or meet us" (9:10), for he believed that the Lord would pass through their midst to destroy them, after which the Deity would withdraw, never to pass through their cities again. That is the real meaning of the threatened famine of the divine word.

OBADIAH

According to the traditions preserved in Genesis, the ancient Israelites acknowledged kinship bonds with their neighbors the Edomites.* This special relationship conditioned Israel to expect friendly treatment from the descendants of Esau, and explains the bitter disappointment unleashed when Edomites betrayed that trust. The shortest book in the canon, Obadiah, which has only one chapter, gives expression to this hostile attitude toward Edom. The message of the book is easily summed up in the taunt that Obadiah hurls against Edom: "As you have done, it shall be done to you,/your deeds shall return on your own head" (Obad. 15b). The first half of this verse applies the principle to all nations, in that it announces the nearness of the day of the Lord. Edom thus becomes a typical example of the way the Deity makes all nations pay for their misdeeds.

Precisely what charges does the prophet bring against Edom, crimes so heinous that they explain the intense hatred registered here? The obvious answer is the refusal to help Judah's citizens escape from attacking Babylonian soldiers in 587 B.C.E., indeed the active involvement of Edomites in aiding the enemy (cf. Lam. 4:21; Ps. 137:7). Obadiah mentions looting of the defenseless city and turning fleeing inhabitants of Judah over to the Babylonians. What is more, these opportunistic Edomites rejoiced over the calamity that befell their neighbors. But these are not the only reasons Obadiah gives for the Deity's retaliation against Edom, for he also characterizes the nation as proud and arrogant. The two sources of its pride were seemingly impregnable defenses in solid rock cliffs and wisdom, for which it was renowned. Obadiah's threat is reminiscent of Amos 9:2–4.

---

*Esau was the supposed ancestor of the Edomites.

Though you soar aloft like the eagle,
though your nest is set among the stars,
thence I will bring you down,
                              says the Lord. (Obad. 4)

The Book of Obadiah consists of two oracles and an appendix (verses 1–14, 15–18, 19–21). The first unit concentrates on Edom, its guilt and its punishment, and the second oracle goes farther afield to include all nations. This broader scope also moves from actual history to the final day of vindication when Zion will be restored to its former glory and when fire will consume Edom. The appendix complicates matters even more, for it mentions several faraway peoples about whom little information is available. The reference to exiles of Jerusalem has assisted in dating this book, but the evidence is by no means conclusive. Since Jer. 49:7–22 and Obad. 1–10 are related, either in a relationship of dependency or as material taken from a common source, a date for the first part of Obadiah depends on the answer one gives to the question raised by the parallel with Jeremiah. Some critics think the strong polemic in the second part of Obadiah reflects the constant struggle between returning exiles and the ancestors of the Samaritans. Although this interpretation of the evidence is probable, we do not possess sufficient knowledge about the history of the two nations to assign absolute dates to this prophecy.

The name Obadiah means "servant of Yahweh," a name that is attested elsewhere in 1 Kings 18:1–16 with reference to an official in Ahab's court who secretly saved the lives of some prophets. It is arguable that the author of this little book that releases bitter feelings against Edom is no servant of the Lord in the sense of the poems in Second Isaiah, but Obadiah's strong words are grounded in a sense of divine justice.

JONAH

It has been said that the ancient Hebrews faced life with their backs to the sea. A possible exception is King Solomon, who is reputed to have aligned himself with Hiram of Tyre in a business venture using ships of Tarshish to bring gold from Ophir and other precious items to Palestine. However, it is not clear whether Israelites actually sailed the fleet, or whether here as in other instances they were content to let Phoenicians handle the shipbuilding and seafaring chores. The only known exception to this aversion for sailing, Jehoshaphat's effort to equip a merchant fleet for royal purposes, is said to have ended in disaster (1 Kings 22:48). A reluctance to risk the high seas was strengthened by mythical understandings of the sea as the personification of evil, or alternatively as the playground for the cavorting of the great sea monster. Jonah's flight from the presence of his Deity becomes even more daring and desperate in light of this widespread attitude toward sailing.

The story, simple and straightforward, needs little amplification. Jonah receives a divine commission to denounce Nineveh for her sins, but instead he flees on a ship that is heading for Tarshish, perhaps Spain. A storm threatens the occupants, who eventually throw a willing Jonah overboard in order to save their own necks, but a large fish swallows him and after three days spews him out on dry land. This time Jonah obeys the Deity's command, warns the citizens of Nineveh that their city will be destroyed in forty days, complains to the Deity and sulks because the city's conversion moves the Deity to compassion, and asks to die. The tale ends with the Deity rebuking him by means of an object lesson. The hero, or antihero, is a prophet; his name is preserved in 2 Kings 14:25 as one who in Jeroboam's day prophesied some victorious engagements with enemies. The book is unique among the prophets, for rather than recording prophetic words or visions it tells a story. Nevertheless, there are comparable narratives about Elijah and Elisha, and to some degree Jeremiah and Isaiah.

Literary Type

What literary type best describes this unusual book? The answers to this question are numerous: a prophetic novel, prophetic legend, allegory, midrash, narrated dogmatics, confession of guilt, and parable.* Because the prophet is the center of attention in only two of the four chapters, the Deity upstaging him elsewhere, and because Jonah is pictured in such negative terms, it seems inappropriate to call the book a prophetic novel or legend. The weakness of the allegorical interpretation is that there are no restraints on the imagination. What objective clues suggest that the fish stands for the exile that swallowed the Jews and later spat them out? While the teaching of the book may correct the claim in Num. 23:19 that the Deity cannot repent and may elaborate Ezekiel's observation that God does not desire anyone's death (Ezek. 18:23), the two verses are not consciously interpreted, as is true in midrash proper. Of course, the theological point of the story is that the Deity is free and compassionate, but the book is hardly narrated dogma. Perhaps farthest from the purpose of the story is the hypothesis that it constitutes an act of repentance on the part of the prophetic movement, through the representative figure Jonah, for in the end Jonah is no closer to the Deity than before. Thus parable is left as the best description of the literary type, although it is more accurate to say that the book *resembles* a parable. Through a vigorous story, punctuated by dialogue, the author clarifies and communicates a religious truth to persons who might be expected to resist the message.

The story is woven from legendary motifs, both Jewish and non-Jewish,

*In an allegory the various features of the story require individual explanations, whereas parables do not presuppose that separate components have distinct, hidden meanings.

and from familiar phrases that appear elsewhere in Psalms. Most of all, the book is conscious artistry. The art can be seen in the repetitions of words and phrases—for example, say, cry, arise, appoint, be afraid, throw, great—as well as in the plays on words. The author draws on Canaanite ideas, sailors' folklore, and widespread notions about miraculous plants, waters that subside when placated by an offering, repentant animals, and the like. Perhaps, too, the persistent motif of a prophet resisting the divine call furnishes material for the author, as well as the sentence, "Who knows, God may yet repent and turn from his fierce anger, so that we perish not?" (Jon. 3:9; cf. Joel 2:14). The second chapter, a prayer that seems out of place in its present context, because it has Jonah thank the Deity for deliverance while still in the fish's belly, abounds in expressions of traditional piety. The twofold allusion to the holy Temple and the denunciation of idolatry offer a clue about the special interests of the person who inserted this prayer into the book, unless the entire chapter is intended to make fun of traditional Jewish piety in the same way the other three chapters ridicule the prophet Jonah.

Message

What, then, does this fascinating story teach? Answers to this question focus on Jonah and on the Deity; if the former, they see him as a representative of a particular kind of prophet or of the entire phenomenon of prophecy. For some critics, the story is gentle satire that is not far from humor, and the intention is to bring a smile of acknowledgment that prophets are, after all, human, but little more. Others understand the figure Jonah as an example of the utter bankruptcy of prophecy, inasmuch as it became more concerned about its own image in the eyes of the people than about condemned human beings. Still others think the purpose of the story is to explain why earlier prophecies against foreign nations had not been fulfilled. The last two answers address a single issue, but from different angles: what prevents one from calling the great prophets who uttered oracles against foreign nations false prophets? Stated another way, why have these threats against the nations failed to materialize, although similar judgmental oracles against Israel and Judah have come true? The response to this problem is little consolation to Israelites, inasmuch as foreigners are depicted as immediately repentant after hearing an extraordinarily brief sermon. "Yet forty days, and Nineveh shall be overthrown!" (Jon. 3:4), comprises just five words in Hebrew. Presumably, the narrator assumes that Jonah spoke to the condemned citizens of Nineveh in his native tongue. Their quick action to avert the disaster is all the more extraordinary. This total conversion of people and animals contrasts sharply with the stubborn resistance that Israel's prophets experienced from those who spoke the same language. A revealing passage in Ezek. 3:4–7 states that foreigners would listen to the prophet although he spoke in his own language, whereas Israel refuses

The Mediterranean Sea at modern Jaffa (ancient Joppa). From this city the prophet Jonah boarded a ship leaving for Tarshish in order to flee from Yahweh.

to heed words that the people clearly understand. This seems to be the viewpoint of the unknown author of the story about Jonah's amazing success as a missionary.

First and foremost, the answer to the question about unfulfilled prophecies against the nations drew attention to the Deity's character rather than to the readiness of the Ninevites to repent. To be sure, the foreigners in the story are depicted as commendable in every way, but the central point lies elsewhere. Although the sacrifice of one man for the benefit of the passengers on the ship does not present the Deity in the best light, the dialogue makes the point forcefully that God is compassionate and that mercy extends beyond the chosen people to embrace her bitterest foe, going as far as the animal kingdom also. The author has Jonah explain his actions as motivated by knowledge that the Deity was "a gracious God and merciful, slow to anger, and abounding in steadfast love, and repentest of evil" (4:2). Here only one side of the ancient statement about the Deity's nature is recited; elsewhere the confession combines mercy and justice, kindness and severity.

Divine Freedom

Another feature of the response to the question about unfulfilled prophecies concentrates on divine freedom. In a sense, that freedom is the decisive issue between the prophet and the Deity: does the prophetic word bind the Deity's hands regardless of changing circumstances? Scholars disagree about the exact nature of early prophecy, whether repentance was the goal or not, but a consensus seems to have formed that at least the later prophets sought to move their audience to action that would possibly cancel the sentence of doom. Accordingly, prophecy was conditional, although some critics insist that the prophetic word automatically set into motion the forces of its own fulfillment. Unfortunately, this viewpoint may result from an overly literalistic reading of prophetic rhetoric. A significant contributor to the sort of thinking that restricted the Deity was the belief in election, the conviction that the Deity chose one nation as a special possession. The message of Jonah places that belief in perspective, and thus it seeks to correct widespread abuse of the concept of election. This point is so important to the book that many interpreters think the work must have been an attack on the narrow exclusivism of the returning exiles during the leadership of Ezra and Nehemiah.

Date

When was the book written? A few clues exist: (1) Nineveh is only a vague memory to the author; (2) the language and customs are appropriate for the fifth and fourth centuries B.C.E.; (3) the author of Second Kings seems not to have known the story; and (4) both Sirach (Ecclus. 49:10) and Tobit (14:4, 8) mention the book. With regard to the first point, it is significant that the author has no idea how large Nineveh was, and indeed even speaks of the King of Nineveh (instead of Assyria). As a matter of fact, Nineveh did not even become the capital of Assyria until the time of Sennacherib, much later than the days of the Jonah mentioned in Second Kings. Furthermore, the author of the book refers to Nineveh in the past tense, which does not make sense until after its collapse in 612. The language of Jonah is closest to Ecclesiastes, which is clearly one of the latest books in the Hebrew Bible. In some respects, the story breathes the same piety as Tobit, particularly in treating the miraculous as a daily occurrence, and it expresses fascination with ancient Assyrian cities.

Theodicy

So far we have avoided the word *theodicy* (a defense of God's justice) in discussing Jonah, but defense of God's justice lies at the heart of the narrative. This is certainly the deeper issue that prompted questions about unfulfilled prophecies against the nations. The author subordinates the divine wrath to a more powerful principle, the Deity's compassion. To the perennial question, "Why?" this storyteller responds in the same way Ezekiel had addressed the issue: God the Creator does not want any creature to perish. This is the religious teaching within the story of Jonah, and preoccupation with the literal historicity of the account threatens to obscure this important message.

MICAH

The prophet Micah was a younger contemporary of Isaiah, and in at least one instance the two southern prophets are credited with the same oracle (Mic. 4:1–4; Isa. 2:2–5), a passage that expresses a universal human desire for peace. It is impossible to determine the authorship of this majestic description of a coming era when instruments of warfare will be transformed into agricultural tools, because either prophet was certainly capable of composing it, or both men may have relied upon an earlier oracle. Despite this bond between Micah and Isaiah, a much stronger link joins Micah with Amos and Hosea. That common thread is the demand for justice in society and antipathy toward official religion.

The structure of the Book of Micah does not assist scholars in the task of determining precisely how much of the book derives from the prophet whose name it bears. The traditional scheme of threats that give way to promises, an arrangement that arose to facilitate the use of scripture in worship, has been doubled in the case of the Book of Micah. Chapters 1–3 contain invective, and chapters 4–5 offer hope for the people of God; likewise 6:1–7:6 contains prophetic denunciations, and 7:7–20 comprises a liturgy that promises divine compassion. Although many critics attribute only the threats to Micah, the matter is not quite so simple. Still, the argument for authenticity based on the "freshness and individuality" of particular sayings is hardly persuasive, because later editors could have achieved these qualities as readily as Micah did. It is far better to acknowledge the difficulty, if not impossibility, of ascertaining authorship in such cases. Exclusive reference to the northern kingdom is yet another matter, and these texts may well come from Micah.

The initial theophany (1:2–7) has strong claims to authenticity, for the object of divine wrath was the capital city, Samaria. Naturally, this prophecy must have preceded the fall of the northern kingdom in 722 B.C.E., because it refers to this event as a future one. The date accords with the superscription in 1:1, which places Micah in the time of three kings of Judah, the last of whom was Hezekiah. It was this ruler who instituted religious reform, removing such sacred images from the Temple as the bronze serpent that for generations had been revered for its powers of healing. Tradition associated this image with the leader Moses and viewed it as a proper sign of divine presence in adversity.

This description of God's self-manifestation that brings destruction in its wake has been applied to Jerusalem, perhaps after Samaria fell. The effect of such adaptation of an earlier oracle would therefore have been greatly enhanced, because the fate of the northern capital was familiar knowledge in Judah. Micah believed that Yahweh's mighty presence spelled doom for the royal city of Samaria, leveling its buildings and destroying its religious objects. In this regard, the prophet saw no fundamental difference between the capitals of the two kingdoms, Israel and Judah, for Jerusalem's fate would be the same as that of Samaria (3:12). This prediction that Zion would be plowed like a field was remembered in Jeremiah's day, and, if the account is historically reliable, provided sufficient precedent of negative prophecy against Jerusalem to save his life (Jer. 26:18). Of course, the religious reform under Josiah in 622 placed Jerusalem at the very center of national religion, inasmuch as all worship was centralized at Zion from that time forward. Hence a denunciation of Jerusalem after 622 was tantamount to rejecting the state cult, whereas Micah's attack fell on one sacred site among many, even though Jerusalem was the state capital and therefore the most important holy place at the time.

The grim announcement about the fate of the two cities must have taken an emotional toll on the prophet, for he seems to have adopted the role of a professional mourner.

> For this I will lament and wail;
>   I will go stripped and naked;
> I will make lamentation like the jackals,
>   and mourning like the ostriches. (Mic. 1:8)

In this willingness to scorn the Hebrew aversion to nakedness, Micah was like his contemporary Isaiah, who for more than three years walked around naked like a prisoner of war as a warning against political rebellion. In this instance, Isaiah was successful in convincing the king that Assyria's might was still very much in place. Micah's aim was to alert officials in Judah to their own vulnerability; subsequent events proved that the prophet had correctly interpreted the historical situation.

The literary forms that Micah adopted were calculated to shock the people into recognition of the peril facing them. For example, he chose a prophetic lawsuit in order to emphasize the crimes that threatened society in his day, and he used the disputation form when the accusation came from his own mouth rather than being presented as divine speech. In addition, Micah employed an entrance liturgy (6:6–8) that seems to have been modeled after priestly instructions intended for pilgrims who journeyed to a sacred place and sought admission into the Deity's presence. Within the debated chapters, the prediction of future happiness achieves prominence, especially in those texts that have the customary beginnings "in that day" and "it shall come to pass in the latter days."

The modern city of Jerusalem. The Dome of the Rock (to the right of center) occupies what is believed to be the site of the Solomonic temple. The present wall dates from the sixteenth century C.E.

Structure

A striking feature of the book is the arrangement of several speeches according to subject matter, a phenomenon that also occurs in the Book of Jeremiah. For instance, Mic. 2:1–5 denounces greedy landowners for lying awake at night devising schemes for stealing the fields and houses of the landed peasantry, as well as for quick and deliberate implementation of those plans. There follows a section concerning the prophet's detractors (2:6–11), people who dislike the content of Micah's message and insist that they are not in harm's way. The basis for their rejection of the prophet's grim words is deeply rooted in religious tradition. For these people Yahweh's very nature is to be compassionate and long-suffering. Micah's retort is both a specific accusation and a caricature. He charges the people with disrobing the peaceful and driving defenseless women from their houses. They prefer a preacher who lacks substance, Micah insists.

> *If a man would go about and utter wind and lies,*
> *saying "I will preach to you of wine and strong drink,"*
> *he would be the preacher for this people! (Mic. 2:11)*

The implication is that reliance on Yahweh's compassion is misguided when the people fail to exercise common decency. Another brief unit that has a single topic is 3:5–8, Micah's dispute with the prophets. He accuses them of varying their message according to the money they receive for their services: peace for food, war against those who offer them no reward. Such charlatans will, in Micah's opinion, come up against divine silence. The seers will no longer experience visions, and diviners will receive no response to their learned inquiry.

The dispute with professional prophets ends on a rather suprising note. Micah expresses his own uniqueness, both as a prophet and as a representative of the people. Unlike the other prophets, Micah is filled with power and the spirit of the Lord, with justice and might (3:8). Such empowerment has a specific purpose—to enable him to speak forthrightly to Israel about its sins. The contrast with Jeremiah's initial confrontation with a rival prophet could not be stronger, for he lacked Micah's assurance that his own word was the correct one in the situation. Such assurance later enveloped Jeremiah and prompted him to action. In Micah's case, too, confidence may have come gradually as a result of further reflection on the nature of prophecy and the character of Israel's God.

A central concern of the prophet is the prerequisite for admission to divine presence and favor. Of one thing Micah is certain: the Deity requires right dealing in society. This requirement means that the inhabitants of Jerusalem are mistaken in their fundamental premise that the Lord will protect the holy city. These perpretrators of violence seem to think that orthodox views are all they need, regardless of their conduct. They say, "Is not the Lord in the midst of us?/No evil shall come upon us" (3:11b). Micah is convinced that they rely on false hope, for corruption has swallowed up their leaders who detest justice and whose greed runs unchecked. As if in response to the issue of divine favor, the entrance liturgy in chapter 6 tries to specify exactly what the Deity expects of humans.

> "With what shall I come before the Lord,
>   and bow myself before God on high?
> Shall I come before him with burnt offerings,
>   with calves a year old?
> Will the Lord be pleased with thousands of rams,
>   with ten thousands of rivers of oil?
> Shall I give my first-born for my transgression,
>   the fruit of my body for the sin of my soul?"
> He has showed you, O man, what is good;
>   and what does the Lord require of you
> but to do justice, and to love kindness,
>   and to walk humbly with your God? (Mic. 6:6–8)

The reference to human sacrifice does not necessarily suggest a date during or after Manasseh's reign, when reversion to this extreme gift seems to have occurred. The liturgy is couched in hyperbole throughout, and thus it moves naturally to ask whether the ultimate sacrifice is nec-

The south wall of the Temple Mount. Archaeological excavations here have uncovered parts of the Herodian city of the first century B.C.E.

essary to secure God's approval. Such a series of rhetorical questions could have arisen at any time, and not just during a revival of human sacrifice. In any event, the summary of human obligation represents an ancient religious ideal: right dealings in society, integrity, and obedient response before God.

The liturgy that concludes the Book of Micah (7:7–20) bears close resemblance to the views that the prophet denounced, for it places emphasis on a forgiving Deity who disregards human sin and proceeds to show steadfast love to the elect people. The allusion to the restoration of the city walls suggests a date after the fall of Jerusalem, at least for 7:11, and other features of the text fit more naturally in a time later than the eighth century. Nevertheless, much of the material in this liturgy has a timeless quality, like the psalms it resembles. Two things deserve special mention. The first is the tendency to hark back to the remote past, both the period of the patriarchs and the memorable experience of the Exodus from Egypt. The other is the play on Micah's name in 7:18, "Who is a God like thee?" This expression recalls the meaning of the Hebrew word Micah, which would be translated, "Who is like Yahweh?" It is also possible that the opening verse of this liturgy contains a conscious reference to Micah's exalted sense of his own power compared with the other prophets. In effect, the liturgy makes a comparable claim for divine protection, even if such favor may lie in the distant future. For this part of the liturgy, at least, judgment precedes divine deliverance, a fact that seems absent from 7:18–20.

The prophet Micah demonstrated remarkable capacity for punning, as can be seen in 1:10–16, where a series of literary puns associates various towns upon whom calamity weighs heavily. The nature of the expected destruction is unclear, although critics naturally think of the Assyrian threats in 711 and 701 as occasions for such a lament. The combined cajolery and summons to lament seem ill-suited for one another, particularly if 7:8–9 belongs to the unit, because there the prophet demonstrates a strong measure of identification with and compassion for the miserable objects of divine judgment.

Religious Views

When one sets aside an interest in the literary features of Micah's utterances in order to focus on their religious significance, a difficult problem quickly inserts itself into the picture. On what foundation did the prophet take a stand against the people and the entire religious establishment? Interpreters of the book often give a sociological answer to this question, when they do not take the claim to divine inspiration at face value. According to this explanation, Micah belonged to the lower class of landowners who suffered at the hands of more affluent citizens of the capital. Because his own values had been shaped by the traditional ideas that sustained this way of life, any threat to the old ways would automatically have provoked his anger. In this view, Micah arose as a defender of the oppressed minority. Critics thus point to the expressions of disgust over the excesses of urban living as natural reaction from one who grew up in a small village. To be sure, Micah came from a town called Moresheth in the foothills about 25 miles southwest of Jerusalem. But that fact alone scarcely explains the literary artistry and theological profundity of the words and visions within the book. Others, therefore, think the prophet bears witness to a wholly new experience of the Deity. Like Amos and Hosea before him, Micah believed that social injustice threatened the very fabric of corporate existence, so much so that the Deity had become intimately involved in human events in order to preserve a small band of faithful devotees. This divine involvement came at considerable expense, and these prophets, especially Hosea and Micah, are careful to draw attention to the suffering that God undergoes. Nevertheless, the Deity does not shrink from bringing destruction to the very people who called upon the name of the Lord. This determination to punish wicked acts gains the victory over a willingness to forgive, even in one whose reputation for compassion is well-known.

What is the nature of the people's offense that demands such extreme reaction from above? Perhaps the most graphic description of their crimes occurs in 3:1–4, which uses the image of cannibalism and threatens the sinners with the worst of all fates, having to rely on their own resources because the Deity no longer listens to their cry for help. Micah charges them with reversing human values; hence they are sinners

> *who tear the skin from off my people,*
> *and their flesh from off their bones;*
> *who eat the flesh of my people,*
> *and flay their skin from off them,*
> *and break their bones in pieces,*
> *and chop them up like meat in a kettle,*
> *like flesh in a caldron. (Mic. 3:2–3)*

Further specifics come from random utterances; in short, powerful people rob the weak of their share in the divine possession, their inheritance in the land. The other type of offense concerns the purity of worship; at issue here is religious syncretism. One text may even have in mind King Hezekiah's purge of the Jerusalem cult (5:10–15), although its scope is much broader. The author has no sympathy for the practice of manipulating hidden powers or bowing down to images fashioned by human hands. Whereas the authorship of this text is suspect, no such doubt attends Micah's prediction concerning the complete obliteration of Samaria's images (1:7).

Elsewhere Micah mentions a crime that had also provoked Amos's anger, namely the use of inaccurate weights and measures that were calculated to cheat customers (6:11). Like his predecessor, Micah threatens guilty persons by means of futility curses.

> *You shall eat, but not be satisfied,*
> *and there shall be hunger in your inward parts;*
> *You shall put away, but not save,*
> *and what you save I will give to the sword.*
> *You shall sow, but not reap;*
> *you shall tread olives, but not anoint yourselves with oil;*
> *you shall tread grapes, but not drink wine. (Mic. 6:14–15)*

There is irony in the thought that those who exercise ingenuity in the quest for riches will experience no substantial gain, and in the end they will have nothing for their trouble.

The Book of Micah contains promises of better things as well as threats; while their origin may be in doubt, none can question the ability of these promises to express human aspirations beyond the present miserable conditions that bore the stamp of divine visitation. The prophecy that Micah and Isaiah have in common expresses the farmer's simple hope that a day will dawn when the dreaded warrior's boot will be banished forever. Various traditions converge in this prophecy, but the mountain of God achieves central position. Here that exalted mountain is identified with Jerusalem, and the Deity who dwells there receives homage from afar. That adoration includes instruction in the sacred lore of the Jews, for foreigners actively seek to learn about the Law and Yahweh's word. This God of Jacob will act to ensure justice, and even powerful foreign nations will submit to the Lord's judgments. The result will usher in universal peace and tranquillity.

> *and they shall beat their swords into plowshares,*
> *and their spears into pruning hooks;*
> *nation shall not lift up sword against nation,*
> *neither shall they learn war any more;*
> *but they shall sit every man under his vine and under his fig tree,*
> *and none shall make them afraid;*
> *for the mouth of the Lord of hosts has spoken. (Mic. 4:3b–4)*

It is curious that the final verse about sitting under a vine and fig tree is not found in the parallel text in Isaiah.

Yet another prophecy concerning a future day has captured the imagination of later readers, for whom the birth of Jesus was the fulfillment of Micah's utterance (5:1–6; 4:14–5:5 in the Hebrew text). Here one reads about the birth of a ruler who, like David, comes from humble origins. It seems that the present misery in which the speaker moves from day to day constitutes birth pangs of the Messiah, whose origin is from ancient days, but that the new situation will witness the return of Israelites to the people of God. Presumably, this prophecy means the restoration of the northern tribes and thus the recovery of a unified nation under a Davidic ruler. Even the mighty Assyrian army will succumb to a coalition of kings who withstand foreign aggression. In one respect this messianic prophecy differs significantly from similar texts in Isaiah 9 and 11. In Micah's scenario the Messiah will actually defeat the Assyrian hordes and set up a system of rulers in the conquered kingdom, whereas in Isaiah's account victory seems to come through unmediated divine action. Some interpreters therefore judge Micah's text to be an earlier version of messianic speculation than the two prophecies that are attributed to Isaiah but often denied to the eighth-century prophet.

A third prophetic utterance belongs to this discussion, although the text stands out in its present context like a ship in the desert. In the midst of Micah's invectives against the people, there occurs a solemn divine promise (2:12–13), which critics usually take to be a later gloss. Here God vows to gather all the elect people who have been scattered hither and yon, so that they can dwell together once more in safety. How will this return to the fold be accomplished? It will result from joint efforts by the earthly and heavenly rulers. A hierarchy of leadership emerges from the procession: God at the head of the line, followed by the king, and then the people themselves.

As we have seen, both promises and threats occur side by side in the Book of Micah. Each type of prophetic utterance throbs with intensity; that is, the bitter invectives are matched by tender promises. Hence it is a mistake to emphasize the stridency of Micah's threats as a barometer to his personality, and it is inappropriate to make sociological judgments on the basis of extreme rhetoric. In short, one does not have to belong to the peasant class in order to react strongly against their subjugation at the hands of powerful landowners. The same caution is necessary with regard to Micah's fondness for martial vocabulary. Such a predilection for military terms no more proves that he was the leader of a military contingent than Hosea's extensive knowledge of baking demonstrates that he belonged to that profession. The harshness of Micah's oracles of judgment and the tenderness of the promises, if they derive from him, arise from something far more profound than a prophet's humble origins. The intense feelings on the part of the prophet correspond to what he perceives to be a sense of divine revulsion for the sinner and a simultaneous constraint on wholesale destruction, reluctance on God's part to leave the people in their misery forever. Although some critics think Yahweh has become a cosmic God in Micah's understanding, this development, if true, does not imply that the Deity has somehow grown more distant.

NAHUM

The prophet Nahum brings together a timeless hymn and a specific historical event, the fall of Nineveh in 612 B.C.E. Both the hymn and the description of human conflict are among the finest examples of poetry in the Hebrew Bible. An ancient confession of the divine attributes that emphasizes compassion, but not at the expense of justice, introduces the sublime manifestation of Israel's God in a whirlwind, with the Deity's feet stirring up dust clouds in the heavens, causing vegetation to wither, and shaking the very foundations of the earth. Nahum, whose name means "One who is comforted," finds reassurance in the belief that the Lord is good to those who take refuge in the Deity and announces that divine punishment of Israel has ended. Now this awesome power will strike the instrument of that punishment, the dreaded Assyrian empire. The rest of the book describes the final battle at Nineveh and pronounces a satirical funeral lament over the fallen city.

The Fall of Nineveh

The poet imagines that he is an eyewitness to the terrible siege and ironically assumes the role of commander, issuing orders to leaderless soldiers and desperately pleading with the waters to halt. Nahum uses matchless images of the city as a fig tree with ripe figs that fall into the mouth of one who shakes it and as a lioness and cubs in their lair waiting for prey to be brought by a plundering lion. The former image represents her present helpless state, the latter her prior way of life when soldiers raided weaker peoples in order to fill the royal treasury. Now the harlot who seduced many nations lies naked, shame having replaced her previous glory,* and the corpses are so many that those who defend the city stumble over them. The protective gates stand wide open, and Nineveh's shepherds sleep the sleep from which none awakes, its princes having fled like locusts.

The opening verse of the book uses two words to characterize the message attributed to Nahum; the first connotes a charge or weighty oracle, and the second emphasizes the visionary nature of the utterance. The initial verse also mentions Elkosh as Nahum's native city, but its location is uncertain. Because of the fervent nationalism in the book, some critics have placed Nahum among false prophets whom Jeremiah attacked or have suggested that he came dangerously close to the boundary between true and false prophecy. This estimate of his message does not do justice to Nahum, whose theology resembles Isaiah's conviction that the Deity would punish Assyria for extending the bounds of its assigned task and whose understanding of human history arose from his belief in a compassionate but just Deity. Like Second Isaiah, Nahum believed that Judah had already endured the Deity's wrath, so that the time had come for divine favor. Perhaps it is noteworthy that Nahum does not appeal to the nation's virtue as deserving kindness but that everything hinges on God's nature.

If Nahum was active during the reform instigated by King Josiah, as most scholars think, this silence with regard to Judah's goodness is significant, for the temptation must have been great in those days to remind the Deity of the people's faithfulness to the newly discovered law book. The outer boundaries for dating Nahum's oracles are 663, the fall of Thebes, and 612, Nineveh's collapse. In his mocking taunt of the Assyrian stronghold, Nahum asks if it thinks it is better than Thebes, which could not withstand Assyrian attack. A certain irony occurs in this grim reminder that it will finally experience the disgrace that others had felt through its cruelty. It is probable that Nahum prophesied during one of two occasions when Nineveh was seriously threatened, around 626 and 612. The first of these was a time of attack by the Medes, but Nineveh managed to resist this frontal assault. It was not so fortunate in 612 when the combined Median and Babylonian forces struck. The book gives evidence of liturgical use, possibly recitation by cultic officials. Some interpreters think the Jewish community may have celebrated Nineveh's fall even after the fact, while others consider the possibility that the book functioned as propaganda for Josiah's rebellion against Assyria.

One feature of the book draws attention to its literary craft. The opening hymn and accompanying theological statement comprise an alphabetic poem, an acrostic, with the initial letters corresponding to the Hebrew alphabet. The poem is not complete, for it only goes through *kaph* (the eleventh letter of the Hebrew alphabet), and some adjustment is required

---

*This punishment of nakedness must be understood from the perspective of persons who thought such exposure was a terrible thing. From a harlot's way of viewing reality, disclosure of nakedness was hardly cause for shame.

to restore that much of its original form. In any event, the partial alphabetic poem suggests that the literary form of the book is important. A number of literary types come together to make a powerful lament, one that approximates a taunt. The prophet Nahum used vision, dirge, taunt, and oracle to arouse feelings of pity and delight. His sense of the dramatic produced the court scene in which the Deity addressed the nation that is comforted and the one whose wound is beyond healing. Similarly, that dramatic flair is responsible for the strong impression that one is actually witnessing desperate efforts to defend the doomed city. Those futile last-minute measures merely serve to demonstrate the power of the Deity who is now at work through Medes and Babylonians, nations so insignificant that they are never even named. By far the most powerful feature of the book, however, arises from a play on the name of the prophet, leading some to think the prophecy may originally have been anonymous. The poet asks two rhetorical questions—"Wasted is Nineveh; who will bemoan her?/whence shall I seek comforters for her?" (Nah. 3:7)—and he answers those questions with the final declaration that none will mourn, because everyone has been victimized by her.

> *All who hear the news of you*
> *clap their hands over you.*
> *For upon whom has not come*
> *your unceasing evil? (Nah. 3:19)*

This scene from Nineveh depicts the desperate measures taken in an unsuccessful defense of Lachish during an attack by Sennacherib's army.

HABAKKUK

A single theme unites the entire Book of Habakkuk in spite of its composite literary form. That theme is the prophet's struggle with the problem of divine justice; the philosopher Gottfried Wilhelm von Leibniz (1646–1716) coined the term *theodicy* (from two Greek words meaning justice of God) to describe this phenomenon. The universal human cry "How long?" establishes the mood from the very beginning, and its sister lament "Why?" prolongs the initial discussion, probing deeper into the dark mystery of the Deity's actions. The answer which the puzzled prophet arrives at, a response he understands as a vision from the Lord, is actually a demand for trusting faithfulness. The hymn in chapter 3 functions both as a source of comfort and as the prophetic confession of confidence regardless of the way things look on the surface.

The arrangement of the book is quite straightforward; it consists of a conversation between the prophet and God, followed by a series of five taunts and a majestic description of Yahweh's coming from Sinai to wreak havoc, an account that evokes in Habakkuk the resolve to wait faithfully until God acts on behalf of the righteous. The dialogue comprises an initial lament (Hab. 1:2–4), the divine response (1:5–11), a second lament (1:12–17), and a vision that serves as the second divine response (2:1–4). The series of taunting sayings has five strophes either introduced by the expression "Woe to" or incorporating these words into the body of the taunt (2:5–19). The psalmlike text in chapter 3 has its own superscription (3:1) and musical notes at the end (3:19c). It also contains a framework within which the hymn is placed (3:2, 16–19).

This unusual arrangement and the content have led interpreters to suggest that the book may have been used regularly in worship. Some critics go a step further, arguing that the whole book was *originally* intended for liturgical use. Habakkuk is therefore understood as a cultic prophet at the Jerusalem sanctuary whose primary concern was to proclaim salvation for the people of Judah. Nevertheless, Habakkuk's nationalism is restrained, because it is tempered by his strong emphasis on faithfulness as the essential human mode of waiting until deliverance comes. In any case, the superscription in 1:1 identifies him as a professional prophet, a *nabi'*, and states that he was charged with a burden (*massa'*).

We possess no further information about the prophet Habakkuk or his family. Even the name has been preserved differently in the Hebrew and Greek texts; in the latter it has the form *ambakoum*. The additions to Daniel in the Apocrypha, specifically Bel and the Dragon, record a legend about Habakkuk. According to the story, the spirit transports the prophet from Judea to Babylon by the hair of his head and sets him down over the lion's den into which Daniel had been thrown. In Habakkuk's hand is food that he had prepared for some reapers in Judea but that he

Cave Four of Qumran, where numerous biblical and other ancient texts were hidden and rediscovered in 1952. The site is on the northwest side of the Dead Sea.

now gives to a hungry Daniel. Then the angel returns Habakkuk to his own country. Of course this narrative lacks historical value except as witness to the devotional speculation about some ancient figures that became common around the second century B.C.E.

Whatever his background, this prophet expresses considerable freedom in the way he handles traditional literary forms. After the lament in 1:2–4 and the divine response in 1:5–11, we expect a confession of confidence in God based on what the prophet has now learned about the Deity's actions. Such an element occurs so often in the Book of Psalms that a statement of assurance is a constitutive component of laments. Furthermore, the usual cause of complaint is some human oppressor, but here Habakkuk points a finger at God. That is not all; the lament and divine response do not stand alone but give birth to futher complaint and a second divine response, this time in the form of a vision.

Complaint and Response

Habakkuk's original lament could arise in virtually any age, for it expresses the perennial frustration decent people feel when injustice runs rampant. Where is God, and what is occupying the Deity's time so that cruelty goes unpunished? If humans take offense from perversion of justice, surely a moral Deity must do the same. The problem, then, is acute:

Why does God refuse to act so as to restore just dealings among women
and men? Has sleep stolen over the Deity, or is the problem greater yet,
one of impotency? Before evil's awesome thrust, has the God of Israel
become powerless? These are the thoughts that one finds sprinkled
throughout comparable laments, and one can suppose that both Habakkuk
and those for whom his words were intended were aware of such dark
reflections. For the moment, however, Habakkuk does not speculate
about the reasons for divine slackness. He is more concerned about the
Deity's timetable and about the suffering the prophet must endure as a
consequence of delayed punishment for malicious deeds.

God's answer to Habakkuk's perplexed question is hardly what the
prophet expected. Indeed, it is so strange that its very form emphasizes
the impossibility of easy acceptance. One can scarcely imagine a divine
response that questions the prophet's ability to believe it, because on
the face of things the Deity has spoken. In truth, unbelief seems out of
place when God is the source of a statement! Here the Deity warns Habakkuk that he will find it hard to believe what his ears hear, so extraordinary is the divine activity. What is that stirring far off that will punish
injustice at long last? It is none other than the emergence to power of
the Neo-Babylonian empire during the last quarter of the seventh century.
The Deity's remarks imply that Habakkuk's field of vision is too limited
to deal with the matter of divine justice, for the whole world is subject
to the Holy One. Already Isaiah had claimed that the God whom Judah
worshipped used Assyria as an instrument of punishment against the
covenant people, but the Book of Habakkuk does not actually make that
assertion here. Instead, the Deity simply states that the Babylonians are
being roused up, and then God proceeds to describe their claim to supremacy in the area of cruelty. In a word, power is their deity.

What comfort is it to learn that God is somehow responsible for stirring
up the Chaldeans? How can they bring relief to the people of Judah?
An answer to these questions may be found by assuming that the Assyrians are the oppressors; the Neo-Babylonian empire was destined to
put an end to the mighty Assyrian threat, first at Nineveh in 612 and
ultimately at Carchemish in 605. If this is the sense of the divine response,
we must imagine a date around 625. On the other hand, the text seems
to imply that these Babylonians have already succeeded in establishing
a reputation for cruelty. For this reason, among others, scholars usually
think that Habakkuk was active between 605 and 598, the occasion of
the first Babylonian invasion of Judah. The wicked one whom Habakkuk
mentions would then be King Jehoiakim rather than the ruler of Assyria,
and that would accord with Jeremiah's attitude toward the Judean king.
If that is the meaning, one could almost anticipate the objection that
follows.

Briefly stated, Habakkuk's argument runs like this: because you, God,
are both pure and permanent, why do you allow cruel people to punish
those who are morally better than they? How can you stand by in silence

when wicked persons swallow up those who are more righteous than they? Better still, why did you fashion people in such a manner that they become as vulnerable to capture as fish to a seine? Will this cruel fisherman never stop emptying his net? Confident that God will have an answer for him, Habakkuk decides to wait until it comes. He situates himself on a tower; unfortunately, we do not know what function this structure served. Was it perhaps a watchtower on the city wall? But then what special significance did an ordinary tower have for the prophetic vocation? A possible answer is that he was watching for the approach of the Babylonian army.

What Habakkuk sees is something quite different from invading soldiers. It is rather a vision, and that vision is accompanied by some specific instructions. The prophet is told to write the vision in plain language so that its content cannot be missed by persons in a hurry or so that the herald can easily read the words while running. Furthermore, Habakkuk receives full assurance that the vision will come to pass, although it may seem long in coming. Hab. 2:4 records the heart of the vision; in short, this verbal image asserts that those who are proud will fall, and those who are righteous will live by remaining faithful. Applied to the immediate context, it seems to suggest that the arrogant Babylonians will also bite the dust, and faithful Judeans will survive enemy invasion. The next verse implies that insatiable lust for power and possessions carries within itself a seed of destruction, for the conqueror must always try to subdue just one more nation. In due time, even a nation as great as Babylon will meet its nemesis.

So far the poet has given highly unusual responses to the problem of divine injustice; in the first place, he has insisted that God stands behind the emergence of Babylon to center stage, and in the second place, he has called faithful people to remain true regardless of circumstances, promising them life for their troubles. The emphasis falls almost completely on human actions, whether cruel beyond belief or faithful against all odds. Nevertheless, Habakkuk now believes that human actions receive their decisive impetus from the Lord, and that belief is ultimately a source of comfort.

Lust for Power

The series of woes that follow seems to reinforce the import of the vision by demonstrating the futility of insatiable lust for power. The five denunciations cover various means of acquiring possessions and therefore control over others. The first warns those who plunder the weak in search of spoil that the time will come when they will themselves be robbed by more powerful plunderers. The second woe oracle addresses those who use force in a vain effort to secure themselves from all harm. It boldly asserts that even the stone and wood that make up the place of refuge will resist such use, crying out for vengeance on the cruel master.

The building of a city at human expense provides the subject matter for the third woe oracle. Such spilled blood will profit them nothing, for in the last resort cities go up in smoke. The fourth woe depends on a play on words: The author speaks about drinking strong wine and the cup of divine wrath. Those who give spirits to their neighbors for personal gain, presumably to satisfy physical lust, will be forced to drink a cup of fury against their wishes. The result will be that these individuals who brought shame on others will suddenly be put to shame. The last woe oracle comprises a scathing indictment of the worship of images. Three arguments against idols are expressed: (1) they are fashioned by human hands; (2) they are wood or stone, hence cannot talk; (3) they are overlaid with precious metals and cannot breathe. The absurdity of such worship thus stands out, in that people worship a creature of their own hands, one that cannot speak so as to provide revelation about the divine world. Here the mockery becomes especially pronounced:

> For the workman trusts in his own creation
>   when he makes dumb idols!
> Woe to him who says to a wooden thing, Awake;
>   to a dumb stone, Arise!
> Can this give revelation?
> Behold, it is overlaid with gold and silver,
>   and there is no breath at all in it. (Hab. 2:18c–19)

A striking feature of these taunts is the presence of two doxologies (verses 14 and 20).

> For the earth will be filled
>   with the knowledge of the glory of the Lord
>   as the waters cover the sea. (Hab. 2:14)

> But the Lord is in his holy temple;
>   let all the earth keep silence before him. (Hab. 2:20)

Vision and Resolve

The final chapter registers Habakkuk's consternation over the message he has received from the Lord and shows how the prophet tempers his fear with firm resolve. Although many scholars think this prayer, hymn, and confession do not belong to the authentic materials from Habakkuk, the issue is considerably more complex. The silence of the Habakkuk Commentary from Qumran with regard to this chapter does nothing to strengthen the case against its authenticity because one can easily give several reasons for the absence of any reference to this material. To be sure, the separate superscription to the chapter does suggest that it may have existed on its own at some time, and the musical notes imply use in worship. Perhaps this liturgical function supplies a clue to the presence of this extra superscription: an authentic text from the prophet Habakkuk was adapted for use in worship.

We cannot be sure whether this chapter is a unity or not. In any case, it seems to make use of an older theophanic tradition (3:3–15); the images are highly reminiscent of Canaanite mythic texts describing the god Baal's battle against the gods of the sea and death. Within the Hebrew Bible this tradition can be seen best in Judges 5, Deuteronomy 33, and Psalm 68. Naturally, the Exodus experience provides the central focal point for the celebration of Yahweh's victory over the forces of chaos. That trampling of the nations is here understood as the supreme expression of Yahweh's saving deeds in Israel's behalf, the benefits of which are now being claimed by the Davidic dynasty: "Thou wentest forth for the salvation of thy people,/for the salvation of thy anointed" (3:13).

Habakkuk's reaction to the vision of an invading Babylonian army is comparable to the earth's reaction to the self-manifestation of Yahweh. Overcome by trembling and sickness, he waits for the disaster that threatens both him and the people (3:16). The final confession of trust in the Lord whose ways are beyond understanding achieves profound spiritual depths that are rarely plumbed in the Bible.

> Though the fig tree do not blossom,
>   nor fruit be on the vines,
> the produce of the olive fail
>   and the fields yield no food,
> the flock be cut off from the fold
>   and there be no herd in the stalls,
> yet I will rejoice in the Lord,
>   I will joy in the God of my salvation.
> God, the Lord, is my strength;
>   he makes my feet like hinds' feet,
>   he makes me tread upon my high places. (Hab. 3:17–19)*

This is the practical response that the prophet Habakkuk offers to the vexing problem of theodicy. In brief, I shall endure adversity in confidence that my feet are firmly planted, and I shall rejoice while doing so. Such is the legacy of the prophet who dared to ask difficult questions and to penetrate beneath the surface of things to a deeper reality.

ZEPHANIAH

Regular payment of tribute to Assyrian kings was not the only disconcerting feature of subject peoples. Equally galling to some individuals was the intrusion of foreign forms of worship into the very center of Judah's religious life. Such a person was the prophet Zephaniah, who seems to have been active just prior to the reforms instituted by Josiah in 621 B.C.E. The cultic abuses and religious syncretism that Zephaniah men-

---

*The image seems to combine the surefootedness of animals accustomed to mountains and victory over one's enemies. The latter sense is derived from the phrase about treading on the backs of enemies, which is at home in Canaanite texts as well as biblical ones.

tions fit nicely into the early years of Josiah's reign while the prophet was still a youth, and this pattern therefore seems to confirm the dating provided by the superscription to the book. A curious aspect of this genealogy is its tracing of the prophet's ancestry as far as four generations; scholars are divided in trying to explain this deviation from the usual pattern. Some think the purpose is to link Zephaniah with royalty, in this case, Hezekiah, although one would expect to find the title king of Judah after the name. Others believe the long genealogy seeks to legitimate the prophet as a full member of the nation, Judah, and thus to remove the impression that his father was an Ethiopian, despite the name Cushi.

Zephaniah is therefore the first prophet that tradition has recalled who broke the silence that enveloped Israel after the death of Isaiah. Those years had seen Hezekiah's reforms erased by pro-Assyrian sentiments in his successors, Manasseh especially, and the stage was set for another purification of worship. In particular, Zephaniah mentions bowing before the host of heaven; swearing by Milcom, the god of the neighboring Ammonites; dressing in foreign clothing; leaping over the threshold; and more generally, priestly and prophetic profaning of what is sacred. In addition, he refers to the idolatrous priests and the remnant of Baal, the latter expression suggesting to some interpreters that Zephaniah may actually have prophesied toward the end of Josiah's reign when only a residue of Baal worshippers remained.

The Day of Wrath

For their faithless conduct these practitioners of alien worship hear threatening words that echo the message of Amos. The Deity has a day of wrath in store for them, a day of darkness and gloom that will encompass the whole earth. Zephaniah's description of the day of the Lord later inspired the medieval Latin poem *Dies irae, dies illa*. He describes that awful time as follows:

> *The great day of the Lord is near,*
>   *near and hastening fast;*
> *the sound of the day of the Lord is bitter,*
>   *the mighty man cries aloud there.*
> *A day of wrath is that day,*
>   *a day of distress and anguish,*
> *a day of ruin and devastation,*
>   *a day of darkness and gloom,*
> *a day of clouds and thick darkness,*
>   *a day of trumpet blast and battle cry*
> *against the fortified cities*
>   *and against the lofty battlements. (Zeph. 1:14–16)*

Zephaniah's elaboration on the effects of this day resembles the illustrations that Amos offered (fleeing from a lion, one meets a bear, or entering the safety of home, one is bitten by a serpent), for he invites the people to a sacrificial banquet in which they become the victims. Here the mention of the king's sons who dress in foreign attire has provoked some discussion, because no reference is made to the king himself. Some interpreters have found support in this text for a later dating of Zephaniah, perhaps even in the reign of Jehoiakim, but others think the verse comes from the period when Josiah was still a minor.

The prophet's unusual power to evoke images that linger in the minds of hearers produced an especially vivid description of the Deity wandering through the streets of Jerusalem, lamp in hand, searching for those who are overcome by a false sense of security, in Zephaniah's words:

> *the men*
> *who are thickening upon their lees,*
> *those who say in their hearts,*
> *"The Lord will not do good,*
> *nor will he do ill." (Zeph. 1:12)*

The use of imagery from wine making is particularly appropriate for the stupor that characterizes these people who have abandoned all hope in the Lord's power to save. The punishment for this indolence recalls ancient futility curses; they shall build houses but will not occupy them and plant vineyards but not drink wine from them.

Like so many of the prophetic books, this one has the structure imposed on it by later collectors. Threats directed at the prophet's own nation are followed by threats against foreign nations, which in turn give way to comforting words for a chosen remnant of God's people. Zephaniah attacks the major power, Assyria, and announces the downfall of an arrogant Nineveh. With striking puns he denounces four cities in Philistia (Gaza, Ashkelon, Ashdod, Ekron), omitting Gath, and likens Moab and Ammon to Sodom and Gomorrah. Ethiopia also finds a place in this denunciation of foreign nations, one that is remarkably reserved about the actual offense for which these peoples will be punished. The only concrete charges are "taunting Israel" and "pride," the latter of which is illustrated by Nineveh's boast: "I am and there is none else" (2:15).

Some scholars think the promises in the book are wholly secondary, but the notion of a righteous remnant who survive the day of wrath already appears in Isaiah, and therefore it seems entirely in order for a thinker like Zephaniah, who comes very close to providing a compendium of prophecy. After all, he does repeat Amos's invitation to seek the Lord, and offers the same faint hope that *perhaps* they may be hidden on the day of wrath. Zephaniah goes one step further than his predecessor Amos, specifying which people he has in mind, the humble of the land. Of course, later ideas have also found their way into these promises, transforming them into full assurance that Jerusalem's inhabitants will become pure and will lie down in peace. Even the belief that the worship of Israel's God will become universal finds expression here.

Yea, at that time I will change the speech of the peoples
to a pure speech,
that all of them may call on the name of the Lord
and serve him with one accord.
From beyond the rivers of Ethiopia
my suppliants, the daughter of my dispersed ones,
shall bring my offering. (Zeph. 3:9–10)

The influence of Ezekiel becomes evident as this promise reaches its climax. The book ends on a positive note: the King of Israel, the Lord dwells in its midst, "a warrior who gives victory," and the lame and the outcast will enjoy special favor.

HAGGAI

At the death of Cyrus's son Cambyses, the Persian empire was plunged into a civil war that lasted from March 522 B.C.E. to November 521. The two main contenders for the throne were Darius and Gaumata, but the eventual winner in this struggle, Darius, boasts of having suppressed numerous rivals. His claim was engraved in full view of all who traveled near the Behistun Rock, an inscription that assisted greatly in the early decipherment of Akkadian wedge-shaped writing, cuneiform. The disturbances that rocked the empire revived fading hopes within the small Jewish community that a new and glorious future was dawning, for the prophet Jeremiah had predicted a restoration after seventy years. If 587, the fall of Jerusalem, is taken as the point of reference for this prophecy, then the civil war in Persia could easily have fueled the flames of expectation within Jewish circles.

Earlier celebration of a new era had proven to be premature, although Cyrus had indeed issued an emancipation decree in 538 that allowed all captives to return home. In this respect, the proclamation by Second Isaiah was accurate, but the extravagant language with which this prophet clothed that comforting word served later to emphasize the disparity between anticipation and reality. A highway in the desert never materialized, nor did rivers flow freely there. As a matter of fact, nature had refused to cooperate in the least with those few people who chose to uproot themselves once more and return to an unknown future in the homeland. Instead of unprecedented prosperity, they experienced hardship in the form of famine and drought. What is more, these exiled peoples returned to learn that others had taken possession of the land during their enforced absence. Some of these new owners were the Jews who never left the country, elsewhere identified as the least desirable citizens in terms of skills, but others were foreigners who had been relocated from other countries that had fallen to the Babylonians. Because all of these people had worked the land for years and had built houses on the ruins left in

587, they strongly resisted the claims of ownership pressed by returning exiles.

From other sources it appears that the inhabitants of Samaria resented these persons who came from far away and intruded in affairs that did not relate to them. The course of this hostility is unclear, although it may have arisen from their own veneration of a sacred altar in Jerusalem, for a cult seems to have continued there despite the burning of the Temple. At least, many scholars reached that conclusion from the story in Jeremiah about pilgrims from the north who were massacred at Mizpah. The existence of a cult in Jerusalem after 587 would also explain the desire on the part of the Samaritans to participate in the restoration of the Temple, a gesture that was rebuffed by the returning exiles. On the other hand, that refusal to accept the offer of assistance from the people in Samaria may have produced resentment on their part that gradually grew into mutual hatred, especially when it was reinforced by religious differences.

A Successful Prophet

Into this explosive situation the prophet Haggai marched, and he began one of the most successful prophetic ministries in the recorded history of the phenomenon, if success can be measured by lasting change that is perceptible to one and all. He believed that all the trouble experienced by the restored community could be blamed on the failure to rebuild the Temple in Jerusalem. The solution, in his eyes, was simple: restore that house, and the new era will finally dawn. His goal, then, was to salvage the dreams that had come to the people through Second Isaiah's poetry, dreams that were quickly vanishing in the bright light of the day. Haggai readily acknowledged the people's disappointment with these poignant words: "You have looked for much, and, lo, it came to little" (Hag. 1:9). The people, on their part, have tried, but all effort seems futile. They sow but reap little; eat but go hungry; drink but are thirsty; clothe themselves but are cold; and earn wages "to put them in a bag with holes" (1:6).

The book that bears Haggai's name comprises two chapters; it is entirely in the third person and appears to be prose, although some interpreters think it may be metrical. The four oracles that make up the book are dated: August 29, 520; October 18, 520; and December 18, 520 (the last two oracles). The first oracle shames the secular and religious officials, Zerubbabel and Joshua, for living in fine houses while neglecting to build a dwelling for the Deity. The point is so persuasive that work began on the Temple a few weeks later, September 21, 520. The second oracle was necessitated by the disappointment that some people experienced when they saw how limited their resources were. The memory of the grandeur of Solomon's Temple overwhelmed them, and their own feeble efforts had produced nothing so majestic. Haggai reassured the people by promising them that the wealth of the nations would flow into their treasury; consequently, there would be no limit to what they could achieve with such vast holdings. After all, he reasoned, silver and gold belong to the Deity.

Priestly Instruction

The third oracle takes the form of priestly instruction; Haggai asks priestly leaders to give a ruling with regard to clean and unclean things. Is uncleanliness made holy by contact with what is pure? The priests say no. Then is cleanliness made ritually unclean if it touches something defiled? The answer, yes. This obscure ruling is then applied to "this people," "this nation," and "every work of their hands" (2:14). Although some critics understand this text as a reference to Samaritans, who are refused access to the atoning work on the Temple, it is more likely a criticism of those among the exiles who believed that the rebuilding of the holy place was making them pure. The prophet rebukes such self-righteousness and warns the workers against carelessness in areas of ritual impurity. A quotation from Amos occurs in Haggai's rationale for this oracle (2:17), for there the argument was made that natural calamity is divine punishment.

The fourth oracle seems calculated to raise the people's expectation still more; Haggai announces the divine readiness to shake the whole world, overthrowing empires and placing Zerubbabel, the governor of Judah, on the throne as ruler of the entire earth. This chosen servant is the Deity's signet ring with which the divine intention will be stamped into the earth. Such blatant messianism must surely have alarmed those within the community who wished to keep peace with Persian authorities, and these people may have found support from a priestly party that feared the loss of their own power resulting from a restored Davidic ruler. In any event, Zerubbabel quickly vanished from the scene, and the high priest took his place. Perhaps it is significant that this is the first time the title "high priest" occurs.

ZECHARIAH

The prophet Haggai was joined by one of priestly descent, if Neh. 12:16 is correct; this co-worker was named Zechariah. His first word is dated October/November 520 B.C.E., the night visions from February 519, and his final word from December 518. Spurred on by prophecies from two men of God, the small community of returning exiles dedicated a restored Temple in 516. They did so with eager expectancy, for they had done their part, and now it was time for the Deity to respond in kind. It is impossible to determine exactly how these hopes were dashed; in any case, it seems that the people were forced to shift the focus of their hopes from the secular realm to the religious, for Persian officials would tolerate considerably more in that domain. This open dimension of Zechariah's proclamation may very well have invited later adjustments; whether invited or not, two independent collections (chapters 9–11 and 12–14) have become attached to the original burden that Zechariah laid on the people. The inscription to these two collections links them to Malachi; it is generally assumed that these three small units were once together, but the third was removed so that there would be twelve books in the collection that has come to be known as the Book of the Twelve Prophets. However, the inscriptions have some important differences that make this assumption highly suspect.

The language of Zechariah is intentionally obscure, partly because he uses a form of communication that employs interpreting angels. This expedient produced economical language that is rich in allusions, which the angel proceeds to explain. The Deity is represented as remote from ordinary human affairs but as one who communicates nonetheless through mediators. Some of Zechariah's images seem to have been drawn from Babylonian culture—for example, the seven eyes of the Lord, which probably refer to the seven planets rather than to the ancient equivalent of the Central Intelligence Agency. The form of these prophetic words, night visions, became immensely popular in subsequent literature, although Zechariah was more prophetic than apocalyptic in ideas. Apocalyptic literature resembles Zechariah in its fondness for angels, its visionary framework, and its understanding of human events as earthly manifestations of a parallel reality in the heavens. Zechariah looks back on a bygone era as a significant time when the Deity proclaimed the future through prophets, but that era has ended, for they are now called former prophets.

Seven Night Visions and Three Action Reports

A series of seven night visions makes up the heart of Zechariah's message. The first vision is of four horses and their riders who patrol the earth. It addresses the abortive hopes that had arisen in connection with the disturbance in Persia but that had been crushed quickly by Darius's restoration of order. That unrest had failed to usher in the new age, and the people of God were forced once more to abandon hope in an immediate transformation of heaven and earth. Zechariah acknowledges their disappointment; he even endows the angel with similar concern, for it quotes Jeremiah's promise that deliverance will come after seventy years and asks about the delay. The Deity answers that things will change for Jerusalem; the brief day of anger is past, for the nations exceeded their authority in punishing Israel. The second vision concerns four horns and smiths, but its meaning is unclear, although it seems to refer to destructive power and the ability to rebuild for the people in Zion. The third vision, a man with a measuring line, concentrates on this city, promising that Jerusalem's population will make walls superfluous but that the Deity will be a protective barrier of fire for its inhabitants. Here, too, Zechariah addresses fundamental problems arising from the exposed nature of an unwalled city.

The fourth vision is preceded by one of three action reports. The high priest, Joshua, stands accused before the angel by Satan, who functions here and in Job as an official who is charged with patrolling the earth in search of genuine righteousness. Joshua concedes that he is guilty and receives divine forgiveness. In this instance sin is characterized as impure garments, which Joshua proceeds to discard in favor of pure clothes. The angel promises the high priest that he will have complete authority over the Temple precincts but that special power is contingent on obedience to the Deity. Zechariah's fourth vision is of seven lamps on a lampstand and two olive trees. The lamps imply divine vigilance, and the two trees represent the secular and religious leaders, Zerubbabel and Joshua, perhaps through heavenly prototypes. Couched within this vision and its interpretation is a reminder that the Deity achieves a goal in ways that are quite different from human force: "Not by might, nor by power, but by my spirit, says the Lord of hosts" (Zech. 4:6). The fifth vision is of a flying scroll, which represents a curse that will descend on everyone who steals or swears falsely. Once again, Zechariah turns to deal with practical matters within the small community, in this instance theft (arising from economic need or hunger?) and subsequent denial that is reinforced by an oath.

The next vision makes a bold assertion: evil has been removed from the land and discarded in Babylon. The prophet sees a basket in which a woman, who is specifically identified as wickedness,* is resting, and two winged women lift the basket and its cargo and bear them away. The angel informs him that a house will be built for her in Babylon, but it is unclear what the object of this ridicule is. Was it a temple in their former land of residence? The final vision returns to the notion of divine patrols, in this instance, four chariots.

The second action report has something to do with crowning a ruler, or possibly two rulers, but the text has been altered, perhaps because of the serious political consequences of such action. It seems that Zerubbabel was crowned as ruler of the community but that he was summarily removed from public office and the authority was therefore shifted to the priestly representative, Joshua. Or it may be that only Joshua was crowned from the start, but the restoration of the Davidic line through Zerubbabel was nurtured by the allusion to his Babylonian name, "the branch."

---

*The attitude toward women in ancient Israel was more complex than this text might suggest. It should also be noted that wisdom was personified as a woman (Proverbs 8; Sirach [Ecclesiasticus] 24).

The third action report continues to address practical ethical and religious matters before the community. Zechariah endeavors to answer a question that some people from Bethel have asked the priests and prophets: when is the appropriate time to fast? His answer shifts away from the proper time for fasting to acts of kindness and mercy, a theme that recurs in chapter 8. The prophetic message of Zechariah ends on a positive note, the promise that Jerusalem will have old men and women sitting in the streets and youngsters playing nearby, and announces a pilgrimage of foreigners to Jerusalem.

Shepherds

Within the poetic material comprising much of Second Zechariah, chapters 9–11, occurs a reference to the Deity's anger against the shepherds; this idea is developed in chapter 11 in a prose passage that is highly obscure. It is said that the cruelty that had run rampant prompted the Deity to appoint a shepherd over the people, but he killed three shepherds in one month. Although this shepherd had augured hope, he actually broke the staff on which was written Grace, and then one called Union. The two staffs symbolized the Deity's covenant and the brotherhood between Judah and Israel.

Contempt for Prophecy

Third Zechariah, chapters 12–14, is perhaps best known for its witness to the contempt for prophecy that arose in at least one circle, apparently because of some connection with idolatry. The author insists that parents are obliged to slay their own sons who decide to enter the prophetic ranks. In that day prophets will be ashamed of their vision and will refuse to admit that they belong to this group. Here the retort that Amos directed to the priest Amaziah is borrowed, but with a different ending: "I am no prophet, I am a tiller of the soil; for the land has been my possession since my youth" (Zech. 13:5). The text concludes with the statement that those prophets who had earlier disfigured their bodies in some way, perhaps during prophetic frenzy, will try to remove those incriminating marks and to laugh off all inquiry with the lame explanation that the wounds resulted from a brawl among friends.

This final collection makes an association that Haggai had made but that Zechariah had carefully avoided, the linking of nature with human deeds. Chapter 14 envisions an annual feast of booths in celebration of which all nations journey to Jerusalem. Those who fail to do so will be punished by a plague and drought. On that day, even the horses will wear bells on which is written, "Holy to the Lord," and every pot in Jerusalem will be sacred.

MALACHI

The book of Malachi consists of six discussion topics and two epilogues, both of which derive from authors different from the anonymous one who wrote the argumentative discourses. The name Malachi seems to be taken from Mal. 3:1, the announcement that God will send a messenger to prepare the way for the Deity. It does not appear to be a personal name, although the Aramaic translation, the Targum, identifies the messenger with Ezra the scribe. So far no instance of this name has survived in any source, despite attempts by some critics to see it as a shortened form of Malkijah, "the Lord is my king."

Discussion Words

The six topics of discussion between the prophet and his audience are (1) Israel's special relationship to the Deity, (2) blemished sacrifices, (3) breach of marriage contracts, (4) doubts about divine retribution, (5) tithes, and (6) doubts concerning the justice of God. In each case the prophet begins with an accusing statement, followed by his presentation of the people's objection, which he then proceeds to refute. He defends Israel's special status by appealing to the appalling conditions in Edom at the moment, for the Deity loves Jacob (Israel) and hates Esau (Edom). The unfavorable economic conditions under which the community chafes are attributed to the very measures designed to save money, specifically the offering of blemished animals to the Deity. The prophet refuses to be impressed by self-righteous boasts that in dire circumstances offerings still are made, and he points out that for sheer numbers and quality of sacrifices foreigners surpass in generosity those who know the Lord. Others interpret this reference to offerings throughout the world as remarkable tolerance, the conviction that God is honored even when the worshipper does not know the name of the true Deity.

The discussion of mixed marriages is unclear, for the image seems also to connote idolatry. Certain features of the argument are beyond doubt; the prophet accuses the people of adultery and divorcing their wives, and he warns that such conduct displeases the Deity. The marriages to foreigners may have been aimed at economic and political security by cementing ties with powerful foreign families surrounding Jerusalem. Although the prophet asks a question that seems to be universalistic, "Have we not all one father? Has not one God created us?" (2:10), he actually has only one people, Israel, in mind. Applied to all peoples, the teaching would endorse rather than condemn mixed marriages.

Two discussions are directed at doubters, people who have begun to question earlier convictions about divine justice. Like Ezekiel, Malachi thinks such skepticism wearies the Deity; he imagines that they say, "Every one who does evil is good in the sight of the Lord, and he delights in them," or they ask, "Where is the God of justice?" (2:17). The prophet reaffirms old beliefs, especially the expectation of a day of the Lord, but he adds some new dimensions to this hope. That day will be preceded by a messenger who will purify the nation of sin, and the Deity is preparing a book of remembrance that will contain the names of all God-fearers. The latter is in all likelihood a redactional comment from a later period.

The discussion word about tithes and offerings makes a connection between sin and natural catastrophes, in this instance a serious drought. The prophet argues that the Deity has withheld rain precisely because the people have robbed God, and he challenges them to submit the Lord to a test. The promise is quite specific: put me to the test and I will pour you out a blessing that will transform the barren fields to overflowing harvests. The promises in Second Isaiah were grander, but they also were less concrete. Even when they did not come to pass exactly as envisioned, it was still possible to believe that the prophecies had been fulfilled. But in the case of the prediction that payment of tithes would bring abundant rain and crops, failure in every specific must have been devastating to those who had subjected the Deity to a test.

The Messenger Elijah

The two appendices affirm that Mosaic law is authoritative for all Israel and identify the messenger with Elijah. The second appendix probably presupposes a continuous chain of prophets similar to those envisioned in Deut. 18:15–18. These two additions imply a collection of the law and the prophets, which are here linked together through the representatives of each, Moses and Elijah. This expectation of the return of Elijah was alive in New Testament times, and an identification of John the Baptist with that messenger occurred in some circles. Likewise the association of Moses and Elijah was made in the New Testament story about the transfiguration of Jesus. Within Judaism the belief that Elijah will return has been kept alive in the Passover seder, when a cup and an empty chair await his coming.

Limited Horizons

It is often noted that the world addressed by the book of Malachi was a limited one, specifically the Jerusalem Temple cult, but that is no reason to dismiss its message as trivial. In all probability, the author's concentration on ritual purity was inspired by the threat posed by syncretistic elements on every hand. In such circumstances the survival of the Jewish community depended on faithfulness to its own distinctiveness. It appears that the all-out effort to rebuild the Temple had only resulted in frustration, inasmuch as the predictions that Haggai and Zechariah linked with the successful building of the Temple did not come to pass. The consequence of this disappointment threatened to destroy the people's faith. If that disillusionment lies behind the doubt that the author seeks to overcome, a date between 500 and 450 B.C.E. seems appropriate for the book. However, such doubt seems to have characterized the people at many stages of their history, so that it is impossible to determine the precise period in which the book arose. Even attempts to date it before Ezra's reforms are not entirely conclusive, because reforms are often short-lived, as seems to have been true of Josiah's and Hezekiah's reforms. Still, the problem of mixed marriage was certainly acute when Ezra came to Jerusalem. There are at least two firm clues about the general period in which the author of Malachi wrote. The book refers to a governor over the area; that reference points to the Persian period when satraps ruled the various localities. The other clue, the existence of the restored Temple, requires a date after 516. Some interpreters think the expression "the Lord of hosts" also points to a late date, but the title was used in early Israel, although it does seem to have become a favorite expression in late texts.

◆ PART THREE ◆

THE WRITINGS

THE collection that falls into the third category, the Writings, is composed of five different types of literature: (1) wisdom, (2) erotic poetry, (3) apocalyptic, (4) lamentation and hymn, and (5) religious history and short stories. The translator of Sirach (Ecclesiasticus) labeled this material "the other books," in addition to the Torah and Prophets, whereas New Testament writers used "Psalms" to designate the third division of the canon. It seems clear that this part of the Hebrew Bible served as a catchall for those additional books that had come to mean a great deal to the religious community by the end of the first century B.C.E. Because wisdom literature stands out as an alien work within the entire canon in the eyes of many, some discussion of this material is essential.

WISDOM IN THE ANCIENT NEAR EAST

The international character of wisdom requires no documentation, for it was a familiar phenomenon in Egypt, Mesopotamia, and Canaan. From the third millennium B.C.E., Egyptian sages instructed others in the difficult aspects of court life; at times the pharaoh is represented as the wise one who leaves a royal testament for his successor, and sometimes the teaching is attributed to viziers who were employed by the king. The ideal toward which students strove was self-control and eloquence. The truly wise individual was the silent one, as opposed to the hot person. In other words, the intelligent court official exercised control over passions, concealing feelings at all times. Moreover, the sage learned when to speak and when to remain silent, practiced restraint, chose words appropriate to the situation, and spoke the truth. It follows that eloquence consisted of timeliness, restraint, propriety, and integrity. The ideal was justice *(ma'at)*, which included the notion of order and truth. In time a strong streak of piety entered Egyptian wisdom, and later still the instructions were democratized, no longer being restricted to the pharaoh's court. For example, *The Instruction of 'Onkhsheshonky* was written for ordinary rural people; it is significant that its style, short proverbs, also differs noticeably from royal instructions, where thematic essays occur regularly. Egyptian wisdom occasionally ventured from proverbial instruction to the dialogue or dispute, which offered serious reflection about the injustices of life. Much more prominent, however, were scribal texts and lists of natural phenomena.

Wisdom in ancient Mesopotamia resembled that in Egypt, although contributing some distinctive features as well. Here the reflective side of wisdom thought came into prominence, particularly the attempt to understand the problem of divine justice. The prototypes for the biblical Job and Ecclesiastes resulted from this kind of Sumerian and neo-Assyrian wisdom. At least two parallels to each book, Job and Ecclesiastes, have survived as testimony to the seriousness with which these sages approached reality. But this wisdom had its lighter side too, as can be seen in the collections of proverbs and in riddles, fables, disputes, and lists. The last category, like its Egyptian conterpart, consisted of encyclopedic data used in educating students. Sumerian wisdom also had its ethical advice that noted scholars handed down to posterity. In Mesopotamia a close link between wisdom and the temple cult is recognizable, and some sages were specialists in interpreting omens. It has even been said that wisdom in Mesopotamia was essentially magic, but this description does not apply to all its forms. As in Egypt, special educational texts arose for the instruction of students, and with them, technical vocabulary such as *father* for teacher and *son* for student.

Canaanite wisdom has not survived, except indirectly through an Akkadian text in which a father offers advice about life's journey to his son who is set to venture forth beyond the safety of home. Of course, there are some allusions to El, the chief god of the pantheon, as wise, and Dan'el is credited with concern for widows and orphans—traditional wisdom language—but this sort of evidence is useless. The claim has been made that the Ebla texts include writings about wisdom, but only time will tell whether that is the case, and if so, how extensive the material is. *The Tale of Ahikar,* which seems to be an Aramaean work, belongs to this discussion, particularly because it contains a number of proverbs and riddles. Unfortunately, Edomite wisdom has not survived, despite the biblical references to this phenomenon. Foreign examples of wisdom also occur in the Book of Proverbs (the brief borrowing from *The Instruction of Amenemope* in 22:17–23:33; the sayings of Agur in 30:1–4; and the teaching of Lemuel's mother in 31:1–9). It is often thought that the numerical proverbs in Prov. 30:11–33 owe something to Canaanite wisdom, but the matter is hardly settled. Nevertheless, the virtual absence of this phenomenon of numerical heightening in Mesopotamian wisdom is striking.

ISRAELITE WISDOM

International wisdom shaped its specific manifestation in Israel, but it did not prevent the emergence of new features. Two things stand out, besides the perfection of the dispute form into a literary masterpiece, the Book of Job. These two new aspects of wisdom are (1) the heightening of religious emphasis within, and indeed the nationalization of, wisdom and (2) the development of hymns about wisdom as a personification, together with the equation of Torah and wisdom. But both of these new departures changed the essence of wisdom, which had been universalistic. All thinking individuals, regardless of their nationality, could inquire about life's inequities and could arrive at the same general conclusions about ethical conduct that is conducive to long life and happiness. The common bond that had held the wisdom enterprise together throughout the ancient world was human inquiry after truth. In late Israelite wisdom, that human initiative was replaced by divine revelation.

Perhaps the reason for this change can be attributed to the crisis that occurred in wisdom throughout the ancient world, a crisis occasioned by the conviction that order was dominant in the universe. Naturally, that conviction depended on belief in a Creator who guided the cosmos in a rational manner. It followed from this that life in accord with the recognizable order of reality would bring prosperity, whereas rebellion against the order would be punished. In time such conviction hardened into dogma, and that development led to a crisis when life failed to correspond to the belief. The earlier optimism about coping with all eventualities soon vanished, and humans found themselves in need of divine compassion. In Israel this sense of dependence linked up with a common theme outside wisdom, and mercy became a comforting divine attribute in late wisdom texts.

A similar feeling of intellectual inadequacy led to the personification of wisdom, for early optimism about the function of the intellect in securing one's existence gave way to an acknowledgment that reason could not achieve its goal at all. The mood changed from optimism to pessimism, largely because death canceled all profit from the application of reason to daily experience. An answer to this denial of wisdom's value was the assertion that human insight has been supplemented by a greater wisdom, the Torah. This Mosaic instruction is thus said to constitute divine instruction, which brings life to those who heed it.

The long path to these specifically Israelite features of wisdom is largely hidden from modern scholars. At least three phases seem to have characterized this phenomenon. In its earliest manifestation, wisdom seems to have existed within the family, where parents instructed their children about practical affairs. Most of the biblical proverbs probably derive from this stage of wisdom, even if they possess signs of later adaptation to a literary context. This parental instruction took place orally, and its content was mostly practical. It seems that a second stage of wisdom was associated with the royal court, possibly Solomon's but certainly Hezekiah's. This claim rests more on analogy from Egypt than on the character of the literature, which gives little evidence of connection with the royal court. The final stage was the educational one when schools first emerged in Israel. The actual date for the beginning of such scribal training is unknown, but we know that Sirach operated a school in 190 B.C.E. It is reasonable to assume that the wisdom literature in the Bible functioned as textbooks in these schools.

A useful way to approach this literature is to take account of its forms, most of which are also found elsewhere. The simplest form is the popular saying, which developed into the aphorism or proverb. Instructions are simply the more self-conscious form of teaching, in which positive and negative reinforcements appear. Numerical proverbs form a special kind, where several related things are joined together and reinforce a single point. Other minor types include anecdote, autobiographical narrative, allegory, prayer, impossible questions, and the like. The gem in Israel's wisdom is its disputation or poetic dialogue, in which the harsher realities of life are examined with great sensitivity. Late Israelite wisdom borrowed various Greek forms of speech (for example, the diatribe and the panegyric, or praise of great individuals).

EROTIC POETRY

Like wisdom, erotic poetry has its origins in earlier cultures, chiefly Egyptian. This poetry resembles the Song of Songs in its use of the terms *brother* and *sister* as synonymous with male and female lovers. The agony and ecstasy of love find expression in both cultures, and the power of sexual attraction is extolled. Egyptian love songs speak of the lover and the beloved on separate sides of a crocodile-infested stream, but they imply that nothing can prevent the lovers from coming together. These poems describe lovesickness and assert that the only medicine the sick person needs is the news that his beloved has come. Although literary dependence of Song of Songs on Egyptian erotic poetry has been claimed, it is better to recognize the universal aspect of such poetry.

APOCALYPTIC

During the struggle to survive as a nation under Syrian persecution, the Book of Daniel was conceived as a literary response to the horrible situation. Its form is that of an apocalyptic book, an unveiling of the future. As we have seen, such works generally reflect a situation of persecution, and the principal reason for their use of symbolic language is to protect the author from detection by authorities. Apocalyptic uses animal imagery, visions, pseudonymity, and astral concepts. Furthermore, it thinks in terms of two ages and assumes that evil has prevailed, at least temporarily. But this kind of thinking also has its hopeful elements: a son of man as redeemer, the establishment of an eternal kingdom, life after death.

LAMENTATION AND HYMNS

The Writings also contain a small collection of laments that arose in connection with the fall of Jerusalem in 587 B.C.E. This literary type is well known in Mesopotamia—for instance, in the lament over the destruction of the city Ur. The Book of Psalms is full of laments as well, but here they are complemented by thanksgiving hymns, for which there are also numerous parallels within Mesopotamian literature. Lyrical poetry thus comprises an important part of the Writings.

RELIGIOUS HISTORY AND SHORT STORIES

The Writings also contain various works that purport to give history, although the religious dimension dominates from beginning to end. The center of attention in three of these works—Chronicles, Ezra, and Nehemiah—is the Jerusalem Temple and its cult. Religious interests actually lead to a whitewashing of history in certain instances, for the aim of the author is to instruct readers morally rather than to record actual history. The dimension of teaching comes further into the forefront in such works as Ruth and Esther, which use story telling as an aid to instruction.

◆ 14 ◆

Psalms

IN the Hebrew Bible the Book of Psalms stands first in the third division, after the Torah and the Prophets. Indeed, for the author of Luke 24:44, Psalms represents the entire third division, the Writings. In one sense, at least, this is entirely proper, for the Psalms are the pulse of Israel's religious life. In them one encounters a rich variety of spiritual sentiment representing the agony and ecstasy of faith. This depository of spirituality arose in daily worship, and it therefore gives voice to vital concerns over the centuries. The central setting for much of this worship, but not all of it, was the Temple of Jerusalem, with its rich ritual. Because this cult originated under royal patronage, it follows that a considerable portion of its liturgy would center on the king and his vital interests. But even these activities within the Temple were of enormous interest to the populace, inasmuch as their social and economic welfare was to a large extent interlaced with royal well-being. Furthermore, numerous psalms are entirely unrelated to the king; in them, as in the others, the later synagogue and church have found a priceless treasury of spiritual prayer and praise.

The subject matter of the psalms is quite diverse, as one would naturally expect in a collection of songs and prayers from different places and times. Hymns extol the Deity's power and goodness, concentrating at great length on the marvels of creation and the saving deeds on Israel's behalf. Laments express grave concern over an absent or angry Deity and the resultant grief imposed on believers, and they give voice to utter confidence that the Lord will hear the complaint and act to restore a right relationship, ultimately removing all sources of discomfort. Songs of trust praise the Deity for faithfulness within a close relationship between Sovereign and subject. Didactic poems recall past moments in the nation's memory in a way that endeavors to profit from examples both positive and negative.

In these songs and prayers one finds sublime expressions of worship and base desires for revenge that spares no one, not even infants. There

292

are ecstatic shouts in which "amen" and "hallelujah" ring out freely, and there are frequent voiceless sighs and loud cries or agony uttered by persons who think life has crushed them without cause. Furthermore, musings about life's vanity intermix with amazement over human grandeur. Nothing seems to have been excluded from the arena of discourse, however unorthodox. Even the supposed thoughts of fools find a place here, although as a foil for better formulations of belief. Freedom of expression is almost boundless, and the believer takes seriously the conviction that the Deity sees and hears everything. Hence one can allow thoughts free rein, confident that they will eventually be purified by the shared relationship. In any event, a positive mood prevails within the Psalter as a whole, for the last word, even in laments, is one of hope.

Such optimism is somewhat surprising when one considers the number of psalms that seem to have arisen in adverse historical circumstances. To be sure, religious people have invariably managed to create escapist theology when faced with persecution, but no hint of such thinking resides in these psalms. In some of them the historical context can be reconstructed to some extent; for example, the Temple lies in ruins and the city walls have crumbled. But most of the psalms offer little assistance toward recovering the actual setting for their composition. The royal psalms, of course, must have arisen during the period of the monarchy, but we possess scant information about actual state affairs in Jerusalem, and much historical reconstruction amounts to conjecture. Some of this educated guessing seems well founded: Psalm 45 as a wedding song; Psalms 24, 47, 93, and 96–99 as songs of divine enthronement; Psalms 2 and 110 as coronation songs; and Psalm 20 as a song to be uttered just prior to departure for battle. For the rest, theories of enthronement and covenant renewal ceremonies have been proposed, although the evidence for either is meager. In short, reliable information about the historical context for the psalms is lacking, and in some respects this lack accords with the situation confronting readers of some other books in the Writings, specifically Job, Proverbs, Ecclesiastes, and Song of Songs.

Although we cannot reconstruct the historical setting of the psalms with confidence, we can rest assured that they represent religious views of many ages. As a matter of fact, at least two psalms (29 and 68) preserve characteristic features of Canaanite literature, suggesting that pre-Israelite traditions have found a way into the Psalter. In another instance (Psalm 104), an Egyptian hymn to the sun god has provided inspiration for the canonical psalm, perhaps mediated through the Canaanite culture (cf. also Psalm 19a). One psalm (18) is also found outside the Psalter in 2 Samuel 22, and this psalm is by no means the only one that stands in biblical books other than Psalms (cf. Exod. 15:1–18; Deut. 32; Judg. 5; 1 Sam. 2:1–10; Jon. 2:3–10; Hab. 3; and elsewhere). As for specifically Israelite material, some psalms are preexilic, others exilic, and a few postexilic.

Naturally, such diverse material does not speak with a single voice.

Perhaps the most noteworthy tension in viewpoint concerns the sacrificial cult, for some psalms openly endorse cultic ritual as a viable means of expressing the relationship between Israel and its Deity, and others criticize the sacrificial cult as an inappropriate response to the Creator of the universe. The remarkable thing is that both attitudes exist in the same book, testimony to the openness of those individuals who selected the traditions and preserved them for posterity.

ORIGIN

Precisely how did this book arise? Some have thought that it constitutes the hymnal of the Temple worship and the prayer book of ancient Israel. This is a useful way of thinking about the Psalter, because it emphasizes the function of the hymns and prayers in daily life. These psalms derive not from a single author but from many. Comprising several independent collections, they represent the accumulation of tradition over successive generations. This diversity is apparent from the fact that the names of various musical guilds are linked with minor collections, despite the tendency to attribute Israel's songs to David, a trend that seems to culminate in a Qumran composition tha credits him with 3,600 psalms and 450 songs. The oldest collection consists of Psalms 3–41, the so-called Davidic Psalter. Of these, only Psalm 33 lacks the superscription linking it to this popular king. A second collection, Psalms 42–89, makes up the Elohistic Psalter, so named because it prefers the general name for the Deity rather than the more specific Yahweh. This collection is itself composite, for it comprises several smaller groups of psalms associated with the names Korah (42–49; 84–85; 87–88), Asaph (50; 73–83), and David (51–65; 68–70). Moreover, in Ps. 72:20 a curious notation occurs, to the effect that the prayers of David are ended. Once these two major collections came together, they became the foundation on which others built (90–150). These additional psalms form clusters according to subject matter (enthronement, 93–99; hallelujah, 104–106; 111–117; 135; 146–150; ascents, 120–134) or association with David (101; 103; 108–110; 138–145). The final stage saw the composition of introductory (1–2) and concluding (150) psalms, as well as the division into five books in imitation of the Torah (I, 1–41; II, 42–72; III, 73–89; IV, 90–106; V, 107–150). Each of these books was then provided with an appropriate concluding doxology (41:13; 72:18–19; 89:52; 106:48; 150). To some extent the additions at this stage transformed the psalms into subjects for meditation and reflection. One small group of psalms stands out because of a peculiar stylistic feature, use of successive letters of the alphabet to introduce each line (9–10, 25, 34, 37, 111, 112, 119, 145). The longest psalm (119) indicates the variety with which this acrostic device was used; at the same time, it gives the impression of artificiality, as opposed to the overwhelming spontaneity elsewhere within the Psalter.

LITERARY TYPES

The chief types of literature in these five books of Psalms are well known from the ancient Near East, albeit they acquire their own peculiar characteristics in the hands of Israelite poets. Hymns, laments, songs of trust, and didactic* compositions make up the Psalter. Of course, various subgenres are readily discernible, but it seems advisable to restrict the major categories to these four. At the same time, we must allow for the possibility that the third category, songs of trust, is actually a component of the lament. In this case the main body of the lament will have disappeared, leaving only the expression of confidence that the Deity has heard the complaint, together with explicit appreciation for a favorable response to an outpouring of grief.

Hymns address the Deity in exalted language, often filled with conscious hyperbole and rhetorical flourish. Adjectives flow freely as poets try to attribute apropriate character and actions to the Creator and Redeemer. Favorite subjects in these hymns are the creation of the universe and the saving deeds that brought Israel into being and sustained it over the years. The hymns praise the Sovereign for restraining the forces of chaos, both natural and social, and they express wonder over the beauty of the natural order. However, they also focus on specific events in the nation's history when survival was assured by what was perceived to be wondrous action on the Deity's part. Of course, many of these hymns belong to the royal cult, lifting up the person of the king before the heavenly ruler and invoking divine blessing for him and his subjects. Some of these give voice to nostalgic feelings about Zion, the sacred city of David. On occasion these hymns even issue in a divine word for the earthly monarch, for it was naturally assumed that the Deity took an active interest in Israel's daily affairs. Often these hymns invite worshippers to enter into a particular cultic act, for which a reason is given, and then the main body of praise follows. Such lively celebration invites popular response in kind, and many hymns make free use of refrains that the people utter after choirs have rendered their praise in song. These hymns suggest that the people took an active part in worship, rather than sitting passively while professional leaders performed. Hymnic language may have been exaggerated, but only by means of such rhetoric could worshippers hope to express the emotions within their innermost being.

Laments were spoken by the community and by individuals. At times even first-person-singular forms may be misleading, inasmuch as the speaker may represent the larger fellowship (cf. Psalm 129). Where the king is involved, a representative function is probable, because he was widely understood as shepherd of the nation. Nevertheless, some indi-

---

*The adjective *didactic* comes from a Greek verb meaning "to teach." It refers to explicit teaching of various kinds, often moral instructions.

vidual laments are exactly that, expressions of personal distress because of sickness, economic depravity, abuse from enemies, or any number of similar undesirable situations. Public laments were often occasioned by national or local disasters such as famine, drought, invasion by enemy soldiers, earthquake, and the like. Private laments were less dramatic but no less distressing for the individual involved. By their very nature, these laments contrast present reality with memories of better days when the Deity smiled on the individual or community. Emphasis falls on the miserable conditions of the worshipper, and various kinds of appeals are voiced, sometimes coming very close to bribery (Ps. 6:5, "For in death there is no remembrance of thee;/in Sheol who can give thee praise?").

The poetic meter of funeral laments is so distinctive that it is easily recognized, whereas the remaining metrical system in the Hebrew Bible is still largely a mystery. The lament consists of three beats followed by two beats, comprising a limping meter. The structure of laments is quite simple; it consists of the complaint and a confession of confidence. The basis for the latter is unclear. Two explanations for the decisive shift from despair to trust are often put forth: a priest or prophet has given a positive answer in the Deity's name, or the worshipper takes a leap of faith. The first explanation naturally reminds one of the story about Hannah's prayer in the sanctuary at Shiloh, for here the old priest Eli gives her a reassuring oracle (1 Sam. 1:9–18).

This certainty of a hearing was so momentous that it produced its own literary type, songs of trust. The bond between worshipper and Deity was so close that it gave rise to frequent expressions of complete trust in divine goodness. These songs do not ignore the darker aspects of reality, but they subsume them under the bright light of a cherished relationship. One of these songs has eked its way into the very soul of Christendom.

> The Lord is my shepherd, I shall not want;
>   he makes me lie down in green pastures.
> He leads me beside still waters;
>   he restores my soul.
> He leads me in paths of righteousness
>   for his name's sake.
>
> Even though I walk through the valley of the shadow of death,
>   I fear no evil;
> for thou art with me;
>   thy rod and thy staff,
>   they comfort me.
>
> Thou preparest a table before me
>   in the presence of my enemies;
> thou anointest my head with oil,
>   my cup overflows.

> *Surely goodness and mercy shall follow me*
>   *all the days of my life;*
> *and I shall dwell in the house of the Lord*
>   *forever. (Ps. 23:1–6)*

The affinities between such expressions of trust and those in laments often make it difficult to discern exactly where the emphasis falls. For example, the opening sentiments in Psalm 139 resemble those in Psalm 23, although the end of the psalm identifies it as a lament. The worshipper moves from a celebration of the Deity's intimate knowledge of humans and from the impossibility of escaping divine presence to a forceful plea that those who work evil be removed from the scene.

The didactic compositions are equally difficult to recognize, and several different kinds of psalms fall into this category to some degree. These poetic compositions have teaching rather than worship as their aim, and they focus on the Torah. Using these criteria, at least three psalms belong to this type (1, 19b, 119). They consciously endeavor to meditate on the religious benefits that befall those who keep the divine statutes. These psalms view the law of Moses as a precious gift, and there is not the slightest hint that anyone thought of the Torah as a burden. Another group of three psalms is often placed in this category and labeled wisdom poetry. These are Psalms 37, 49, and 73, all of which wrestle with the vexing

The remains of the synagogue at Capernaum. The origins of synagogues remain obscure, although they must have sprung up to provide a place for studying the Torah.

problem of divine justice. The first affirms traditional belief that the universe operates according to a principle of reward and punishment, whereas the other two raise significant objections to such a simple approach to reality. The inadequacy of this fourth category is further shown by the running account of Israel's history that occurs in many psalms, for a didactic purpose must surely lie behind this particular feature. It follows that a satisfactory description of all these psalms has yet to be found, and alternatives such as wisdom psalms or learned psalmography fare no better.

AUTHORSHIP

Because the psalms arose over a long period of Israelite history, it is out of the question to attribute them to a single author. Nevertheless, an early tradition about David's musical talent sprang up, leaving its mark on the prophet Amos (6:5), on the Deuteronomistic historian or his sources (2 Sam. 1:17–27; 3:33–34; 23:1–7), and on the Chronicler. As time went by, a desire expressed itself to associate David with as many of the individual psalms as possible, even when their content often ruled out such an association. Naturally, David did not write those psalms which presuppose the existence of the Temple or which grieve over its destruction. This tendency to link David with the psalms did not result in a complete suppression of other names; as a result, a few chosen psalmists compete with David for authorship. These are Ethan and Heman, the sons of Korah; Asaph; Moses (90); and Solomon (127).

Although the earliest Jewish understanding of the expression l^{e}dawid was of authorship, modern interpreters have recognized a different meaning in the superscription. The preposition can mean "belonging to" and thus connote authorship, but it also has another sense, "pertaining to." The same preposition occurs in Canaanite literature with the names Keret, Aqhat, and Ba'al. Obviously, authorship is not being claimed in the third instance, for the reference is to deity. The meaning must be something like "pertaining to the Davidic collection." This interpretation would agree with a normal use of the preposition, namely "for." In this case the psalm was written for a particular collection that was in some way intended as a tribute to the king. In 2 Chron. 20:19 and 1 Chron. 15:16–24 there is a tradition about a guild of singers, the Korahites, along with Temple musicians and singers, Asaph, Ethan, and Heman. It is possible that the psalms linked with these professional musicians were sung by the respective Temple choir.

Inasmuch as the earliest readers of the Psalter understood the expression l^{e}dawid in terms of authorship, they endeavored to provide details about his private life that would illuminate the individual psalms. Accordingly, thirteen superscriptions give occasions in David's life when he was thought to have composed these particular psalms. For instance, the heading to Psalm 3 identifies the occasion for this lament as David's flight from his son Absalom; Psalm 34 is said to have been occasioned by David's clever pretense at madness so as to escape from Abimelech; and Psalm 51 is thought to have been prompted by Nathan's rebuke of the king for his adulterous conduct with Bathsheba. The fact that the last of these alludes to the ruined walls of Jerusalem and questions the necessity for sacrifice did not prevent this editor from connecting Psalm 51 with David and from an even more specific locating of these confessions of guilt in the king's life.

In many cases the headings to psalms contain musical notes, many of which are not fully understood today. A few of them seem straight forward: for the director or choirmaster, interlude (selah), song (mizmor), popular song (maskil), and lament (shiggayon). Others apparently refer to a particular tune ("Hind of the Dawn," "Dove on Far-off Terebinths") or musical note ("Upon the Eighth.") In some instances the headings identify certain psalms as belonging to a collection for ascents, or they link them with affirmation (amen) or shouts (hallelujah). The first group is often associated with pilgrimages to Jerusalem, but the respective psalms are strangely silent about such a journey. For this reason it seems wise to think of them as a group of psalms that were sung when priests and choirs ascended the steps in the Temple.

Because of the very nature of the material, it is virtually impossible to date most of the psalms. At best there are sufficient clues to permit an approximate dating—for example, the references to a ruined city and Temple, which require a date after 587 B.C.E. One remarkable lament looks back over the enforced residence in Babylon and recalls certain features of that unhappy period.

> By the waters of Babylon,
>   there we sat down and wept,
>   when we remembered Zion.
> On the willows there
>   we hung up our lyres.
> For there our captors
>   required of us songs,
> and our tormentors, mirth, saying,
>   "Sing us one of the songs of Zion!"
>
> How shall we sing the Lord's song
>   in a foreign land?
> If I forget you, O Jerusalem,
>   let my right hand wither!
> Let my tongue cleave to the roof of my mouth,
>   if I do not remember you,
> if I do not set Jerusalem
>   above my highest joy! (Ps. 137:1–6)

The vividness of the events surrounding the fall of Jerusalem was kept alive by the conclusion to this psalm (137:7–9), which pronounces blessing on anyone who dashes Edomite infants against rocks.

Prior to the discovery of the hymn scroll from Qumran, the trend was to date many psalms as late as possible. Some scholars even thought that a substantial number was composed during the Maccabean period in the second century B.C.E. The marked difference between canonical psalms and those from Qumran has resulted in a reverse tendency, the attempt to place many psalms in the early period of the monarchy. The Qumran hymns (hodayot) differ in many respects, but perhaps most importantly in language. In one respect, religious fervor, they rival the biblical psalms. One salutary effect of this psalm scroll has been the stifling of earlier tendencies to view "late Judaism" as characterized by dry legalism devoid of genuine spirituality. Another collection of psalms, the Psalms of Solomon, compiled during the first century B.C.E., was excluded from the canon, presumably because it was already closed. This exclusion suggests that the new trend among scholars is warranted, but it does not rule out actual composition of biblical psalms in the postexilic period, nor does it exclude redactional activity by persons associated with traditions preserved by the Chronicler.

USE

At least three primary settings of the psalms suggest an equal number of uses. These prayers and hymns were used in the Temple ritual, in royal functions, and in the private devotions of countless Israelites. Belonging to the first group are prayers on sacrificial occasions when incense and daily offerings were presented to the Deity. According to 1 Chron. 16:4–7, David appointed Asaph and his brethren to be musicians and singers in the temple worship, and by the first century C.E. certain psalms were used before daily prayer and the morning sacrifice. The Talmud links Psalms 113–118 with celebration of the Passover, and Matt. 26:30 refers to the singing of a hymn on this solemn occasion. Although the latter text does not identify the hymn as one of the psalms, such an implication seems reasonable.

Numerous psalms seem to have been specifically composed for use by the royal cult. In the life of Israel's king there were frequent occasions when he enlisted the Deity's blessing, and often these ceremonies were public. Such ceremonial occasions include the initial coronation, annual enthronements, weddings, processionals, offerings, and consulting the Deity before important military or economic ventures. Then, of course, kings addressed the Deity on behalf of the people in times of national disaster. Of special interest is the epithalamium, or wedding song, that probably celebrates Ahab's marriage to the Tyrian princess Jezebel. Here alone in the psalms is the king probably called a god (45:5). The song concludes with an address to the bride, assuring her that she will receive far more than she has left in Phoenicia.

Hear, O daughter, consider, and incline your ear;
forget your people and your father's house;
and the king will desire your beauty.
Since he is your Lord, bow to him;
the people of Tyre will sue your favor with gifts,
the richest of the people with all kinds of wealth.

The princess is decked in her chamber with gold-woven robes;
in many-colored robes she is led to the king,
with her virgin companions, her escort, in her train.
With joy and gladness they are led along
as they enter the palace of the king.

Instead of your fathers shall be your sons;
you will make them princes in all the earth.
I will cause your name to be celebrated in all generations;
therefore the peoples will praise you for ever and ever. (Ps. 45:10–17)

At least two psalms seem to have functioned as entrance liturgies (15 and 24), and the second of these is frequently linked with the story about David's removal of the ark from its temporary resting place to Jerusalem. Both psalms were probably used by officiating priests to ensure the righteousness of worshippers and, from their perspective, to protect the people from divine anger. Psalm 24 restricts admission to the sacred precincts; only those who have clean hands and a pure heart, who do not lift up their soul to what is false or swear deceitfully, can stand in the holy place (24:4).

The other entrance liturgy, Psalm 15, is clearly addressed to the ordinary citizen. Its demands are considerable, and in contrast to those in Psalm 24, they focus on human relationships (honesty, abstaining from slander, lending money without charging interest, refusing a bribe, and so forth). Like Psalm 15, many others served private citizens in their moments of prayer and praise, whether in the context of the sacrificial system or later when that form of worship was temporarily abolished. These psalms express the full range of human emotions, and some of them achieve remarkable heights of spiritual insight.

I lift up my eyes to the hills.
From whence does my help come?
My help comes from the Lord,
who made heaven and earth.

He will not let your foot be moved,
he who keeps you will not slumber.
Behold, he who keeps Israel
will neither slumber nor sleep.

> *The Lord is your keeper;*
>   *the Lord is your shade*
> *on your right hand.*
>   *The sun shall not smite you by day,*
> *nor the moon by night.*
>
>   *The Lord will keep you from all evil;*
> *he will keep your life.*
>   *The Lord will keep*
> *your going out and your coming in*
>   *from this time forth and for evermore. (Ps. 121:1–8)*

A less exalted view can be observed in the frequent cries for the return of the Deity, whose absence has permitted a triumph of wicked persons. Still other psalms meditate on the human condition and reflect on the religious heritage transmitted from parents to children. Such psalms may originally have been composed with the entire community in mind, but they were readily adapted for private use.

RELIGIOUS CONTENT

From the preceding discussion it is obvious that the spiritual content of the psalms commends them to modern readers who value ancient efforts to understand the nature of religious experience. Then, as now, competing voices vied for acceptance, and no single answer to life's anomalies silenced all alternative responses. As noted above, alongside psalms that live and breathe cultic religion stand others which view the entire sacrificial apparatus as superfluous.

> *I will accept no bull from your house,*
>   *nor he-goat from your folds.*
> *For every beast of the forest is mine,*
>   *the cattle on a thousand hills.*
> *I know all the birds of the air,*
>   *and all that moves in the field is mine.*
>
> *If I were hungry, I would not tell you;*
>   *for the world and all that is in it is mine.*
> *Do I eat the flesh of bulls,*
>   *or drink the blood of goats?*
> *Offer to God a sacrifice of thanksgiving,*
>   *and pay your vows to the Most High;*
> *and call upon me in the day of trouble;*
>   *I will deliver you, and you shall glorify me. (Ps. 50:9–15)*

In the same book some psalms endorse anthropological views that place humans just slightly below deity, and other psalms dwell on life's ephemerality.

When I look at the heavens, the work of thy fingers.
  the moon and the stars which thou hast established;
what is man that thou art mindful of him,
  and the son of man, that thou dost care for him?

Yet thou hast made him a little less than God,
  and dost crown him with glory and honor. (Ps. 8:3–5)

Lord, let me know my end,
  and what is the measure of my days;
let me know how fleeting my life is!
Behold, thou hast made my days a few handbreadths,   Selah
  and my lifetime is nothing in thy sight.
Surely every man stands as a mere breath!
  Surely man goes about as a shadow!
Surely for nought are they in turmoil;
  man heaps up, and knows not who will gather! (Ps. 39:4–6)

Whereas some psalms protest divine inactivity, others are confident that the Deity is so compassionate that the tears of the afflicted are preserved in a container (56:8) and their number is recorded in a book. While one psalmist looks back over a long life and cannot remember having seen a single instance of wicked individuals prospering (Psalm 37), another begins by affirming divine goodness to the upright but concludes by redefining the goodness of God (Psalm 73). This matchless testimony of one who found faith tested to the limit and who proceeded to purify a perplexed heart and to adjust changing beliefs to accord with experience comes very close to endorsing existence in God's presence after death.

When my soul was embittered,
  when I was pricked in heart,
I was stupid and ignorant,
  I was like a beast toward thee.
Nevertheless I am continually with thee;
  thou dost hold my right hand.
Thou dost guide me with thy counsel,
  and afterward thou wilt receive me to glory.
Whom have I in heaven but thee?
  And there is nothing upon earth that I desire besides thee.
My flesh and my heart may fail,
  but God is the strength of my heart and my portion for ever.
    (Ps. 73:21–26)

◆ 15 ◆

Job

THE conviction that the universe was governed by a rational principle of order commended itself to ancient sages, largely because
it enabled them to construct an elaborate system of thought that
seemed to make sense of reality as they perceived it. To be sure, not
every individual experience accorded with this newfound belief, but its
application to society in general was thought to confirm the principle
despite occasional flaws of minor consequence. The comforting idea of
a harmonious universe soon became axiomatic throughout the ancient
Near East. One important by-product of this axiom was the doctrine of
reward and retribution—that is, the certainty that a virtuous deed was
rewarded and a wicked act was punished. The specific manner in which
reward and punishment were believed to have taken place is unclear,
although it seems probable that direct action on the Deity's part was
envisioned. Nevertheless, some texts have seemed to suggest that the
act itself set into motion the forces appropriate to the deed, punishment
for evil and reward for virtuous acts.

This belief in reward and retribution was unable to endure the constant
questions that arose as individual worth came to be valued more and
more, nor was it adequate to explain societal revolts, the ruinous consequences of invading soldiers, or natural disasters. Slowly the dogma
gave way before sharp attack by revolutionary minds, first in Mesopotamia
and Egypt, later in ancient Israel. The resulting crisis in wisdom produced
a significant body of literature. The oldest, a Sumerian "Job," describes
the suffering of an individual and defends the deity by asserting that
humans are sinful by birth. A later version, *I Will Praise the Lord of
Wisdom*, describes the misfortunes of a Job figure and entertains the
possibility that what humans value is despised by the gods. However,
the sufferer makes proper appeal to them within the cult, and they reward
him by appearing in splendor. Healing naturally follows. A third text
from Mesopotamia is the *Babylonian Theodicy*, a dispute between a suf-

ferer and his friend. This polite acrostic has the orthodox friend concede that the deity does sometimes permit minor irritations to befall good people, whereas the sufferer moves considerably beyond this in attacking the Deity for creating humans somewhat less than perfect. Egyptian discussion literature is formally less akin to Job, but its content is similar. Essentially, this outcry complains that the gods have allowed an upheaval in society, reversing all values and causing undeserved suffering everywhere.

In Israel the crisis erupted after much dissent on the part of courageous individuals. Their voices can be heard throughout the different traditions that eventually became canonical. Much of this dissent came from the period after Jerusalem's fall when divine promises seemed to have become bankrupt. In the story about the destruction of Sodom and Gomorrah, Abraham asks whether the Judge of all earth will act justly. In another text, Gideon complains to an angel that the Lord has ceased to deal favorably with Israel. The prophet Habakkuk wonders just how long God will sit idly while wickedness thrives, and Jeremiah accuses his trusted Friend of betraying him by taking advantage of his weakness and innocence. In perhaps the most ironic touch of all, Jonah becomes angry at the Lord because Nineveh was spared as a result of repentant action. Justice, in Jonah's mind, required punishment for the evil city, and nothing, not even repentance, should get in the way of divine wrath. The Deuteronomistic historian's grand portrayal of the past was actually an attempt to respond to the crisis generated by unexpected harvests for one's labor, perhaps seen nowhere so dramatically as in Josiah's death, which must have dealt the final blow to the dogma of reward and punishment. These isolated voices seem to have achieved unison in the circle of tradition from which the Book of Job sprang.

STRUCTURE OF THE BOOK

The most striking external feature of Israel's response to a crisis within the ancient world view is the combination of prose and poetry into a single literary work. The prologue and epilogue consist of measured prose that functions as a framework for the poetry. The prose, albeit brief, introduces the problem and offers a frame of reference for the argument that follows. It resembles an envelope into which the poetry is inserted, and although the two are related, each is an entity in itself. The long poetic material comprises the bulk of the book. Distinctive viewpoints characterize the prose and the poetry. Attempts to harmonize the two have not been successful, although they have often been ingenious. In simplified form the difference in the depiction of the hero is decisive. Job in the prose is a model of patience; the poetic portrayal of Job is a defiant rebel. Other important differences follow from this, making it difficult if not impossible to understand the book as a whole. Furthermore, several additions to the poetry complicate the interpreter's task.

Prologue and Epilogue

The prologue (chapters 1–2) is made up of five scenes that alternate from earth to heaven. The opening scene introduces the hero and declares him worthy of adulation. The second scene confirms Job's virtue by having the Deity praise him as a person who is both moral and religious. The third scene puts Job to a test that consists of the loss of his possessions, including all ten children. The fourth scene has the Deity reaffirm confidence in Job's virtue despite Satan's skepticism, but a second test is granted. The fifth scene depicts the gravity of this further test when illness strikes Job's very skin and drives him away from home and friends. Job responds to his loss of possessions by continuing to praise the Deity: "Naked I came from my mother's womb, and naked shall I return; the Lord gave, and the Lord has taken away; blessed be the name of the Lord" (Job 1:21). Likewise his reaction to personal sickness and to his wife's urging that he end it all by cursing God is consistent with the earlier response: "Shall we receive good at the hand of God, and shall we not receive evil?" (2:10b). Lest anyone fail to recognize Job's exemplary conduct in these trying circumstances, the narrator conveniently absolves him of any guilt, first with a blanket statement ("In all this Job did not sin or charge God with wrong," 1:22) and after that with something a little more specific ("In all this Job did not sin with his lips," 2:10c). The prologue ends with a visit by Job's three friends, who are silent now but who will have much to say in the poetic section.

The epilogue returns to these friends and has the Deity charge them with misrepresenting the facts where God is concerned. Job's intercession stills the divine anger against them and inaugurates his own recovery and a twofold restoration of everything except sons and daughters, where the original number is thought adequate. The story ends where it began, in an idyllic land of harmony and plenty. Job has faithfully withstood both tests and in so doing has proved that righteousness does exist without thought of reward. In demonstrating disinterested righteousness he has shown that religion can survive any threat, and by his response to undeserved suffering Job has provided an example for others who find themselves in similar circumstances.

Debate

The poetic section of the Book of Job consists of a debate between Job and his three friends (chapters 3–31), a monologue by a person named Elihu (32–37), and two divine speeches, each of which provokes repentent words from Job (38–42:6). The dispute between Job and his friends

(Eliphaz, Bildad, and Zophar) lasts three rounds, although the speeches in the third cycle have been disturbed, leaving a hopelessly confused culmination to their controversy. Job begins with a curse on the day of his birth (chapter 3) and concludes with a self-imprecation calling down divine wrath on his head if he is guilty of any crime although he painstakingly denies any guilt (chapter 31). The curse resembles laments within the Psalter, and the self-imprecation has frequently been compared with negative confessions in Egyptian and Mesopotamian cultic literature. Job's argument throughout the speeches is that he is innocent of any wickedness grievous enough to warrant the suffering that has befallen him, and hence the Deity is at fault. He seems unable to decide whether God has forsaken him and cannot be found or whether the Deity has singled him out for target practice and mercilessly oppresses a faithful servant.

The friends do not press their arguments in a manner that permits one to make clear distinctions among them, except of the most superficial kind. Eliphaz seems more respectful of Job, Bildad less so, and Zophar least of all. They all agree that Job is undermining the very foundation on which their world view stands. The heat of their words derives from this awareness that a loss to Job will ultimately mean the collapse of their world. For this reason they are willing to exalt deity almost beyond human imagination; at least that is what happens when they question whether human deeds affect the Deity at all or not. Their implicit answer, sometimes explicit, is that God remains oblivious to earthly events. Eliphaz surely thinks differently, for he describes a numinous experience that terrified him at the same time that it made him aware of a spoken word from beyond: "Can mortal man be righteous before God?/Can a man be pure before his Maker?" (4:17). Nevertheless, Eliphaz uses this experience to assert the claim that humans are by nature corrupt. Such exalting of the Deity does not prevent the friends from advising Job to repent, for they are confident that such prayer will bring an end to his present misery. On one point Job and his friends possess a single mind: they take for granted the dogma of reward and punishment. Although Job openly calls it into question, his argument against the Deity loses all force once the dogma is discarded, for then the causal connection between sin and suffering is broken.

Neither Job's argument nor that of his friends progresses toward a suitable climax, although in Job's case emotional thresholds do occur. In the first he resolves to argue his case with God if it costs his life, comforted nevertheless by the belief that no sinner can stand before the Deity (13:13–16). In the second text he returns to the idea of an arbitrator, which he earlier rejected, and now seems virtually certain that the vindicator will take up his cause. A corrupt text makes it impossible to determine exactly what Job means here, whether vindication will take place at the moment of death or beyond that event (19:23–29). The background of this imagery is beyond dispute. Job thinks of the kinsman whose responsibility is to avenge the death of a family member. While Job's expression of hope has been compared to a Canaanite liturgical shout acknowledging Baal's resuscitation, and the allusion to engraving on a rock has seemed to envision a feat like that represented by the Behistun Inscription, such parallels are rivaled by the spiritual power of this confession placed in the mouth of one who has reached the end of his rope. Step by step Job has turned away from human comforters in his quest for more convincing answers to his questions. The poem in chapter 28, which marvels at human ingenuity where the search for precious minerals is concerned, denies that wisdom can be found among humans on earth or in Sheol. Only God has access to it, the poem insists; in a curious non sequitur, the final verse identifies wisdom with religious experience, which is available to everyone. Chapters 29 and 30 are almost an exercise in nostalgia. Job looks back on his former life and recalls what it was like when he was honored by one and all, and he contrasts that time with his present misery. The next chapter is his bold challenge to the Deity, by which Job hopes to force a response. The challenge takes the form of a series of oaths: if I have done such and such, then let so and so happen to me. The ethical "code" in these verses is remarkable for its concentration on social obligation, purity of thought as well as deed, and ritual purity.

Elihu's and God's Speeches

With his affirmation of innocence Job commits himself to a trial before an impartial jury. He fully expects the Deity to take the witness stand. Instead, an angry young man renews the friends' accusations against Job that have already worn his patience thin (chapters 32–37). Repeating many of their words and phrases, Elihu makes one point in various ways. Suffering for which there is no suitable explanation is sent by the Deity as a test. Of course the purpose of such tests, in Elihu's thinking, is to refine character and to educate the suffering individual. In due time the Almighty does appear to Job, and as the mere mortal had suspected, the effect is terrifying beyond words. The Deity addresses Job with some questions, as if he were a schoolboy, and challenges him to answer. Moreover, the voice from the tempest inquires whether Job, who has presumed to criticize the way the universe is currently operating, can govern it himself. The divine speeches do not address a single issue that Job has singled out for discussion. Instead, they celebrate the wonders of nature, many of which have nothing to do with human beings. Job wishes to discuss the issue of justice; the Deity talks about power. Naturally, Job surrenders before such an awesome display and confesses his smallness, which was never at issue. At this point divine speech continues, this time singing the majestic powers of the hippopotamus and croc-

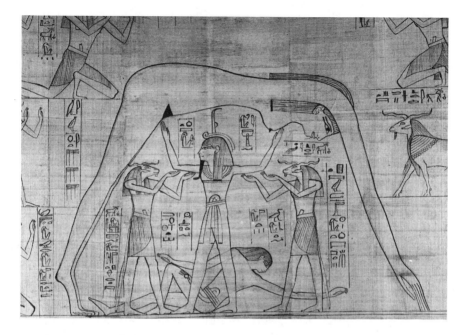

This vignette on a copy of the "Book of the Dead" shows the sky goddess Nut as the heavens arched over earth and being supported by the air god Shu, while Geb, the earth god, lies at his feet.

odile, which seem to be visible representations of the mythological chaos monster that appears in hymnic literature throughout the ancient Near East. Once more Job dares to respond, and this time he claims that his previous knowledge of Deity was derivative, whereas the immediacy of sight characterizes his newfound knowledge. Therefore, he despises himself and repents in dust and ashes. He who launched the poem with a curse has ended it with fresh awareness of his finitude. The one who boldly marched into divine presence has now lost all pretensions to titanism. But Job still has no answer to the problem with which he began this dangerous journey.

AUTHORSHIP

The preceding survey of the contents of the Book of Job acknowledges its composite nature. The first decision any interpreter must make concerns the authorship of the narrative account. Did the author of the poetry write this prose framework? Three possibilities are often entertained: the poet wrote the story; the poet borrowed it and adapted the account for his purpose, or a later author inserted the prose into the poet's finished

work. The differences between the prose and poetry render a claim of
unitary authorship highly suspect. Besides the difference in style, the
presentation of Job as submissive in the story and defiant in the poem
is decisive for many interpreters. Other important differences, such as
the names for Deity, the orientation of the author, and the patriarchal
setting of the story, point to different ages of composition and different
authors. On the other hand, the poem requires some stage setting; otherwise, it begins in the middle of things without sufficient explanation
for the lament or the dispute. This necessity for an explanatory framework
rules out the third option. It follows that the second alternative offers
the best explanation of the facts. The poet used an old story to introduce
the problem to be treated in the poetic dispute.

There are signs that this story has undergone considerable development. First of all, it appears that the earliest version did not know about
the second test, Job's illness, because the epilogue ignores this fact completely. Second, the story seems to confuse visits by Job's relatives and
by his three friends. It is therefore probable that the relatives originally
played the role of temptors. Third, the earliest version would not have
mentioned the Satan figure, which first appears in the sixth century B.C.E.
Some features of the story are quite old, and this fact accords with the
choice of the name Job, which occurs alongside Noah and Daniel in
Ezekiel 14, where ancient heroes are mentioned. Like Dan'el, which is
found in Canaanite texts, the name Job is well known in the ancient
world. Furthermore, the description of Job's possessions in the prologue
and the mention of a *qesitah* (coin) in the epilogue, as well as Job's role
in offering sacrifices, are either indications of antiquity or evidence of
conscious archaizing on the author's part.

The poetic composition also gives evidence of multiple authorship.
In the three cycles of debates, certain hymnic passages have often been
viewed with suspicion, but there is no compelling reason to exclude them
from the original poem, with the possible exception of 9:5–10. Entirely
different is chapter 28, the exquisite hymn about wisdom's inaccessibility.
The poem anticipates the answer in the divine speeches and therefore
seems inappropriate in its present position, and it has a different understanding of wisdom from that of the poet who composed the rest of
the book. Because the friends believe that they have access to theological
wisdom, this poem cannot represent a lost speech by one of them, nor
can it be their summary argument. Some interpreters have sought to retain
the poem as original by ascribing a psychological purpose to it. In their
view, the hymn serves as a sort of interlude between the end of the debate
between Job and his friends, and the initial challenge to God (chapters
29–31). The poem therefore emphasizes the failure of human wisdom
and points forward to the true source of wisdom from whom Job will
shortly hear much.

The Elihu material (chapters 32–37) is usually taken as secondary, largely because he is ignored in the divine speeches and in the framework. Besides, Elihu marches onto the stage precisely when the poem has dramatically prepared for the Deity's appearance. On the basis of Elihu's familiarity with the argument in the three cycles of debates, one can safely conclude that the author of chapters 32–37 had access to the earlier poem and modeled Elihu's speeches on them. Assessments of his contribution vary from high praise to scorn; those critics who fall into the latter category are largely offended by Elihu's bombastic rhetoric and inflated ego. Others attribute less significance to the manner in which he speaks than to the essential message within the rhetorical flourish, which they attribute to brash youth. For these interpreters, Elihu offers an important response to the question that Job has raised: suffering purifies and is educational. Some scholars think that the poet of the book composed the Elihu materials later and inserted them into the original composition. The actual differences in style and thought between the original poem and the later supplement are then explained as the natural consequence of time's passage.* The alternative approach to the Elihu speeches accords better with what is known about the handling of texts in ancient Israel. Accordingly, a later traditionist sought to address Job's problem from the standpoint of a subsequent era, when sacred texts were quoted and commented upon in light of the community's faith.

The existence of two divine speeches and two responses by Job is somewhat disconcerting, especially because the second address by the Deity seems like carping and because Job's vow to speak only once is quickly broken. Within the divine speeches the descriptions of the hippopotamus and crocodile do not conform to the style of the other references to creatures of the wild. This difference may indicate that these two poems are secondary, and the addition of a second divine speech produced the necessity for two responses by Job.

Literary Types

It seems likely, therefore, that several hands have contributed to the final form of the book. Any attempt to discover a single literary category to describe the complete work seems destined to fail, for the book is unique. In its external form, it resembles other literary compositions in the ancient world. If the prose and poetry are taken together, the book is best characterized as a disputation. In the disputation form, a prose narrative introduces a problem, which is then treated in debate form, and a resolution is ultimately given by a deity. On the other hand, if one considers the poem in isolation, the category of lament accurately describes the initial

---

*An example from modern times has been cited, namely Johann Wolfgang von Goethe's *Faust*. The two parts of this masterpiece were written about fifty years apart by the same poet. However, the subject matter also affected the style of the two parts significantly, so the issue is complex indeed.

dialogue. Further precision is also possible, inasmuch as parallels to Job from the ancient Near East function as a model of an answered lament. The purpose of such compositions is to offer examples for others who find themselves engulfed in suffering for which there is no suitable explanation. By studying these texts, the individual discovers appropriate responses to suffering and thus profits from the experience of others.

Although dispute and lament are the categories that apply to the larger composition, these two literary types by no means exhaust the possibilities for describing the smaller units within the book. These subgenres include hymns, lawsuits, nature wisdom, a theophany (divine self-manifestation), and an oath of innocence. Even within the dialogue that constitutes the dispute there are proverbial sayings, impossible questions, and other types of wisdom. The final solution to the problem with which Job wrestles mightily comes from traditional Israelite faith rather than from rational thought typical of the sages. In reality, then, the book draws upon literary types from many different circles: legal, prophetic, wisdom, and so forth. Furthermore, the author demonstrates a knowledge of international wisdom but exercizes individual initiative in composing a poem that can only be explained on its own terms.

Date

Where and when did the author live? The book is set in patriarchal times somewhere to the east, presumably in Edom. The problem and the manner of dealing with it point to the exilic or postexilic period, when the individual moved into the forefront to a greater degree then in earlier times. The language is rich in Aramaisms, and while this feature is no clear proof of lateness, it does strengthen the case already being formed on the basis of perspective. The experience of the exile seems to lie behind the powerful laments, some of which may treat Job as representing the nation's extreme suffering. The Satan figure coincides with the early development of this notion in the late sixth century, when an office or function is envisioned rather than a proper name. In addition, the rigid insistence on a rational principle behind the order of the universe, which furnishes the intellectual position with which the author takes issue, seems to have hardened in the way other texts describe it to have done in the sixth century. All of this suggests a date for the poem in the late sixth or early fifth century.

Indications of the actual home of the author are inferential, at best. The references to marshes and their flora and fauna point to Egypt for this material, but such descriptions of the crocodile and hippopotamus are part of international wisdom. The use of the divine name Eloah is associated with Teman in northwest Arabia, but this, too, may result from the author's desire to put the hero in a bygone era before the name Yahweh was known, according to the viewpoint reflected in the Priestly source. Furthermore, non-Israelites were supposed to avoid the special name for the Deity. It is interesting that the Septuagint links Job with Jobab, king of Edom, mentioned in Gen. 36:33, and that Lam. 4:21 associates Uz with Edom. In all probability the Israelite author of the book of Job chose Edom as the setting for this poem because of its reputation as a center of wisdom.

TEACHING

The author addresses two aspects of a single problem; one is theoretical and the other is practical. The first concerns the problem of theodicy—that is, the question of divine justice. The second deals with the way in which one responds to suffering. In essence these are the fundamental questions of reality: can faith survive in a world where assurances of rational order have vanished, and what is the appropriate behavioral response in such a harsh environment? What answers to these two questions does the author offer?

Divine Justice

To begin with, the poet refuses to subscribe to the axiom that wisdom governs the world in a rational manner that humans can recognize through use of reason. This claim, which lay at the heart of the intellectual endeavor undertaken by the sages, is held up to close scrutiny and discarded as a lie. Job refuses to submit to a doctrine that his own experience contradicts. In insisting that personal experience is the ultimate criterion of truth, he exalts individual insight over impersonal collective theory. The friends demonstrate the cruel extremes to which theory divorced from actual experience may go. Although Job's abandoning of the comforting theory comes slowly and at considerable price, in the end he sees clearly the utter impossibility of ascribing justice to reality as he knows it. At last when the Deity breaks the oppressive silence, Job's understanding of the situation remains unscathed, for nothing in the speeches seems directed at restoring Job's confidence in divine justice. In short, the dominant theme of these speeches is the inscrutable divine act, and here lies a direct link with the character of the Deity's conduct in the prose narrative. The sovereign of the universe is not subject to human ideas about what constitutes justice. This is the message that the poet proclaims with unusual force.

Once the poet abandons belief in an orderly universe and recognizes the inevitable presence of an inscrutable factor in all of reality, a further issue rises to haunt serious inquiry. Is it possible to retain faith in Deity any longer? Perhaps a better formulation of the issue is less theoretical: given the unpredictable character of the Deity, can obedient faith survive? The answer which the poet gives to this question is a resounding yes, but this response leaves the realm of rational thought in favor of irrational paradox. Job's submission before a questioning Deity can hardly satisfy anyone who subscribes to the sufficiency of the intellect in resolving the human dilemma. Indeed, his confession that all previous knowledge of the Deity was secondhand scarcely harmonizes with the assertions about him in the story or with his own authentic memory within the poetry. If the poet directs his message to the learned representatives of wisdom, as seems likely because of the nature of the problem being examined and the presuppositions that come under attack, they must surely have found the final answer inadequate. The surrender of faith cannot be submitted to intellectual analysis and is therefore philosophically unsatisfactory.

To judge from the nature of the poet's argument, it seems likely that the horizon of wisdom informed the world from which he spoke. In other words, the author belonged to the intellectual group whose teachings are pronounced bankrupt. If this statement is indeed true, it suggests that the author of the book came to prefer the irrational dimension of reality when discussing divine activity and its repercussions for humans. For this unknown poet the power of faith transformed mystery into a relationship with deity that acknowledged divine sovereignty and human transience. In effect, the problem of theodicy is given up, and at the same time humans are assured that they may bring their doubts and even accusations before the Sovereign One, confident that such daring thoughts will not call down the wrath of God on them. However, they are given no assurance that answers will be forthcoming. Quite the contrary, for in the final analysis Job does not receive a single answer to his relentless questioning.

Response to Suffering

The other problem that the Book of Job takes up is more practical, and therefore it is one for which a definite answer can be found. Given the arbitrary way in which the universe operates, undeserved suffering strikes most people sooner or later. What should their response be when this unwelcome guest arrives? The book considers various answers to this question, for Job's friends and Elihu have definite views on this score. As it turns out, Job's final submission is exactly what the friends encouraged him to do. In a word, confess your sins and submit to God's sovereign will. But Job's conduct offers yet another response to the question, and the poet seems to have recommended this sort of action as well. Job pours out his soul to the Deity. To be sure, he does this in anger and desperation, but he directs his dark thoughts to God. The implications of such boldness are mind-boggling, for his courage springs from a conviction that a relationship with Deity permits honest expression of feelings and thoughts regardless of their nature.* Nevertheless, the poet carefully avoids any hint that Job could always depend on the Deity to answer when summoned, for presumption based on personal relationships can result in a dogma that enslaves Deity just as readily as presumption about the operation of a principle of reward and punishment.

*This issue has recently come to the fore in theological discusssion. See my *A Whirlpool of Torment* (Philadelphia: Fortress Press, 1984), Robert Davidson, *Courage to Doubt* (Philadelphia: S.C.M., 1983); and Sam E. Balentine, *The Hiddenness of God* (Oxford: Oxford University Press, 1983).

• 16 •

Proverbs

THE Hebrew word *m^eshalim*, usually translated "proverbs," covers a wide range of sayings. It is used to designate similitudes, popular sayings, literary aphorisms, taunt songs, bywords, allegories, discourses, and much more. The meaning of the root *mshl* seems to suggest that similitude or likeness was the original connotation, although some interpreters have preferred the sense of "a ruling word," that is, "a powerful expression." Its use to represent the diverse sayings in the Book of Proverbs is naturally an extended one, for there are actually very few pure proverbs in this large collection. Alongside brief statements that ring true and linger in the memory once they have achieved poetic form, lengthy discourses and conscious instruction abound. This remarkable formal difference points to more than one setting for these sayings.

If we begin with the simple truth statement and seek to recover its original setting, we are obliged to consider the presuppositions of those who took an active interest in coining witty observations about reality. For them the secrets of the universe itself lay hidden within nature and in the ordinary events of life. These valuable mysteries were put there by the Creator as a gesture of good will, and as a further act of kindness the universe was attuned to these secrets. The lucky persons who discovered these hidden secrets thereby achieved harmony with the order of the world. An obvious consequence of this success in ferreting out life's mysteries was happiness, for such good things as health, children, wealth, honor, and length of days followed. The wish to live in harmony with divine order was a religious and ethical impulse, rather than mere self-interest. Those individuals who spurned the attempt to find the hidden insights and who refused to profit from others' discoveries were not simply fools; they were also wicked, because they undermined the order of society and nature itself.

KINDS OF FOOLS

The sages took great care to identify wicked persons and to distinguish various kinds of fools. Their terminology is rich indeed, and this variety must have evolved from considerable study and reflection. In all, eight different kinds of fools are mentioned in the Book of Proverbs.

1. *pethi*—a naive, untutored individual
2. *k^esil*—a person who is innately stupid
3. *'^ewil*—one who is persistently obstinate
4. *sakal*—one who persists in folly
5. *ba'ar*—a crude individual
6. *nabal*—a brutal, depraved person
7. *holel*—an irrational madman
8. *lets*—an inveterate talker who values his opinions excessively

The first of these presented an opportunity for those sages who desired to test their own persuasive power, inasmuch as the untutored individual simply lacked exposure to learning. Like an innocent and inexperienced youth, this person was vulnerable to influence from companions, whether for good or ill. For the other seven kinds of fools the wise had nothing but contempt, which they freely dispensed in their sayings.

TYPES OF KNOWLEDGE

The discovery of hidden truths and the application of these insights to daily experience was by no means a simple task. The fundamental means for achieving this knowledge was analogy. By studying nature and human behavior, one arrived at certain insights about the way things worked, but these perceptions had to be transferred from one realm to another on the assumption that what was true in nature was equally true in society. Moreover, just as there was a spatial transfer, so a temporal one also seemed appropriate. If an insight was true in a past generation, it must also be valid for the present. The recognition of legitimate analogies required extensive observation, tabulation of initial impressions, and the drawing of conclusions. A first stage seems to have been the mere listing of items that resembled one another in some way; eventually this approach produced a branch of knowledge known as onomasticons (noun lists), the forerunner of modern encyclopedias. Although this phase of the sages' enterprise is well represented in ancient Egypt and Mesopotamia, it has contributed only scattered sayings among the canonical proverbs.

Once the sages compiled sufficient data with which to work, they set about trying to recognize patterns that seemed to recur in similar circumstances. The next step was to express that relationship in poetic language that was easily remembered. In time a third stage came to dominate the thought of the sages, now teachers. That was the furnishing of powerful reinforcements for the sayings, which therefore brought about a radical transformation of truth statements to instructions or which more often resulted in the actual substitution of exhortation and warnings for simple observations about the way things appeared to be. It is possible that the two kinds of sayings, truth statement and instruction, arose in total isolation from one another. If this assessment of the situation is correct it would demand separate settings for each. Although it may be somewhat misleading if pressed, the association of truth statements with popular composition and instructions with professional teachers may possess merit.

Mastery of language was essential both to formulate a truth statement that would capture the hearer's imagination and to produce a persuasive instruction. Rhetoric therefore came into play wherever individuals sought to cope with everyday affairs and to assist others in that enterprise. Four components characterized ancient rhetoric: the right word, the correct moment, truth, and restraint. Eloquence alone did not suffice for the right word, inasmuch as some circumstances called for silence. No words, however soothing, would assuage a grieving heart, and no response to a fool would escape a trap laid by wielders of opposing proverbs (the sage has either stooped to the level of the opponent or has allowed a fool to have the last word, Prov. 26:4–5). It was therefore necessary to study the situation before speaking and to choose the opportune moment for reply.

> To make an apt answer is a joy to a man,
>   and a word in season, how good it is! (Prov. 15:23)
>
> A word fitly spoken
>   is like apples of gold in a setting of silver. (Prov. 25:11)

One's manner of speaking sometimes provided a valuable clue about character, particularly when accompanied by telltale bodily movements.

> A worthless person, a wicked man,
>   goes about with crooked speech,
> winks with his eyes, scrapes with his feet,
>   points with his finger,
> with perverted heart devises evil,
>   continually sowing discord . . . . (Prov. 6:12–14)

The last two elements of rhetoric, truth and restraint, indicate the sages' conviction that character was essential to powerful speech. The word had to be trustworthy, and truthful words flowed from the mouths of honest persons. In their understanding of reality, only truth arrived safely into harbor and escaped the normal process of decay (1 Esd. 4:38–41).

In addition, the word had to be modest, one that avoided extremes of passion or intellectual claim.

LIMITS TO KNOWLEDGE

The need to be modest is significant for yet another reason. From earliest times, it seems, the sages recognized that the Deity had imposed certain limits to what could be known. This important reminder of divine freedom does not appear to have evoked consternation among those who first observed its effects for human actions, although later thinkers like the authors of Job and Ecclesiastes certainly registered dismay over their inability to find absolute certainty. How different are the sayings in the Book of Proverbs that draw attention to the incalculable aspects in all human affairs!

> No wisdom, no understanding, no counsel,
>   can avail against the Lord.
> The horse is made ready for the day of battle,
>   but the victory belongs to the Lord. (Prov. 21:30–31)
>
> A man's steps are ordered by the Lord;
>   how then can man understand his way? (Prov. 20:24)

In every situation there is the possibility that the best laid plans may go awry, and these sayings merely acknowledge this fact.

Because communicating insights to others was of enormous importance to sages, they naturally developed sophisticated means of achieving their goal. Besides formulating strong supporting arguments positively (exhortations) and negatively (warnings), they fashioned a wide range of persuasive devices in which puns, rhetorical questions, anecdote, allegory, imagined speech, humor, satire, and so much more found free expression. Above all, they seized the opportunity to reinforce their teachings by means of religious sentiment. Hence, they promised divine favor for one way of life and threatened those who opted for the opposite mode of conduct with the Deity's swift punishment. In what was perhaps their most effective stroke of fortune, the sages developed the idea of wisdom as a desirable woman who actively sought to win the affections of young men. Of course, this manner of thinking opened the door for imagining an opponent, folly, who seduced her suitors and led them to the grave.

The Book of Proverbs comprises the final product of this intellectual enterprise in ancient Israel, except for scattered sayings in Ecclesiastes and Job. As we shall subsequently see, Sirach (Ecclesiasticus) represents a significant transition within Israelite wisdom, despite his use of sayings that resemble those in Proverbs. Even where the two books contain sayings that are similar in form and content, there is always one decisive difference. The Book of Proverbs is the product of many thinkers, whereas Ecclesiasticus derives from a single teacher, Jesus son of Sirach. That information is important in view of Sirach's pride of authorship, which is wholly absent from the canonical writings.

COLLECTIONS

Headings within the Book of Proverbs identify at least seven separate collections, and there are actually more than that.

1. Chapters 1–9, The Proverbs of Solomon, son of David, king of Israel
2. 10:1–22:16, The Proverbs of Solomon
3. 22:17–24:22, The Sayings of the Wise
4. 24:23–34, More Sayings of the Wise
5. Chapters 25–29, More Proverbs of Solomon transcribed by the men of Hezekiah, king of Judah
6. 30:1–33, Sayings of Agur son of Jakeh from Massa
7. 31:1–31, Sayings of Lemuel, king of Massa, which his mother taught him

In all likelihood, the first heading is intended for the entire book; an earlier heading may have dropped out at this time, unless the same person who wrote 1:1 also compiled the initial collection of sayings in chapters 1–9. The second and third collections each contain two sections with different authors, if differences in form imply separate authorship. Chapters 10–15 stand together in form, whereas 16:1–22:16 makes up a distinct group of sayings. Similarly, 22:17–23:11 differs markedly from 23:12–24:22. Again, the fifth collection seems to comprise two separate ones, chapters 25–27 and 28–29. Collections 6 and 7 are equally composite, although in the first of these it is difficult to know where Agur's words end (verse 14 at the latest, but probably verse 4, to which a corrective supplement has been attached). A clear break occurs in chapter 31 after verse 9, and the alphabetic poem in verses 10–31 is obviously an entity in itself.

Solomon as a Sage

The overwhelming majority of these sayings is attributed to Solomon, although two non-Israelite authors, Agur and Lemuel's mother, are credited with minor contributions. The latter fact is remarkable only if one ignores the international context of wisdom literature. As for the attribution of the major collections to Solomon, this phenomenon merely continues a trend that we have noticed with regard to the Torah and Psalms where Moses and David are credited with the respective collections of tradition. In the Psalms, alternative authorship for individual sections is also granted, and that statement is true of Proverbs as well. The tradition that Solomon composed proverbs and songs is preserved in First Kings:

> He also uttered three thousand proverbs; and his songs were a thousand and five. He spoke of trees, from the cedar that is in Lebanon to the hyssop that grows out of the wall; he spoke also of beasts, and of birds, and of reptiles, and of fish. (1 Kings 4:32–33)

The astonishing thing about this tradition is the lack of congruity between the content of the sayings within the Solomonic collections and the subject matter described in this narrative account. Only a small number of sayings have anything to do with trees, beasts, birds, reptiles, and fish.

We are on firmer ground when attempting to evaluate the reliability of the allusion to certain functionaries during King Hezekiah's reign (second half of the eighth century). It is conceivable that this tradition arose in those circles that created the legendary material about this king that is preserved in the Book of Isaiah, but the existence of a scribal profession at Hezekiah's court is entirely possible. The content of Proverbs 25–29 does nothing to detract from this supposition, for this collection seems to house some of the oldest material in the entire book. Another collection that rivals it in antiquity must be 10:1–22:16, and it is difficult to determine which of the two is earlier. The two foreign collections may be even older, if the similarities with Canaanite literature offer a clue for dating these sayings.

The latest collection is certainly chapters 1–9, which reveal considerable development in form and in content. Brief essays appear in which a truth statement sometimes reinforces the argument (1:8–19, where verse 17 contains the supporting argument), or a rhetorical question functions as a declarative statement (6:20–35, where verses 27–28 make a forceful point). The first of these warns against associating with undesirable companions and argues that a trap that is openly visible to the intended victim will naturally catch nothing. The second text asks young men to consider two flames, the indispensable light of parental instruction and the destructive fire of lust. The danger of misdirected passion is then brought out with unforgettable clarity.

> Can a man carry fire in his bosom
> and his clothes not be burned?
> Or can one walk upon hot coals
> and his feet not be scorched? (Prov. 6:27–28)

This initial collection also shows an advancement in the area of religious reflection, particularly the elevation of piety as the presupposition and goal of knowledge and the personification of wisdom as an agent of creation and communicator of life.

Because of the diverse nature of the separate collections, it is necessary to examine them one by one before attempting a general analysis of the book. A consideration of formal aspects of each collection, as well as specific content, will enable one to extract dominant themes that occur in a single collection or throughout the book. This process in turn may give some clues about various settings for this literature and about the individuals who composed and preserved these sayings.

The first collection opens with an introduction that applies to the entire book (1:2–7). The religious character of this initial collection sets it apart, as do conscious efforts to persuade youngsters through brief essays. The didactic purpose is particularly visible in the numerous rhetorical devices employed: anecdote, allegory-like images, rhetorical questions, direct address ("my son"), and vivid description. A dominant mood surfaces as a result of constant warnings against an adulteress, and the attractiveness of her blandishments is scarcely concealed from young eyes. For example, a brief description of Dame Folly demonstrates her amazing facility with seductive phrases when it has her say: "Stolen water is sweet,/and bread eaten in secret is pleasant" (9:17). The instructions in this collection return to the theme of the foreign woman again and again, leaving the impression that the young people for whom these teachings were intended needed constant warning lest they fall into her pit. The picture of Dame Wisdom as architect of an unusual banquet hall and her special role prior to creation find no point of contact with the sayings in the other collections.

The second major collection (10:1–22:16) is less easily described because it consists of discrete sayings that are complete in themselves. Rarely do these one-line statements give evidence of conscious arrangement into larger units, except in the broadest sense possible. For instance, chapters 10–15 prefer antithetic parallelism ("A soft answer turns away wrath,/but a harsh word stirs up anger," 15:1) whereas 16:1–22:16 has a relatively equal number of synonymous, antithetic, and synthetic parallelisms. Only one saying of the 375 in this collection departs from the two-line form, and it has three lines (19:7). The scope of these sayings is as wide as life itself, but a few recurring topics are pride, laziness, passion, deceit, gossip, and their opposites. Here and there similitudes occur ("Like a gold ring in a swine's snout/is a beautiful woman without discretion," 11:22), as well as "better" sayings ("Better is a dry morsel with quiet/than a house full of feasting with strife," 17:1).

To some degree the third collection (22:17–24:22) resembles the first. Egyptian influence is widely acknowledged in both. It includes the notion of righteousness as the foundation of the throne; the picture of wisdom holding life in one hand, riches and honor in the other; the garland on the head; personified wisdom; the goddess (Ma'at) who played at creation; and much more that is also found in chapters 1–9. Egyptian wisdom has also contributed eleven sayings from *The Instruction of Amenemope* in 22:17–24:22 and, of course, the introduction to the borrowed material, 22:7–21. Brief paragraph units emerge in this third collection, and direct address returns to prominence, after being almost completely absent in 10:1–22:16. Unlike the second collection, the third seldom uses the various types of parallelism, preferring exquisite metaphors. In one extended essay the plight of drunkards is described with great pathos (23:29–35).

The fourth collection (24:23–34) lacks parallelism except for verses 30, 32, and 34, but it employs both exhortation and admonition. It displays a relationship with the first collection in that a brief saying from 6:10–11 is used as a traditionally sanctioned message that reinforces an anecdote denouncing laziness.

> *I passed by the field of a sluggard*
> *by the vineyard of a man without sense;*
> *and lo, it was all overgrown with thorns;*
> *the ground was covered with nettles,*
> *and its stone wall was broken down.*
> *Then I saw and considered it;*
> *I looked and received instruction,*
> *"A little sleep, a little slumber,*
> *a little folding of the hands to rest,"*
> *and poverty will come upon you like a robber,*
> *and want like an armed man. (Prov. 24:30–34)*

The fifth collection (chapters 25–29) resembles the second in its fondness for antithetic parallelism but strikes out on its own in its use of comparative statements. These similitudes draw freely from society at large and demonstrate keen powers of perception.

> *Like clouds and wind without rain*
> *is a man who boasts of a gift he does not give. (Prov. 25:14)*

> *Like snow in summer or rain in harvest,*
> *so honor is not fitting for a fool. (Prov. 26:1)*

> *Like a roaring lion or a charging bear*
> *is a wicked ruler over a poor people. (Prov. 28:15)*

A noteworthy feature of this collection is its occasional observations about kings. Because the entire collection is said to have been copied at the royal court, one would naturally expect to find frequent sayings that apply specifically to this setting. Such is by no means the case, although there are some significant sayings of this nature.

> *It is the glory of God to conceal things,*
> *but the glory of kings is to search things out.*
> *As the heavens for height, and the earth for depth,*
> *so the mind of kings is unsearchable. (Prov. 25:2–3; cf. verses 4–7)*

The sixth collection (30:1–33) juxtaposes skeptical reflections about human knowledge and faith assertions that culminate in a devout prayer.

The collection also brings together several numerical sayings about un-quenchable thirst, phenomena that defy explanation, situations in which certain persons become intolerable, small things that achieve unexpected results, and proud parading by humans and animals. Near the center lies a striking description of a wanton woman.

> *This is the way of an adulteress:*
> *she eats, and wipes her mouth,*
> *and says, "I have done no wrong." (Prov. 30:20)*

The final collection (31:1–31) resembles Egyptian instructions to a ruler, and the emphasis on royal justice echoes a common theme throughout the ancient Near East. The Queen Mother's manner of in-struction comes very close to harangue, but intimate language corrects that impression. Two subjects occupy her mind: sexual misconduct and drunkenness. The alphabetic poem celebrating the virtues of a good wife brings the entire book to a fitting close. Some interpreters have under-stood this poem as praise of Dame Wisdom, although there is no explicit reference to the woman who appeared with such frequency in the initial collection. This unusual poem must surely function as a corrective to the somewhat negative picture of women drawn by many of the sayings throughout the book. This celebrated wife's reputation is wholly secular until the very end, where a religious note erupts: "Charm is deceitful and beauty is vain,/ but a woman who fears the Lord is to be praised" (31:30). Perhaps a choice between the two understandings of this poem is unnecessary. It may praise both Dame Wisdom and virtuous women of exceptional skill and industry. In any event, the poem acknowledges that many women have done excellently, a point that deserves to be highlighted.

THEMES

Because the individual sayings in these collections arose over a long period of time and in diverse circumstances, differences of viewpoint and interest have naturally manifested themselves. Furthermore, to some extent the final editor shaped the overall content of the book by providing an introduction and an initial collection in which certain themes recur frequently. Although the most prominent themes, the fear of the Lord and personified wisdom, recede into the background after the first col-lection, memory of them persists in readers' minds after they have turned to entirely different content. It is difficult, therefore, to recover earlier themes that may have possessed equal cogency. Perhaps a clue that will assist in this search lies concealed in the images for wisdom and folly. The goal of understanding was life, and the end of ignorance was death. Hence these sayings and instructions speak about a way of life or a path leading to life, and alternatively they envision a tree of life. Of course, there is an opposite path that leads to destruction. The wise travel along the former path, and fools walk on the latter. Stated another way, the righteous go on the way to life, and the wicked crowd the path to destruction.

It is certain that the sages acknowledged the reality of death for everyone, good or evil. They did not overlook the fact that all people actually close their eyes in death. Moreover, they did not believe that survival in Sheol was anything but an unenviable state. What, then, did they mean by insisting that wisdom enabled one to find life whereas ignorance resulted in death? Life and death must function symbolically for them. To obtain life means to surround oneself with those things that enhance well-being: a good name, respectable family, good health, and adequate wealth. Those individuals who chose death opted for a pattern of behavior that endangered themselves and others. Such wicked persons inflicted suffering on innocent ones and brought about their own premature demise. Lacking honor, they sowed discord in their own household as well as in others, and they were punished in their bodies and also with loss of possessions.

With this understanding of reality the sages set out to make a necessary distinction between two opposing standards of conduct, but they inevitably oversimplified things. Believing that the Deity rewarded virtue and punished vice in the present life, the sages naturally thought one could tell at a glance whether an individual were wise or foolish. By and large, the criteria for divine blessing were thought to be visible to the naked eye, and the same was true of the means by which to recognize a reprobate. Over the years this insight was pushed to the limit, and little room was left for exceptional cases, despite the important admission that the human mind could grasp only partial truth. The need to clarify their own standing compared with a societal group that rejected their way of life seems to have produced considerable thought and many observations in the literature that has survived.

Observation of Reality

There is little doubt that the sages valued certain kinds of conduct: obedience to one's parents, self-control, generosity, and humility. They had contempt for the opposite types of behavior: disrespect for parents, a hot temper, refusal to help others, pride. In their effort to recommend the path to life and to discredit its opposite, the wise carefully observed everyday life and drew lessons from experience. Often these descriptions of conduct, whether commendable or otherwise, possess unusual objectivity.

One man gives freely, yet grows all the richer;
*   another withholds what he should give, and only suffers want. (Prov. 11:24)*

From the fruit of his words a man is satisfied with good,
  and the work of man's hand comes back to him. (Prov. 12:14)

One man pretends to be rich, yet has nothing;
  another pretends to be poor, yet has great wealth.
The ransom of a man's life is his wealth,
  but a poor man has no means of redemption. (Prov. 13:7–8)

The poor is disliked even by his neighbor,
  but the rich has many friends. (Prov. 14:20)

A worker's appetite works for him;
  his mouth urges him on. (Prov. 16:26)

A man's gift makes room for him
  and brings him before great men. (Prov. 18:16)

The poor use entreaties,
  but the rich answer roughly. (Prov. 18:23)

"It is bad, it is bad," says the buyer;
  but when he goes away, then he boasts. (Prov. 20:14)

The glory of young men is their strength,
  but the beauty of old men is their gray hair. (Prov. 20:29)

The rich rules over the poor,
  and the borrower is the slave of the lender. (Prov. 22:7)

Presumably, such observations about human nature were at first morally neutral, although they would have participated in the presuppositions of those who shaped their form and content. It is conceivable that their inclusion in the collection attributed to Solomon has altered their impact in some measure, and the moralizing tone of the initial collection has carried this refashioning by context even further. Nevertheless, these brief observations still have a distinctive character that is all the more remarkable because of the "secular" atmosphere pervading the sayings.

Education

By far the majority of sayings consciously sought to provide the way of life that the sages subscribed to and to discredit its opposite. At the forefront of their discussion lies the notion of obedience. That includes two fundamentally different types of authority to which sages subjected themselves. One was parental authority; the other was divine sovereignty. However, the two were often intertwined, for parents enjoined their children to be faithful in religious observance as well as to perform ordinary duties within a household. Responsibility toward parents lasted until their death, and did not disappear simply because the years brought shortness of temper or physical frailty. The effectiveness of the right start in life was taken for granted: "Train up a child in the way he should go,/ and when he is old he will not depart from it" (22:6).

Proper training of children included generous use of physical punishment. The familiar aphorism, "Spare the rod and spoil the child," seems to have led to much corporal punishment, both at home and at school. Abundant evidence exists for the use of whippings in Egyptian and Mesopotamian schools, and although Israelite literature is almost totally silent with regard to schools, many interpreters have plausibly assumed their existence in Israel. In any event the sages certainly believed that the whip was effective in reinforcing positive teaching. However, they insisted that a verbal rebuke was more appropriate in some circumstances, particularly when an intelligent person was being punished. Moreover, the sages realized that a beating was wasted on some fools. Knowing when to use the stick therefore required careful thought and consideration of the probable consequences. For some people it seemed that a sound thrashing accomplished wonders: "Blows that wound cleanse away evil;/strokes make clean the innermost parts" (20:30). Loving parents applied physical punishment because they wanted to secure their children from external threats to survival. It was even thought that the Deity used chastening as a means of demonstrating love.

> My son, do not despise the Lord's discipline
>   or be weary of his reproof,
> for the Lord reproves him whom he loves,
>   as a father the son in whom he delights. (Prov. 3:11–12)

The Hebrew word *musar* (discipline) meant far more than physical beating or verbal rebuke. By discipline the Israelite also meant a body of teaching that enriched life. This instruction had to be mastered through hard study, and Israel's youth, like those in Egypt and in Mesopotamia, were often easily distracted from their study. To hold their attention, teachers devoted much energy to choosing language that captured the imagination of youth. Failing in this endeavor, the elders could always resort to stronger means of exerting pressure.

Self-control

One clear indication that discipline had achieved its goal was self-control, particularly in one's speech. This form of discipline meant complete mastery over the tongue, so that it did not inflict unwarranted pain on others. The individual who had achieved self-control exercised restraint in speech and valued truth above everything else. But this individual also subdued physical desires, especially excessive appetite for food and forbidden sexual pleasure. In Egypt this emphasis on governing the passions was so important that it resulted in technical terms for the wise as "silent ones" and fools as "heated ones." By these expressions they signified control over one's temper and an inability to restrain anger. Experience taught sages in Egypt and in Israel that it was far better to conceal one's inner attitude in many situations. Without giving any indication

of their true feelings, they could use calculated rational thinking to considerable advantage. Such self-control was especially important for young
officials at the royal court, where tipping one's hand could have disastrous
consequences. Here, too, mastery of sexual lust was obligatory, lest one
compromise the position of trust and provoke punishment for improper
conduct. Israel's teachers believed that achieving mastery over the passions required colossal effort and that a soldier was no stronger than the
individual who practiced self-control: "He who is slow to anger is better
than the mighty,/and he who rules his spirit than he who takes a city"
(16:32; cf. 24:5–6). Although this task of subduing passion required individual effort, at least in one respect those who were fortunate in marriage had a distinct advantage.

> He who finds a wife finds a good thing,
>   and obtains favor from the Lord. (Prov. 18:22)
> House and wealth are inherited from fathers,
>   but a prudent wife is from the Lord. (Prov. 19:14)

Unlucky persons in marriage wandered around and sighed, or they went
from nest to nest like a stray bird. Such individuals seem to have been
the unhappy objects of caustic tongues, for several comparative statements
describe the sad lot of husbands whose wives constantly nagged them:
"It is better to live in a corner of the housetop/than in a house shared
with a contentious woman" (21:9; 25:24).

Such teachings take as their starting point the self-interest of the individual. It should occasion little surprise that the impression of calculated rational action leaps to the forefront. What is somewhat surprising,
therefore, is the occasional admonition to transcend selfish interests so
that others will benefit from an act of kindness. It seems that the sages
recognized ambiguity where riches and poverty were concerned, and
they sought to improve the living standards of those whose misfortune
was not self-imposed.

> He who oppresses a poor man insults his Maker,
>   but he who is kind to the needy honors him. (Prov. 14:31)

> He who is kind to the poor lends to the Lord,
>   and he will repay him for his deed. (Prov. 19:17)

These specific instructions about the path to life were offered because
Israel's teachers believed that inner resolve was rewarded by external
support for those good intentions. Accumulated wisdom functioned as a
social force that reinforced individual effort.

> discretion will watch over you;
>   understanding will guard you;
> delivering you from the way of evil,
>   from men of perverted speech .... (Prov. 2:11–12)

Wisdom, personified as a woman, was thought to have stood watch over the wise while they slept. With this notion the sages arrived remarkably close to the modern concept of culture or "ethos," the powerful network of sanctions that individuals of a given culture assimilate as naturally as they eat and breathe.

Conduct to Avoid

An inordinate amount of attention was focused on the path to destruction, as if Israel's youth seemed inclined in that direction. In this respect the sages' attitude agreed with oft-expressed prophetic assessments and with the negative interpretation of Israelite history by the Deuteronomistic historians. Such unflattering views of human nature need to be placed in context lest a jaundiced understanding of ancient Israel result. Perhaps it will help to prevent such an unfortunate misunderstanding if a single principle is kept in mind: it is the truly virtuous person who is always most sensitive to imperfection. If this observation holds true, it suggests that such negative assessments bear witness first and foremost to a scrupulous conscience. In what particular areas did the sages recognize threats to a life of wisdom?

SEXUAL TEMPTATION

To judge from the frequency of warnings against the foreign woman, it seems that sexual temptation was almost an obsession with the teachers, at least those who compiled chapters 1–9. The references to the foreign woman may echo a particular kind of temptation, the Mesopotamian fertility worship that confronted Israel in exile. But that cultic dimension has largely been erased, and the emphasis now falls on adultery. The attacks on this temptation achieve remarkable power. In one, the author paints a vivid picture of an adulteress stalking her prey and enticing him into her chamber with promises of a night of pleasure. The warning ends with an explosive observation that the young man does not know that it will cost him his life (7:6–23). Another text seeks to combat such seductive promises with equally desirable ones from appropriate sources.

> Drink water from your own cistern,
>   flowing water from your own well.
> Should your springs be scattered abroad,
>   streams of water in the streets?
> Let them be for yourself alone,
>   and not for strangers with you.
> Let your fountain be blessed,
>   and rejoice in the wife of your youth,
>   a lovely hind, a graceful doe. (Prov. 5:15–19a)

LAZINESS

A second threat to wise conduct was laziness; the observations about sloth are often full of humor and sarcasm. An exquisite image likens a sluggard's turning on his bed to a door turning on its hinges, and another describes a person who puts his hand in a food bowl but is too lazy to feed himself. Many of these sayings derive from a rural setting, where certain chores must be performed in season if one expects to reap a successful harvest in due time. The indolent refuse to plan ahead, and they are therefore unprepared when calamity strikes. Sometimes such laziness is rationalized in strange ways, as when the sluggard refuses to leave the security of a house for fear that a lion is lurking outside. The teachers insisted that such individuals should look at something far smaller than the lion.

> Go to the ant, O sluggard;
>   consider her ways, and be wise.
> Without having any chief,
>   officer or ruler,
> she prepares her food in summer,
>   and gathers her sustenance in harvest.
> How long will you lie there, O sluggard?
>   When will you arise from your sleep? (Prov. 6:6–9)

DRUNKENNESS

The disastrous effects of laziness were slow in coming, whereas the evil consequences of drunken abandon dawned quickly. Like women, wine enriched life. But both could become occasions for one's destruction. The sages warned against excessive use of strong drink, although they conceded that wine should be given to condemned criminals and to miserable creatures who wanted to forget their poverty. Others needed a clear mind so that their judicial decisions would be fair.

SLANDER

Another danger that sages warned against was gossip and slander, indeed any misuse of speech.

> When words are many, transgression is not lacking,
>   but he who restrains his lips is prudent. (Prov. 10:19)

> The words of a whisperer are like delicious morsels;
>   they go down into the inner parts of the body. (Prov. 18:8)

> There are six things which the Lord hates,
>   seven which are an abomination to him:
> haughty eyes, a lying tongue,
>   and hands that shed innocent blood,
> a heart that devises wicked plans,
>   feet that make haste to run to evil,

> *a false witness who breathes out lies,*
> *and a man who sows discord among brothers. (Prov. 6:16–19)*

When individuals succumb to these four threats they develop an attitude that is haughty. This proud spirit offends the Deity, who desires humility. When pride comes, then comes a fall. On the other hand, those who learn obedience and self-control must guard themselves against pride in their achievements. In principle at least, the sages recognized the necessity for humility, although their attitude toward fools could scarcely be likened to humility.

SETTING

The background for these sayings and instructions seems to include more than one setting. As we have seen, it is customary to think of at least three contexts for this material: the family, the royal court, and the scribal school. Similarly, it is supposed that each of these settings produced its own special sayings with distinctive features in form and content. Unfortunately, the precise characteristics of clan, royal, and theological wisdom escape detection, and scholars are forced to form suitable hypotheses that will explain the evidence that has survived. At present no general explanation for all the evidence has won consensus, partly because of editorial reworking of older material to give it a stronger religious flavor. If indeed such an alteration of earlier sayings has occurred, it raises the question whether such a thematic analysis as the one offered here applies to the sages in general or merely to the final collection of sayings and instructions. An alternative approach would have been to analyze each collection independently. The perspective followed in this book is a compromise: it proceeds first with a description of the separate collections and then endeavors to offer a more comprehensive treatment of the world view to which the compilers of these traditions subscribed.

Perhaps the clearest expression of this particular problem occurs in the sayings attributed to the Arabian skeptic Agur (30:1–9?). The first four verses appear to be one of the strongest criticisms of wisdom's excessive claims in the canonical literature. The choice of vocabulary seems to be highly polemical, for it echoes prophetic and priestly oracular formulas. In addition, the opening verse apparently denies the existence of God and speaks of the consequence of such thinking, specifically an inability to cope. The following verses use expressions from creation hymns, but these ideas become support for a reminder that all knowledge is limited. The final taunt, "Surely you know!" bristles with irony. But then a different voice interrupts the train of thought; it is actually a combination of two partial verses from Israel's hymnic tradition. The next verse warns against adding to his words, and verses 7–9 offer a devout prayer.

Two things I ask of thee . . .
  give me neither poverty nor riches;
  feed me with the food that is needful for me,
lest I be full, and deny thee,
  and say, "Who is the Lord?"
or lest I be poor, and steal,
  and profane the name of my God. (Prov. 30:7–9)

To put the above question in another way: what is the setting for these verses? So far the situation that evoked this powerful text is unclear, and its meaning is therefore subject to much debate. The teachers who compiled and preserved the several collections in Proverbs have succeeded in one important respect. They have reminded their modern counterparts that the right starting point in any intellectual endeavor is crucial.

• 17 •

Ruth

ABRAHAM is not the only person in the Hebrew Scriptures who
ventured to another country from his home and from those who
gave him birth. In this respect Ruth's journey from Moab to nearby
Judah represents the same daring and comparable devotion. In Abraham's
case the devotion is presented as obedient response to a deity's command;
in Ruth's, loyalty to a mother-in-law prompted the action. The narrator
of the short story about this foreign woman has Boaz, the principal male
character in the narrative, call attention to this resemblance between the
Moabitess and the father of the Hebrew people. Such remarkable openness toward a foreigner characterizes the entire story, which succeeds
in artfully describing plot, character, and movement without introducing
a villain at all. Naturally, interpreters have compared this positive attitude
toward marriage between a Hebrew and a Moabitess with the hostile
position that Ezra and Nehemiah took and have viewed the book of Ruth
as an attack against their harsh measures that required the dissolution
of interracial marriages.

Like Abraham, Ruth occupies a prominent place in Israel's genealogy;
she is said to be an ancestor of King David. That bold claim appears at
the end of the story, and scholars generally agree that this genealogy is
a later addition. The reason for the supplement is not clear, although
several possibilities have come to mind. The addition provides the missing legend of David's birth; it explains why David fled with his parents
to Moab; or it attempts to explain the circumstances surrounding David's
actual foreign ancestry. None of these explanations is entirely satisfactory,
although the last one seems to have some merit because it is unlikely
that anyone would have succeeded in promoting the idea that David
came from a union between an Israelite and a foreign woman. The link
between him and the Moabitess must therefore have been a historical
fact.

Of course, the original purpose of the beautiful story is different from the use to which this genealogy puts it. Was it written to counteract the measures implemented by Ezra and Nehemiah, or is another purpose more central to its composition? Admittedly, the narrative offers a powerful critique of narrow attitudes in certain circles within postexilic Judaism. In essence it recognizes admirable traits in a foreign woman, and it thereby supports marriage between an Israelite and a person of another nation. However, some critics have insisted that an absence of open polemic within the story make this interpretation of its purpose suspect.

PURPOSE

If the critics who say that the Book of Ruth does not support intermarriage are right, what is the intention of the narrative? At the heart of the story is the theme of fidelity and its rewards. For some, the narrative is an edifying tale about a young woman who remains faithful to her mother-in-law and receives full recompense for her conduct. Furthermore, the story is rich in religious sentiment; some commentators even assert that it deals with the hidden God in a manner similar to the Joseph narrative. The latter claim scarcely accords with the facts, for the story abounds in references to divine activity. The narrator states that the Deity brought food to a land that had known famine and that the Lord gave Ruth a son. Naomi, the mother-in-law, accuses the Deity of wielding a strong hand against her, one that afflicted her and sent calamity, and notes that this powerful Lord brought her back to Bethlehem empty. Boaz greets his field hands with a pious blessing; he expresses to Ruth the hope that the Deity will give her a full reward for her faithfulness to Naomi; he asks that the Lord bless her; and he swears by the Deity that he will accept his responsibility to act as her redeemer. Finally, the people pronounce a blessing on Ruth in which they wish multiple offspring for her, as was true of Rachel and Leah. Such frequent reference to the Deity suggests that scholars have exaggerated the hidden aspect of divine providence in this story. Is it likely that an author who speaks so freely about the Deity intended to describe the hidden activity of God? Perhaps the choice of the expression, "she happened to come to the part of the field belonging to Boaz," has no deep theological significance but recognizes the element of chance in human experience.

THEME: EMPTINESS AND FULLNESS

Central to the story is the movement from emptiness to fullness. The emptiness occurs first in the natural realm, driving a family from Judah to Moab in search of food. The loss of social and cultural ties follows, and then the emptiness on a personal level and in the family, for the husband dies, as do his two sons some ten years later. However, rumor that the famine in Judah has passed prompts Naomi to return at the beginning of the barley harvest. The rest of the story traces the manner in which the emptiness experienced by Naomi is replaced by ample food and by a grandson whom she holds in her bosom as the story ends.

One feature of the narrative continues to perplex interpreters, partly because of the peculiar circumstances surrounding the custom. Like the story of Judah and Tamar in Genesis 38, this narrative about Ruth deals with the issue of levirate marriage, according to which the brother of the deceased was obligated to marry the widow if she had no children and to provide progeny for the dead brother. In this instance that obligation is set alongside the requirement to redeem property of the deceased so that it will remain in the family. The custom of taking off a sandal to disavow one's obligation does not accord with the law of the levirate in Deut. 25:5–10. As a matter of fact, the story has some loose edges: Boaz is not aware that he is the redeemer, and must be reminded of this fact, at which point we learn that another person is the next of kin. Furthermore, the possession of a tract of land at Naomi's disposal would seem to rule out the need for Ruth to glean in Boaz's fields like a pauper. Again, while the whole town has heard about Ruth's faithfulness, the unnamed redeemer seems to be ignorant of this complicating factor in purchasing Elimelech's property.

The means by which Naomi and Ruth seek to persuade Boaz to spread his skirt over the Moabite maiden is story telling at its best. The language is highly erotic, but without explicit reference that might offend some ears. Indeed, the entire episode is silent about the extent of their actual intimacy during the first nocturnal meeting. Ruth's language leaves no doubt about her intentions, and her boldness in uncovering him invites daring on Boaz's part, but the narrator leaves the rest to the imagination. One incidental remark by Boaz does introduce an interesting element into the relationship: he praises the beautiful young woman for her choice of an old man when she could have sought out some young person of means.

The narrator's attention to vocabulary is particularly noticeable in the symbolic names of the characters in the story: Naomi (peaceful), Ruth (companion), Boaz (in him is strength or quickness), Mahlon (sickness), Chilion (consumption), Orpah (disloyal). A similar appropriateness of names does not characterize the genealogy, for the child born to Boaz and Ruth should by right belong to Ruth's dead husband, Mahlon. It follows that the name the people bestow on the infant ignores the levirate law the story has just exalted.

The introduction to this story puts the events in the time of the Judges. For this reason the Greek translators placed the book after Judges, whereas in the Hebrew Bible it appears among the writings. The language of the story and its content seem to fit best into the postexilic period, which accords with the position of the book in the Hebrew canon. The custom of removing the sandal is explained for an audience that is no longer familiar with the practice, and the introductory formula in the book is reminiscent of the Deuteronomistic expression. The language has a number of Aramaisms, and the openness toward foreigners seems to suggest an origin in the fifth century B.C.E. However, the author may very well have used older materials. Because the story revolves around the issue of food, whether inadequate for survival or a bountiful harvest, it came to be used in the synagogue liturgy as the scroll for the feast of Weeks, the wheat harvest and forerunner of the Christian Pentecost. As for the genealogy, its similarity with 1 Chron. 2:4–15 may indicate an origin as late as the fourth century.

Few moments in biblical literature are as touching as the scene in which Ruth expresses her resolve to accompany her mother-in-law wherever their common destiny will lead them.

> Entreat me not to leave you or to return from following you; for where you go I will go, and where you lodge I will lodge; your people shall be my people, and your God my God; where you die I will die, and there I will be buried. May the Lord do so to me and more also if even death parts me from you. (Ruth 1:16–17)

Here is no theology of a hidden Deity. Instead, this is a sublime celebration of faithfulness on the part of a foreign woman for her mother-in-law. While the Deity may guide their actions and grant them success, the emphasis falls rather on the bold actions the two women undertake to secure their future.

✦ 18 ✦

Song of Songs

T HE whole world is not worth the day on which the Song of Songs was given to Israel; all the Writings are holy, and the Song of Songs is the holy of holies." Thus Rabbi Akiba, who lived in the first half of the second century C.E., expressed his esteem for this book despite its abuse by those who sang its erotic poetry in local taverns. A glance at the songs preserved in this collection easily reveals the reasons for Akiba's remark and the use to which pleasure-seeking youth put the poems. The songs praise love as a passion rivaling death, and they examine the agony and ecstasy of sexual desire. Precisely for the latter reason, these songs are at home wherever love stirs itself. Such powerful feelings erupt wholly unexpectedly in various circumstances, for physical desire knows no limits. Akiba's assessment of this book is all the more remarkable when one considers the potential for abuse. Perhaps that high regard arose from his knowledge of love's grandeur, a mystery that justifies any sacrifice.

The title of the book is a Hebrew idiom that means "the best song." The superscription associates these songs with King Solomon, either as author or as the one to whom they are dedicated. Dependence on the tradition in 1 Kings 4:32 (5:12 in the Hebrew text), which attributes 1,005 songs to Solomon, seems likely. Elsewhere within the songs this king is mentioned, twice in a poem describing his wedding procession and later in an uncomplimentary remark about Solomon's extensive harem. In this mild rebuke of the king, the lover boasts that his one beloved is preferable to Solomon's thousand women, whose care must be entrusted to others. In one song the woman thinks the king has brought her into his chamber; in another song she imagines that her lover is in a royal chariot and that she sits beside him as they go for a ride in the country. The second description of the young woman concludes with the observation that a king is held captive in her tresses. Even similes within the poetry sometimes

337

allude to Solomon—for instance, the reference to the woman's tanned
skin that was dark like the curtains of Solomon.

ROYAL IMAGERY

What is the place of royal imagery in common love songs? That question
has engendered considerable discussion. Three answers have vied for
acceptance: (1) the cultic, (2) the dramatic, and (3) the symbolic. In the
first of these, the songs are understood as part of a sacred marriage ceremony in the ancient Mesopotamian world. The union of a king and a
sacred priestess, earthly representatives of Tammuz and Ishtar,* was
thought to assure an ordered and properous society for the coming year.
The songs praised these two in erotic language that stimulated sexual
desire in all who heard them and thereby contributed to the well-being
of society. The second answer, the dramatic, takes two forms, in one of
which Solomon is the villain. A shepherd addresses his beloved, who in
turn sings to him, and a chorus of young women sing to both lovers as
they struggle to gain one another's love. Alternatively, Solomon takes
into his harem a young maiden, the Shulammite, who loves a shepherd;
she remains faithful to her rustic lover until the king must eventually
return her to him. The third answer, the symbolic, views the songs as
love poetry that was used to celebrate a wedding during which the bride
was addressed as queen and the groom was called king.

    None of these explanations is entirely satisfactory. The first comes up
against the question, how could such foreign cultic material have entered
Jewish circles and gained acceptance, once purged of recognizable pagan
features? While it does appear likely that the Tammuz cult entered Judah
during Manasseh's long reign, so that in popular religion the Jewish people worshipped the dying and rising vegetation deity, it seems highly
unlikely that this myth could have entered the canon even in disguised
form such as erotic poetry. The dramatic interpretation makes sense of
the alternating voices within the songs but ignores the ancient concepts
of royalty and of a woman's status in marriage. In short, it represents a
modern romantic understanding of things that is remote from ancient
reality. The symbolic view rests on research into Arab customs in Syria.
The analogy between these customs and the situation presupposed in
the songs is illuminating, but it breaks down in the end. The practice of
describing the bodies of bride and groom occurs in both, but nowhere
in the biblical poetry is the bride identified as a queen. Furthermore,
the biblical songs lack progression toward ultimate union in marriage.

---

*Tammuz and Ishtar were Mesopotamian dying and rising gods associated with fertility
and vegetation.

EROTIC POETRY

It seems better, therefore, to classify these poems as erotic songs, nothing more. They are not restricted to a marriage ceremony, for the lovers enjoy one another intimately almost from the outset. The poems constitute an anthology of independent love songs, although they have been brought together on the basis of refrains, themes and catchwords. For example, the same refrain occurs three times:

> I adjure you. O daughters of Jerusalem,
>   by the gazelles or the hinds of the field,
> that you stir not up nor awaken love
>   until it please. (Song of Songs 2:7; 3:5; 8:4)

Similarities with Egyptian love poetry are striking, especially the reference to the beloved as sister, but the universality of such literature makes direct literary dependence unlikely. The songs express a longing for an absent lover, describe the beauty of the beloved, boast about the beloved's assets, complain about conventional restrictions on freedom of physical expression, and recount private thoughts and actions.

Modern readers find the imagery in the songs to be somewhat strange in certain cases. What do a young woman's teeth have to do with ewes which bear twins, and what lover wants to be told that her hair is like a flock of goats, or that her nose is like a tower of Lebanon? The poet captures a single feature of the beloved in these images and endeavors to communicate the idea. Expressed more prosaically, her teeth sparkle, her hair is wavy, her nose is graceful. The images come largely from nature, especially those used in describing the woman. Precious metals predominate in the songs characterizing the man, although images from the natural realm also occur (eyes like doves, cheeks like beds of spices, lips like lilies). The praise of the man starts at the head and ends with the legs, only to return to his sweet speech. In contrast, one song praising the woman begins at the head and stops with the breasts, which are called two fawns or a mountain of myrrh and a hill of frankincense. The other song starts with the sandals and concludes with an allusion to a king who is held captive in her flowing locks.

The poems acknowledge love's agony, for that too seems universal. The lover vanishes and the young woman must search for him during the night; she does so at considerable risk. In one poem she escapes harassment, but in another song the watchmen seize her mantle and beat her. This desperate woman enlists the help of other maidens in searching for her lover, for she will not rest until she finds him. The notion that sickness overtakes one whose beloved has gone occurs in one song, and this idea echoes an Egyptian song that insists that the presence of the sick man's beloved is the only medicine he needs. These songs also acknowledge the power inherent within a woman's eyes, for they succeed in ravishing the man's heart with a single glance. Small wonder he pleads with her to turn away her eyes, for they disturb him.

The virtue of young women is celebrated in song also. Such images as a garden locked and a fountain sealed connote the virginal state. This symbolism was well-known throughout the ancient world, and it appeared in popular proverbs and in cultic songs. Here in the biblical text an invitation goes out to the winds:

> Awake, O north wind,
>   and come, O south wind!
> Blow upon my garden,
>   let its fragrance be wafted abroad.
> Let my beloved come to his garden,
>   and eat its choicest fruits. (Song of Songs 4:16)

The young man gladly accepts her invitation, eating and drinking freely. The union of the lovers is encouraged, either by the chorus or by the editor who intrudes elsewhere to observe that love is powerful like death.

> Set me as a seal upon your heart,
>   as a seal upon your arm;
> for love is strong as death,
>   jealousy is cruel as the grave.
> Its flashes are flashes of fire,
>   a most vehement flame.
> Many waters cannot quench love,
>   neither can floods drown it.
> If a man offered for love
>   all the wealth of his house
>   it would be utterly scorned. (Song of Songs 8:6–7)

RESISTANCE TO EROTICISM

In the history of Judaism and Christianity a mighty effort to extinguish the flame has taken place in the form of allegorical interpretation. The songs were viewed within Judaism as an allegory about God's love for Israel, and early Christian interpreters saw in them a portrayal of Jesus' love for the church or for the individual soul. This refusal to accept the songs as spontaneous expressions of sexual desire and confessions of love indicates that within both religions there is a reluctance to accept the implications of the priestly claim in Genesis 1 that everything that God created is very good. The authors of these songs had a healthier view of sexuality by far than did later allegorists. The former sang enthusiastically, vividly but with good taste, about the bittersweet joys of love. Because the sexual attraction rivals death in its power, Akiba's judgment about the songs is both realistic and profound.

The songs in this collection may have arisen over the course of many years, but their final compilation took place in late postexilic times. Echoes from an earlier period seem to persist in the present form of the songs, although the most compelling one, the allusion to Tirzah, the ancient northern capital, may simply have been chosen for its symbolic meaning (pleasant). The language and syntax in the songs point to a late period of composition, particularly the shortened relative particle* and loanwords from Persia and Greece. A number of features suggest to some interpreters the probability that the songs were literary from the outset and that they are the product of a cultured circle of poets. Because the setting of the songs is rural and the time is spring, this scroll came to be read in the synagogue during Passover, the festival that recalled Israel's deliverance from Egyptian expressions of hatred.

---

*The usual relative particle in Hebrew is *'asher* (who, which). In the late Book of Ecclesiastes the short preformative *sh^e* is also used frequently.

Ecclesiastes

THE right word or deed for the occasion comes very close to sum-
ming up the fundamental concept in international wisdom. The
various intellectual enterprises undertaken by the sages arose
during their search for ways of discovering when to speak or act in a
given manner. Their goal, of course, was to master their own fate by
bringing their actions into harmony with what they perceived to be the
rational principle ordering the universe. The author of the Book of Job
began a devastating attack on this preoccupation with wisdom, and the
Book of Ecclesiastes carries this attack to its ultimate conclusion. The
author of this latter work, who will be called Ecclesiastes to avoid repeated use of the longer expression, "the author of Ecclesiastes," insisted
that the supposed certainty that the sages claimed for their endeavor was
actually a delusion.

> When I applied my mind to know wisdom . . . then I saw all the work of
> God, that man cannot find out the work that is done under the sun. However
> much man may toil in seeking, he will not find it out; even though a wise
> man claims to know, he cannot find it out. (Eccles. 8:16–17)

On the basis of the expression in Daniel, "those who know the times,"
it appears that a science of the times, which played an important role in
international wisdom, was beginning to emerge in Israelite circles also.
Ecclesiastes subscribes to the belief that there is a correct time for everything, but he refuses to take the next step toward securing one's existence
through wisdom. This goal cannot be achieved, he insists, because at
the end of every intellectual endeavor there is an element of the unknown: "That which is, is far off, and deep, very deep; who can find it
out?" (7:24). It is difficult to imagine a more devastating attack on ancient
wisdom, if Ecclesiastes is correct. Nevertheless, Ecclesiastes does not
go so far that he rejects the entire wisdom enterprise, for it is acknowledged to have limited utility. What Ecclesiastes rejects is the claim that

wisdom yields absolute, as opposed to relative, benefits. For this reason Ecclesiastes may be viewed as a critic from within the wisdom establishment who reminds its representatives of limits that reality itself imposes on their efforts. Others see his work as a total repudiation of wisdom as a means of insulating humans from harm. In this book alone within the Hebrew Bible, with the possible exception of Song of Songs, practical experience is the measure of all truth.

Personal observation taught Ecclesiastes that death imposes an absolute limit on all living things. What seems to have disturbed him most about this awareness was the additional perception that the messenger of death did not single out the virtuous for a better reward than the wicked. One fate befell everyone, wise or fool, human or animal. Furthermore, that unwelcome visitor came unannounced, and no amount of effort could ever succeed in discovering what lay in the future. At the moment of creation the Deity had seen to it that the future would always be hidden, for humans were endowed with a sense of eternity, but a knowledge of the complete picture was withheld from them. "He has made everything beautiful in its time; also he has put eternity into man's mind, yet so that he cannot find out what God has done from the beginning to the end" (3:11). This inability to know anything that would secure one's future was painful to Ecclesiastes, who went so far as to confess hatred for life. It is ironical that this scroll came to be read in the synagogue during the feast of Tabernacles (Booths).

AUTHORSHIP AND DATE

The author of the book speaks several times in the first person and identifies himself as Qoheleth, son of David, king in Jerusalem. The only person who fits this description is Solomon, but nowhere else has his name been preserved as Qoheleth. The word is feminine, in keeping with other Hebrew terms denoting a profession (for example, *soperet*, "writer," in Ezra 2:55; Neh. 7:57). "Qoheleth" comes from a root that means to assemble or to gather, so it is natural to assume that a function of gathering is implied. The usual explanation links this person with the task of assembling people to a public meeting place or synagogue, although less religious interpretations have also been proposed, such as gatherer of wives or assembler of truth sayings. The Greek name Ecclesiastes derives from the supposed association between the form Qoheleth and its equivalent in Greek (*ecclesia:* a gathering).

The ascription of the book to Solomon is literary fiction; its source is undoubtedly Egyptian wisdom literature, where aged pharaohs conveyed their "testament" to successors. A number of factors indicate that the author did not intend this attribution of authorship to be taken literally. If the references to all those kings who preceded him in Jerusalem failed

to alert readers to this bit of literary fiction, the stance from which he
wrote must surely have revealed the claim for what it was. Conceivably,
readers may not have been aware that only David preceded Solomon as
king in Jerusalem, but even the least alert of them could hardly have
missed the fact that Ecclesiastes wrote from the viewpoint of a subject
rather than from the perspective of a ruler. Then a final blow to the illusion of Solomonic authorship is struck in the first supplement to the
book, which identifies Ecclesiastes as a professional teacher:

> Besides being wise [a *hakam*], the Preacher also taught the people knowl-
> edge, weighing and studying and arranging proverbs with great care. The
> Preacher sought to find pleasing words, and uprightly he wrote words of
> truth. (Eccles. 12:9–10)

The reason Ecclesiastes introduced this literary fiction from Egyptian
wisdom was transparent to early rabbinic interpreters who recognized
the principle that wealth and social position enhance a speaker's authority. Quite simply, only someone like Solomon had the resources to
test life as fully as Ecclesiastes envisions in 2:1–26.

Modern interpreters reject Solomonic authorship of the book for other
reasons as well. One critic stated the matter as dramatically as possible:
if Solomon wrote Ecclesiastes, then a history of the Hebrew language
cannot be written. The language of the book is the latest in the Hebrew
Bible; in some ways the style and vocabulary are closer to Mishnaic Hebrew* than to classical Hebrew. Furthermore, an abundance of Aramaisms has led to a theory that the book is a translation into Hebrew. Persian
and Greek loanwords confirm the suspicion that Ecclesiastes is one of
the latest books in the canon. Arguments from content (a crisis within
wisdom, cyclical thinking, a threat from Hellenism), although always difficult to assess, lead to the same conclusion: Ecclesiastes wrote at some
time during the third or early second century B.C.E. Fragments of the
book from Qumran seem to warn against dating Ecclesiastes much later
than the third century. It is not certain whether Sirach knew the book
or not; however, a strong case has been made for understanding Wisd.
of Sol. 2:1–11 as polemic against a perversion of Ecclesiastes' teaching.

The place of composition is undoubtedly Palestine, although some
have thought the Egyptian influence points to Alexandria, where a flourishing Jewish community existed. Certain features of the language have
seemed to indicate Phoenicia, but the weight of evidence inclines toward
Jerusalem as Ecclesiastes' home. The author's environment is clearly
Palestinian: boundary walls and quarrying; fountains and cisterns; wind,
clouds, and rain; the structure of houses; and so forth. References to a
king or ruler are part of international wisdom and do not require a setting
in which an actual king ruled the land.

---

* The Mishnah, the first portion of the Talmud, contains legal and homiletic teachings
preserved orally alongside the actual exposition of scripture, the Midrash.

How much of the present book derives from Ecclesiastes' hand? Opinions vary with regard to the actual extent of editorial retouching, but virtually everyone agrees that some additions have made their way into the text. At minimum, these later insertions include the superscription (1:1) and two epilogues (12:9–12; 12:13–14). The first epilogue commends the author as a trustworthy guide, while at the same time implying that not everyone was pleased with such efforts. The second epilogue submits Ecclesiastes' radical skepticism to the powerful corrective within traditional theological wisdom. Moreover, in a few places within the body of the text skeptical viewpoints are nullified by orthodox statements, especially where the traditional view of reward and retribution came under attack (3:17; 7:18; 8:12–13; 11:9b). Because of the aphoristic nature of Ecclesiastes' thought, it is conceivable that competing viewpoints existed in his own mind, particularly if the collected sayings comprise a sort of diary into which he has entered the thoughts of a lifetime. But the manner in which traditional sayings interrupt the train of thought makes this interpretation of the facts unlikely.

An interpretive refrain opens and closes the book proper: "Vanity of vanities, says the Preacher,/vanity of vanities! All is vanity" (1:2; 12:8). Whether this refrain derives from Ecclesiastes or from a subsequent glossarist can scarcely be decided. It has even been proposed that someone other than Ecclesiastes provided a framework for his thought by introducing a poem in 1:3–11 to match 12:1–7. In favor of this suggestion is the unusual form of 1:12, which seems to mark the beginnings of Ecclesiastes' teaching. Nevertheless, the search for an underlying structure to the book has yielded no compelling scheme, despite the presence of valuable clues such as recurring refrains. The amazing thing is the impression of unity that pervades the book when so many factors combine to undermine this possibility. In short, even the present form of the book has a unity of theme and mood, and the introductory and concluding refrain captures both: "Vanity of vanities, says the Preacher,/ vanity of vanities! All is vanity." The Hebrew idiom is the equivalent of the superlative, hence the supreme vanity, and the root meaning is "breath," and therefore something fleeting and insubstantial.

LITERARY FORMS

The literary fiction of a royal testament is but one of several categories that Ecclesiastes uses. Perhaps the leading literary type is reflection, first person reports in the form of autobiographical narration. Such reflections contribute to an impression of objectivity that to some degree tempers the subjective conclusions being presented. In these larger units Ecclesiastes frequently resorts to personal references about considering, taking note of, drawing conclusions, and the like. The effect is to emphasize the rational, cognitive dimension of his observations. Often the final insight that Ecclesiastes arrives at by careful observation and considered thought is fixed in the pithy form of a truth saying or a popular maxim. Sometimes it is hard to tell whether he cites traditional wisdom that he proceeds to refute or alter in a significant way, or whether the truth saying is his own contribution.

Ecclesiastes also expresses himself in the manner of traditional sages, using "better" sayings, counsels, anecdote, allegory, and more. Occasionally, he develops an earlier form in directions that are dramatically richer, particularly with respect to the poem in chapter 12, which contains an allegory describing the waning years in exquisite images of a house, a human body, and a storm:

> Remember also your Creator in the days of your youth, before the evil days come, and the years draw nigh, when you will say, "I have no pleasure in them"; before the sun and the light, and the moon, and the stars are darkened and the clouds return after the rain; in the day when the keepers of the house tremble, and the strong men are bent, and the grinders cease because they are few, and those that look through the windows are dimmed, and the doors on the street are shut; when the sound of the grinding is low, and one rises up at the voice of a bird, and all the daughters of song are brought low; they are afraid also of what is high, and terrors are in the way; the almond tree blossoms, the grasshopper drags itself along and desire fails; because man goes to his eternal home, and the mourners go about the streets; before the silver cord is snapped, or the golden bowl is broken, or the pitcher is broken at the fountain, or the wheel broken at the cistern, and the dust returns to the earth as it was, and the spirit returns to God who gave it. (Eccles. 12:1–7)

Although not all the images are fully understood, enough of them are transparent to convey the powerful impact of this description of old age and death. Sight fails, knees shake, the body shrinks, teeth fall out, hearing is impaired, the voice loses its tonal quality, sleeplessness and loss of appetite for food and sex characterize existence, the hair turns white, and death signals the return to dust when the breath goes back to its original source.

Often Ecclesiastes quotes a maxim to great advantage. Some examples of popular sayings indicate a sense of humor and clever turns of phrase.

> For as the crackling of thorns under a pot,
>   so is the laughter of fools;
>   this also is vanity. (Eccles. 7:6)

> But he who is joined with all the living has hope,
>   for a living dog is better than a dead lion. (Eccles. 9:4)

> What is crooked cannot be made straight,
>   and what is lacking cannot be numbered. (Eccles. 1:15)

A press from Capernaum. Flour mills and oil presses were used to provide daily necessities.

As the addition of the words, "this also is vanity," in 7:6 shows, Ecclesiastes did not permit laughter to linger as a last impression. His preference for a darker mood permeates a "better" saying.

> *It is better to go to the house of mourning*
> *than to go to the house of feasting;*
> *for this is the end of all men,*
> *and the living will lay it to heart. (Eccles. 7:2)*

Is the situation different when Ecclesiastes gets around to offering advice? Among the many counsels, one stands out because of its frequent appearance, albeit in a variety of expressions.

> Go, eat your bread with enjoyment, and drink your wine with a merry
> heart; for God has already approved what you do.
> Let your garments be always white; let not oil be lacking on your head.
> Enjoy life with the wife whom you love, all the days of your vain
> life. . . . (Eccles. 9:7–9a)

To answer the question about the offering of advice, it is necessary to
consider Ecclesiastes' message.

TEACHING

The rejection of wisdom's power to secure one's existence did not propel
Ecclesiastes into a position of denying the existence of the Deity. Belief
in a Creator seems to have been built into the very foundation of the
wisdom enterprise, both in Israel and among its neighbors. Indeed, the
idea of reward and retribution seems to require a sovereign mind behind
the ordering of the universe. Ecclesiastes subscribed to belief in the
Creator but refused to accept the implication that the sages drew from
that conviction. One consequence of this departure from traditional wisdom was to render the category of Deity virtually useless as far as daily
life was concerned. "For God is in heaven, and you upon earth; therefore
let your words be few" (5:2b). The distant God could not be relied upon
in time of danger, loneliness, or at any occasion when divine presence
was desired. Chance, not a benevolent Deity, controlled human destiny.

> Again, I say that under the sun the race is not to the swift, nor the battle
> to the strong, nor bread to the wise, nor riches to the intelligent, nor favor
> to the men of skill; but time and chance happen to them all. (Eccles. 9:11).

Such thinking signaled an end to prayer, a refusal to enter into dialogue
with the transcendent one. Death, not God, was decisive.

Nevertheless, Ecclesiastes' retention of the idea of God allowed him
to credit the Deity with enormous generosity. In reality, it is simply Ecclesiastes' way of saying that if something occurs the Deity must have
willed it. Therefore, whatever good thing happens falls under the heading
of "a gift of God," just as misfortune is labeled a mischance or fate. Ecclesiastes encourages young people to enjoy life while they have the
vigor to do so, and he identifies one's lot in life as a portion granted from
the Creator. Nevertheless, Ecclesiastes resents the inability to move into
a position of control over what comes one's way, for the status of a recipient of gifts is always that of a dependent. Moreover, even the positive
counsel invariably rests under a dark cloud, which Ecclesiastes seems
eager to focus upon. Not all interpreters agree that the spotlight falls on
the ominous cloud. For some, Ecclesiastes' heart beats excitedly when
the subject of enjoyment is introduced, and he is described as a messenger
of joy.

A fragment of a clay tablet preserving an Assyrian version of the Eleventh Tablet of the Gilgamesh Epic. In this story Siduri advises Gilgamesh to enjoy life; she uses language very similar to that in Ecclesiastes.

Ecclesiastes' self-centeredness is beyond question, but in this regard he has merely adopted the perspective of wisdom literature. Yet there are occasions when the suffering of the oppressed moves him to a twice-repeated lament over an absence of comforters and when madness and wicked deeds in others evokes an observation that a stillborn is more fortunate. In one text he comes very close to recognizing a necessary corrective to his rugged individualism, for Ecclesiastes perceives the advantage of having a friend in certain circumstances (4:9–12). But the social conscience of Israel's prophets does not awaken in him.

Instead, a radical sense of emptiness and of sameness fills Ecclesiastes' mind to the limit. The refrains heighten this sense, as do the leading words that recur with great frequency (*vanity, lot, toil, gain,* and so forth). Besides the thematic refrain about vanity there is the additional allusion to striving after wind. Then, too, statements like "cannot find" and "does not know" leave their mark on the entire book. One can readily understand how Ecclesiastes arrived at such a position when nothing enabled him to determine whether divine love or hate awaited and when it appeared that the Deity arranged human experience with the sole intention of demonstrating that people are mere beasts. To some critics, it seems that in him the nerve of faith had atrophied, and ennui had set up camp. For others, Ecclesiastes is an honest thinker who describes the human dilemma with astonishing accuracy. This ambiguity that grips contemporary interpreters of the book has a long history, perhaps fueled by the rabbinic claim that Solomon wrote this book during his dotage, as well as by the tenacious refusal to give up its canonical status.

· 20 ·

Lamentations

THOSE inhabitants of Judah and Jerusalem who stayed behind after the fall of the capital to the Babylonians in 587 B.C.E. felt the necessity of releasing pent-up emotions, for they were suddenly trapped by a crisis of faith that threatened their deepest convictions. Their spiritual leaders had assured them in the Deity's name that the royal throne would always have a descendant of David as shepherd of the people, but now that office no longer existed. Their most able prophet had promised divine protection for the city in which the Holy One of Israel resided, but now that city and its sanctuary lay in ruins. Their teachers had sworn that obedience would result in prosperity, but now compassionate women boiled their own infants to stave off death from starvation.

Without doubt, the ancient promises had proven false. What possible explanation existed for the collapse of cherished beliefs? Had Judah's religious instructors misled the people, causing them to place their trust in illusions? Was the old promise about a Davidic ruler nothing more than political propaganda, the solidifying of a regime through divine sanction? Was the tradition about Zion's indestructability merely a pious scheme to secure its prestige and to acquire power for the crown and priesthood? Was the optimistic hope that religious reform assured divine protection no more than an effort to gain support for Josiah's revolt against Babylon? Answers to these questions were essential if faith were to survive among those who imagined that the Deity had constructed a cloud between them and their God so that prayer could not penetrate to its intended auditor.

EXPLANATION FOR JERUSALEM'S FALL

Of course, the obvious explanation for the calamity that had struck the city and its inhabitants was that they had sinned. This response is freely

351

offered, although at one point the blame is laid on the previous generation, whose crimes have fallen on the children's shoulders. But what about the other two promises, related as they are? The divine promise about David is unconditional, and the improbability that Israel's God would allow someone to invade the divine residence makes the tradition of Zion's inviolability entirely believable. The inability to imagine suitable responses to these dilemmas must have prompted the intense wail that characterizes the five laments in this book.

ALPHABETIC FORM

The author, or perhaps authors, chose a traditional form for expressing grief, the funeral lament, but combined it with the individual and communal complaints that occur frequently in the Psalms. A striking feature of the five laments, loosely defined, is their acrostic form, although the final one is alphabetic only in the sense that it has twenty-two verses, the same number as the letters in the Hebrew alphabet. The other four chapters vary the acrostic form: in chapters 1 and 2, the first verse in each three-strophe unit begins with a letter of the alphabet in sequences; in chapter 3, all three verses in the unit begin with the appropriate letter of the alphabet; and in chapter 4 the first verse in a two-verse unit begins with the letter of the alphabet in sequence. From the reversal of the order of two letters (pe and ayin) in chapters 2, 3, and 4, it seems likely that the sequence of the Hebrew alphabet had not been firmly fixed by the time these poems were composed.

Why did the author(s) choose the acrostic device, which places such constraints on poetry? Interpreters have offered several explanations for this highly artificial device: it aids the memory; it has magical power; or it represents completion. Only the last of these seems likely, because the alphabetic form is evident to the eye and not the ear, and it scarcely assists in retention, and because there is no evidence that the ancient Israelites viewed alphabetic verse as magical. The poet seems to have selected the device with the intention of conveying the impression of exhaustiveness; the emotional expression fathoms the heights and the depths, the length and the breadth of reality from *a* to *z*.

The specifics of that grief know no bounds; extreme misery grips society as lawlessness invades its ranks. Children beg for bread in vain; adults exchange their valued objects for bread; they pay money for wood and water; famine prevails. Women and virgins are raped in the streets, elders are treated with contempt, princes are executed, slaves rule, and aliens have taken over the real estate. The sanctuary lies in ruins, and none comes to the appointed feasts. Priests sigh and prophets wait in vain for visions from on high. The usual signs of a well-ordered society have vanished: elders no longer come to the gates, and the young sing and dance to music no more. Instead, jackals prowl in search of prey.

The western wall of the city of Jerusalem, a portion of which is known today as the wailing wall.

Such physical suffering has its corollary in spiritual turmoil. The Deity has become like a lion or a bear, actively inflicting suffering. Or God has become an enemy archer who uses the citizens of Jerusalem as a target. In anger the Lord has trodden a winepress and withdrawn from human contact, so that there is no comforter and none to deliver the dying people. Much of this imagery occurs in chapter 3, which seems to have no relationship with the fall of Jerusalem but registers timeless spiritual torment. Such individual complaints comprise a large part of the book of Psalms and appear elsewhere frequently, particularly in Job and in Jeremiah's so-called confessions. The final word of such individual complaints is a resounding "nevertheless" of faith, although, of course, such a confession of confidence is missing from Job and Jeremiah. The poet meditates on the divine character and finds hope. God's steadfast love endures forever, is new every morning; the Lord is good to those who wait expectantly. Although good and evil come from the Most High, making complaint inappropriate, the Deity assumes the initiative in penetrating the cloud. The result is a comforting divine word, "Do not fear."

By using a traditional individual complaint the poet has integrated the shriek of agony that rises in the other four laments into the nation's liturgical tradition. In this way the author suggests an answer to the implicit question: "Where do we go from here?" Nevertheless, the poet who composed the final chapter refuses to permit a return of easy promises, because, after all, they were the occasion for the present misery. The book ends, therefore, on a sober note, the possibility that the Deity has forgotten Judah. Although the poet continues to address the Deity, the appeal for restoration includes the possibility that God has utterly rejected those who desperately need a deliverer.

The book of Lamentations is the festival scroll that is read in synagogue worship on the 9th of Ab in commemoration of Nebuchadnezzar's destruction of the Temple in Jerusalem, as well as the burning of the second Temple by Titus in 70 C.E. The Greek translation, the Septuagint, contains a superscription identifying Jeremiah as the author, a view that is probably based on the observation in 2 Chron. 35:25 that the prophet composed a lament on the occasion of Josiah's death. This link between Jeremiah and Lamentations is historically inaccurate, for he would hardly have blamed the events on the father's sins, or accused all prophets of false visions, or placed hope in Egypt. Nevertheless, the author was probably a survivor of the events surrounding 587, and these five complaints represent profound wrestling with reality. Here is no retreat into false assurances and no shrugging of shoulders in despair. However, the expression of grief makes no secret of its unresolved nature; the time for hope has passed, and the author is uncertain whether it will ever be different.

• 21 •

Esther

NOT every threat to Jewish survival originated with the supreme
ruler in a nation. Sometimes lesser officials, greedy for power
and recognition, used their influence with royalty to accomplish
their own nefarious schemes. This situation unfolds in the literary gem
Esther, a scroll that is read by the Jewish community during the feast of
Purim. Because the survival of the Jewish people is "an obligation of
the first magnitude," it naturally follows that the story that deals with
this issue is immensely popular within Judaism. The high esteem that
the book of Esther enjoys explains why it is called *the* scroll. This appreciation for the book even gave rise to the notion that the scroll will
join the Torah as the only written canonical works that will survive into
the age of the Messiah. By and large, Christians have not shared this
high regard for the book, partly because of its secular character and partly
because of its extreme nationalism.

This historical novella describes a plot to exterminate the Jewish population in the Persian empire, which extended from India to Egypt. In
effect, the goal was the elimination of Judaism, and all because one individual had personal animosity for a Jew. The story traces that private
struggle through its escalation into armed conflict and a dramatic reversal
of fortune. A series of banquets sets the stage for a life-and-death struggle
in which Jewish participants take their lives in their own hands and control their destiny without any reference to the Deity. This constant round
of feasting serves to accentuate the gravity of the struggle, and it is perhaps
happy irony that the Talmud enjoins drinking wine during Purim until
one cannot distinguish between "Blessed be Mordecai" and "Cursed be
Haman."

355

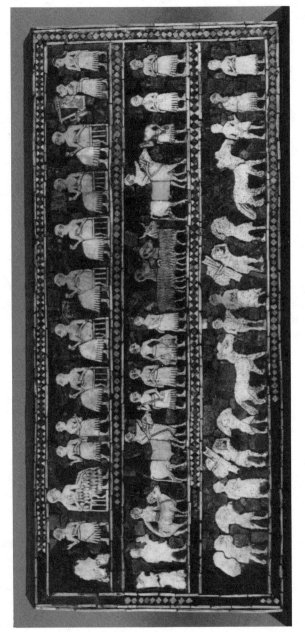

The Peace Panel from ancient Ur (twenty-fifth century), the reputed home of Abraham, portrays a royal victory and its accompanying celebration in the form of a banquet.

356

FEASTING

The story begins with feasting throughout the Persian provinces, a feast that lasts for 180 days, followed by a week-long lavish affair at Susa, the winter citadel of the Persian king, Ahasu-erus. Parallel to this latter celebration is a banquet that Vashti, the queen, hosts for the women of Susa. Later the new queen, Esther, gives two dinner parties to which she invites only two persons, the king and her enemy Haman. Then after she has exposed her foe for what he is, and his plot to slaughter the Jews has been frustrated by effective counterslaughter, the story ends with a two-day celebration of the feast of Purim in commemoration of Haman's having cast the lot *(Pur)* to decide the specific day on which to slay the Jews, a day that actually brought victory to the intended victims.

The villain is the chief advisor to the king, and his genealogy links this ambitious vizier with Agag, Saul's enemy and a member of the hated Amalekites who, according to Exod. 17:16, are destined to be blotted out forever. His nemesis is Mordecai, apparently a palace gatekeeper and a descendant of Kish, Saul's father. This Jew overhears a plot to assassinate the king and informs the threatened ruler through his one link with royalty, his adopted cousin Hadassah. This beautiful woman, also called Esther, had replaced a disgraced queen, Vashti, who had dared to refuse her king's request that she display her beauty at a royal banquet. Haman is promoted for no specified reason, and only one thing mars his total satisfaction: Mordecai the Jew refuses to bow before him. Hence the scheme to eradicate all Jews. Then, acting on advice from his wife and friends, he builds a gallows and proceeds to a banquet, only to suffer exposure of his plot and false accusation that he is attempting to rape the queen. Naturally, someone suggests that he be hanged on the gallows he has prepared for Mordecai, and it is done.

The king appears in the guise of a puppet who is manipulated by persons closest to him. After Vashti insults him by refusing to come when bidden, he asks his advisers what the law permits him to do, and he accepts their humorous assessment that her action is an affront to every male in the kingdom, an offense that must quickly be set right by a royal decree that each man rule over his household as lord. After Mordecai saved the king's life, Ahasu-erus neglected to reward him until a sleepless night prompted the reading of his records and pointed to unfinished business. When Haman wanted to destroy his enemy, he persuaded Ahasu-erus to go along with the massacre, but the king declined the colossal bribe of approximately $18 million that was to come from plundering the Jews. In the end the king bowed to the wishes of his queen and her uncle, who replaced Haman as second in rank. In at least one incident, Ahasu-erus jumped to a wrong conclusion and sentenced Haman to death for rape, although the unfortunate man was clinging to Esther and begging for his life. The irony could hardly be more extreme as Haman, the enemy of the Jews, pleads for his life to a Jewess who had withheld her identity from the king.

THE VILLAIN

The turning point in the story, Haman's mistaken assumption that the king intended to honor him and his advice as to what should be done for this recipient of royal favor, is a fine example of dramatic irony. Haman is therefore responsible for the specifics of his own humiliation at the very moment when he expected to be exalted above everyone else. The audacity of his response is overwhelming, for he comes just short of requesting the kingship. As it is, he suggests that clothing which the king has worn be placed on the lucky person and that he ride on a horse that Ahasu-erus has ridden. His humiliation is complete when he must parade through the winter capital calling everyone's attention to Mordecai as the king's favorite. When he returns home from this ordeal, it seems that even his wife has turned against him, for she utters a dark prophecy concerning the futility of competing with a Jew.

In this personal struggle for supremacy Mordecai consciously refuses to obey the royal decree that everyone pay respect to Haman, but he inexplicably escapes the king's wrath. Vashti is not so fortunate, perhaps because the story required her disappearance so that Mordecai would have access to the king through his adopted daughter. Esther's route to this royal bed takes her to a beauty contest from which she emerges as the loveliest virgin in all of Persia. In a sense she represents those Jews in favored circumstances who were in danger of complete assimilation; by reminding her of the illusion of safety that quickly vanishes, Mordecai persuades his daughter to risk her life for her people. Although some interpreters understand his words, "relief and deliverance will rise for the Jews from another quarter"* (Esther 4:14), as a veiled reference to the Deity, that theory is unlikely because Mordecai would imply that assistance would arise from a deity other than Israel's God. Moreover, the secular atmosphere of the story is total, even when Esther requests that every Jew in Susa fast on her behalf for three days. Here the absence of any reference to prayer is astonishing, and it only confirms the suspicion that the author intended to address Israel's survival as a problem that it must meet without divine help.

Nevertheless, the inclusion of this book in the canon places it under the umbrella of divine providence, just as the author's own readers would

---

*In later Judaism the divine name was used less and less. In its place various substitutes were used, one of which was the word translated "quarter" here (maqom). The New Testament witnesses to this preference for substitute expressions for the Deity.

likely have perceived the hidden activity of their God as the decisive factor in this conflict. Thus Esther's courageous words, "if I perish, I perish," when she boldly breaks the law and appears unbidden before the king, are not mere resignation, especially when understood within the context of a community's faith. Unlike the three men in Daniel who utter similar words, Esther does not introduce any dimension into the picture other than the human one. The absence of the religious dimension throughout the book was quickly corrected however, for the Greek translation has 107 additional verses that introduce traditional piety into this secular story.

ADDITIONS IN THE SEPTUAGINT

The additions are not all of this kind, for some of them fill out the story with greater detail. The following additions occur in Esther: after 1:1, Mordecai's dream and the plan to assassinate Ahasu-erus; after 3:13, the royal decree that Jews are to be exterminated on the 13th of Adar; after 4:17, prayers by Mordecai and Esther; after 5:27, the king's reception of Esther; after 8:12, the royal edict in favor of the Jews; and after 10:3, the interpretation of Mordecai's dream and a final note about the date on which the Greek translation arrived in Egypt.

HISTORICAL INACCURACY

Use of the term "historical novella" in the preceding discussion may strike readers of the biblical book as strange, inasmuch as the author gives the appearance of historical accuracy to the story. The general culture is described correctly, frequent dates and names of even minor characters who play no role are given, and a formula like the one in the canonical Kings implies that the material derives from royal chronicles. But the historical inaccuracies far outweigh these few features of verisimilitude, which are essential in effective historical fiction anyway. The author's knowledge of Persian succession leaves something to be desired, for the story has Xerxes I (Ahasu-erus) succeed Nebuchadnezzar or possibly his successor. If Mordecai had really gone into exile in 597 B.C.E., he would have been about 120 years old during Xerxes' reign (485–465), and Esther would hardly have been a beautiful young virgin. Furthermore, Xerxes I had no wife named Esther; as a matter of fact, she was called Amestris. Of course, we can suppose that, like Artaxerxes II, who is reputed to have had a concubine for every day in the year, Xerxes I could have had a concubine whose name was Esther. The story describes her, however, as the chief wife, and her Jewish origin overlooks the strict hereditary requirements for a Persian queen. Moreover, the names Esther and Mordecai are Babylonian rather than Elamite; these seem to be personal names, although they are based on the names of the deities Ishtar and Marduk. The first of these is a goddess of love, the second is the patron deity of Babylon. Again, at the same time when Ahasu-erus was supposed to be hosting a series of banquets, he was actually engaged in a disastrous battle with the Greeks that eventuated in the defeat at Salamis.

LITERARY ASPECTS

The story abounds in literary features whose purpose is to enrich the narrative rather than to present exact facts. For example, the bribe that Haman offered his king has been estimated as half the annual income of the Persian empire. Of course, no rational ruler would grant subjects, Jew or non-Jew, permission to kill more than 75,000 citizens in a single day. Nor is anyone likely to construct gallows 83 feet high, even if hatred for the intended victim is gnawing at his insides and propels him to extreme actions. The story, rich in drama and hyperbole, has its lighter moments, such as the elaborate perfumings that prepare Esther for the first encounter with the king. It makes use of several fairy-tale motifs: a sleepless king; a ruler who desires to show off his queen's beauty (cf. the Greek historian Herodotus's account of Gyges); a king who offers his lovely wife a gift "up to half his kingdom"; and the rise of an orphaned daughter to a place of honor beside the king. All its attempts at historical exactness pale before the dominant characteristic of the book, its literary craft.

Even literary polish fails at one point, the complex discussion of the celebration of Purim in two localities, presumably in the Eastern Diaspora* and in Jerusalem. This section (9:20–32) attempts to legislate the precise days for observing the feast of Purim and the manner of celebration. In all probability, this Persian festival arose as a pagan celebration, possibly on the occasion of the New Year, and was subsequently taken over into Judaism. It seems that Jews in the provinces kept the festival on the 14th of Adar, whereas those in Susa observed it on the following day. An easy resolution to the problem was to observe both days. As an expression of gratitude, gifts were to be exchanged and, in addition, some were to be bestowed on the poor.

Although the story of Esther is woven together with considerable skill, there are some indications that the individual narratives may once have existed independently. Each of the stories stands on its own: Vashti's refusal to appear before a drunken court, Mordecai's discovery of a

---

*The word *Diaspora* has become a technical expression for the dispersion of Jews, in this instance throughout Babylon.

planned palace revolt and rise to power, Esther's success in a beauty contest, and Haman's aspirations to power and bitter disappointment. However, these stories now comprise a nearly flawless narrative that moves from the ridiculous to the self-sacrificial. In many respects the finished product resembles the Books of Daniel and Judith, but each one contributes its particular view about the most effective Jewish response to external threat.

ORIGIN OF THE BOOK

When was the author of this secular narrative active? As in most cases of biblical books, the matter is extremely complicated. A few observations seem in order, although their value is not always of equal weight. Sirach does not mention Esther in his praise of famous men (Ecclesiasticus 44–50), but he does not include any women in this survey of notable biblical persons. Esther is the only canonical book that has not shown up in some form among the documents at Qumran. On the other hand, the style of the book is not that of the noncanonical scrolls from the Dead Sea area. Unlike Daniel, which has several Greek words, Esther seems to be entirely free of this Hellenistic influence, unless it has occurred in another form, the Greek concept of a woman's erotic power. Perhaps most surprising of all, the book is completely silent about some of the themes that seem to dominate other literary compositions of the second century B.C.E.: apocalyptic expectations, prayer, a legalistic understanding of the Torah, and so forth. One thing appears certain; the author lives in an age that is far removed from the Persian period, for memory of that time has become highly inaccurate. The early period of Seleucid persecution therefore offers a realistic time for someone to offer a response such as this book to that crisis. However, there may have been earlier crises that could have elicited such a response, so it is perhaps wise to leave open the matter of dating it.

An origin during the persecution that Antiochus IV Epiphanes set into motion would explain the ferocity of the spirit released within this book. Not content with a single day's slaughter of the enemy, the Jews repeat the performance a second day. Persons who enjoy religious freedom and cannot imagine any threat to their survival as an ethnic group may quickly condemn this ferocity as the inevitable poison that infects a persecuted people, but surely more can be said than that. It is remarkable that the author takes pains to absolve the Jews of any charge that they profited financially from the killings, although it would have been legal for them to do so. To be sure, this notion may represent conscious recollection of the divine prohibition against taking plunder in the battle against Haman's ancestor Agag, king of the Amalekites. But there may be more in this twice-repeated phrase: "But they laid no hands on the plunder"

(9:10–15). The author implies that Jews should take up arms for one purpose only: to defend the nation against annihilation. The voice of nationalism is certainly heard in this story, but it is tempered by a spirit of self-sacrifice on behalf of an endangered populace. It may be that this unknown author has actualized the religious expectations associated with the end of time by subsuming them wholly under a political solution to the Syrian threat. If that is indeed the case, others quickly raised their voices in favor of traditional hopes that relief and assistance would arise from on high. That conforting thought does not seem to have found a haven in the mind of the person who wrote the book of Esther.

◆ 22 ◆

Daniel

T HE collapse of the Judean state in 587 B.C.E. marked the end of its independent political existence, with one brief exception during the years 145–63 B.C.E. when the Maccabees gained control of its destiny at the expense of Syrian rulers, the Seleucids. For more than four hundred years the covenant people had little reason for boasting, despite some grandiose promises by the unknown poet whom we call Second Isaiah and by the two prophets Haggai and Zechariah, who inspired the disappointed people to rebuild the Temple in Jerusalem. In this endeavor, nostalgia surfaced as a problem of immense significance, for the new sacred edifice could not compare with Solomon's architectural achievement for the worship of Israel's God. The brutal reality pressed itself on the people again and again: the glory that was Israel's lay in the past. Small wonder the poet who announced a new exodus urged the people to forget former things and to anticipate the new acts of deliverance that Cyrus would set into motion. But the fresh experiences never quite measured up to the memories of what had characterized Israel's earlier existence, and, as always, frequent telling of the sacred stories resulted in numerous embellishments that only encouraged the tendency to live in the past.

One aspect of this veneration of heroes from earlier days was the elevating of ancient prophets who had warned the nations Israel and Judah that the Deity intended to punish them for failing to practice justice and for religious infidelity. The prophecies of doom against the northern and southern kingdoms had come true, and in the the process the prophetic vocations of these individuals had been vindicated. But these same prophets had predicted comparable judgment against the great empires of their day, and these prophecies had not yet been fulfilled. Slowly the conviction grew that in the near future the Deity intended to put an end to these powerful forces of evil. A sense of expectancy filled the air as nations competed for supremacy, and all the while the covenant people

363

watched to see what these struggles meant for a displaced people and for those few exiles who had returned to Judah.

SETTING

The Book of Daniel was written in a time of expectancy. It begins with the destruction of Jerusalem and ends with a prophecy about the dawning of the kingdom of God on earth. At the heart of the book stands a prophecy about this kingdom, and the pulsebeat is occasioned by the attempt to determine the exact time for the end.. The means of discovering this date was the study of ancient prophecy in the light of contemporary events. It seemed to the author that history was winding to a close, and every announcement of hostile engagement must have been electrifying for a community awaiting the end. So far, however, only human forces were locked in struggle, but any moment that situation could change, and this entry of warriors from a heavenly realm would mark the beginning of the end. Although the last days would be a period of great testing for the saints of the Most High, these holy ones believed they would finally inherit the kingdom. Then nothing in the past, not even Solomon's glory, would compare favorably with the present moment.

ANCIENT PROPHECY

The decisive prophecy that the author seeks to understand, chapter 2, speaks of a human figure with head of gold, breast and arms of silver, belly and thighs of bronze, legs of iron, and feet partly of iron, partly of clay. A stone, quarried by the Deity, smites this image and shatters it; then that stone becomes a huge mountain filling the whole earth. Just as the Israelites thought their own history was in decline, so this author believed the kingdoms of the world were becoming successively worse. This decline is the meaning of the mixture of metals in the figure of a man. Whereas the head was pure gold, the feet were iron and clay. Here we have a version of the ancient notion that civilization has become pro-gressively worse, the four ages being gold, silver, bronze, and iron. The prophecy, which came as a dream, proclaims the collapse of world powers as a supernatural accomplishment, but it does not specify who will benefit from the Deity's entrance into the human drama, nor does the dream specify the date for this overthrow of earthly might. Another dream, chapter 7, expresses the same idea in different words. Four beasts, a lion, a bear, a leopard, and an unspecified dragon-like monster, arise from the great sea, the symbol for chaos in ancient thought.* The last one emerges

---

*The Book of Revelation concludes with an exquisite vision of a new heaven and new earth, in which it is said that there was no more sea. The point is that evil has been van-quished forever.

victorious, and its ten horns and one little horn occasion comment. Then God, the Ancient of Days, ascends a throne and opens the books in judgment. The dragon is slain, the others prolonged for a season, and a person resembling a son of man descends from heaven and receives an everlasting kingdom. The rest of the book is mostly concerned about the meaning of this dream and its consequences for the Jewish people. In this way the prophecy was made to describe their own historical situation; as a result, the book can be dated almost exactly.

DATE

The four kingdoms of the prophecy are the Babylonians, Medes, Persians, and Greeks. On the basis of some earlier erroneous prophecies by Isaiah (13:17; 21:2) and Jeremiah (51:11, 28) that the Medes would defeat the Babylonians, this author assumed that there must actually have been a Median kingdom that succeeded the mighty Babylonians. As a matter of fact, the Persians under Cyrus took Babylon without a fight. The ten horns of the fourth beast represent the Diadochi who succeeded Alexander the Great, and the little horn signifies the Seleucid ruler Antiochus IV Epiphanes. This king desecrated the Temple in Jerusalem and proceeded to make Judaism an illicit religion. The author describes Antiochus's actions correctly until the year 168 B.C.E., but from that time historical inaccuracies take over. What is more, the author does not know about Antiochus's death in 164. The obvious conclusion is that at precisely this point the author begins real prophecy, and all the rest is past history. The date of composition was therefore between 168 and 164.

This understanding of the date for the final compilation of the book, which explains the fact that Sirach does not refer to Daniel in Ecclesiasticus 44–50, is reinforced by the language and content. The curious use of Aramaic and Hebrew has defied explanation so far, although the most likely explanation is that the court tales circulated orally in Aramaic for some time before the author used them and wrote chapter 7, his own interpretation of the prophecy in chapter 2, as a suitable transition to the more specific attempts in chapters 8–12 to apply this prophetic word to contemporary events. Naturally, the court stories required an introduction, and this was written in Hebrew, the language of the author. The court stories are in Imperial Aramaic rather than an earlier form of the language. It is still a mystery, however, why the Aramaic passage breaks into the middle of a sentence, although the author may imitate Ezra and Nehemiah in presenting "documents" in their original language.

CONTENT

The content of the book includes ideas that are the latest in the Hebrew Bible—for example, the belief in the resurrection and a personal angel who watches over the Jewish people. Furthermore, the medium of communication, the use of dreams and visions to interpret history, is a late development, even though it links up with comparable material in the Joseph narrative. Certainly the emphasis on animals to represent the kingdoms of the ancient Near East and the unusual imagery associated with them characterize a particular kind of literature from the second century onward. That literary type, apocalyptic, purports to unveil the future and therefore attributes the interpretation of visions to heavenly figures. Because this literature assumes that it makes use of earlier prophecies that spoke to the present moment, it is attributed to an ancient figure, in this instance, Daniel. In the Canaanite epic *Dan'el and Aqhat*, Dan'el is a king who looks after the well-being of widows and orphans, and in Ezekiel he is associated with Job and Noah. The spelling of the hero's name in these court tales and visions is different, Daniel rather than Dan'el, but an association with the ancient hero may well have been intended. A consequence of this identification of a figure from the past as the author of the current book is the notion that it has been sealed for centuries. This sequestration also implies that the material is reserved for a special group of people and is therefore esoteric knowledge. In this way the long delay between the time of the original prophecy and its actual fulfillment is given a rational explanation, and a rationale is provided for the emergence of an old book years later. This also explains the sustained effort to attribute the revelation to an angel and to depict Daniel as frequently confused and unable to grasp the meaning of the visions.

Perhaps the attribution of the book to Daniel arose from another kind of reasoning, the assumption that a correspondence existed between the beginning and the end of time. The belief that the course of human affairs was moving in a great circle seems to have gripped the ancient world. It has been called the myth of the eternal return.* According to this view of things, the end time corresponds to the beginning time. Therefore, a prominent participant in that earlier era would be expected to understand what must inevitably take place at the end of time. If the hero Daniel were thought to have lived in that formative period, he would naturally have been a logical choice to play the role of prophet of things to come. Later literature chose Enoch as the premier visionary, because according to tradition he had never died, but it also viewed many others in this light: Moses, Noah, Abraham, Baruch, Ezra, and so forth.

---

*To some extent ancient Israel seems to have entertained the notion that history would make one great revolution, so that the beginning of time corresponded to the end of time. But this cyclical understanding of reality, usually attributed to the Greeks, was not understood as an exact equivalence, for the end time in rabbinic thought certainly introduced new elements into the picture.

AMBIVALENCE TOWARD FOREIGNERS

A striking feature of the book is its ambivalence toward foreigners in the court stories, whereas the second half has a loathing for them. In fact, the Greek translation paints the foreign rulers and other officials in much darker colors, indicating the intense feelings of hostility that seem to have overtaken many Jews. These early stories about Daniel and his three friends at pagan courts must have arisen when life among the exiles was difficult but not yet impossible; this situation changed decidedly during the persecution by Antiochus IV, for at that time many faithful Jews were required to lay down their lives rather than shift religious loyalties. In one respect the whole book represents a united front; the focus of history no longer centers on Israel and Judah. Actually, the covenant people stand on the perimeter of world events, and other nations occupy center stage. The most the exiles can do is offer advice through gifted individuals like Daniel, Shadrach, Meshach, and Abednego.

OLDER COURT STORIES

The exiles at the royal court undergo various trials but always emerge from danger unscathed. Daniel successfully tells Nebuchadnezzar his dream and its meaning, although the wisest of the king's counselors had said that none but the gods could do such a thing. The story makes no secret of the means by which Daniel acquired the necessary information, for it reports that the Deity revealed this matter to him. Daniel's three friends refuse to compromise their faith by bowing before a golden image, and they survive being thrown into a furnace. In this story we hear of a strange figure like a son of the gods who joins them in the fire, and when the three emerge from it they are completely unharmed. Again Daniel interprets the king's dream that announced that he would become a madman living among animals for a time, and once more Nebuchadnezzar acknowledges the superiority of Daniel's God. In another story Daniel explains the meaning of some writing that mysteriously appears on the wall during a banquet when Belshazzar and his court drink from sacred vessels that had been stolen from the Temple in Jerusalem. The final court tale reports that malicious courtiers seek to harm Daniel by persuading Darius to pass a law requiring everyone to worship him alone for a month. Of course, Daniel continues to pray three times a day toward Jerusalem and is therefore thrown into a lion's den, despite the king's efforts to frustrate his own law. This time, too, the Deity comes to the rescue, Daniel walks out of the den unhurt, and his enemies and their families are executed.

These earlier stories once circulated independently, for they have not

The inscription on this mina weight states that it is an exact copy of a weight from the time of Nebuchadnezzar II (605–562). A mina was the equivalent of sixty shekels. The inscription on the wall in the story about Belshazzar contains a pun on this word (mene, mene, tekel and parsin).

been integrated very effectively, although they do indicate planned structuring. This unevenness appears most clearly in the presentation of the king, who converts to the Jewish faith more than once, as if the earlier recognition of the Deity's power had never taken place. Moreover, Daniel must be introduced at the court twice, although his first success as an interpreter of dreams should have made his name familiar to the king. Besides these inconsistencies, there are dates that do not correspond, and one story mentions Daniel's three friends even though they do not play any role in the chapter, just as he does not appear in chapter 3.

The introduction is essential to the stories as they now exist, for it prepares for the one narrative in which heroes other than Daniel appear. This introduction achieves something far more important, however, for it shifts the historical context from the problems in exile to perils facing

Judeans in the second century. In short, Antiochus IV had forbidden Jewish subjects to live according to their dietary laws, the very thing that set them apart from their neighbors and contributed to their survival as a distinct people. The author's answer to this decree from a despotic ruler, whose policies were so insane that he was nicknamed Epimanes (the madman), was cleverly disguised in the story about Daniel and his three friends who were brought to a foreign court and who insisted on keeping the dietary laws despite any risk it might entail. In this story the four thrive on their own special food, for their Deity made them prosper. The message is that Jews in Antiochus IV's day should continue to keep the dietary laws, trusting all the while in divine protection.

This appeal to faithfulness is the central theme of all the court tales. No risk is to too great where religious allegiance is concerned, even if one's life has to be forfeited. That point almost jumps out at readers in the response by the three men who choose a fiery furnace rather than abandon their God. They grant the possibility that the flames may snuff out their lives, but they also insist that the God whom they serve is able to rescue them. Whether they live or die, they will not alter their conduct. The other stories do not state the point in so many words, but the heroes speak by their actions. For example, no law issued by a human ruler takes precedence over one's conscience. Prayer, the flame that keeps religious devotion alive regardless of earthly circumstances, must go on whatever the cost. Therefore, Daniel bows the knee and worships his God as before, and the Deity does not forsake him in time of need.

DREAMS AND VISIONS

The second half of the book takes a somewhat more realistic view of the situation, perhaps in acknowledgment of the many martyrs who died when they risked everything. Such was the danger inherent in the hero legends about Daniel and his three friends. Reality was considerably more brutal for the ordinary Judeans who dared to defy a king. The author of the dreams and visions in chapters 8–12 recognizes the agony that faithfulness to the Deity will bring, and he allows for a brief period when the battle will appear to go in favor of the evil ones. Nevertheless, this author is decidedly less realistic in an optimism that the heavenly forces will decide the issue in favor of the Jews. Furthermore, the writer introduces a bold hope for some individuals who had laid down their lives for a worthy cause. These unfortunate ones who had hoped in vain would now experience the power of the resurrection. Whereas Ezekiel dared to believe that the spirit could revive a dead nation, this author takes an unprecedented step to apply that miracle on an individual scale. By New Testament times this assertion became a divisive issue separating religious parties, the Pharisees endorsing belief in a resurrection and the Sadducees rejecting it.

Catacombs at Beth-she'arim, an extensive burial place in postbiblical times.

PRAYER

In chapter 9 a long liturgical prayer is preserved; scholars generally consider it secondary because there are striking similarities between this prayer and those in 1 Kings 8, Ezra 9, and Nehemiah 9. These similarities suggest that the author uses traditional phrases that worshipping congregations would have known and appreciated. The emphasis falls on human guilt and divine compassion, and appeal is made on the basis of the Deity's reputation. In short, the defeat of the Jews will foster the belief that their God was too weak to protect them, and foreigners will therefore mock the Deity. The prayer also looks back over the long history of Israel's relationship with its God, confessing sins but reminding the Deity of "his servants the prophets" and mentioning Moses and the Law. Of course, the deliverance from Egyptian bondage and the resulting elevation of the divine name are singled out in this historical retrospect. A single aim seems to characterize this prayer—to elicit divine mercy. That purpose becomes evident when the appeal is made that the Deity shine on the sanctuary "for thy sake" and not because of human merit. One can only imagine the horror that must have overtaken the Jews when Antiochus IV offered swine's meat on the sacred altar in the Jerusalem Temple. This act was "the abomination that makes desolate," a phrase that occurs more than once in the book of Daniel.

The earlier court tales also contain evidence of traditional piety and even some special prophetic themes. Two of these are pratically note-worthy, the denunciation of pride and the appeal to the king that he change his ways and begin to implement social justice. The form of the appeal differs from the prophetic word, but the content is similar.

> Therefore, O king, let my counsel be acceptable to you; break off your sins by practicing righteousness, and your iniquities by showing mercy to the oppressed, that there may perhaps be a lengthening of your tranquility. (Dan. 4:27)

The occasion for this advice is the king's exalted sense of his own worth, which led him to think that he was the tree of life that sustained all creatures. For this arrogance, he is driven away from civilization for a definite period of time. This story may have been about Nabonidus, the Babylonian ruler who neglected his duties and lost his kingdom to the Persians, for some evidence from Qumran points in this direction. This evidence is a fragment of a prayer attributed to Nabonidus that was dis-covered near the Dead Sea. However, Eusebius of Caesarea preserves a tradition about Nebuchadnezzar's madness, so the issue is not so simple. The absence of the motif of pride in the Qumran text has seemed to indicate that a tradition about Nabonidus has been transferred to Ne-buchadnezzar in the court stories recorded in Daniel.

Although the stories may originally have functioned largely as enter-tainment, the instructional intent seems to have been there from the out-set. They make a single point in various ways: human destiny rests in the Deity's hands and not in the power of monarchs. The importance of this theme could hardly be overstated in the days when Antiochus IV seemed to hold the fate of the Jewish people in his powerful hands. The stories about Daniel and the three friends assert in no uncertain terms that the Most High watches over those who remain faithful to their Lord. The final word will be spoken by the Ancient of Days, who bestows the kingdom on the saints of the Most High.

FOLKLORE

An interesting feature of this consoling word is its use of folklore and mythic material from various cultures. The reference to the Ancient of Days echoes Canaanite texts that identify the deity El with these words, and the strange vision of a ram and a he-goat seems to derive from ancient Babylonian astrology, which uses these animals to identify signs in the zodiac. Three of the beasts in another vision—the lion, bear, and leop-ard—were the dreaded predators of Palestine. Nevertheless, these crea-tures are equipped with the additional wings and heads that often appear in Mesopotamian iconography. In the story about Belshazzar's feast, the folklore motif of spirit writing occurs. It follows that the author draws on materials from different cultures to communicate with fellow Jews in the second century B.C.E. This eclecticism suggests that the second part of the book, at least, presupposes a sophisticated audience, a probability that its esoteric character seems to confirm.

SETTING THE DATE FOR THE END OF TIME

The author of Daniel inadvertently set into motion a trend that has surfaced throughout Jewish and Christian history since the second century B.C.E.—the attempt to determine the exact date for the end of time. In the case of this initial calculation, a mistake was made, someone later made a new estimate, and the two stand sidy by side. The original author believed that the end would come in 1,290 days after Antiochus IV desecrated the Temple, but another date seeks to extend that period to 1,335 days, unless the two dates represent two different ways of reckoning calendar years. Like all such efforts to know more than the human brain is capable of grasping, this calculation ended in failure. An unfortunate by-product of such counting of the day is the inevitable strain on faith when the predicted day for the end of time arrives and things go on as usual. The other result of such thinking is the danger of precipitate military action in the mistaken belief that the Deity will enter the foray and usher in the kingdom. The later Jewish revolt against Rome seems to have been fueled by this sort of thinking.

In the Hebrew Bible the book of Daniel appears in the Writings, the third division of the canon, whereas the Greek translation, the Septuagint, places it among the Prophets. One can readily understand why the book was associated with prophecy, despite the absence of the usual formulas from that body of literature. The later prophetic books became more and more concerned with certain themes that are central to apocalyptic, such as the day of the Lord's judgment for the nations and salvation for a remnant of Israel. In a very real sense, apocalyptic carries on these emphases within prophecy. It is therefore highly probable that prophecy gave birth to this kind of literature, and the supposed similarities between apocalyptic and wisdom literature are more apparent than real. The position of the book within the Hebrew Bible suggests that by the second century B.C.E. the prophetic portion of the canon was already complete, and the entry of a new book was no longer admissible to those who made such decisions. The fact that the fragments of Daniel from Qumran are not written in the style of Hebrew normal for the canon confirms this assessment of the situation.

TRIVIALIZATION

Perhaps more than any other book, Daniel has been trivialized by religious enthusiasts whose sole interest seems to rest in identifying contemporary political figures who are destined to play a dubious role in the final battle just before the Deity wraps up history. The book does not deserve such a fate, for it constitutes a powerful testimony to faithful conduct in the midst of almost unbearable persecution. If the message that the author sought to leave with his fellow Jews appears to be a flight into metaphysics and a retreat from reality, it is because the times were difficult indeed. But that message was also one of courage and resolute conduct in serving the Most High. The imagery may be bizarre, and the stories unrealistic, but both arose from a vital faith in the Lord of history. To be sure, the author was mistaken in viewing the confrontation with Antiochus IV as the final battle that would usher in the kingdom, but more importantly, the writer recognized the responsibility to serve God faithfully regardless of the circumstances. This is the legacy bequeathed by the author of the Book of Daniel, and not some mistaken timetable about the last days.

· 23 ·

Ezra-Nehemiah

CHRONICLES, Ezra, and Nehemiah reflect a common style and similar interests, leading interpreters to think that one person, or perhaps a school of thought, stands behind all three works. The central emphasis lies on priestly elements in society and their official duties, and piety pervades every aspect of communal life. Moreover, a harsh attitude toward foreigners colors the account, except in depictions of Persian rulers, who are described as partial to the Jewish exiles who hazarded the long journey from Mesopotamia to Jerusalem. In the face of threatened assimilation into the local population, extreme measures commended themselves to the small group who endeavored to repopulate the Judean capital and to restore worship of the ancient Deity thought to have chosen Jerusalem as a special dwelling place.

The author of these three works, the Chronicler, had access to some written sources from which to compile the account in Ezra and Nehemiah. The extent of these sources and their reliability have occasioned extensive debate, and so far no consensus has formed. A surface reading seems to indicate at least the following sources: (1) an account of the early efforts to restore the community from 538 to 516 B.C.E., (2) some memoirs associated with Ezra the scribe; and (3) memoirs of Nehemiah. In addition, various governmental decrees, lists of sacred vessels and people who returned from exile, and lists of those who married foreigners give the impression that the Chronicler consulted official documents in compiling authentic history. Closer examination has raised doubt about the historical reliability of the materials and the final product constructed from them.

Utter chronological confusion exists in both books. The events of 538–516 have been fused with those associated with 458–420, and the relative order of Ezra and Nehemiah may have been reversed. The first six chapters in Ezra recount the story of initial efforts by Zerubbabel and Jeshua to reconstitute worship in the Temple at Jerusalem. This narrative downplays Sheshbazzar's contribution in favor of leaders some seventeen

374

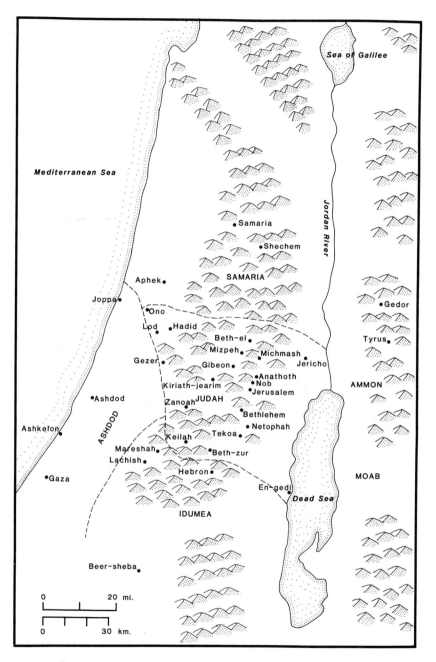

The Land of Judah in the days of the return (c. 440 B.C.E.*)*

years later during the prophetic ministries of Haggai and Zechariah. The lists of sacred vessels that were returned to Jerusalem, whence they had been taken by Nebuchadnezzar in 587, stands a better chance of being authentic than the list of people who made the long journey to that city, which seems inflated in the same way numbers are regularly exaggerated in Chronicles. Nehemiah's memoirs seem to be a genuine written source, perhaps a defense of an official who had been wrongly accused and a prayer aimed at redress for this individual. Parallels to this memorial exist in Egyptian biographical inscriptions;* however, Nehemiah's intention is less self-glorification than self-vindication. In some ways the Ezra memoirs resemble those by Nehemiah, but their authenticity has fallen under attack in some circles. Indeed, a few critics have gone so far as to question Ezra's actual existence, viewing the stories about him as a figment of the Chronicler's imagination.

SEQUENCE

The narrative about Ezra breaks off in the middle, only to recur in the latter part of the book of Nehemiah. This treatment of the two men as if they were contemporaries presents a problem. According to the chronology within the text, Ezra preceded Nehemiah by several years. Ezra's arrival in Jerusalem is dated in the seventh year of Artaxerxes I Longimanus (458), whereas Nehemiah came to Judah in 445. For various reasons many scholars reverse the sequence, placing Ezra's arrival in the seventh year of Artaxerxes II (398). The essential reasons for this bold hypothesis are as follows: a certain Johanan, the son or grandson of Eliashib, is mentioned in Ezra, but evidence from the Jewish colony at Elephantine places him in Judah about 410; for thirteen years Ezra delayed the task for which he came to Jerusalem; when Nehemiah arrived in Jerusalem the walls were not built, and the city was sparsely inhabited; Nehemiah had to repeat Ezra's harsh measures aimed at dissolving marriages between Jews and non-Jews; Nehemiah never mentions Ezra, and blames his predecessors for the corrupt situation in Judah; local officials exercised authority during Nehemiah's stay in Jerusalem; and a list of high priests is mentioned. A third theory has been put forth recently, one based on ancient sabbatical years. This mode of calculation yields the years 430–429 for Ezra's arrival.

The evidence for any theory is hardly overwhelming, although probability seems to rest on the side of those who reverse the order of the two men. Nevertheless, there may very well have been two Johanans, as there seem to have been several Sanballats in Samaria. Moreover,

---

*The purpose of these inscriptions was to impress the deities and thus to assure a place in the next life for the individual whose exploits are enumerated.

The excavated wall of Jerusalem believed to date from the time of Hezekiah (eighth century B.C.E.*).*

religious reforms are often short-lived, and life in Judah was difficult in those years, considerations which may explain the conditions that prevailed when Nehemiah arrived. The prophet Isaiah never mentioned Micah, who was active in his day, and Hosea did not refer to Amos. It follows that Nehemiah's failure to mention Ezra may not be significant at all. Furthermore, it seems unlikely that either Ezra or Nehemiah really exercised the degree of authority that is attributed to them. In short, Nehemiah's limited secular authority and fiscal resources explain the arduous circumstances under which the city wall was built. The same goes for Ezra, who exercised religious leadership but whose power to command obedience was minimal. Hence, the long delay in implementing the work for which he left a comfortable life in Persia to endure unknown hardships in Judah is understandable.

THE REBUILDING OF THE TEMPLE

The two books chronicle the events surrounding the rebuilding of the Temple between 521 and 516 (Ezra 1–6) and the work of Ezra and Nehemiah (Ezra 7–10, Nehemiah 1–13). A considerable segment of Ezra is written in Imperial Aramaic (4:8–6:18, 7:12–26), and there is a curious shift from first to third person within the memoirs. This narrative feature occurs elsewhere in late texts, specifically Tobit and the Aramaic story of Ahikar. Perhaps the memoirs are more extensive than those texts employing the first person. If so, Ezra 10 may belong to Ezra's memoirs, and Nehemiah 10, 12:27–43, and 13 may complete Nehemiah's self-defense. Because he alludes to having returned to Persia in 433 and says that he came back to Jerusalem before Artaxerxes' death (424), it is conceivable that Nehemiah was recalled by Persian officials because of charges against him by local citizens.

PIETY

The Chronicler's distinctive piety finds expression in the two books, particularly in the prayers preserved in chapter 9 of each. Here the sins of the community are confessed, the Deity's forgiveness is sought, and the long history of divine solicitude for Israel is recalled. One feature of the Chronicler's attitude toward cultic purity brought untold suffering to many families within the community. The threat of religious syncretism and ethnic assimilation prompted Ezra and Nehemiah to demand that every marriage between a Jew and a foreigner be dissolved. This narrow view grew out of a historical situation in which the Jewish faith faced a serious threat to its very survival. Where the heart of religion is understood as the Temple cult and where priestly purity is the dominant concept, the harsh measures implemented by Nehemiah and Ezra seem to be a logical means of addressing a vexing problem. That this extreme action was not taken without strong resistance arising from circles where quite different presuppositions reigned becomes clear if one turns to such books as Ruth and Jonah.

NATIONALISM

Modern readers often react coolly to the provincial attitudes that governed Ezra and Nehemiah's conduct. The dissolution of marriages, the cruel treatment of children who spoke a language other than Hebrew or Aramaic, the refusal of assistance from worshippers of the Lord who had remained in the homeland, the enforced reading of the Law while the people shivered in a cold rain—such behavior on the part of religious and secular leaders hardly commends these books to contemporary Jews or Christians. Nevertheless, these two men believed that the new law in Ezra's hand, presumably the whole Pentateuch, reflected divine will for the community, and they risked their lives in an all-out effort to turn the written word into actual reality. In light of extreme resistance from hostile neighbors, Nehemiah's repeated appeal to the Deity for remembrance becomes understandable. Nehemiah's accomplishment in building a wall around Jerusalem has become an ironic symbol prompting many interpreters to remember him for evil rather than for good. That result is indeed unfortunate. The history of Christianity is also marked by attempts to establish a holy community that were characterized by extreme cruelty.

• 24 •

Chronicles

THE fall of Jerusalem in 587 B.C.E. marked the end of the Davidic monarchy, and about fifty years later when a few of the exiled peoples returned to their former capital they were unable to reconstitute life as it once had been. An attempt to restore kingship during the brief period when the prophets Haggai and Zechariah burst on the scene and successfully inspired the people to rebuild the Temple in Jerusalem came to grief, for Persian authorities seem to have acted quickly to extinguish such messianic fervor. Unable to recover a significant aspect of their past—specifically, political kingship—the disappointed people focused their energies on the religious institution that had set them apart from foreigners among whom they lived. If these former exiles were not permitted to have a king from the Davidic line, at least they could worship freely. Political aspirations thus receded into the background, and cultic matters took precedence in the community.

It therefore seemed proper to offer an adequate legitimation for the Temple cult that had assumed such importance to the community, especially because a rival group in Samaria challenged the religious hierarchy at Jerusalem. The unknown author of Chronicles took up that task of providing a legitimate rationale for the centrality of the Jerusalemite cult. In doing so, this individual was able to capitalize on a growing "Davidic mystique" in a way that exalted David at Solomon's expense. It almost seems that this author thought David's chief interest lay in making plans for the construction of the Temple and for organizing cultic life in its precincts.

PLOWING OLD FURROWS

Of course, the Chronicler covers ground that others had already plowed, often in great detail. It appears that the author used Samuel and Kings as a primary source, frequently recounting stories that parallel those in the Deuteronomistic history. Although numerous sources are mentioned in the course of the Chronicler's history, the two main ones, royal chronicles and prophetic utterances, actually comprise one work, Samuel-Kings. However, the Chronicler extends the history beyond the exile of King Jehoiachin in 597 B.C.E. and subsequent events surrounding Jerusalem's fall in 587, for these things lay in the distant past. Various sources came into play for this more recent history, particularly the memoirs of Nehemiah and Ezra. It is usually thought that these three separate books once constituted a single work by the Chronicler, but strong arguments have recently been made for viewing Ezra and Nehemiah as separate works.

It is immediately apparent that Chronicles has no claim to objective reporting of history, but the difference in this regard between Samuel-Kings and Chronicles is only one of degree. The author of Chronicles exercises considerable liberty with sources and offers a selective rendering of the facts that heightens the miraculous where Temple personnel are involved. Levitical priests merely have to pray and sing, whereupon enemy forces become confused, smite themselves, and leave their booty lying on the ground for Judeans to confiscate. A similar attitude toward actual history allowed the Chronicler to describe David as a king who was preoccupied with the building of the Temple and with organizing its music. The excuse David offers for all this effort is that Solomon is just a lad and will therefore need plenty of advice from an older, experienced individual.

The Temple personnel were responsible for more than the daily sacrifice, the many festivals, and their accompanying music. Teaching, which seems to have played an important role among priests from early times, came into prominence within the exilic and postexilic Jewish community. Naturally, the Chronicler introduced this element into the history that was written for this new community. The form of this instruction has come to be known as Levitical preaching, and it lies at the heart of Chronicles. This type of preaching was so decisive for the Chronicler that it has spread to the speeches placed in the mouths of prophets and kings. The same spirit and themes dominate the prayers that are sprinkled throughout the Chronicler's work.

OMISSIONS AND ALTERATIONS

One feature of Chronicles has occasioned considerable discussion, much of it negative. The author omitted those episodes in David's life that discredited him, in particular the adulterous affair with Bathsheba and murder of her husband, Uriah, as well as the pathetic account of turmoil within the royal household. Some interpreters view this omission as an attempt to whitewash the Judean king, but others point out that a full account is in Second Samuel, a source that the Chronicler used without making any effort to conceal it. In effect, his frequent citations from chronicles of Judah's kings almost invite readers to consult them. If this observation is correct and the Chronicler really expected readers to consult a work that by now must have gained considerable authority, the omission of flaws within David's character in the Chronicler's history may have resulted from a desire to concentrate on the king's admirable qualities, because he is exalted as founder and organizer of the Temple cult.

At times, however, the Chronicler simply altered the truth in a way that goes beyond discreet silence about a popular king's weaker moments. Nevertheless, this altering of the facts functions theologically in the same way that materials to support a particular view of history are used by the author of Samuel-Kings. A specific instance of the Chronicler's rewriting of historical events concerns the notorious Judean king Manasseh, who acquired a reputation for religious apostasy because of his close ties with Assyria. This ruler had occupied the throne in Jerusalem longer than any other king, despite his relaxed attitude toward Assyrian religious customs. For the Chronicler, who applied the principle of reward and retribution to individuals rather than to nations as the Deuteronomistic historian had done, Manasseh's long reign constituted a problem. Why did Israel's God permit this wicked king to thrive for so many years? An answer concentrated on divine compassion and patience: the Lord knew that Manasseh would eventually repent of his misdeeds. Therefore, the Chronicler introduces the wholly unrealistic account of this king's conversion toward the end of his life. The apocryphal Prayer of Manasseh takes this idea further in the direction of the piety prevailing in the era just before the end of the Hebrew Bible.

Another incident reveals just how the Chronicler touched up the portrait of Judah's kings according to a vision of how things should have been. Josiah met an early death at the hands of Pharaoh Necho despite the Judean's obedience to the divine will and his valiant efforts to reform the nation. Whereas the Deuteronomistic author passed over in silence what must have brought immense anguish to many troubled thinkers, specifically an early violent death for one who, in most eyes, deserved much more favor from the Deity, the Chronicler offers an explanation for Josiah's execution. That incident resulted from his refusal to pay heed to a prophetic oracle. By adding this little bit of extra information, the Chronicler managed to reinforce the theory of reward and retribution that Josiah's early death had thrown into question.

As a matter of fact, the Chronicler credits Israel's prophets with far more success in dealing with kings than occurs in other sources. One gets the impression that prophecy is remembered as something from the past, and its representatives have acquired certain features often associated with holy persons. One reason for this elevation of prophecy may be the Chronicler's desire to demonstrate the Deity's active control of everyday affairs. In a word, history is shaped so as to show that a theocracy has come into existence. Through a series of chosen representatives— kings such as David, Solomon, Jehoshaphat, Hezekiah, and Josiah who listened to prophets and obeyed the divine will—the way has been prepared for a society that is ruled by God. That community now exists, in the Chronicler's opinion, and the Temple personnel mediate the divine will to a repentent people. With God in control, the community no longer needs a Davidic ruler on the throne. The ancient struggle between royal and priestly authority has issued in a victory for the religious leaders, thanks to the Persian government.

It has been suggested that the Chronicler sought to undercut claims made by a hostile community in Samaria. Certain features of the Chronicler's work seem to support such an interpretation. Instead of tracing the history of the northern kingdom, the Chronicler ignores this important nation except in the few places where Judah's story interacts with it. This aversion to facts pertaining to the northern kingdom may explain the curious beginning chapters, which comprise a genealogy from Adam to Saul's death. In this manner the community at Samaria is deprived of any material within the Chronicler's account of world history that might legitimate its own claims to be the true people of God, although of course the genealogy of the northern tribes is included in First Chronicles 1–9.

HISTORICAL CONSIDERATIONS

In certain instances the Chronicler has preserved factual data that fill in some gaps in historical description. For example, Josiah's reform seems to have begun about ten years before the discovery of the law book within the Temple ruins. If this chronology is indeed correct, it implies that Hilkiah's discovery of a scroll, probably Deuteronomy, was occasioned by the religious reform rather than giving birth to it. Such an understanding of the facts may strengthen the claim that this scroll was actually produced for the occasion; in other words, it was written to give divine authority to Josiah's political revolt against Assyria and the accompanying religious reforms. The Chronicler also offers a credible explanation for Josiah's death beyond the one aimed at defending a theory of reward and retribution. Josiah seems to have sacrificed his life in a futile attempt to prevent Pharaoh Necho from reaching Carchemish in time to assist the Assyrian army in its stand against a combined Babylonian and Median force.

These reliable data relate to other kings as well. We learn about an aqueduct dug by Hezekiah's engineers in anticipation of rebelling against

Assyria, and we are provided a list of fortresses for the defense of Judean cities. Moreover, a plausible reason is given for a visit to Jerusalem during Hezekiah's days by an embassy from the Babylonian ruler, Merodach-baladan. These representatives of a foreign king came to Jerusalem to arrange a treaty with Hezekiah that would strengthen Merodach-baladan's resistance against Assyria. Even some names have been preserved in their original form, Merib-baal and Eshbaal, whereas the Deuteronomist replaced the despised *baal* ending with the Hebrew word *bosheth* (shame), giving these names as Mephibosheth and Ish-bosheth. Nevertheless, the Chronicler handled the facts loosely in most cases, and that laxity has caused suspicion about the treatment of Nehemiah and Ezra.

Perhaps the tendency on the Chronicler's part to paint the past in terms of a particular theology reached its fullest expression in the story about David's census, for which the Deity is thought to have punished the people grievously. According to the Chronicler, Satan tempted David to number the people, presumably for military purposes, whereas the parallel account in Second Samuel 24 credits the Deity with this command to take a census. Obviously, the older account reflected badly on Israel's God, and the Chronicler lived at a later time when an alternative explanation for evil had come into vogue. Therefore, this new version of the census blames Satan for inciting David to act in a manner that angered the Deity. In this way the story comes to emphasize divine compassion rather than caprice.

MORALIZING

The Chronicler's comments about the deaths of Saul and Uzziah also illustrate this tendency to moralize. King Saul died because he consulted a medium, and Uzziah contracted leprosy as punishment for a cultic transgression. With examples like these the Chronicler sought to strengthen a theory about reward and retribution that had increasingly fallen under attack. In a sense this author continued a trend that had been set long before, and in doing so the Chronicler successfully counteracted religious apostasy and compiled an exalted narrative account of a community that believed the Deity ruled over its daily existence. As in the case of the Deuteronomistic "historian," the facts functioned in the service of religious instruction. Both works should be evaluated in terms of their success toward achieving this goal; if that is done, the Chronicler's standing will increase greatly, and perhaps this much-maligned author will be less subject to accusations of deceit and legal-mindedness.

It may then be possible to appreciate Chronicles as a response to a religious situation in which faithfulness to the ancient Deity had become difficult. The Chronicler linked past and present, and in the process ironed out some wrinkles in Judah's sacred memory. The impulse that "distorted the facts" can hardly be faulted: it was a desire to strengthen the faithful for whom world history had collapsed more and more into a Temple cult and its sacred moments. For the Chronicler, this holy community was the Creator's intention, and the events that brought it about resulted from a happy coincidence of divine activity and obedient human response.

• PART FOUR •

THE DEUTEROCANONICAL LITERATURE

TO judge from the literature composed during roughly the last two centuries B.C.E., radical changes were taking place in the life and thought of the Jewish communities. Partly because Jews found themselves scattered in several directions, Jerusalem soon became but one of at least three intellectual and religious centers, the other two being Alexandria and the region to which Judeans had been dispersed during Babylonian domination. The earlier unifying function of the Temple in Jerusalem temporarily vanished with its destruction in 587, and new forms of worship soon made their appearance. Above all, the dominant presence of Greek language, custom, and thought forced Jews to come to terms with altogether different understandings of reality. It is significant that the Jewish literature of this period has survived almost solely in the Greek language, with the exception of sectarian writings from the area near the Dead Sea. This Jewish literature in Greek was first attached to the Septuagint, a translation of the Hebrew Bible into Greek. In due time the additional books became known as the Apocrypha, or hidden books, and were at first popular among Jews in Alexandria but eventually fell into disfavor because of their popularity with a rival group, the Christians. Their survival is largely due to this Christian appreciation for earlier Jewish writings in Greek.

Precisely what sort of changes occurred in this important period of Jewish history? What is possibly the most noticeable shift seems to have come as a natural result of trends set into motion by Nehemiah and Ezra during the second half of the fifth century B.C.E. Their attention to the Torah as the decisive factor in daily life must have given rise to a coterie of specialists whose sole task was to issue rulings concerning the correct requirements of the law. Thus a priestly aristocracy became indispensable once Torah observance achieved signal importance. To educate the people about the demands of and rewards for Torah observance, a new kind of literature was needed. Hence popular stories were conceived in which

387

heroes and heroines exemplified the kind of daily conduct characterizing one who practiced obedience to Torah. Naturally, such exemplary behavior was not easy, which the devotional legends do not attempt to gloss over. The centrality of prayer stands out, but deeds of kindness toward others assume almost equal prominence. So does purity of worship, that is, the avoidance of various forms of idolatry. The attacks on idolatry are particularly harsh, suggesting that this issue must have caused much grief in Jewish circles. Another issue that generated considerable consternation was purity of blood, indicating a desire to marry within the Jewish community itself. Of course, these two issues were closely related, since non-Jews presented a threat by introducing alien worship into the family circle.

Another far-reaching change in Jewish perception resulted from the decisive shift in the power base from earlier times when Israel was able to wield some influence on the international scene. The days of David, Solomon, and the Omrides had long since vanished, and all hope of self-determination seemed lost. It appeared that Israel's moment of glory lay in the distant past, and foreign empires with huge armies threatened to crush anyone who dared to challenge their might. What was one to make of faith claims about the Lord's sovereignty and the choice of Israel for special destiny? Why had the forces of evil gained sway, and when would Yahweh rise to do battle against them? Such were the burning questions that forced themselves on the minds and hearts of devout Jews again and again.

Therefore, a new type of literature came into being—apocalyptic—and anxious souls reflected on the meaning of existence in an evil world. Behind this literature burns the conviction that a bright prospect is in store for the elect despite present misery; apocalyptic literature aims to unveil the future and thus to offer a ray of hope for a chastened people. In due time historical events seemed to reverse the recent trend, hurling tiny Judah once more into a position of religious and political independence. Naturally, an accurate account of these momentous events had to be written; thus the ancient history of Israel as recorded in the Hebrew Bible came into being once more, tracing events into the late second century. An unusual feature of this new history is its pathetic dimension, exhibiting a conscious desire to emphasize martyrdom and the emotional suffering to which the pious are submitted.

Not every shift in perspective is so serious, for these Jewish writers show a remarkable capacity to laugh in difficult times. Indeed, a new means of expressing faith in the literature of this period resembles modern detective stories. In such narratives a prophet succeeds in exposing wicked judges or empty religious claims. Although the laughter may approach mockery, it is not entirely mean spirited. At times humor intrudes where one expects serious history, and entertainment seizes the initiative. One example of contest literature poses the question, "What is strongest?"

and elevates woman above wine and sovereign, partly atoning for the negative attitude toward women in some of this literature.

In some ways the most significant change during this period is the way wisdom is integrated into the religious traditions of earlier Israel. This change comes about in two important stages; the equating of wisdom and Torah and the identification of wisdom with the divine spirit that inspired great men of the past, especially prophets, priests and kings. Even the exodus from Egypt is interpreted as the direct result of divine wisdom. What is more, the Jewish idea of wisdom is also related to Stoic notions of a rational principle governing the universe, and thoroughly Greek philosophical concepts enter the discussion of Jewish wisdom. Nevertheless, one of these wisdom books retains its original Hebraic flavor, continuing the trend in Proverbs 1–9 toward extensive discussion of proverblike sentences, resulting in instructional literature.

In short, the last two centuries B.C.E. and the first century of the Common Era brought decisive changes to Jewish history and faith. Life in the dispersion was beset with new temptations and new opportunities, not the least of which can be summed up with the word Hellenization. To retain their individuality, Jews focused their lives on the observance of Torah, and this led to scribal-priestly resurgence, consciousness of sin and penitence, and joy over piety and deeds of kindness. The watchword came to be purity, both in faith and in lineage. But such striving for holiness did not automatically change history, personal or national. The problem of evil remained the perennial threat to belief, giving birth to a masterpiece of theological reflection. The sheer burden of history did not destroy the Jewish capacity for laughter, and in the end a compromise was worked out so that Greek and Hebraic ideas could stand alongside one another. It is to this literature that we now turn.

• 25 •

First Esdras

THE Book of First Esdras, also called Third Ezra, is essentially a
Greek translation of the final part of Second Chronicles, all of Ezra,
and a small segment of Nehemiah. The only substantive addition
is a story about a contest at the royal court (1 Esd. 3:1–5:3). The book's
purpose seems to be concentrated on reforms within the Jerusalem cult;
it emphasizes the contributions of Josiah, Zerubbabel, and Ezra. Just as
Sirach overlooks the work of Ezra, First Esdras ignores Nehemiah's activity in Jerusalem. There is some historical confusion here, particularly
the merging of Sheshbazzar and Zerubbabel, although the former returned the sacred vessels to Jerusalem and laid the foundation for the
Temple in the time of Cyrus, and the latter succeeded in restoring the
Temple under Darius about twenty years later. The historian Josephus*
followed the account in First Esdras, and therefore its date must be prior
to 90 C.E. Most interpreters assume that the book was written in the late
second century B.C.E. A striking feature is its ending, which breaks off
in the middle of a sentence.

The contest of Darius's guards is an exquisite example of literature in
Greek, but Hebrew and Persian influence on some features of the story,
at least, is generally acknowledged. The contest has been adapted to the
Jewish setting by the addition of the words, "that is, Zerubbabel," which
identify the hero with the Jewish court figure who returned to Jerusalem
during Darius's reign. Then, of course, a lengthy section has been added
to the actual story, which ends in 4:41. The purpose of this material is
to state how Zerubbabel attained the king's favor. Its contradiction of
2:1–14 seems not to have bothered the author. We shall concentrate on
the contest itself. It concerns the question, what is strongest? The three

---

*The Jewish general Josephus surrendered to Rome during the first revolt in 66–70 C.E.
and was richly rewarded; he later devoted his time in Rome to writing about Jewish history,
his most significant works being *Jewish Wars* and *Antiquities*.

guards answer: wine, the king, woman, and truth. Their defense of these answers constitutes matchless rhetoric.

The first speech defends wine as strongest of all. It describes the powerful effect of wine on human thought and action. Those who get their fill of wine cease to think rationally; they act in complete disregard for sociological distinctions; they undergo altered psychic states; they lose all contact with reality; they turn their backs on custom; and they sacrifice their most valuable capacity, memory. But these points are made concretely; the pictures of drunken behavior are unforgettable. Under wine's power people think poorly; kings and orphans become equal; pain and unpleasant realities are forgotten; even paupers think they are millionaires; brothers fight with one another; and nobody recalls what happened when wine's influence has subsided. It follows that wine destroys the essence of humans, their capacity to think, to make discriminating judgments, and to remember. Thus the link with the past is severed, and the present moment, distorted by wine, is mere illusion.

The defense of king as strongest begins by noting how a royal figure merely tells soldiers to risk their lives and they do so, but it extends the scope of royal authority to include those subjects who pay taxes. All subjects, whether professional soldiers or ordinary citizens, carry out the ruler's slightest wish. In this connection one comes upon a passage that strongly resembles the polarities in Ecclesiastes about a time for everything. Only those things that fell within the jurisdiction of royalty are selected for inclusion here.

> If he tells them to kill, they kill;
> if he tells them to release, they release;
> if he tells them to attack, they attack;
> if he tells them to lay waste, they lay waste;
> if he tells them to build, they build;
> if he tells them to cut down, they cut down;
> if he tells them to plant, they plant. (1 Esd. 4:7–9).

The speech emphasizes subjects' willingness to turn over to a king the fruit of their own labor, and yet he is only one man. Although this powerful person is vulnerable, because he must eat and sleep, no one dares to raise a hand against the sovereign. It is curious that this concession of the king's vulnerability is not seized by the next speaker, but then a similar admission that wine's power wears off is also ignored.

The defense of woman as strongest starts with the declaration that women give birth to kings and to those who plant vineyards, but the argument ends with an anecdote about the king and his favorite mistress. Men cannot exist without women, just as they owe their existence to women. Furthermore, men readily drop their most valuable possessions, even gold and silver, and stare openmouthed at a beautiful woman. When love conquers a man, he turns his back on primary relations—parents and country—and thinks only of his wife. Men will face any danger bravely, whether wild animals or the raging sea, in order to gain treasures and to lay them at women's feet. Indeed, love for women has driven men mad; others have become enslaved, perished, or lost all honor because of women. As a clinching argument, the speaker tells about the king's amorous conduct when Apame took his crown, placed it on her lovely head, and slapped her sovereign. He, in turn, was miserable until she smiled on him, and the ruler found himself flattering her. With this democratizing of the king came the necessity for the people to judge who the winner was, for the king had become subject to a woman.

The third speech has two answers, for even strong women die. So do kings and vineyards, for all earthly things are ephemeral. The earth, heaven, and sun are mighty testimonies to one who is greater than they, God the lord of truth. Only truth endures and is strong forever. At a number of places it appears that there may actually have been four speeches at one time, besides the praise of truth. The fourth speech would have praised men, with special emphasis on their extraordinary achievements.

The speeches abound in rhetorical questions that function to gain the audience's agreement. They also make use of certain images with unusual effect—for example, the words "and with open mouth stare at her," which applies both to men who are overwhelmed by a beautiful woman walking by and to the king who looks at his favorite mistress, Apame, after she has just teasingly slapped him. The contest is thus an appropriate text for the entertainment of a royal court. From various sources it is clear that such occasions as banquets and similar gatherings encouraged intellectual activity similar to that represented in this contest.* Its preservation is therefore a happy accident. Although most interpreters think its origin is Greek or Persian, strong links with the Hebraic tradition suggest that its author may have been Jewish, albeit a thoroughly Hellenized one insofar as linguistic ability is concerned.

*See the Mesopotamian *Dialogue between a Master and his Slave*, as well as *The Epistle of Aristeas*, a Jewish composition.

◆ 26 ◆

Second Esdras

TOWARD the end of the first century C.E., a deeply sensitive Jewish author reflected on the human problem and left an apocalypse for posterity. That remarkable work (chapters 3–14) later attracted Christian additions (chapters 1–2, 15–16). In this form Second Esdras, also called Fourth Ezra, became enormously popular within the Christian community. The author reveals the shattering effect of the Roman victory in 70 C.E., when Jerusalem was left in ruins. Naturally, these disturbing events raised the oldest and shortest religious question of all, why? In a series of seven visions the author probes the depths of despair and the heights of hope. The first three visions are characterized by profound skepticism, and the last three are filled with divine promise. The fourth vision provides a transition from inquiry and complaint to confident hope. The clue to this hope rests in the twice-mentioned assurance of divine concern for the human race: "For you come far short of being able to love my creation more than I love it" (2 Esd. 8:47).

The initial "vision" deals with the anthropological problem of human depravity (3:1–5:19). Because we all possess an evil heart,* why has Jerusalem suffered divine recrimination? Surely there is no evidence that its conqueror, Babylon (a symbol for Rome), was morally superior. An angel, Uriel, responds by reminding the author that humans cannot solve terrestrial problems, much less these which concern divine intention: "Go, weigh for me the weight of fire, or measure for me a measure of wind, or call back for me the day that is past" (4:5). Undaunted by Ezra's protest that no human is capable of doing these things, the angel reminds him that fire, wind, and the day are accessible to one and all. Had Uriel wished, it could have asked much more difficult questions such as the

---

*From the fact that the Hebrew words for heart and inclination had two different spellings for each expression, it was concluded that humans have two propensities, one good and the other evil. The latter, called the evil *yetser*, was believed to have entered infants, whereas the good inclination did not arrive until the age of twelve.

exits of hell or entrances of paradise. When the angel gives an object lesson that suggests that Ezra has overstepped his limits, Ezra protests that he has raised legitimate issues and wonders why he was endowed with the power of understanding if he is not permitted to use it. The problem raised by a Roman victory over Israel is a matter of here and now. The angel implies that a time of harvest is fixed for the evil seed's produce, and Ezra inquiries, how long? To this question Uriel responds that just as human birth comes at its appointed time, so will the divine harvest.

The second "vision" (5:20–6:34) takes up the issue of election, asking why the Deity abandoned the chosen nation to other nations. The angel asks Ezra if he loves Israel more than his Maker does and poses a series of impossible tasks.

> Count up for me those who have not yet come,
> and gather for me the scattered raindrops,
> and make the withered flowers bloom again for me;
> open for me the closed chambers, and bring forth
> for me the winds shut up in them, or show me the
> picture of a voice; and then I will explain
> to you the travail that you ask to understand. (2 Esd. 5:36–37).

Again the angelic interpreter offers no solution but assures Ezra that the age approaches the end, with people now morally and physically inferior to earlier ones. Ezra wonders why everyone could not have lived at the same time, but the angel insists that, like a pregnant woman, the earth can only give forth its creatures in sequence.

If Israel is indeed God's chosen people, why does she not enjoy the earth's bounty? That is the issue that surfaces in the third "vision" (6:35–9:25), which represents Ezra as rebuking Adam for introducing sin into human experience and condemning all subsequent generations to perfidy. "O Adam, what have you done? For though it was you who sinned, the fall was not yours alone, but ours also who are your descendants" (7:49). In a similar rebuke of earth, Ezra concludes that it would have been better if the dust had never been formed, for then no human mind could have been made from it (7:63). The angel's announcement that the world was created for the sake of a few people provides little comfort for Ezra, who knows that freedom of choice allows most people to transgress the law. The angel emphasizes the narrow and difficult entry into life, and assures Ezra that Israel's portion lies in the next world. The unhappy fate facing the masses troubles Ezra, who insists that most people will miss out on the good things in this world and in the next. Uriel rebukes him sharply: "You are not a better judge than God, or wiser than the Most High! Let many perish who are now living, rather than that the law of God which is set before them be disregarded!" (7:19–20). Here two opposing views of reality call attention to a pressing question: is human personality more valuable than religious institutions and the sacred objects they spawn? In this context, too, the angel describes the order of the righteous and the order of the sinner in the next life. In essence, this section portrays the contrasting fates of the two groups. This "vision" ends with enforced silence on Ezra's part; the angel justifies this prohibition of further questions by asserting that everyone was provided a choice, and no one can escape blame for exercising that freedom.

The fourth vision (9:26–10:59) begins with lamentation and ends in splendor; it therefore provides a suitable transition from the first three complaints to the last three promises. Ezra sees a woman mourning the loss of a son who was born to her late in life and died on his wedding day; the angel explains that the woman represents Jerusalem. Suddenly, a transformation takes place, and the Holy City shines in all its glory. Such is the hope that awaits Zion, provided that the people acknowledge God's decree to have been just.

The fifth and sixth visions interpret Daniel 7. In the fifth (10:60–12:51) an eagle rises out of the sea and disappears when confronted by a lion of the forest. The eagle symbolizes the fourth world empire, Rome, which goes down in defeat before the Messiah. The sixth vision (13:1–58) is about a man who emerges from the sea and destroys an army by his fiery breath. The victorious one then calls a peaceful army to himself. The angel explains that the man represents the Messiah, who destroys pagan armies and gathers the lost ten tribes of Israel.

The final vision (14:1–48) deals with some unfinished business before Ezra is taken up into heaven. He is ordered to restore the Scriptures that were believed to have perished when the Babylonians destroyed Jerusalem. Under divine inspiration Ezra dictates to his five assistants for forty days, and at the end of this period they make twenty-four books public but reserve seventy additional books for the wise. This explanation for the rise of the deuterocanonical books includes the observation that they represented a major change in the Hebrew script, from the old to square script. The author's appreciation for these seventy books is boundless: "For in them is the spring of understanding, the fountain of wisdom, and the river of knowledge" (14:47). This praise of the seventy books did not come at the expense of the twenty-four, for the author was capable of an all-encompassing love.

The angel's argument that precious things, like gold, are rare must surely apply to sensitive spirits like this unknown author's. The profound struggle to understand the human situation is reminiscent of Job, but the answer that the angel offers in Second Esdras is altogether different. Judaism has turned otherworldly, so that the believer's hope transcends the present life. Nevertheless, the problem has become greater than personal or even national injustice; for this author, it is the human problem. Why will only a few people obtain bliss? In this case, the revelation of the Deity's compassion (Exod. 34:6–7) is robbed of its power, and intercession is depleted of its effect. The angel insists that all persons must assume responsibility for their actions, just as all must be born for themselves. Faced with the anthropological problem of the human heart, which has been corrupted by an evil inclination, Ezra refuses to be consoled by assurances that he is one of the few who will achieve life.

The answers that this book offers are less impressive than the witness to an agonizing spirit. The appeal to divine sovereignty is no solution at all, for it evades the moral issue altogether. How can a moral and kind Deity allow evil to triumph? The second response is not an explanation but a promise. The Messiah will prevail at last, and God's people will find rest. To be sure, the strong emphasis on freedom of choice goes a long way toward reducing the Deity's responsibility for the sorry state of affairs, but the human propensity toward evil requires a more adequate explanation.

The Christian additions to the book shift the promise to the church and apply the hope of the resurrection to those who accept the Son. Israel is therefore reckoned to have been abandoned by its God, and Mother Church replaces Mother Zion. The prophetic tradition comes to the fore, with specific mention of the entire division of the Latter Prophets except for Ezekiel. The ethical imperative follows:

> Guard the rights of the widow, secure justice for the fatherless, give to the needy, defend the orphan, clothe the naked, care for the injured and the weak, do not ridicule a lame man, protect the maimed, and let the blind man have a vision of my splendor. Protect the old and the young within your walls; when you find any who are dead, commit them to the grave and mark it, and I will give you the first place in my resurrection. (2 Esd. 2:20–23)

In addition, there is a promise that evil powers will soon fall. Perhaps this reminder that agony of spirit should issue in concrete deeds of kindness provides yet another response to the perplexing human situation. Only in this way way will blind persons catch a vision of divine splendor.

◆ 27 ◆

Tobit

TWO themes lie at the heart of the short story entitled Tobit. The first is the obligation to provide a proper burial for the dead, and the second, perhaps the thrust of the book, is the duty to marry within one's own family group. The two community concerns are illustrated by the personal histories of a father, Tobit, and his son Tobias. The father demonstrates his unusual charity by giving a burial to an executed compatriot, at great personal risk, because the act was clearly a defiant one in the king's eyes. For his trouble he suffers blindness and subsequent poverty, even to the point of praying for death. Tobit's son rescues his cousin Sarah from comparable distress that also prompted her to consider suicide. For some reason unknown to her, seven husbands had died on their wedding night. In the end she abandons the thought out of love for her father and pours out her grief in prayer. Tobias and Sarah marry, thus assuring the integrity of the social group that is threatened in a foreign land. The angel Raphael, whose name means "God heals," assists Tobias in driving off a demon, Asmodeus (the destroyer), who has slain the seven previous husbands on Sarah's wedding night.

The weaving of these two themes into a unified story is achieved with admirable skill. The literary gem combines exquisite narration (told initially in the first person but subsequently becoming a third-person account), speeches, prayers, and ethical advice. It uses a motif of the grateful dead, which is widely employed in various forms within folklore, but also introduces Persian demonology and angelology into the Palestinian context. Furthermore, the narrative mentions Ahikar, the oriental sage whose life and teachings are celebrated in various wisdom texts, especially one that was discovered at Elephantine. In addition, the story of Tobit preserves the well-known Golden Rule, albeit in negative form: "And what you hate, do not do to anyone" (Tob. 4:15a).

In a way the suffering of Tobit and Sarah resembles the test through which Job passed before confessing that the experience taught him the

A menorah (seven-branched candle holder), an oft-used symbol in synagogues.

truth about the Deity, as opposed to secondhand knowledge. One may even speak of undeserved suffering in these instances, for the pious Tobit does nothing to deserve the evil that befalls him, and Sarah is equally innocent, for she cannot be held responsible for a demon's lust directed at her exceptional beauty. Both Tobit and Sarah plead for relief from their suffering and shame, but they do not blame the Deity for injustice. Indeed, Tobit's advice to his son who is setting out on a long journey is strangely silent with regard to the contradiction between his own belief and the facts. The promise of prosperity for good deeds seems hollow when one examines Tobit's misfortune. Clearly, the emphasis of the story obscures the deeper dimensions of reality that the Book of Job examines in an original way. In one respect, however, Tobit and Job are very much alike. Both are less than kind to their wives. In Tobit's case, he suspects his wife, Anna, of impropriety when she brings home a goat that was given to her in addition to her wages. Thoroughly shamed by her husband's suspicion that she has stolen the kid and hurt by his refusal to believe her story, Anna does not remain silent: "Where are your charities and your righteous deeds? You seem to know everything!" (2:14). Job's suspicion was directed at his sons, but his harsh rebuke fell on his wife's ears.

Magic plays a decisive role in the reversal of fortunes for Tobit and Sarah. In the former instance, fish gall is applied to Tobit's eyes and he regains his sight. In the latter case, the heart and liver of a fish combine with incense to drive the demon all the way to Egypt, the supposed land of magic. Naturally, this was no ordinary fish, for it almost devoured Tobias before he succeeded in killing it. The book also contains some unusual features such as the dog that mysteriously accompanies Tobias and Raphael, without contributing anything to the story. Some interpreters have pointed to a similar feature in the epic about Odysseus. For Israelites the dog was an impure animal (Isa. 66:3; compare Deut. 23:18 in which a male prostitute is called a dog); hence, its presence here is extraordinary. So, too, is the approval of offerings on a grave, which is forbidden in the Mosaic law (Deut. 26:14).

The author is guilty of some historical and geographical inaccuracies, and he gives little indication of wanting the book to be taken seriously as history. It confuses Assyrian kings, gives hopelessly impossible dates for Tobit's exile, and indicates an ignorance of Mesopotamian topography. Nevertheless, it quotes canonical tradition freely (Amos 8:10), but sometimes incorrectly (Nah. 3:7 is attributed to Jonah). Moreover, the author refers to the Law and the Prophets, implying that at least these two divisions of the canon are closed, and designates the former as the "Book of Moses." The piety is thoroughly Jewish, with the primary focus on the things that characterize the third to the first centuries B.C.E. Tobit's remarks about the Temple as being less grand than its original must be dated before 20 B.C.E., for Herod's reconstruction of the Temple could hardly be called inferior. The original language was probably Aramaic or Hebrew; fragments of the book in both languages have been found at Qumran. Three recensions in Greek have survived, for the book was immensely popular within the church, which valued its emphasis on marriage and the family.

The scene in which Tobias's parents await his return, fearing the worst, is especially perceptive. While the son and his bride celebrate an extended wedding feast of fourteen days, the father counts the days and thinks of various reasons for the son's absence: he has been detained, or Gabael has died and no one has the authority to give Tobias the money that his father has left in Gabael's care. Noting her husband's distress, Anna, like Sisera's mother in the initial lament of Judg. 5:28, assumes that her son has perished. Her cry reflects the bond between a mother and child, one that is even closer than that of husband and wife: "Am I not distressed, my child, that I let you go, you who are the light of my eyes?" (10:5). Tobit's efforts at quieting her fears fail, and she takes up his own opening words: "*Be still* and stop deceiving me; my child has perished" (10:7). Therefore Anna goes daily to the road by which her son and the angel had departed, watching to catch a glimpse of her son again. For the duration of the feast, she does not eat during the day and mourns by night.

Another component of the story is the attempt to place Tobit in a royal court, which is reminiscent of the Book of Daniel. However, there it was essential to the plot. Tobit is a buyer of provisions for the Assyrian king, Shalmaneser, but falls into disfavor when Sennacherib, his son (!) comes to power. This king executes Judeans, and Tobit buries them. For his charities he has to flee and loses all his possessions. Later Sennacherib's sons assassinate their father, and things change under Esarhaddon, who appoints Tobit's nephew Ahikar second in command. Ahikar intercedes and convinces the king to permit his uncle's return. Once again Tobit defies royal policy and buries a corpse, for which he becomes blind when his impure state requires him to sleep outside the city and sparrow droppings fall in his eyes. For part of the eight years that Tobit is blind, Ahikar takes care of him, but then he leaves town. In the end, Tobit warns his son and the new wife to move away from Nineveh, for it will surely fall as the prophet Jonah (Nahum!) said.

Raphael's final speech, in which he reveals his identity to father and son, combines wisdom sayings with self-revelation. The angel speaks about guarding a king's secrets but disclosing God's works, and encourages prayer when it is accompanied by fasting, almsgiving, and righteousness. The advice can be summarized in a sentence: Do good, and evil will not overtake you. Lest Tobit and his son misunderstand, Raphael states that he only appeared to be corporeal; they actually beheld a vision.

Some aspects of the story reveal sensitivity to the smallest detail. One of the finest touches is the report that Sarah's father proceeded to dig a grave for Tobias on his wedding night so as to conceal his death and thus avoid further shame. In this little anecdote one sees the awful effect of seven deaths within the family, for Raguel has abandoned hope. In yet another episode the story expresses the depth of sorrow by having maidens make fun of the unfortunate Sarah, accusing her of murdering her several husbands. The Book of Job likewise uses this technique to great effect.

The curious attempt to link the Ahikar story to Tobit underlines the fact that counsel occupies an important position in the book. Nadin, Ahikar's adopted son, who in the words of this author was brought from darkness into light, betrayed his father in the Assyrian court, leading to his flight and lengthy exile. The last chapter of Tobit reports that the wicked son paid for his deeds, a statement that seems to sum up much of the advice within the book. An Akkadian wisdom text discovered in Canaan resembles Tobit's advice to his son who is embarking on life's journey.* This section in Tobit (4:3–21) concludes with the promise of great wealth "if you fear God and refrain from every sin and do what is pleasing in his sight" (4:21). Raphael's advice resembles this section, as does Anna's rebuke of Tobit:

> Why have you sent our child away? Is he not the staff of our hands as he goes in and out before us? *Do not add money to money,* but consider it rubbish as compared to our child. For the life that is given to us by the Lord is enough for us. (5:17–20)

---

*Shakespeare uses the same literary convention in Polonius's speech to his son Laertes. The image of a journey is an apt one for life, and it has been used often.

• 28 •

Judith

THE Book of Judith is a brief historical novel about a heroic woman who delivers a besieged city by using her powers of seduction. Like the Book of Esther, this story is characterized by extreme nationalism and deals with the way physical beauty enables individuals to emerge unscathed from threatened extermination. Unlike that book, the narrative about Judith is deeply religious. Even the siege of the unknown city Bethulia, perhaps a symbol for "house of God," is understood as a divine test in Judith's initial speech (Jth. 8:11–27). Here she rebukes the terrified citizens of Bethulia for putting the Deity to a test and insists that they are the ones who are being tested.

> You are putting the Lord Almighty to the test—but you will never know anything! You cannot plumb the depths of the human heart, nor find out what a man is thinking; how do you expect to search out God, who made all these things, and find out his mind or comprehend his thought? . . . Do not try to bind the purposes of the Lord our God; for God is not like man, to be threatened, nor like a human being, to be won over by pleading. (Jth. 8:13–14, 16)

Drawing upon ancient stories about the patriarchs, Judith proceeds to interpret the presence of enemy soldiers as a divine scourge, the lash that love wields on those who draw near in love. Although Judith urges prayer and patient waiting, her own course of action indicates that she also believed that the Deity helps those who help themselves.

The plot is simple. Nebuchadnezzar demands that the west, including the Jews, join him in waging war against Arphaxad, but they refuse to acknowledge his lordship. The furious king sends his general, Holofernes, against the west; the attacking army numbers 120,000 infantrymen and 12,000 archers on horseback. All nations acquiesce except the Jews, whereupon Holofernes asks a certain Ammonite, Achior, why the Jews resist; he gives a lecture on the history of Israel, together with a prophecy that so long as the Jews remain sinless they cannot be defeated, for God defends them. Some soldiers deliver Achior to Bethulia, and others seize the water supply, intending to force the thirsty citizens into surrender. The officials decide to wait five days for divine assistance. A prominent widow, Judith, rebukes them for testing God and persuades them to let her take matters into her own hands. Dressing in her most enticing clothes, she goes outside the city, accompanied by her maid. An enemy patrol escorts the two women to Holofernes' tent, and Judith succeeds in convincing him that she has forsaken her people because they are on the verge of committing a terrible sin, for which God will punish them through Holofernes. Assuring him that she will know the moment when they sin and will communicate that fact to Holofernes, who can then attack the city and take it without losing a single soldier or hearing a dog growl, Judith gains permission to leave the camp each night for the purpose of bathing and praying. Having thus assured a means of escape, Judith promises Holofernes her sexual favors, but he gets drunk in anticipation of pleasure, and she cuts off his head. Placing the head in a food basket, along with the canopy for his bed, Judith and her maid leave the tent and return to Bethulia, whereupon the leaderless enemy soldiers are routed and Judith sings a song in praise of God. Although many wish to marry Judith, she remains a widow until her death, and the people of Israel have peace for a long time thereafter.

The book is a strange mixture of confused history and fiction, much like Genesis 14. The first seven chapters seem particularly problematic. Anachronisms and historical inaccuracies abound, as well as a carnival of names that further complicates matters, almost implying deliberate historical confusion. Nebuchadnezzar is identified as king of Assyria, rather than Babylon, and the Jews are said to have recently returned from exile. As for Holofernes and Bagoas, it seems that two generals by these names (Orophernes and Bagoas) served under the Persian ruler Artaxerxes III Ochus who waged a campaign against Phoenicia and Egypt about 350 B.C.E. Nevertheless, the march by Holofernes' army, 300 miles in three days, is incredible, and the geography is equally unrealistic.

Several things point to a date considerably later than this time: the vague memory of earlier events, the mention of Titans, the reference to an olive wreath, the presence of a deliberative body called the senate, and the strong emphasis on observance of dietary laws.* It seems that the lower limit is the reign of Alexander Jannaeus (102–76 B.C.E.), when the coastal cities Jamnia and Ashdod were annexed by Judea. The original language was probably Hebrew, but this work has been lost; the Greek text has survived in four recensions. During the Middle Ages this book's popularity led to the composition of interpretive (midrashic) additions. From early times the book has been associated with the festival of Hanukkah.

---

*The Titans and the olive wreath as a reward in the gymnasium are Greek, whereas the assembly and dietary laws are entirely Jewish but appear quite late.

Some features of the book are generally considered offensive, apart from its complete disregard for a specific prohibition in Mosaic law. Achior the Ammonite converts to Judaism after witnessing Judith's trophy of war, despite the warning in Deut. 23:3 against permitting any Ammonite or Moabite to enter the assembly. One could interpret this verse literally as inoperative after the tenth generation, or four hundred years. The means by which Judith achieved her goal has occasioned considerable comment, ranging from those who think seduction in itself is immoral to those who also view calculated murder as heinous conduct. Justice can only be done to the story by setting it within the Maccabean period when Judaism's survival was at stake. Holofernes' demand that the people worship Nebuchadnezzar may actually point to Antiochus IV. In that context both its nationalism and its unusual ethics appear in an altogether different light.*

The story also possesses its lighter side, which is almost obscured by the subject itself. Judith's speech to Holofernes is full of hidden meanings, and the comment by the enemy soldiers who discovered Holofernes' torso is humorous: "For look, here is Holofernes lying on the ground, and his head is not on him!" (14:18). Humorous, also, is the way in which Holofernes' head was secretly carried out of camp in a food basket. Various aspects of the story were chosen for their capacity to evoke pleasure in Jewish audiences, particularly the enemy soldiers' remarks about Judith's ravishing beauty.

> And they marveled at her beauty, and admired the Israelites, judging them by her, and every one said to his neighbor, "Who can despise these people, who have women like this among them? Surely not a man of them had better be left alive, for if we let them go they will be able to ensnare the whole world!" (Jth. 10:19)

The dialogue is especially rich throughout the latter part of the book. Judith's initial comments to enemy soldiers recall a comparable speech by Hushai during Absalom's rebellion against his father David. Judith identifies herself as a Hebrew—her name means Jewess—and explains her departure as an unwillingness to be devoured. Then she adds the following:

> I am on my way to the presence of Holofernes the commander of your army, to give him a true report; and I will show him a way by which he can go and capture all the hill country without losing one of his men, captured or slain. (Jth. 10:13)

Confronting Holofernes for the first time, Judith pretends to be awed by his splendor, which she describes in royal imagery: "For we have heard of your wisdom and skill, and it is reported throughout the whole world

---

*In this area it is easy to forget that ancient peoples had different understandings of reality from modern ideals about right and wrong. Perhaps ancient ideals also differed from actual practice.

that you are the one good man in the whole kingdom, thoroughly informed and marvelous in military strategy" (11:8). When summoned by him for a night of pleasure, she seems more eager than he. "Who am I, to refuse my lord? Surely whatever pleases him I will do at once, and it will be a joy to me until the day of my death!" (12:14).

Sensual imagery is not all Judith is capable of evoking. Her piety is equally passionate. She prays regularly, and her deep devotion to the Deity sets her apart as a singularly devout person. Therefore, the extreme risk that she took was all the more noteworthy, and her strong claim to have escaped compromise insofar as her virtue is concerned makes that point most tellingly. Judith's prayers recall her ancestors' extreme action in avenging the rape of Dinah and praise the warrior Deity.

> For thy power depends not upon numbers, nor thy might upon men of strength; for thou art God of the lowly, helper of the oppressed, upholder of the weak, protector of the forlorn, savior of those without hope. Hear, O hear me, God of my father, God of the inheritance of Israel, Lord of heaven and earth, Creator of the waters, King of all thy creation, hear my prayer! (Jth. 9:11–12)

Even as she held Holofernes' sword over the sleeping general, Judith paused long enough to pray. Her legacy, therefore, is more than heroism akin to Jael, for Judith is a model of piety as well, observing the dietary laws within an enemy camp and committing her cause to the Deity in fervent supplication and praise.

◆ 29 ◆

Additions to the Book of Esther

U NIQUE among the books of the Hebrew Scriptures stands Esther, which lacks any direct reference to the Deity. That poverty with respect to the religious dimension of reality was corrected in the Greek version, which contains 107 extra verses. These additions consist of a dream and its interpretation, an exposure of a plot to assassinate the king, prayers by both Mordecai and Esther, a letter that purports to represent the Persian ruler's edict that placed Jews throughout the empire in peril and one that reverses the royal decree, and a story about the queen's appearance before the king without having been summoned. The additions contain drama, legitimation of historical "facts," and religious sentiment.

Mordecai dreams of a struggle between two dragons, who symbolize him and Haman, and of a tiny spring that becomes a huge river, which represents Esther. Having overheard a conspiracy against the king, Mordecai reports the matter and ingratiates himself with the sovereign, who bestows favor on his loyal subject. Naturally, the king's letter fits in badly with this information, for the one who saved his life is now endangered by royal action. Mordecai's prayer acknowledges that he would readily have kissed the soles of Haman's feet to save Israel but professes his resolve not to bow down before anyone but God. Esther tells the Deity that she has rejoiced in God alone since becoming the queen and confesses that she loathes the bed of the uncircumcised. When she goes to see the king unbidden, she possesses supernatural beauty that prompts him to say that the law does not apply to her and to act solicitously toward her. The earlier description of Esther's self-abasement serves as a foil to God's exaltation of her. The king's second letter accuses Haman of villainy and praises Mordecai as "our savior and perpetual benefactor." The final addition identifies Lysimachus as translator of this entire book into Greek in the year 78–77 B.C.E.

◆ 30 ◆

The Wisdom of Solomon

THE extent to which Greek style and ideas permeated Jewish wisdom in the first century is evident in the Wisdom of Solomon, about which Jerome* wrote that "even the style of the book stinks of Greek eloquence." This claim is based on far more than such obvious features as explicit mention of the four cardinal virtues (self-control, prudence, justice, and courage, Wisd. of Sol. 8:7) or of a preexistent soul that burdens the body. The author draws freely on Hellenistic concepts, often using them to refute traditional Jewish beliefs or to broaden Hebraic teaching in quite specific ways. The use of technical language and concepts from Greek philosophy is loose and uncritical, as if the author had simply been alert to popular ideas of the day. Naturally, the claim of Solomonic authorship cannot be taken seriously, for the Hebraic elements in the book are minimal, and the original language was Greek. Like Ecclesiastes, which also purports to be written by Solomon, this book alternates between third- and first-person narration. Both books combine poetry and prose, as well. In the Wisdom of Solomon the first few chapters maintain an illusion of poetry through parallel verse form, but discourse eventually prevails, and narrative characterizes the final chapters.

The structure of the book is relatively simple. It consists of three parts: (1) the justice and mercy of God, 1:1–6:11; (2) wisdom, the bride, 6:12–9:18; and (3) wisdom and justice in Israel's history, 10:1–19:22. The central thesis is that wisdom profits those who acquire her, despite arguments to the contrary, for the Deity is both sovereign and just. The author seeks to defend this conviction against "faulty logic," represented by persons who see life's meaning only in terms of the present moment, and promises rich rewards that wisdom freely bestows on those who love her. The

---

*Jerome was the translator who rendered the Hebrew text into Latin (the Latin Vulgate) in the early fifth century C.E.

accusations become harsh at times, especially when mocking the prevailing popular ideas about idols. Still, the dominant mood is one of fervent appeal to follow a way of life characterized by wisdom.

Who was the intended audience? Scholars generally give a twofold answer to this question, asserting that the author addressed Jews and Egyptians. In this view, the first part of the book is intended as a refutation of apostate Jews, whereas the section on wisdom and the attack on idolatry are aimed at Egyptian rulers. It seems more likely that the whole book was written to Jews, for the fiction of rulers hardly requires actual pagan kings as readers, and the language in the section on idolatry seems more appropriate as confirmation of Jewish beliefs than as refutation of Egyptian beliefs intended for pagan ears. Such abuse would have convinced few pagans, for their own thinkers had already recognized the dangerous excesses of idol worship, and few people really would have recognized themselves in the description that appears in this book. Everything within the three sections is understandable as a fervent appeal to Jews in Alexandria, who were exposed on every hand to Greek concepts and practices.

The precise date of the book is uncertain, although linguistic evidence points to the late first century B.C.E. or the early decades of the Common Era. The author does not seem to know Philo, the Jewish philosopher who lived in Alexandria from 25 B.C.E. to 40 C.E. However, on the basis of the theological argument in the book, one would think that the author had never heard of Job, for the valuable contributions of this radical thinker are ignored. Some interpreters assert that a similar silence occurs with respect to Ecclesiastes, although others understand the argument in chapter 2 as direct attack on individuals who have perverted Ecclesiastes' teaching about enjoying life. Similarities between the Wisdom of Solomon and the epistles of St. Paul can be understood in one of two ways, either as direct influence on the Apostle or as common education.

There is little doubt that the author of the Wisdom of Solomon embraced Greek thinking as an appropriate medium for the expression of religious belief. The proof from history, a sort of midrash on the Exodus event, makes effective use of a device called syncrisis wherein contrasts between the Deity's treatment of Israelites and Egyptians are isolated for religious reflection. Seven contrasts came to mind: (1) the Deity slaked Israel's thirst but gave Egyptians blood to drink; (2) Israelites ate quail, but odious insects spoiled the Egyptians' appetite; (3) God delivered Israel from fiery serpents and punished Egypt with insect bites; (4) snowlike manna benefited Israelites, but snow and ice (hail) were harmful to Egyptians; (5) a pillar of fire illuminated the night for Israel, but darkness overcame the land of Egypt; (6) the Deity protected Israel's firstborn but slaughtered Egyptian children; and (7) Israelites walked through the Reed Sea on dry land, whereas Pharaoh's army was drowned by the surging sea.

Another stylistic device is sorites, the linking together of an argument in a chain structure. This Hellenistic feature occurs in chapter 6.

> *The beginning of wisdom is the most sincere desire for instruction,*
> *and concern for instruction is love of her,*
> *and love of her is the keeping of her laws,*
> *and giving heed to her laws is the assurance of immortality,*
> *and immortality brings one near to God;*
> *so the desire for wisdom leads to a kingdom. (Wisd. of Sol. 6:17–20)*

In addition, there is the practice of stringing together a long list of adjectives that describe character, a practice that Paul also used with reference to virtues and vices. In the Wisdom of Solomon, the bride, wisdom, is described in the following manner:

> For in her there is a spirit that is intelligent, holy, unique, manifold, subtle, mobile, clear, unpolluted, distinct, invulnerable, loving the good, keen, irresistible, beneficent, humane, steadfast, sure, free from anxiety, all-powerful, overseeing all, and penetrating through all spirits that are intelligent and pure and most subtle. (Wisd. of Sol. 7:22b–23)

The thought of the book is fully as Greek as the style. This Hellenistic perspective extends to a description of the curriculum available at the time. The teacher is wisdom, and her subjects include philosophy, physics, history, astronomy, zoology, religion, botany, and medicine (7:17–22). That is not all, for she is called an initiate in the knowledge of God, and for this reason wisdom offers instruction in the mystery cults that flourished at the time. Perhaps that is a reasonable deduction from 2:22, which denies such esoteric knowledge to the sinners whose hope rested in this life only. For the author of the Wisdom of Solomon, death was not the end, inasmuch as humans were endowed with an immortal soul. Two explanations for evil are therefore given, the one Hebraic and the other Hellenic. The first was that the devil led people astray, and in this form one recognizes a sharp departure from the original story about a serpent who beguiled Eve. The second explanation centers on materiality; the sin of humans consists of the fact that they have bodies, which in themselves are evil.

One consequence of this attitude toward corporeality is the reshaping of earlier Hebraic teachings. Material possessions no longer constitute divine rewards, for an otherworldliness suddenly enters Jewish thought. Childlessness with virtue is now more important than children, and eunuchs can rejoice if they possess goodness. Furthermore, the attitude toward longevity now changes, and a long life is not seen as proof of righteousness. Instead, an early death is understood as the Deity's way of testing believers or delivering someone from temptation before a fatal lapse occurs. With all this comes a remarkable shift in the nature of religion itself. Whereas doubt played an important role in Hebraic religious expression, it is no longer considered appropriate. Now the worshipper is expected to silence those questioning thoughts that functioned as creative fountains from which ancient Hebraic thinkers freely drank.

The author takes pains to defend the Deity's justice against doubters who reasoned that life's brevity requires instant gratification at any cost. Their use of thematic language from Ecclesiastes seems certain, including the enjoyment of creation during youth, drinking wine and anointing themselves with perfumes, the idea that this is their portion and lot, and the belief that death is the end, both of one's existence and of memory. The passage echoes dominant words from Ecclesiastes, so much so that it is difficult to escape the suspicion that the author has in mind some persons who have perverted Ecclesiastes' teaching. Their viewpoint is dismissed as faulty reasoning, and justice is affirmed.

The author's crowning argument derives from a belief in immortality. Because we shall survive death, it matters little whether that termination of life in the body comes early or late. With a single stroke of the pen most arguments against divine justice are nullified. Ancient Israelites did not reckon with life after death, and therefore they were obliged to defend the Deity's conduct in terms of earthly circumstances. The author recognizes no conflict between sovereignty and justice, thus renewing Isaiah's argument that the creature cannot complain to the Creator. Great stress falls on divine compassion, at times in almost bizzare form, as when the Deity is said to have chosen a humane manner of slaying Egyptians rather than turning wild beasts loose on them.

The notion of an elect people permeates the author's thought. Israel is the Deity's favorite, just as Solomon is the husband of the bride, wisdom.

> But thou our God, art kind and true,
> patient, and ruling all things in mercy.
> For even if we sin we are thine, knowing thy power;
> but we will not sin, because we know that we are accounted thine.
> (Wisd. of Sol. 15:1–2)

Divine favor is not limited to the elect nation, however, for the sovereign Deity judges with mildness and gives foreigners ample time to repent. This idea is developed at length in the midrashic treatment of the events associated with the Exodus. This story must have required extensive reinterpretation once Jews settled in Alexandria, for the core event in their faith presented Egyptians in a very unfavorable way. Such sacred texts could hardly have ingratiated the Jews to Egyptians in the first century B.C.E.

If the section on idolatry (13:1–15:17) actually functioned as apologetic literature, its effectiveness was seriously impaired by a misunderstanding of such worship. It would not be the first time this happened, for Second Isaiah's mockery of idolatry suffers from a comparable unwillingness to recognize the positive features of this practice. The author of the Wisdom of Solomon offers three explanations for the origin of idolatry: vanity, grief, and aesthetics. Desire to pay proper respect to a distant ruler prompted subjects to fashion idols in the emperor's likeness. Or a grief-stricken father carved an idol as a permanent memorial to a dead child. Alternatively, the love of beauty led to a craft that proved lucrative as well as creative.

The author gives these people credit for recognizing beauty in the created world but scolds them for stopping short of seeing the Creator behind nature itself. Their right intuition had failed to prevent sexual perversion, a charge that occurs in extremely harsh language. Here the origin of fornication is linked to the concept of idolatry inasmuch as the sullying of marriage beds is explained as the direct consequence of such worship. The idol's inability to do anything comes in for special ridicule:

> When he prays about possessions and his marriage and children,
> he is not ashamed to address a lifeless thing.
> For health he appeals to a thing that is weak;
> for life he prays to a thing that is dead;
> for aid he entreats a thing that is utterly inexperienced;
> for a prosperous journey, a thing that cannot take a step;
> for money-making and work and success with his hands
> he asks strength of a thing whose hands have no strength.
> (Wisd. of Sol. 13:17–19)

The culminating argument is that worshippers are superior to the object of adoration, for the one who prays to a dead idol has life.

The ideas in the Wisdom of Solomon are in no way unique. For example, Euhemerus of Messene explained the origin of idolatry in terms of emperor worship and a grieving father, whereas various philosophers of the day ridiculed such worship in similar language. Moreover, points of contact between the Wisdom of Solomon and several philosophical or religious systems of the time are easily perceived. The Stoic idea of wisdom as the ordering principle of a harmonious universe occurs in this book, but the author differs from Stoic thinkers in recognizing the place of miracles in altering the nature of reality. There are also sections in the book that remind one of gnosticism and dualism, two powerful intellectual movements at the beginning of the Common Era. The description of wisdom as an emanation of the glory of the Almighty and a reflection of eternal light (7:22–27) is very much like later gnosticism, and the otherworldly emphasis approximates the teachings at Qumran, where an ethical dualism prevails, and with it a lingering pessimism. It is significant that the ancient Hebraic notion of Sheol has yielded to a concept of Hades, with the accompanying belief in the afterlife as a place of punishment. In addition, the praise of wisdom resembles the language in hymns to the Egyptian goddess Isis.

Of course, the author also reflects knowledge of the biblical tradition.

Sometimes, as in the idea of the image of God, the earlier concept is transformed into something quite different. At other times the older teaching remains reasonably intact—for example, the numerical saying in Prov. 30:18–19 about mysterious movement by a ship, eagle, serpent, and two lovers. This proverb appears in Wisd. of Sol. 5:9–12, with the omission of the final reference and the substitution of an arrow for a serpent. However, this discourse on movement without a trace leads into an allusion to the mystery of birth, which is understood as the loss of previous virtue. From these examples it is clear that the biblical material serves as a source for theological reflection. The use to which the author puts the story about Solomon illustrates this point. Here the king's choice of wisdom is set within an erotic context, which sees knowledge as the ultimate partner in life. Accordingly, Solomon's prayer for wisdom is highlighted, and his example is lifted up for others to follow. Nevertheless, differences quickly appear when Solomon boasts that a pure soul befell him, and when he discounts human reason.

> *For the reasoning of mortals is worthless,*
> *and our designs are likely to fail,*
> *for a perishable body weighs down the soul,*
> *and this earthly tent burdens the thoughtful mind. (Wisd. of Sol. 9:14–15)*

The author of Ecclesiastes would readily have concurred in the negative assessment of reason, but the rationale here provided is one that belongs in Alexandria rather than in Palestine.

◆ 31 ◆

Sirach

BY the beginning of the second century the bankruptcy of biblical wisdom had become evident, largely through incisive critiques by the unknown authors of Job and Ecclesiastes. For the former, revelation replaced human reason in the final analysis, and faith prevailed. Ecclesiastes exalts personal observation and reflection while insisting that wisdom cannot uncover life's mystery or equip one successfully to come to terms with death. Both authors rejected extravagant claims that in their enthusiasm wisdom's guardians had advanced; at the same time, the authors of Job and Ecclesiastes recognized that relative gains could be had through the use of reason.

Jews in second-century Palestine and Alexandria faced a dilemma in reconciling religious claims and experience. Exposure to the Greek philosophical tradition taught them an appreciation for biblical wisdom, which resembled it in many ways. How could they recover this valuable legacy without abandoning the distinctive features of their faith, elements that were strangely absent from wisdom literature? An answer to this question would not come easily, for any adequate resolution of the problem from which the query arose had to satisfy competing factions. There were traditionalists, who looked on wisdom literature as impoverished because it nowhere takes into account the special relationship between Israel and the Lord. But others, perhaps comprising the bulk of the younger generation, valued the product of universalistic thinking inasmuch as it placed tiny Judah on the world scene intellectually.

The Book of Sirach (Ecclesiasticus) offers a response to this difficult problem. It reveals a transition within Israelite wisdom, a fusing of traditional faith with worldly wisdom. The lesson from the Book of Job seems to have weighed heavily on the mind of the person who brought together these two quite different understandings of reality, specifically that no really satisfactory explanation for life's enigmas could afford to exclude the element of divine initiative. Of course, this acknowledgment opens the way for the mystery of revelation in the living present, terrifying and grand beyond belief. The initial collection in the Book of Proverbs offered an additional clue: religious faith is the presupposition and goal of all knowledge. From these two starting points, a self-manifesting deity and wisdom as the human expression of spiritual devotion, it was a small step to hymnic adoration of a compassionate deity and to equating true wisdom with the law that was thought to have issued from the mouth of this Holy One. In essence, the scribe dons a prayer shawl, and wisdom takes her seat within the worshipping community.

AUTHORSHIP

Greek pride of authorship has made a firm contribution to biblical scholarship in the case of Sirach, for the author identifies himself by name.

> *Instruction in understanding and knowledge*
> *I have written in this book.*
> *Jesus the son of Sirach, son of Eleazar, of Jerusalem,*
> *who out of his heart poured forth wisdom. (Ecclus. 50:27)*

Although the text varies appreciably in the form of this self-introduction, it is customary to call the author Sirach or Ben Sira, the Ben meaning "son of." Sirach also provides the information that he operates a school, to which he invites prospective students.

> *Draw near to me, you who are untaught,*
> *and lodge in my school.*
> *Why do you say you are lacking in these things,*
> *and why are your souls very thirsty? . . .*
> *Get instruction with a large sum of silver,*
> *and you will gain by it much gold. (Ecclus. 51:23–24, 28)*

Elsewhere Sirach concedes that his school's product requires leisure for its acquisition, though the similarity between this text and the Egyptian "Satire on the Trades" may mean that Sirach has not fully assimilated this view of manual labor, for in 7:15 he recommends it. Nevertheless, Sirach emphasizes the depletion of energy resulting from the work of farmers, craftsmen, smiths, and potters while honoring them for maintaining the fabric of the world. Unlike these people who work with their hands, the fortunate individuals who devote themselves to the study of the law of the Most High will serve rulers and travel to foreign lands (38:24–39:5). Sirach does not ignore the dangers inherent in travel, but he bears personal testimony to the advantages of experience gained through exposure to other places and different cultures (34:9–12).

Further information about the actual date of Sirach's activity comes from two sources; the praise of Simon the high priest in 50:1–21 and the prologue to the book. The first identifies Onias as the father of Simon but leaves unresolved the actual Simon who is the subject of such lavish praise, since at least two high priests had this name. The prologue settles that question in favor of Simon II, who was high priest about 219–196. Written by Sirach's grandson, the prologue states that Jesus (Hebrew, Joshua) had devoted himself to the "law and the prophets and the other books of our fathers" and acknowledges that his grandfather had tried his own hand at literary composition. The result was a book of such worth that Sirach's grandson translated it from Hebrew into Greek for the benefit of Jews in Egypt. For his arrival in Egypt he gives the year 132 B.C.E. (the thirty-eighth year of Ptolemy VII Euergetes). From this precise information it is possible to calculate that Sirach wrote his book in the decade between 190 and 180 B.C.E.

It seems that Sirach wrote the book in two stages, unless his repeated references to making instruction and pouring out teaching like prophecy are mere rhetoric. In context he seems to imply that the scope of his literary effort exceeded his original expectation (24:20–34). Both he and his grandson emphasize the value of his instruction beyond Sirach's private edification. The structure of the book corresponds to its evolution: each part begins with a poem praising wisdom. In the first instance the teacher sings its praises, and in the second wisdom proclaims its own virtues. A suitable hymn to the Deity concludes the work, and its entirety commends Sirach to prospective students. Perhaps Sirach's failure to have his book accepted into the canon explains the corrupt state of the text, which exists in quite divergent traditions. Some assistance in assessing the different readings has come from comparatively recent Hebrew manuscript discoveries, the latest of which were found at Qumran and at the fortress at Massada.

SETTING

In all likelihood, Sirach located his center of learning in Jerusalem, partly to be near those who wielded power and partly to attract wealthy students. Some interpreters have found support for such an assumption in the fact that Sirach must have actually witnessed the high priest Simon as he led worship in the temple at Jerusalem, but of course visitors from other towns may also have shared in this experience that seems to have made a lasting impression on Sirach. Assuming that Jerusalem was the scene of Sirach's activity, what was the general ethos at the beginning of the second century? The situation roughly twenty-five years later is very well known, for this marks the beginning of the Maccabean revolt against Syrian rule. The intolerable burden that Antiochus IV Epiphanes laid on the Jewish people is unknown to Sirach, although he does express great hostility for Samaritans and makes a fervent appeal to the Deity for decisive action that will punish foreign nations and restore the tribes of Israel. Sirach's concern is not simply that Jerusalem be exalted, for he explicitly mentions yet another benefit of such saving action: the renewed signs of divine favor and the hastening of the day of salvation will eventuate in the recounting of God's mighty deeds (36:1–17). This reference to foreigners is too general to be of much help in clarifying the political situation during Sirach's time. Scholars are left with the necessity of reconstructing the setting by piecing together bits and pieces from the entire book.

One of the surest clues in this effort is the presence of conscious polemic in which Sirach aims at correcting views that he considers misguided or perverse. Such evidence seems to indicate that idolatry was flourishing, that renewed interest in divination was manifest, and that wicked persons had launched a concerted effort at denying divine justice. Sirach ridicules images to which homage is paid as useless because they can neither eat nor smell the offering of fruit. Their impotency is likened to that of a eunuch who embraces a maiden and groans (30:18–20). Dreams are still another matter. Sirach recognizes their deceptive quality, admitting that they give wings to fools, but he also remembers that in Israel's sacred story dreams sometimes conveyed messages from the Deity, and this recollection prompts him to qualify his rejection of them. The decisive thing for Sirach is the instigator of the dream; like omens and divination that originate in a human desire to know the future, dreams of this nature give false hope (34:1–8).

Outright denial of divine justice by an outspoken group of detractors prompted considerable reflection on Sirach's part. Here and there he cites his opponents' opinions and endeavors to refute them decisively. In defending the traditional claim that God rules the world justly, Sirach drew on arguments used earlier by various individuals—suffering as education, vicarious suffering, justice prevailing in the end, and so forth. Nevertheless, he also introduced at least two new ones, although they were well known to Greek defenders of theodicy. The first was the view that the universe had been created in complementary pairs, the one good and the other evil. It naturally followed that nature itself rewarded virtue and punished wickedness. The other new answer entered the inner world of the psyche; Sirach argued that anxiety functioned as punishment for evil. With these two responses to the problem of evil Sirach moved into metaphysics and psychology. It seems that he was never fully satisfied with any of these solutions to the problem, whether traditional or innovative, and that his final answer was a leap of faith, which he expresses in prayer and hymnic praise.

Above all, Sirach emphasizes divine compassion. Apparent delays in punishing the wicked arise from the Deity's mercy. This theme is so important to Sirach that he actually quotes David's memorable reply to the Lord when the threat of destruction hovered overhead:

> *Let us fall into the hands of the Lord,*
>   *but not into the hands of men;*
> *for as his majesty is,*
>   *so also is his mercy. (Ecclus. 2:18; cf. 2 Sam. 24:14)*

Moreover, when Sirach contemplates the brevity of life, he returns to this theme of divine mercy.

> *Like a drop of water from the sea and a grain of sand*
>   *so are a few years in the day of eternity.*
> *Therefore the Lord is patient with them*
>   *and pours out his mercy upon them. (Ecclus. 18:10–11)*

This conviction that the Lord is merciful enables Sirach to invoke that blessing in prayer and to encourage others to rejoice in God's mercy, which the last two verses of the book relate to the problem of divine justice. In short, humans must reckon with a different timetable from their own, one that is sustained by the Deity's compassion for creatures who are subject to death. Surprisingly, Sirach is able to deal with the topic of death almost lightheartedly.

> *Remember my doom, for yours is like it:*
> *yesterday it was mine, and today it is yours. (Ecclus. 38:22)*

> *All living beings become old like a garment,*
> *for the decree from of old is,*
> *"you must surely die." (Ecclus. 14:17)*

Sirach's use of the image of leaves falling from a tree to describe death has been taken as evidence of dependence on Egyptian wisdom, but the idea is one that might readily occur to any reflective individual.

CONTENT

The form in which Sirach chose to express himself is borrowed from the Book of Proverbs, especially the first collection where didactic units occur. More often than not Sirach engages in extensive discussion of a given topic: discipline (30:1–13), physicians (38:1–15), poverty and wealth (4:1–10), drunkenness (31:25–31), wicked wives and headstrong daughters (26:6–12), the enjoyment of good things (14:11–19), and much more. Although he freely uses the old address "my son," he shows himself adept at new departures, particularly in highly developed refrains that link individual sayings into a coherent unit. Whereas earlier teachers had respected the proverb's power of communication, Sirach rarely leaves an isolated saying on its own, preferring rather to explain its sense. As a result he seems to recognize more ambiguity in truth sayings than earlier sages did.

There is one who keeps silent because he has no answer,
*   while another keeps silent because he knows when to speak. (Ecclus. 20:6)*

O death, how bitter is the reminder of you
*   to one who lives at peace among his possessions . . . .*
O death, how welcome is your sentence
*   to one who is in need and is failing in strength,*
*   very old and distracted over everything;*
*   to one who is contrary, and has lost his patience! (Ecclus. 41:1–2)*

Nevertheless, Sirach demonstrates unusual skill in coining unforgettable maxims.

A new friend is like new wine;
*   when it has aged you will drink it with pleasure. (Ecclus. 9:10b)*

A poor man is honored for his knowledge,
*   while a rich man is honored for his wealth. (Ecclus. 10:30)*

A rich man does wrong, and he even adds reproaches;
*   a poor man suffers wrong, and he must add apologies. (Ecclus. 13:3)*

As a stake is driven firmly into a fissure between stones,
*   so sin is wedged in between selling and buying. (Ecclus. 27:2)*

Sometimes Sirach seems even to transform an earlier proverbial feature entirely; the following sayings are recognizable variants of numerical or graded proverbs.

The sand of the sea, the drops of rain,
*   and the days of eternity—who can count them?*
The height of heaven, the breadth of the earth,
*   the abyss, and wisdom—who can search them out? (Ecclus. 1:2–3)*

Still, Sirach retains the graded numerical saying in several instances.

There is one literary form that Sirach seems to have derived from Greek sources. That is his panegyric on famous men (chapters 44–50). Beginning with Enoch, Sirach sings the praises of men who belonged to Israel's sacred story. Pride of position falls to Aaron, and, or course, to the high priest in Sirach's own day. One puzzling omission from this list is the name Ezra. Noteworthy are the references to Isaiah, Jeremiah, Ezekiel, and the twelve minor prophets, an indicaton that by Sirach's day at least the first two divisions of the canon were substantially in their present form.

It has been said that, for Sirach subjectively, wisdom is the fear of God, and objectively, wisdom is the law of Moses. Precisely where the emphasis fell is a debated issue. Did Sirach subordinate wisdom to the fear of God and the law? Certainly it appears so if one presses such images for the fear of God as root, garland, and crown of wisdom. That impression is strengthened by the explicit identification of wisdom with the Mosaic law. On one occasion Sirach declared that nothing was better than the fear of the Lord or sweeter than to heed the commandments (23:27). Whatever the answer to this difficult question about priority may be, there is much evidence to suggest that Sirach's first love was the priestly ritual and its splendid ceremonial dress.

Nevertheless, Sirach was also a teacher who painstakingly devised instruction for others, and that fact must not be forgotten in assessing the relative importance for him of religion and wisdom. Like the author of Proverbs 8, Sirach also believed that the Lord created wisdom and poured her out on favored individuals. But Sirach moved far beyond that earlier author's position to astonishing assertions: like a mist wisdom issued from the mouth of the Most High and covered the whole earth; she endowed representatives among all peoples with her gift; she sought a resting place and eventually lodged in Israel after receiving a special command from the Creator; there she thrived and benefited all who hungered and thirsted for knowledge (24:1–22).

In one area Sirach's legacy is a dubious one. He seems determined to present women in the worst light possible. Accordingly, he did not shrink from asserting that the birth of a daughter is a loss (22:3) or from blaming sin and death on a woman (25:24). Apparently, he suspected the morals of far too many wives and daughters.

> As a thirsty wayfarer opens his mouth
>   and drinks from any water near him,
> so will she sit in front of every post
>   and open her quiver to the arrow. (Ecclus. 26:12)

Perhaps the best commentary on his observation about the birth of a daughter comes from Sirach's discussion of all the secret anxieties that fathers experienced over daughters' virginity (42:9–10). Whereas Ecclesiastes thought women were only one thousandth worse than men, Sirach made the preposterous claim that a man's wickedness is better than a woman's goodness (42:14). Such lack of generosity is so overwhelming that the occasional references to good wives almost lie buried in a sea of forgetfulness (26:1–4).

The direct connection between sin and sickness survived attack by the Book of Job. In Sirach's day the place of physicians within society was complicated by lingering belief that sickness was punishment for sin. If that were true, anyone who interfered in this process incurred divine wrath. What were doctors supposed to do in such a situation? Sirach defended the right of physicians to carry out their profession; his reasoning was that they made use of medicines that the Creator provided in roots and herbs. Furthermore, physicians called upon the Deity to assist them in the healing process. Thus far, Sirach embraced concepts that were in keeping with the times. But in the end he reverted to the older notion of a direct association between illness and sin (38:1–12).

The task that Sirach set for himself was no easy one. In the process of bringing wisdom from the periphery of faith into the sphere of orthodoxy he failed to remove all the rough edges. In spite of these features of his thought that are not fully integrated into the whole, Sirach's contribution to the intellectual and spiritual life of the early second century was enormous. Had he chosen to remain silent, one of his own truth sayings would surely have risen to haunt him.

> *Hidden wisdom and unseen treasure,*
>   *what advantage is there in either of them? (Ecclus. 20:30)*

◆ 32 ◆

Baruch

THE Book of Baruch consists of a national penitential prayer (Bar. 1:15–3:8), a hymn about wisdom (3:9–4:4), and words of lamentation and consolation (4:5–5:9). These three parts are introduced by a narrative that attributes the book to Jeremiah's scribe Baruch (1:1–14). A shift from prose into poetry takes place after the prayer; other features of the text suggest different authors for the poetry and prose. The most noteworthy argument for at least two hands is the name for the Deity—Yahweh in the prose, God in the poetry. Whereas Yahweh occurs nearly fifty times in the prose, it never occurs in the poetry, where titles like the Holy One, the Everlasting, and the Everlasting Savior appear.

The confessional prayer is inspired by a similar one in Dan. 9:4–19, although the focus is on the exilic situation rather than on the cessation of the Temple cult. Emphasis falls on the righteousness of the Deity and Israel's culpability, particularly in refusing to obey the prophets or the Mosaic Law. In true Deuteronomistic language, the author mentions the fulfillment of prophecy in the lives of the people, on the one hand, and the decisive acts of God in their behalf, on the other hand. Moreover, arguments from various psalms find their way into this prayer—for instance, the absence of praise for Yahweh in Sheol. In addition, ancient threats and promises are recalled, from Moses' to Jeremiah's promise that the Lord will establish an everlasting covenant and give Israel and Judah a new heart. A rehearsal of Yahweh's victory over Egypt's might brings to memory the past history when things were different; its purpose appears to be the fostering of hope in those who are here invited to confess their sins and to pray for deliverance.

The confessional prayer is introduced by a brief section in prose (1:1–14). This introduction identifies Baruch as the author and reports that the people in exile sent a collection of money and a copy of the Law to their compatriots who were still in Jerusalem at the time. The date is given as 582 B.C.E., the fifth year after Jerusalem's destruction. The narrative mentions a high priest named Jehoiakim, who is otherwise unknown. Like Daniel, the author confuses the relationship between Nebuchadnezzar and Belshazzar, Nabonidus's son. More importantly, the introduction states that Baruch took the sacred vessels that the Babylonian king had carried off to Babylon, in order to return them to Judah. Naturally, this tradition about the return of the vessels differs from the canonical explanation for their return under Sheshbazzar.

The praise of wisdom borrows freely from Job 28 and Sirach 24, although wisdom is the object of the search rather than the active searcher who appears in the latter text. The long stay in captivity is understood as evidence that the people have forsaken wisdom. Hence, they are growing old in an alien country. The rhetorical questions in Job 28 return here: "Who has found her place?" None has done so among mortals; no youth, no foreigner renowned for knowledge, and no giant has achieved wisdom. "Who has gone up into heaven, and taken her, and brought her down from the clouds? Who has gone over the sea, and found her, and will buy her for pure gold?" (3:29–30). The answer: God alone has found her and knows her. But this generous One bestowed wisdom on Israel, specifically the Mosaic Law. Here the very different views of Job and Sirach come together into one.

The final section draws inspiration from Lamentations and Second Isaiah. The initial segment acknowledges divine punishment and expresses the author's helplessness save as an intercessor. A note of encouragement then enters the picture, an exhortation to pray expectantly, for those who receive divine favor shall soon see salvation. The thrice-repeated words, "Take courage, my children [O Jerusalem]," announce the imminent day when the one who sent calamity will replace it with peace. Jerusalem is invited to look eastward, whence her children will come, and to put off her garments of mourning, replacing them with robes of righteousness. A changed status will require a name change, as the mother-in-law of Ruth knew so well. Now the children of Jerusalem will be called "Peace of righteousness and glory of godliness." The words of encouragement end by renewing Second Isaiah's memorable promises about the level highway on which the returning exiles will walk. Here, however, God carries the fortunate people in glory, as on a royal throne: "For God has ordered that every high mountain and the everlasting hills be made low and the valleys filled up, to make level ground, so that Israel may walk safely in the glory of God" (5:7). The book concludes with the people residing in the shade, awaiting divine leadership.

When was this book written? Despite the implication that the Temple at Jerusalem was functioning, the prose gives evidence of a late date. To be sure, a Hebrew original of the book seems certain. The influence of Daniel 9 and Sirach (Ecclesiasticus) 24 point to the late second century B.C.E. at the earliest. If Nebuchadnezzar is a cipher for Antiochus IV and

Jehoiakim for Alcimus,* this late dating is confirmed. However, it is impossible to set a firm date for any one of the three segments in the book. In any event this book is but further proof of Baruch's immense popularity in the second and first centuries B.C.E., particularly in apocalyptic circles. His association with Babylonian exile is strange, inasmuch as Jer. 43:6 indicates that Baruch accompanied the prophet into Egypt.

*The high priest Alcimus in Jerusalem during the second century B.C.E. turned against the pious Hasidim and slaughtered sixty of them in a single day.

◆ 33 ◆

The Letter of Jeremiah

CCORDING to the Book of Jeremiah, the prophet sent a letter
to the exiles in Babylon containing words of encouragement and
advice on how to adjust to a long captivity. A much later author
in exile was inspired by this reference to Jeremiah's letter; the result
was a polemic against idolatry that arose at some time during the first
century B.C.E. The unknown author extends the period in exile to seven
generations; if we allow forty years for each generation, the date for an
expected return is 317 B.C.E. This individual supplied a continuation of
the attack on idolatry in Jer. 10:2–15, as well as similar mockery in Second
Isaiah.

The central thrust of the Letter of Jeremiah is that idols are lifeless
and helpless fabricated objects, hence not worthy of adoration by people
who are themselves stronger. The author makes the same point in various
ways, hoping to unite the disconnected attacks by means of a refrain.
Although the actual words in the refrain vary slightly, it draws a conclusion from the foregoing observations that the worship of idols is pointless.
At times the refrain consists of a declaration and an exhortation; at other
times it is a rhetorical question that functions as an emphatic statement.
The consistent presence of a verb of cognition maintains the illusion of
an intellectual argument that defies refutation—for example, "Since you
know by these things that they are not gods, do not fear them" (Letter
of Jer. 6:29).

Most of the ridicule deals with the idols' helplessness. They cannot
see, feel, speak, breathe, walk, pick themselves up, or do anything that
ordinary humans take for granted. Consequently, the gods are vulnerable
to theft, despite the dagger and axe in their hands, to fire, dust, invading
armies, and wild animals. The gods are subjected to the indignity of birds
perching on them, and they are touched by women during their impurity.
Avaricious priests steal from the helpless gods and use the money to pay
prostitutes for their favors. Prostitution flourishes in their presence, and

424

the gods cannot even require payment of vows when people renege on promises.

Some arguments focus on the inability of the idols to perform the kinds of deeds for which Israel's God was well known. They cannot give rain to thirsty citizens, help widows and orphans, give sight to the blind, or avenge an injustice. Others call attention to the worthless aspect of idols, which fulfill no useful function. A door prevents entry by a robber, and a pillar holds a structure up, but idols contribute nothing of value to society. Furthermore, they actually deceive people by their very makeup, for inside the gold cover is ordinary wood. If gods depend on humans to move them from place to place and to protect them from fire, then wild beasts are actually superior to idols. Such is the reasoning of the author who composed this book.

An interesting feature of this letter is its acceptance of stellar luminaries, whereas Second Isaiah rejected astral cults along with other kinds of idolatry. The subservience of sun, moon, and stars to divine command is taken for granted in this late text. Another unusual characteristic of the letter is the obscure illustration about competition among prostitutes, which seems to have two points. It criticizes the integral connection between sacral prostitution and idolatry, and it implies that a similar competition occurs among the gods for human adoration. If, indeed, that is the intention of the reference to prostitutes who boast of their own superior attractiveness, it ridicules the aesthetic dimension associated with idolatry.

The reference to the gods' impotence uses the Akkadian name Bel, which occurs also in Isa. 46:1, in Jer. 50:2, and in the additions to Daniel. In the Letter of Jeremiah the point concerns the futility of praying to Bel, for the god cannot hear prayer.

One can readily appreciate the force of such arguments for exiled peoples who watched processions in which sacred priests marched through the streets with their gods on their shoulders. After all, these gods had demonstrated their extraordinary power by giving Judeans into the hands of the Babylonians, or so it seemed. That apparent potency is the reason for the repeated assurance that the subject peoples need not fear these gods. Noteworthy is the author's failure to introduce direct statements about Israel's Deity and to praise the Lord for possessing those qualities that were missing from the idols. The closest thing to such language occurs in the introduction, which explains the exile as punishment by the God whom Judah must worship and which promises angelic protection in distant Babylonia.

Israel's critics of idolatry never really penetrated to the heart of the matter, largely because they refused to distinguish between a cult object and its referent. The abusive attack on objects fashioned by human hands is effective only if pagans worshipped those material things, wood and clay, gold and silver. However, these gods merely symbolized the in-

visible realities which humans call God, and for this reason all such attacks as those in the Letter of Jeremiah, the Wisdom of Solomon, Second
Isaiah, and Jer. 10:2–15 ultimately lack cogency. Their value lies in correcting cruder aspects of worship, from which no religion can ever free
itself completely.

◆ 34 ◆

Additions to Daniel

T HE Greek text of the Book of Daniel is considerably longer than the Hebrew. The additions, which later entered the Latin text as well, comprise three separate works: (1) the Prayer of Azariah and the Song of the Three Young Men; (2) Susanna; and (3) Bel and the Dragon. In the first of these, the prayer is separated from the song by a prose narrative about efforts by the king's servants to increase the heat of the furnace, which were thwarted by the angel of the Lord who joined the three in the fire. The first and third were probably written in Hebrew or Aramaic, but the second may have been composed in Greek, because it has some puns that occur in this language but not in Semitic equivalents. It is possible that a translator introduced the puns, so one cannot be entirely certain about the original language.

THE PRAYER OF AZARIAH AND THE SONG OF THE THREE YOUNG MEN

The Prayer of Azariah is unsuitable for its context, for it confesses sin although Azariah (the Hebrew name of Abednego) has faithfully kept the Law at risk of death. In truth, the prayer constitutes a national song of lament; the plural form stands out in the setting, although Azariah may speak for his companions too. The content is not even remotely related to the situation of the three young men. Instead of thanking the Deity for wondrously preserving them in the furnace, the prayer pleads for the nation's survival. It acknowledges the sorry state of the nation, which has become leaderless and few in number, but dares to hope that a contrite heart will make a decisive difference. The song, which in some respects is modeled on Psalms 136 and 148, invokes the whole universe to praise the Lord. After opening with a doxology, the hymn calls on heaven, earth, and Israel to bless the Lord. In the second half of each

427

verse a refrain occurs after each summons to praise, "Sing praise to him and highly exalt him for ever." Verse 66 relates the song to the context, referring to the three young men by name and praising the Deity for delivering them from the fiery furnace.

SUSANNA

This little story about a faithful Jewish woman who resisted seduction and was rescued from death by a young prophet is a thing of beauty. Susanna, whose name means lily, aroused the passions of two Jewish judges who regularly came to her husband's house. At first the two men secretly spied on her when she walked in her garden, but when they met one another in compromising places, they confessed their lust. Then the two men devised a scheme to enjoy Susanna' body, and they proceeded to implement it. Approaching her while she was bathing, they demanded that she submit to them or they would testify that she was caught in adultery with a young man who fled. Since the testimony of two men was binding in court, and adultery was punishable by death, they naturally assumed that Susanna would choose to lie with them. Instead, she preferred death to dishonor, and the men successfully pled their case before a court of justice. Susanna lifted up her voice to heaven and appealed to a higher court. Then a young Daniel, whose name means "god has judged," stopped the proceedings with a prophetic oracle. Given permission to interrogate the two men separately, Daniel cast verbal abuse on each man and demanded to know under what kind of tree the adultery took place. One judge said a mastic tree, the other an evergreen oak. The names provided the basis for a pun, which can be rendered in English by, "Under a clove tree . . . the angel will cleave you"; "Under a yew tree . . . the angel will hew you asunder." Daniel informed the people that the judges had contradicted themselves; a new trial was conducted, and the men were executed according to the Law.

The narrator is careful to describe Susanna as a God-fearing woman, and her speech reinforces this idea. When faced with a choice of adultery or death, she said:

> I am hemmed in on every side. For if I do this thing, it is death for me; and if I do not, I shall not escape your hands. I choose not to do it and to fall into your hands, rather than to sin in the sight of the Lord. (Sus. 22–23)

Once sentence had been given, Susanna prayed:

> O eternal God, who dost discern what is secret, who art aware of all things before they come to be, thou knowest that these men have borne false witness against me. And now I am to die! Yet I have done none of the things that they have wickedly invented against me! (Sus. 42–43)

The earlier story about Joseph's refusal to lie with Potiphar's wife deals with the same issue, but the court tale is democratized in Susanna. Moreover, the roles are reversed, for it is the woman who is innocent. Here the enemy is not a foreigner, but two respected Jewish citizens. The central themes are marital fidelity and divine protection for those who maintain their integrity. Because it deals with a youthful Daniel, this story appears at the beginning of the Book of Daniel in Theodotion's recension.

BEL AND THE DRAGON

Like the story of Susanna, the two short stories in Bel and the Dragon depict Daniel as a kind of Sherlock Holmes, although engaged in detective work on behalf of religion. The first episode tells how Daniel proves to Cyrus, his king, that the statue-god Bel does not eat the offerings placed before it and hence is powerless. Daniel secretly scatters ashes on the floor of the temple, which is then locked. The priests of Bel enter the room by secret doors, accompanied by their families, and consume the food. The next day their tracks betray them, and they are executed. Daniel then destroys the temple.

The other episode tells how Daniel feeds the great dragon a special mixture of pitch, fat, and hair, causing it to explode. The people demand that Daniel be given to them, and the king reluctantly yields to their wishes. They throw him into a lion's den, where seven lions accustomed to eating humans are waiting. In faraway Judea the prophet Habakkuk prepares a meal for reapers in the field, but the Spirit transports him to Babylon, food in hand, and Habakkuk gives the food to Daniel. Afterward Habakkuk is returned to Judea, Daniel is released from the lion's den unharmed, and his accusers are thrown into it and perish.

◆ 35 ◆

The Prayer of Manasseh

T HE extraordinarily long reign of Manasseh in Judah posed a problem for those who subscribed to the belief that justice prevails in
society, for this king was remembered as one who actively fostered
apostasy from the Lord. To be sure, a historical explanation for his introduction of Assyrian deities in Judah is near to hand. As an Assyrian
vassal, Manasseh had no choice but to promote the official religion of
his sovereign. Nevertheless, the Deuteronomistic conviction that the
Deity rewarded virtue and punished vice did not seem to apply in this
case. The Chronicler offered an explanation for this apparent oversight
on the Deity's part: toward the end of his life Manasseh repented of his
sins (2 Chron. 33:11–13). This note further states that the king composed
a prayer of repentance while in exile. At a later time someone provided
a suitable prayer for individuals who had abandoned the faith and who
wished to return to the fold.

The prayer begins with hymnic invocation, offers a personal confession, begs for forgiveness, expresses confidence in a positive divine response, and expresses appreciation in appropriate praise. The language
is full of traditional expressions, although one unusual image occurs: "and
now I bend the knee of my heart, beseeching thee for thy kindness" (Pr.
of Man. 11). We cannot be certain when this poem was written or what
its original language was, but it probably arose in the first century B.C.E.,
perhaps in Greek.

430

◆ 36 ◆

First Maccabees

THE primary historical source for the events associated with the Maccabean revolt against Seleucid oppression is First Maccabees. This book covers the events from 175 B.C.E., the coronation of Antiochus IV Epiphanes, to the death of Simon in 134. Its opening verses look back on the achievements of Alexander the Great, and its conclusion indicates that an account of John Hyrcanus's deeds is readily available. The book tells about the initial act of revolt by Mattathias of Modin, a priest whose five sons later distinguished themselves for valor (chapter 2), and recounts the battles of Judas Maccabeus (1 Macc. 3:1–9:22), Jonathan (9:23–12:53), and Simon (13:1–16:18). It is filled with documents, letters, and reported conversations that give the appearance of being official. In this respect as in many others, the book resembles Chronicles-Ezra-Nehemiah; perhaps its intention was to continue the history of Judah into the late second century. However, the treatment of the Hasmonaean high priesthood suggests that the real purpose of the book was to offer a legitimation for that priestly order. Nevertheless, the author subjects the high priesthood to the Great Assembly, a policy-making body.

First Maccabees combines historical narrative and fervent piety, much of which is influenced by the stories within the Deuteronomistic history and Chronicles. Although the miraculous element is never actually acknowledged, the Maccabees pray before engaging the enemy in battle and praise the Deity afterward. Their battles are understood as holy war, at least in a modified form, and the outcome of conflict is directly related to the religious state of the people. The scheme is reminiscent of the pattern underlying the Book of Judges; when Israel sins, it goes down in defeat before its enemies, but when it is righteous, its foes fall in large numbers. Nevertheless, a disastrous decision to refrain from fighting on the sabbath was reversed; it became painfully clear that victory over the oppressors required strong and decisive action on the part of Israel's faithful few.

Sprinkled throughout the book are poetic passages and highly developed rhetoric, particularly patriotic addresses. Often these sections make free use of older biblical material. Even the speeches frequently draw on ancient stories about heroes in battle, thus linking the conflict against the Seleucids with earlier struggles against the forces of evil. To prevent an act of apostasy in Modin, Mattathias kills a Jew who has come forward to offer a sacrifice, as well as a Syrian officer. The bold murder on Mattathias's part is likened to Phinehas's zeal by which the Aaronite priesthood was established. The point is that the Hasmonaean priesthood rested on a similar act of zeal for the Lord.

The author of First Maccabees never introduces the hope of resurrection, which finds a place in the Book of Daniel as an answer to the problem of premature death in a devout cause. Instead, the emphasis falls on faithfulness despite the cost. Human courage, rather than divine intervention, is the central theme in this account. The author occasionally acknowledges that a leader of Israel erred; Simon's faults are therefore brought to light, but the greatness of his deeds more than compensates for these mistakes. It seems that the author is eager to depict the warriors as a religious community and not merely as heroic soldiers.

Whereas the author's attitude to the Greeks is hostile, it is quite different where Romans are concerned (8:14–16). The former are responsible for the Seleucid empire, which under Antiochus IV Epiphanes determines to eradicate Judaism. On the other hand, Roman support for the Hasmonaeans seems forthcoming. This positive view of Rome sets the lower limit for dating First Maccabees, because such an attitude toward the Romans is inconceivable after Ptolemy's conquest of Palestine in 63 B.C.E. The book chronicles the endless intrigues and struggles for power within Israel and in the Seleucid empire. Toward the end of the Maccabean period, rivalry for the Seleucid throne provided an opportunity for the Jewish leader to support the eventual victor, but this kind of politics is always dangerous, as Jonathan found out to his ruin.

The Maccabean struggle was for religious and secular freedom. Antiochus IV Epiphanes, whom the Jews nicknamed Epimanes (madman), proscribed the practice of Judaism. His goal was to Hellenize his kingdom completely. It is reported that many Jews supported this policy, largely because of the cultural advantages associated with the Greek way of life. Others resisted to the death. That is the story which the author of First Maccabees wishes to tell. The victory over Nicanor and the annual celebration of that event signals the mood of the book. Suffering comes to some Jews, but the people of God have the last word, for the Deity is on their side. Hence, they must realize that, "It is not on the size of the army that victory in battle depends, but strength comes from Heaven" (3:19). Therefore, it is said that Judas reinstated the ancient practice of excluding from military service those "who were building houses, or were betrothed, or were planting vineyards, or were fainthearted" (3:56).

The continuity with the past is broken at one point, however; prophecy has ceased (4:46; 9:27; 14:41), and the people do not know what to do about the stones that once comprised the sacred altar in Jerusalem. Nevertheless, the achievement of Simon is compared favorably with that of Solomon, whose era was also not noted for its prophets. According to a poem in 14:4–15, Simon brought to fulfillment the long-awaited promise of a day when everyone would sit under a vine or fig tree and there would be none to make them afraid (14:12). The struggle has thus achieved religious and political freedom; hence, there is no need to continue the story into John Hyrcanus's reign. It is significant that a group of Hasids came to the support of the Maccabeans in the early stages of the conflict. The later Pharisees sprang from this group, eventually assuming repsonsibility for shaping the religious destiny of Judaism.

◆ 37 ◆

Second Maccabees

TOWARD the end of the second century B.C.E., a certain Jason of Cyrene wrote a "historical" work that comprised five volumes. Second Maccabees is an abridgment of that literary composition; two letters from Palestinian Jews to their Egyptian compatriots precede the excerpt. Their intention is, first, to ask the Jews in Egypt to celebrate the rededication of the Temple in Jerusalem and, second, to recount the miraculous preservation of sacred fire, together with the fulfillment of written prophecy, both of which legitimate the new festival of Hanukkah. The epitomist states the purpose of summarizing the contents of a much longer work: the aim is to aid in memorization, to make the material conveniently accessible, and to entertain readers. Other purposes may have guided the author, such as providing a covert attack on the Hasmonaean priesthood by emphasizing Judas Maccabeus at others' expense. Perhaps, too, the concentration on the Temple at Jerusalem implicitly rejects the rival temple that Onias built at Leontopolis in Egypt.

In any event, the Jerusalem Temple is the central topic of the story. The whole book revolves around the initial threat to the Temple occasioned by Helidorus's attempt to remove its treasures, the later desecration of its sacred altar by Antiochus IV, its liberation from profanation, and the rededication of a purified altar. Thus the author's subject matter is restricted to the struggle for religious freedom, a limitation that may explain why the book stops where it does without narrating the events that achieved political independence for the Judean state. Because the emphasis is on sacred history, the story abounds in supernatural manifestations. The Deity protects the Temple by sending flying horses and angels, and similar agents fight the Jews' battles and shield Judas from harm.

The style of writing is typical of "pathetic" history. It appeals to the emotions of readers by extravagant rhetoric, sensationalism, and exposed feelings of characters. The suffering of martyrs is a favorite topic, and

434

their agony is depicted in extreme language. The aged Eleazar chooses to die an exemplary death as a martyr, and the noble Razis tears out his own entrails and hurls them away. Two mothers who circumcised their sons are paraded with their children hanging around their necks, and are then thrown over a wall. Another mother encourages her seven sons to give their lives rather than yield to apostasy, and she gladly follows them in martyrdom. The depiction of this cruelty leaves nothing to the imagination, and one reads of tongues and limbs being cut off and of martyrs being fried in a pan. When the story of such atrocities ends, readers may think, like the epitomist, that enough has been said about tortures.

Another feature of this work is its explicit moralizing. Indeed, the function of the martyrdoms is to bring about a change in the Deity's treatment of the Jews. Sin has been atoned for, and now mercy is appropriate. Antiochus IV's profanation of the Temple in Jerusalem is specifically blamed on the people's sin, and when the battle against some Idumeans goes badly for some Jews a reason is discovered: every dead Jew was secretly wearing a sacred token of the idols of Jamnia. Such moralizing is not always woven into the fabric of the story, for the epitomist interrupts the narrative from time to time with moralizing comments.

Perhaps it is significant that this evocation of feelings ventures in new directions at two points. Here for the first time we encounter the idea that the Deity created the world from nothing (2 Macc. 7:28), although the language is not expressed in its absolute form. Here, too, is the notion of intercession for the living and the dead (12:43), with the concomitant belief in eternal life or damnation (7:9, 14). Furthermore, hope in the resurrection of the body is firmly fixed in the thought of the epitomist (7:11; 14:46). Naturally, the problem of martyrdom required this resolution of injustice. Indeed, these heroes seem eager to die so that they can enter eternal joy sooner; at least, they are allowed to express such hopes freely.

Despite the serious subject matter, occasional pieces of humor can be found in the book. After Helidorus's unhappy experience with supernatural defenders of the Temple at Jerusalem, he informs the Syrian king that he has discovered a perfect way of dealing with perpetrators of sedition. These enemies of the government can be sent against the Jewish Temple and they will return home suitably scourged, if they escape at all. Elsewhere the author describes a man named Auranus as "advanced in years and no less advanced in folly" (4:40). An element of the ludicrous appears in the lingering description of Antiochus IV's death. One reads about a pitiable man whose stench drives away even the bravest soldiers, a helpless king who is desperately willing to try anything, even conversion to Judaism, to stay alive. This is the same person who is portrayed elsewhere as so arrogant that he thought he could sail on the land and walk on the sea.

Although Second Maccabees has decidedly less historical value than First Maccabees, not all details in Second Maccabees are fictional. Despite its confused chronology, Second Maccabees provides valuable information about the situation in Jerusalem during the time of Antiochus IV. The picture is not very pretty; two individuals, Jason and Menelaus, bid for the office of high priest, and many Jews seem ready to abandon their religion completely. From this representation of the religious situation, it becomes clear that the crisis in the second century B.C.E. was considerably more complex than First Maccabees seems to imply.

The differences between First and Second Maccabees are nonetheless significant. Whereas the former was written in Hebrew, the latter was composed in Greek. The relationship between the two books has been compared to that of Samuel-Kings and Chronicles-Ezra-Nehemiah. Neither First Maccabees nor Second Maccabees writes objective history, but the former is generally more reliable than the latter. Because the two books deal with the same events in a major portion of the narrative (1 Macc. 1:10–7:50; 2 Macc. 5–15), the differences in perspective are easily recognized. Although First Maccabees carries the story down to the time of John Hyrcanus (175–134 B.C.E.) and Second Maccabees stops with Judas Maccabeus (180–160), the actual date of the epitomist cannot be much earlier than 60 B.C.E.

From Cherished Word
to Holy Scriptures

THE emergence of a collection of writings with normative value for religious life within the Israelite community is inexplicable apart from a conviction that the Deity had made known the divine will in word and deed. Belief in inspired utterance therefore lies at the center of the development of a canon. However, the spoken word vouchsafed to Israel was attributed to an exclusive Deity, an idea which led to a further conviction that the people of God were also chosen from among the nations. It naturally followed that the Deity's revelation was unique and hence worthy of preservation, at first mainly through oral recital but eventually in written form. Generation after generation told the sacred story and sang Yahweh's praises, or when circumstances forbade the confessing of traditional faith the community asked penetrating questions and poured forth heartfelt agony in prayer and lament. In this way each generation examined its legacy and constantly reshaped the convictions by which the community lived. The result was a living tradition, one in which old and new understandings existed alongside one another, even when from modern perspectives they seem mutually exclusive. In due time cherished texts became the exclusive standard by which all belief and action were judged. At that moment they assumed the role of a canon, a measuring stick or norm; the first known reference to these writings as "Holy Scriptures" occurs toward the end of the first century B.C.E. in 2 Macc. 8:23. However, the Hebrew canon as we know it was finalized in several stages; consequently, the process of canonization was far more complex than one might think.

INSPIRED UTTERANCE

The idea that inspiration lay behind the poetic expression, whether mediated by priest, prophet, or sage, and the conviction that stories about the elect people were sacred led to a desire to retain these diverse words

437

for posterity. Select groups committed to memory those traditions that best expressed their own understanding of religious experience. Priests recorded their instructions about the proper way to carry out the sacrificial ritual, and they drew up ethical injunctions and legal codes that gave concrete expression to the divine will for daily conduct. Judges amassed a wealth of decisions about communal living. Prophets declared the Deity's will in judgment and grace, and their utterances were memorized and committed to writing by "disciples," some of whom continued the master's agenda so self-consciously that one may properly speak of a school of thought. Officials at various cultic centers devised their own liturgical traditions and entrance requirements. Jerusalem, in particular, developed a flourishing royal theology often designed to promote the well-being of the Davidic dynasty. When the northern sanctuaries lost their constituency as a result of Assyrian deportation, many of these vital traditions migrated south. The reform movement in Josiah's era further centralized these diverse memories at a single sanctuary, Jerusalem.

ALL ISRAEL

Over the centuries, traditions that originally applied exclusively to one group were broadened and became the sacred memory of all Israel. Even material that once belonged to foreign peoples was adapted to Israel's special understanding of reality. In the end, rival perspectives enjoyed equal dissemination, and differences were largely ignored by those who increasingly searched tradition from the past for an authentic expression of the divine will. Apocalyptists thus looked to the remote past as inherently superior, and this view extended beyond their circles. Postexilic prophets, too, spoke almost nostalgically of the former prophets, and others consciously quoted previous texts and inaugurated the earliest stage of midrashic interpretation. This attention to the inspired utterance over the centuries sprang from a conviction that the divine word would ultimately achieve its goal.

TORAH

The development of the cherished traditions into Holy Scriptures came gradually. First, the Torah achieved canonical status in the worshipping community, perhaps by the fifth century B.C.E. Although they are but two of many contributing factors, the Josianic reform and Ezra's activity deserve notice here. For the first time in history, a book, Deuteronomy, became the constitution by which the state determined to carry out its daily policy, if not in practice, at least in theory. Ezra's contribution was to enlarge the Law for the restored community, so that the Torah became the norm for all decisions. The move to viewing the entire Pentateuch as revelation par excellence naturally followed. In Judaism the Torah stands as the supreme canonical revelation, and the other two divisions of Scripture derive their authority from these five books.

PROPHECY

The fixing of the prophetic books occurred in two distinct stages. The Former Prophets, known by a designation that arose in the eighth century C.E., achieved final form by the fourth century B.C.E., for Chronicles was relegated to the Writings. In all probability, these "historical" books were taken as the sequel to the narrative of Israel's beginnings that appears in the Torah. Because the Book of Daniel was placed in the third divison, it follows that by the time of its composition the Latter Prophets had achieved final form. Two prophetic texts are instructive, for they specify how the Books of Isaiah and Jeremiah came to be written down. In Isa. 8:16 the prophet announces that the Deity has instructed him to bind up the testimonies, presumably the inspired utterances, and to seal them for safekeeping among those who have been taught, usually designated disciples. Jeremiah 36 tells how the prophet dictated his previous oracles to his scribe Baruch, and when that scroll was reduced to ashes, Jeremiah repeated the process, adding more words this time. Moreover, the later veneration of ancient prophets issued in quotations by those lesser prophets who wished to revere the memory of their favorite inspired person, and apocalyptic thinkers searched earlier prophecies for clues that would enable them to calculate the course of history in their own time. The latter Prophets was a fixed entity by the beginning of the second century B.C.E., for Sirach (Ecclesiasticus) refers to the entire collection: Isaiah, Jeremiah, Ezekiel, and the Twelve.

WRITINGS

The third division of the canon remained fluid for several centuries, although the Prologue to Sirach (c. 132 B.C.E.) mentions three separate groups of revered works: the Torah, the Prophets, and "the other books." Eventually these "other books" became known in Judaism as the Writings; alternatively, the early Church Fathers called them the Hagiographa (holy writings). Their order varied, but pride of place always went to Psalms, with Job and Proverbs vying for second place. By the sixth century C.E. the five festal scrolls were brought together, and after the twelfth century they stood in this order: Song of Songs, Ruth, Lamentations, Ecclesiastes, and Esther. The sequence is thus determined by the festivals with which they are associated, Passover, Pentecost, 9th of Ab (mourning over Jerusalem's destruction), Booths, and Purim, respectively. From time to time questions arose within Judaism about certain of these books (Ecclesiastes, Song of Songs, Esther), but their essential worth and place among the sacred literature seems never to have been seriously challenged. Questions also arose about Ezekiel, because the legislation in chapters 40–48 differs from Mosaic law. The lame responses to the queries show how deeply revered these writings were and suggest that these books enjoyed popular esteem. After all, the decisive issue was whether or not the people at large considered a book sacred.

The evidence on which this reconstruction rests is quite diverse, and the conclusions disregard the traditional claim in 2 Esd. 14:18–48. Here it is stated that Ezra dictated to five assistants for forty days, and thus he restored the twenty-four canonical books that burned when Jerusalem fell to the Babylonians. In addition, it is reported, he dictated the contents of seventy books that were reserved for the wise. The purpose of this claim was to secure the authority of this second group, among which Second Esdras itself resided. Other sources refer to twenty-two books instead of twenty-four, perhaps in imitation of the twenty-two letters of the Hebrew alphabet. This number of books is arrived at by counting Ruth with Judges and Lamentations with Jeremiah. The traditional number, twenty-four, is achieved in the following way: Torah (5); Joshua, Judges, Samuel, Kings (4); Isaiah, Jeremiah, Ezekiel, the Twelve (4); and the Writings, including Psalms, Job, Proverbs, Five Scrolls, Daniel, Ezra-Nehemiah, Chronicles (11). The New Testament attests the threefold division, and a discussion of the actual contents of the canon took place among Jewish leaders at the so-called synod of Jamnia (c. 90 C.E.). By then the canon was already closed. Josephus, a Jewish historian at the Roman court, and Philo, a Jewish philosopher and theologian in Alexandria, confirm the existence of a canon that consisted of precisely these twenty-four books. Josephus goes further, listing four criteria for selecting sacred writings: (1) inspiration; (2) the specific number, twenty-four; (3) holiness; and (4) individual Hebrew consonants that were sacrosanct. In his mind, the period of inspiration extended from Moses to Artaxerxes I, the age of Ezra. This view soon became traditional, thus ruling out anything that betrayed a date of composition later than Ezra. In Jewish literature *Yedaim III.5* and the Babylonian Talmudic tract *Baba bathra 14b–15a* record similar information about the canon, those books which defile the hands (that is, they are holy).

PRESSURE TO CLOSE THE CANON

The necessity for closing the canon seems to have arisen from within and from without; sectarian movements within Judaism and the perceived threat from Christianity forced Jewish leaders to restrict its sacred books.

Apocalpytic groups were composing ever-new calculations of the future, often appealing to revelations in the name of Moses' predecessors. Hence, newly written books were attributed to Abraham, Adam, Enoch, and many others. The discoveries from Qumran throw considerable light on the vigor of sectarian movements, particularly in composing their own sacred books alongside those writings which they shared with Judaism generally. In Alexandria a flourishing Jewish community adopted a tolerant attitude toward sacred books, especially because composition in Greek was for them no obstacle. Among the Samaritans a rival version of the Torah existed, and even a history of that sect began to take shape. With the rise of Christianity and the composition of its own sacred books, alongside the Jewish canon, a situation developed in which urgent action seemed desirable. The closing of the canon was the response to internal and external pressure. The increasing dominance of the Pharisees made this move possible. This final fixing of the canon occurred during the period from about 100 B.C.E. to 100 C.E.

The decision to restrict the number of sacred books was to some extent precipitated by the translation into Greek of first the Torah and later the Prophets and Writings. According to a legend preserved in the Letter of Aristeas (c. 100 B.C.E.), the Egyptian ruler Ptolemy II Philadelphus commissioned seventy-two Jewish scribes to translate the Torah for the famous library at Alexandria. After forty days in complete isolation, the translators emerged with exactly identical renderings into Greek. There is some truth in this account: the Greek translation that received its name from the roughly seventy men (Septuagint) was made by several different persons in Alexandria during the third century B.C.E. As these Jewish people enlarged their own collection of writings, it became considerably more extensive than the Jewish canon in Palestine. Some of these additional books became particularly popular within the young Christian community, which took over the Jewish scriptures in Greek translation.

AN OPEN ATTITUDE

The New Testament follows the Septuagint in its generous attitude toward other writings, although it already acknowledges the threefold divisions for the Jewish canon (the third division is called Psalms after its initial book). The same formula is used in the new Testament for canonical books and for noncanonical writings. As the early church spread throughout the Hellenistic world, it manifested a preference for the Alexandrian translation of Hebrew into Greek. In this way the church adopted several books that do not appear in the Palestinian canon. These deuterocanonical books entered the Vulgate, a Latin translation made by Jerome between 390 and 405 C.E. Since the sixteenth century, these additional writings have been called the Apocrypha (hidden). They appeared in most English Bibles until the 1820s; the negative attitude toward them in the Reformed Church was a factor in the decision to print only those books that were in the Hebrew Bible. The Roman Catholic Church views them much more positively, and the Eastern Orthodox Church is ambiguous about the matter, accepting only some of the books. Martin Luther adopted a neutral stance, one that recognized their worth for edification.

The period just before the birth of Christianity saw the composition of considerably more literary works than these few deuterocanonical ones. Sirach implies that he thinks of his own contribution to knowledge as inspired, perhaps on a par with the canonical books. Clearly, the manuscripts from the region of the Dead Sea functioned as authoritative texts for the Essene community, although these sectarians also viewed the Hebrew canon as sacred. Fragments of every biblical book except Esther were found in the caves where they were preserved, sealed in clay pots, for more than two thousand years. Besides a complete manuscript of the Book of Isaiah and another nearly complete one, these caves yielded several compositions that were peculiar to this group, especially a "Manual of Discipline," "Thanksgiving Hymns," a "Temple Scroll," and "The Wars of the sons of Light against the Sons of Darkness." Besides these recently discovered manuscripts, there are many other literary works that have been known for some time. These works are usually identified as Pseudepigrapha, mainly because many of them purport to be written by worthy figures of antiquity, hence are pseudonymous. Because this charge of pseudonymity applies to only some of these works, a more appropriate title is noncanonical books. The Christian Church later produced its own canon and dozens of books besides. These latter works belong to the New Testament Apocrypha.

TRANSLATIONS

Once the Hebrew Bible achieved the status of canon, that is, the norm for faith and conduct for the Jewish people, its accuracy in transmission took on added significance. The Torah was shared with the Samaritan community; about 6,000 variants exist between the two recensions, but most of them are simply spelling differences. The main substantive difference concerns the place in which the Deity put the divine name, which the Samaritan version identifies with Mt. Gerizim near Shechem. In almost 1,900 places, the Samaritan manuscript agrees with the Septuagint against the Hebrew Bible. As the Jewish communities began to speak Aramaic more and more, Hebrew fell into disuse except as the language of sacred literature. This necessitated the writing of Aramaic translations of the Bible; these are called Targums. Two Targums are well known:

Targum Onkelos (on the Torah) and Targum Jonathan (on the Prophets). These Aramaic works are largely sermonic paraphrases, rather than actual translations. A Syriac translation of the Hebrew Bible (called the Peshitto, the simple rendering) has strong affinities with the Targums, but its complex text does not enable scholars to decide whether or not this Syriac version was the product of a Jewish or a Christian translator.

The Septuagint was not the only translation into Greek. Three versions of the Septuagint arose, each apparently representing a particular principle of translation. Aquila's version was strictly literal, in keeping with a growing belief among Jews, championed by Rabbi Aqiba, that every consonant of the Bible was inspired. Theodotion's translation was closer to a paraphrase, whereas Symmachus adopted a perspective somewhere between these two extremes. Perhaps the fragmentary nature of these translations makes such a description as this premature. Early renderings of the Septuagint into Latin (Vetus Latina and Itala) were eventually replaced by Jerome's translation, the Vulgate (common, vernacular). This important translation was based on Hebrew manuscripts as well as Aramaic versions, which did not ingratiate Jerome to the Christian theologian, Augustine. The danger of so many translations was that the original content of the Hebrew Bible would vanish from memory. That did not happen, thanks to the great care with which Jewish scholars preserved their literary treasure.

SCRIPTS

The earliest written Hebrew texts were in an old Phoenician script, which has survived in several important nonbiblical inscriptions. The cursive, or old script, contained three pairs of similar consonants, so that uninentional errors sometimes entered the text (the letters *b* and *r*, *m* and *n*, *ch* and *h*). This script gave way to the Assyrian square script by the second century B.C.E. at the very latest, although the archaic script was used for some biblical manuscripts at Qumran and for revolutionary writings as late as the second century of the Common Era. The square script, which modern Hebrew Bibles use, has some letters that resemble each other (*b* and *k*, *n* and *g*, *r* and *d*, *ch* and *h*), giving rise to mistakes in transmission. In the earliest period, writing of biblical manuscripts was by pen and ink on leather, papyrus, or parchment. The codex, or book form, came into use during the second century C.E. The Hebrew Bible originally had no vowels, and the breaks between words were not always indicated. Occasionally, incorrect division of words has produced an erroneous text, for example Amos 6:12 ("Does one plow with oxen?" which should read, "Does one plow the sea with oxen?")

Saint Catherine's Monastery, located at the foot of what is traditionally considered to be Mt. Sinai. One of the oldest Greek manuscripts of the Bible, Codex Sinaiticus (fourth century C.E.), was discovered here. The manuscript is now in the British Museum.

SOPHERIM AND MASSORETES

The task of establishing a fixed consonantal text fell to the Sopherim (Scribes) who made notes about dubious words, introduced corrections and abbreviations, and commented on unusual forms. In addition, the Sopherim omitted certain expressions, mainly those which in their eyes were theologically offensive or which were sexually explicit. For the most part these changes were either for the sake of euphemism or to defend the Deity's honor. The Sopherim were succeeded by Massoretes (Transmitters), who handled the Hebrew text from c. 500–1000 C.E. To these scholars we are indebted for a system of vocalization. Two vowel systems arose and competed for widespread use, the Babylonian and the Tiberian. Eventually the latter system enjoyed greater support, and it has prevailed to this day. In addition to supplying the Hebrew text with vowel signs, the Massoretes also made copious notes in the margins and at the end of Hebrew manuscripts, and they developed a system known as *Ketib-Qere'* (Written-Read) by which an error in the text was allowed to stand, but a correct form was read during worship. They also designated the divine name Yahweh as a perpetual form of *Ketib-Qere'*, for the vowels of the word Lord were pronounced. This attempt to avoid the use of the divine name out of reverence later gave rise to the tetragrammaton form Jehovah, which combines the consonants of one word with the vowels of another word.

MANUSCRIPT TRADITIONS

In time two families, Ben Asher and Ben Naphtali, representing different text traditions, gained ascendancy. The eminent Jewish philosopher Maimonides threw his weight behind the text tradition preserved by Ben Asher, and the Jewish community followed his lead. The oldest complete Hebrew manuscript from this text tradition is in Leningrad and dates from 1008. A slightly earlier manuscript, the Aleppo Codex, comes from the tenth century, but it is partially destroyed. There are also two older manuscripts of the Prophets, one in Cairo from 895, and the other in Leningrad from 847. Before the discovery of the biblical manuscripts from the region of the Dead Sea, scholars relied almost completely on rather late manuscripts. The remarkable Qumran finds push the manuscript tradition back over twelve hundred years. The great similarity between the medieval text of Isaiah and the Qumran Isaiah scroll has caused renewed appreciation for the care with which the Sopherim and the Massoretes transmitted the Hebrew Bible.

One other feature of the Hebrew text deserves comment. There were originally no indications of chapters or verses. Gradually the Torah was divided into open and closed paragraphs for reading in synagogue worship; the Babylonian Jewish community preferred fifty-four paragraphs for an annual lunar cycle, while the Tiberian cycle was repeated every three years (154 paragraphs). Chapter divisions derive from Stephen Langton of Canterbury (thirteenth century C.E.) and verse enumeration first entered the Old Testament in 1571. Naturally, these innovations bear witness to the continued use of the Hebrew Scriptures as valuable guides to worship and action. To hear this story in such a way that it evokes a faithful response is both a priceless gift and an awesome responsibility.

Selected Bibliography

SECTIONS 1–3 of this bibliography have been chosen because they can be read profitably by beginning students. An occasional entry is marked by an asterisk, indicating that the treatment is more advanced but nevertheless understandable to discriminating readers who lack a knowledge of ancient languages. Sections 4 and 5 provide suggestions for further reading in several areas. Many of these books are highly technical, but students will find in them a wealth of information that will enable them to pursue virtually any interest. Because the literature in this field is vast, I have endeavored to offer a representative sample of writings in the discipline.

1. The Bible as Literature

Ackerman, James, et al., eds. *Literary Interpretations of Biblical Narratives.* 2 vols. Nashville: Abingdon, 1974 and 1982. Essays by several scholars on biblical texts. The aim is to demonstrate the importance of studying the Bible from a literary perspective.

Alonso-Schökel, Luis. "Narrative Structures in the Book of Judith." In *The Center for Hermeneutical Studies in Hellenistic and Modern Culture, Colloquy 11,* 1–20. Berkeley, Calif., 1975. A perceptive analysis of the structure of the Book of Judith; the author of this essay has done pioneer research in the literary understanding of scripture, particularly in translating the Bible.

Alter, Robert. *The Art of Biblical Narrative.* New York: Basic Books, Inc., 1981. An indispensable work by one whose specialty is literary cirticism rather than biblical studies. The book is flawed by two things: an unnecessary polemical tone and inadequate knowledge about the discipline the author wished to further.

Auerbach, Erich. *Mimesis.* Princeton, N.J.: Princeton University Press, 1953. The chapter entitled "Odysseus' Scar" contrasts Greek (Homeric) narrative art with Hebraic, as seen in the story about the sacrifice of Isaac. Its value lies more in the sensitive analysis of Genesis 22 than in the generalizations about Hebraic and Hellenic narrative art.

446

Barr, James. "Reading the Bible as Literature." *Bulletin of the John Rylands Library* 56 (1973): 10–33. A leading philologian offers a careful assessment of the strengths and weaknesses of the literary approach, especially valuable because biblical scholars use the adjective to designate source criticism as well as to indicate narrative or poetic art.

Craven, Toni. *Artistry and Faith in the Book of Judith*. Chico, Calif.: Scholars Press, 1983. Uses music theory to illuminate the literary structure of the book, and shows how theology is communicated by the mode of expression.

Crenshaw, James L. *Samson*. Atlanta: John Knox Press, 1978; and London: S.P.C.K., 1979. Shows how literary analysis, called aesthetic criticism here, complements other approaches. Compares John Milton's *Samson Agonistes* with the biblical understanding of Samson.

Crenshaw, James L. *A Whirlpool of Torment*. Philadelphia: Fortress Press, 1984. A literary and theological analysis of the offering of Isaac, Jeremiah's confessions, Job, Ecclesiastes, and Psalm 73.

Crenshaw, James L. "The Contest of Darius' Guards (1 Esdras 3:1–5:3). In *Images of Men and God*, edited by Burke O. Long, 74–88. Sheffield: Almond Press, 1981. Examines the composition of the Greek text comprising speeches in defense of wine, the king, women, and truth as the strongest thing in the world.

Fishbane, Michael. *Texts and Texture*. New York: Schocken Books, 1979. Close readings of selected texts from the Hebrew Bible by one whose knowledge of rabbinic literature enriches the discussion appreciably.

Fokkelman, J. P. *Narrative Art in Genesis*. Assen, the Netherlands: Van Gorcum, 1975. The first of four projected volumes that are intended to provide an alternative to traditional approaches; rather than serving as complementary analysis.

Frye, Northrop. *The Great Code*. New York: Harcourt Brace Jovanovich, 1982. Resembles typological treatments of the two testaments in the ancient church, although updated by material from the history of religions. Traces various links between the Hebrew Bible and the New Testament.

Good, Edwin M. *Irony in the Old Testament*. Philadelphia: Westminster Press, 1965. An early attempt to introduce literary categories into the study of certain key texts.

*Good, Edwin M. "The Unfilled Sea: Style and Meaning in Ecclesiastes 1:2–11." *Israelite Wisdom*, edited by John Gammie et al., 59–73. Missoula, Mont.: Scholars Press, 1978. Draws on music composition theory to show how the Hebrew poet composed the poem in Ecclesiastes 1.

Gunn, David. *The Story of King David*. Sheffield: Journal for the Study of the Old Testament, 1978. *The Fate of King Saul*. Sheffield: Journal for the Study of the Old Testament, 1980. An important presentation of the narrative features in the stories about Israel's first two kings. The author's training in classics enables him to understand the complex problem of moving from literature to history.

Kermode, Frank. *The Sense of an Ending*. New York: Oxford University Press, 1966. Traces the sense of expectance in narratives to biblical eschatology, the conviction that history is progressing toward a climax, an ending.

Kikawada, Isaac M., and Quinn, Arthur. *Before Abraham Was*. Nashville: Abingdon Press, 1985. Stresses the essential literary unity of Genesis as an alternative to the documentary hypothesis.

Miscall, Peter D. *The Workings of Old Testament Narrative*. Philadelphia and Chico: Fortress Press and Scholars Press, 1983. The emphasis falls on the undecidability of the text, its ambivalence in character portrayal, and the necessity for an open reading.

Polzin, Robert. *Moses and the Deuteronomist*. New York: Seabury Press, 1980. The function of authorial interruptions, or frame-breaks, in narrative is emphasized in this interesting analysis.

Robertson, David. *The Old Testament and the Literary Critic*. Philadelphia: Fortress Press, 1977. This discussion of literary criticism is marred by an assumption that Hebrew literature operates on the level of a child's mentality, whereas Greek literature is appropriate for adults.

Sandmel, Samuel. *The Enjoyment of Scripture*. New York: Oxford University Press, 1972. A lively presentation of the content of the Hebrew Bible, its humor and felicity of expression.

Thompson, Leonard L. *A More Fantastic Country*. Englewood Cliffs, N.J.: Prentice-Hall, 1978. A popular treatment of the two Testaments, emphasizing their exquisite metaphors and similes.

Trible, Phyllis. *God and the Rehtoric of Sexuality*. Philadelphia: Fortress Press, 1978. Feminist concerns inform this significant analysis of various stories (for example, the garden of Eden, Ruth, Song of Songs).

Trible, Phyllis. *Texts of Terror*. Philadelphia: Fortress Press, 1984. Further close readings of biblical texts dealing with women.

Weiss, Meir. *The Story of Job's Beginning*. Jerusalem: Magnes Press, 1983. Psychological and literary dimensions combine in this important discussion of the prose in the Book of Job.

2. Theological Interpretation

Barr, James. *Old and New in Interpretation*. London: S.C.M., 1965. *The Bible in the Modern World*. London: Harper & Row, 1973. *Fundamentalism*. Philadelphia: Westminster Press, 1981. Important discussion of the difficult task of presenting biblical insights to contemporary readers, with warnings against excessive emphasis on the historical dimension and with valuable contributions to the understanding of inspiration and revelation.

Buber, Martin. *On the Bible*. New York: Schocken, 1968. A collection of essays on various aspects of the Hebrew Bible; "The Heart Determines," a treatment of Psalm 73, reveals the author's literary and theological sensitivity.

Carroll, Robert. *From Chaos to Covenant*. New York: Crossroad, 1981. A provocative examination of the way the tradition ascribed to Jeremiah was shaped by later concerns of the exile and postexilic communities.

Crenshaw, James L., ed. *Theodicy in the Old Testament*. Philadelphia: Fortress Press; and London: S.P.C.K., 1983. These essays by various scholars discuss the problem of evil in ancient Israelite thought.

*Eichrodt, Walther. *A Theology of the Old Testament*, translated by J. A. Baker. 2 vols. Philadelphia: Westminster Press, 1961. The classic study of Old Testament theology, written from a systematic approach and using the idea of the covenant as the unifying theme.

Fretheim, Terrence. *The Suffering God*. Philadelphia: Fortress Press, 1984. Examines the powerful biblical notion that the Deity participates in the suffering that engulfs humans.

Hanson, Paul D. *The Diversity of Scripture.* Philadelphia: Fortress Press, 1982. Emphasizes the plurality of views within the Hebrew Bible and draws conclusions about modern Christian efforts to appropriate ancient insights.

Harrelson, Walter. *The Ten Commandments and Human Rights.* Philadelphia: Fortress Press, 1981. A theological assessment of the Decalogue paves the way for a study of contemporary efforts to preserve fundamental human rights throughout the world.

Klein, Ralph W. *Israel in Exile.* Philadelphia: Fortress Press, 1979. Discussess the important period when Israel's earlier traditions were transformed by a new historical situation.

Miskotte, Kornelius. *When the Gods Are Silent.* New York: Harper & Row, 1967. The theme of divine silence in world literature, with special focus on the speaking One who revealed divine mystery to Israel.

Nicholson, Ernest W. *Preaching to the Exiles.* Oxford: Basil Blackwell, 1970. A theological analysis of the prose traditions within the Book of Jeremiah.

Rad, Gerhard von. *Moses.* London: Lutherworth Press, 1960. This little book is a model of clarity, illustrating von Rad's special approach to the Bible (tradition history).

*Rad, Gerhard von. *Old Testament Theology.* 2 vols. New York: Harper, 1962 and 1965. Examines the theologies of the various traditions within the Hebrew Bible (the Yahwist, Elohist, Priestly Writer, Deuteronomist, Chronicler, prophecy, wisdom, apocalyptic).

Terrien, Samuel. *The Elusive Presence.* New York: Harper & Row, 1978. Uses the idea of divine presence in the cult as the central theme of the Bible; the adjective "elusive" indicates that the Deity always concealed fundamental mystery.

Vawter, Bruce. *Job and Jonah.* New York: Paulist Press, 1983. A perceptive analysis of two books that signal the collapse of wisdom and prophecy as definitive responses to life's ambiguities.

Zimmerli, Walther. *Man and His Hope in the Old Testament,* Naperville, Ill.: A. R. Allenson; and London: S.C.M., 1971. Looks at the language of hope within the Hebrew Bible.

*Zimmerli, Walther. *Old Testament Theology in Outline.* Atlanta: John Knox Press, 1978. The significance of divine self-presentation lies at the center of this important study, and with it, the freedom of God.

3. Canonical Divisions

A. THE TORAH

Anderson, Bernhard W., ed. *Creation in the Old Testament.* Philadelphia: Fortress Press: and London: SCM, 1984. An anthology of important articles on the subject of creation as it was understood by ancient Israelite thinkers.

Anderson, Bernhard W. *Creation versus Chaos.* New York: Association Press, 1967. A popular discussion of biblical ideas about creation.

Blenkinsopp, Joseph. *Wisdom and Law in the Old Testament.* Oxford: Oxford University Press, 1983. Compares the different approaches of these two types of literature, noting substantial lines of connection.

Gunkel, Herrmann. *The Legends of Genesis.* New York: Schocken, 1901. Constitutes the introduction to Gunkel's classic commentary *Die Genesis* (Göttingen: Vandenhoeck & Ruprecht, 1969) a pioneer work in form criticism, like his commentary on Psalms.

Holt, John. *The Patriarchs of Israel.* Nashville: Vanderbilt University Press, 1964. One of the few nontechnical studies of this difficult subject, although somewhat dated.

Nicholson, Ernest W. *Deuteronomy and Tradition.* Philadelphia: Fortress Press, 1967. Studies the rhetoric of the book and attempts to determine what groups contributed to its growth.

Rad, Gerhard von. *Deuteronomy.* Philadelphia: Westminster Press, 1979. *Studies in Deuteronomy.* Chicago: Regnery, 1953. A popular commentary and an examination of the sermonic features of Deuteronomy, which are associated with Levites from the north.

*Rad, Gerhard von. *Genesis.* London: S.C.M., 1979. A theological commentary, filled with profound insights.

*Seters, John van. *Abraham in History and Tradition.* New Haven, Conn.: Yale University Press, 1975. This controversial analysis of the materials about Abraham emphasizes their relatively late date and historical unreliability.

Westermann, Claus. *The Genesis Accounts of Creation.* Philadelphia: Fortress Press, 1967. Popular treatment of various creation narratives.

Westermann, Claus. *The Promises to the Fathers: Studies on the Patriarchal Narratives.* Philadelphia: Fortress Press, 1980.

Zimmerli, Walther. *The Law and the Prophets.* Oxford: B. Blackwell, 1965. Claims that biblical prophets based their theological arguments on an understanding of Yahweh that derives from the Torah.

B. The Prophets

Blenkinsopp, Joseph. *A History of Prophecy in Israel.* Philadelphia: Westminster Press, 1983. A solid, though conventional, analysis of the prophetic phenomenon in ancient Israel.

Buber, Martin. *The Prophetic Faith,* New York: Macmillan, 1949. Stresses theological aspects of biblical prophecy and emphasizes the prophetic interpretation of history.

*Carroll, Robert. *When Prophecy Failed.* London: S.C.M., 1979. An interdisciplinary study of prophetic literature from the perspective of cognitive dissonance, the reshaping of mistaken hopes in the light of changed circumstances.

*Crenshaw, James L. *Prophetic Conflict.* Berlin and New York: Walter de Gruyter, 1971. A study of the problem generated by opposing prophetic voices; this book assesses the different criteria in the Hebrew Bible for distinguishing between true and false prophets.

*Gottwald, Norman K. *All the Kingdoms of the Earth.* New York: Harper & Row, 1964. A valuable analysis of the historical context for eighth-century B.C.E. prophecy.

Heschel, Abraham J. *The Prophets.* 2 vols. New York: Harper & Row, 1969, 1971. Emphasizes the divine pathos.

Koch, Klaus. *The Prophets.* 2 vols. Philadelphia: Fortress Press, 1982, 1984. Innovative and theoretical, this significant examination of biblical prophecy is filled with insights. The treatment of "apocalyptic" texts is particularly illuminating.

*Lindblom, Johannes. *Prophecy in Ancient Israel.* Philadelphia: Muhlenberg Press, 1963. A classic, though dated, treatment of the prophetic phenomenon.

Overholt, Thomas W. *The Threat of Falsehood.* London: S.C.M., 1970. Examines the conflict between Jeremiah and prophets who opposed his understanding of the religious situation.

Petersen, David L. *The Roles of Israel's Prophets.* Sheffield: Journal for the Study of the Old Testament, 1981. A sociological approach to prophecy.

Rad, Gerhard von. *The Message of the Prophets.* New York: Harper & Row, 1972. In most essentials this treatment of the prophetic literature appears in *Old Testament Theology,* vol. 2 (listed in section 2).

Scott, R. B. Y. *The Relevance of the Prophets,* rev. ed. New York: Macmillan, 1968. A popular study of biblical prophecy.

*Wilson, Robert. *Prophets and Society in Ancient Israel.* Philadelphia: Fortress Press, 1980. Comprehensive treatment of prophecy in the ancient Near East, with emphasis on "central" and "peripheral" features of the phenomenon. Distinguishes between a northern and a southern prophetic tradition.

C. THE WRITINGS

(1) Wisdom Literature

Brueggemann, Walter. *In Man We Trust.* Richmond: John Knox Press, 1972. Views wisdom literature in the light of the Deity's vote of confidence in humans, the commission to master the world.

Crenshaw, James L. *Old Testament Wisdom.* Atlanta: John Knox Press; and London: S.C.M., 1981. A comprehensive introduction to wisdom thinking and to the literature it produced, both in the Bible and in ancient Egypt and Mesopotamia.

*Fichtner, Johannes. *Die altorientalische Weisheit in ihrer israelitisch-jüdischen Ausprägung.* Giessen: Alfred Töpelmann, 1933. A classic analysis of Israel's wisdom in its various manifestations.

Lambert, William L. *Babylonian Wisdom Literature.* Oxford: Clarendon Press, 1960. A valuable translation and discussion of proverbs and reflective literature comparable to the books of Job and Ecclesiastes.

Morgan, Donn F. *Wisdom in the Old Testament Traditions.* Atlanta: John Knox Press, 1982. Examines the relationships between wisdom literature and other parts of the Hebrew Bible.

Murphy, Roland E. *Wisdom Literature.* Grand Rapids, Mich.: Eerdmans, 1982. Classifies the individual units within the wisdom literature, broadly understood, according to the different genres represented.

Perdue, Leo G. *Wisdom and Cult.* Missoula, Mont.: Scholars Press, 1977. Considers the role of the cult in the formation of wisdom literature, as well as the sages' attitude toward cultic religion. Looks at the wider context in ancient Egypt and Mesopotamia.

*Rad, Gerhard von. *Wisdom in Israel.* Nashville: Abingdon Press, 1972. Stresses the influence of Yahwism on biblical wisdom and the limits to knowledge. Argues that apocalyptic derives from wisdom rather than from prophecy.

Rylaarsdam, J. Coert. *Revelation in Jewish Wisdom Literature.* Chicago: University of Chicago Press, 1946. Develops the thesis that a concept of grace gradually entered Jewish wisdom as the result of waning confidence in human ability.

*Schmid, Hans Heinrich. *Wesen und Geschichte der Weisheit*. Berlin and New York: Walter de Gruyter, 1966. An important study of the crisis that developed within wisdom throughout the ancient Near East when belief in exact reward and punishment crystallized into dogma.

Scott, R. B. Y. *The Way of Wisdom in the Old Testament*. New York: Macmillan, 1971. A popular introduction to wisdom literature, with special attention to the contrast between optimistic and pessimistic viewpoints.

Thompson, J. M. *The Form and Function of Proverbs in Ancient Israel*. The Hague: Mouton, 1974. Comparative literature from various cultures illuminates the external form and essential use of aphoristic sayings.

*Wilken, Robert, ed. *Aspects of Wisdom in Judaism and Early Christianity*. Notre Dame, Ind.: University of Notre Dame Press, 1975. A significant collection of essays on late Jewish and early Christian texts.

Williams, James G. *Those Who Ponder Proverbs*. Sheffield: Almond Press, 1981. An analysis of aphoristic wisdom in the two testaments from the standpoint of contemporary linguistic theory.

(2) Apocalyptic Literature

Frost, Stanely. *Old Testament Apocalyptic*. London: Epworth Press, 1952. A standard examination of the characteristics of Israelite apocalyptic.

Hanson, Paul D. *The Dawn of Apocalyptic*. Philadelphia: Fortress Press, 1982. Develops the thesis of competing parties within ancient Judaism, particularly a hierocratic (priestly) group, and gives extensive analysis of apocalyptic literature according to its various stages.

Hanson, Paul D., ed. *Visionaries and their Apocalypses*. Philadelphia and London: Fortress Press, 1983. Collected essays on apocalyptic literature by several scholars.

Koch, Klaus. *The Rediscovery of Apocalyptic*. Naperville, Ill.: A. R. Allenson, 1972. Perceptive discussion of apocalyptic language and imagery characterizes this important study.

Rowley, Harold Henry. *The Relevance of Apocalyptic*. London: Lutterworth Press, 1963. A beginner's guide to the world view of apocalyptic texts.

*Russell, D. S. *The Method and Message of Old Testament Apocalyptic*. Philadelphia: Westminster Press, 1964. A comprehensive treatment of the language and thought of biblical apocalyptic.

*Stone, Michael E. *Scriptures, Sects, and Visions*. Philadelphia: Fortress Press, 1980. Covers the period from Ezra to the second Jewish revolt in 132 C.E.

4. The History of Israel and the Ancient Near East

Ackroyd, Peter. *Exile and Restoration*. Philadelphia: Westminster Press, 1968.

Aharoni, Y. *The Archaeology of the Land of Israel*. Philadelphia: Westminster Press, 1982.

Aharoni, Y. *The Land of the Bible*. Philadelphia: Westminster Press, 1979.

Bright, John. *A History of Israel*, 3rd ed. Philadelphia: Westminster Press, 1981. A standard conservative work.

Jacobsen, Thorkild. *The Treasures of Darkness*. New Haven, Conn.: Yale University Press, 1976. Systematic analysis of Mesopotamian religious thought.

Filson, Floyd V. and G. E. Wright, eds. *The Westminster Historical Atlas to the Bible*. Philadelphia: Westminster Press, 1956.

Jagersma, H. *A History of Israel in the Old Testament Period*. Philadelphia: Fortress Press, 1983. Succinct assessment of the relevant historical data.

Lichtheim, Miriam. *Ancient Egyptian Literature*. 3 vols. Berkeley, Calif.: University of California Press, 1973, 1976, 1980. Translations and copious notes on numerous texts.

May, Herbert G. *The Oxford Bible Atlas*. London and New York: Oxford University Press, 1974.

Miller, J. Maxwell, and John Hayes, eds. *Israelite and Judean History*. Philadelphia: Westminster Press, 1967. Covers the whole range of the historical study of ancient Israel.

Murphy-O'Connor, Jerome. *The Holy Land: An Archaeological Guide from Earliest Times to 1700*. London: Oxford University Press, 1980.

Noth, Martin. *The History of Israel*. Philadelphia: Westminster Press, 1960. *The Old Testament World*. London: A.& C. Black, 1966. A thorough treatment of Israelite history and of the international context for those events.

Pedersen, Johannes. *Israel*. 4 vols. London: Oxford University Press, 1973. A psychology of ancient Israelite thinking, with valuable discussions of concepts such as blessing, curse, peace, and the like.

Pritchard, James B., ed. *Ancient Near Eastern Texts*, 3rd ed. Princeton, N.J.: Princeton University, 1969. *The Ancient Near East in Pictures*, 2nd ed. Princeton, N.J.: Princeton University, 1969. Indispensable translations of texts related to the Old Testament, as well as pictures illustrating every aspect of daily life.

Simpson, William Kelly, ed. *The Literature of Ancient Egypt*. New Haven, Conn.: Yale University Press, 1973. Translations of important texts from ancient Egypt.

Vaux, Roland de. *Ancient Israel*. New York: McGraw-Hill, 1961. Discusses Israel's life and institutions.

Vaux, Roland de. *The Early History of Israel*. London: 1978.

5. Interpretation

A. INTRODUCTIONS TO THE OLD TESTAMENT

Anderson, Bernhard W. *Understanding the Old Testament*, 3rd ed. Englewood Cliffs, N.J.: Prentice-Hall, 1975. Combines historical and theological approaches for beginning students.

Bentzen, Aage. *Introduction to the Old Testament*. Copenhagen, 1957. Contains a valuable discussion of the forms of literature.

Childs, Brevard S. *Introduction to the Old Testament as Scripture*. Philadelphia: Fortress Press, 1979. Develops an approach called canon criticism, in which the present form of the canon is theologically normative.

Eissfeldt, Otto. *The Old Testament: An Introduction*. New York: Harper & Row, 1965. An exhaustive study of the Hebrew Bible and intertestamental literature; the most valuable resource available.

Fohrer, Georg. *Introduction to the Old Testament*. Nashville: Abingdon Press, 1968. The introductory sections on prophecy and wisdom are particularly good.

Gottwald, Norman K. *A Light to the Nations*. New York: Harper & Brothers, 1959. A solid literary approach for beginners.

Gottwald, Norman K. *The Hebrew Bible: A Socio-Literary Introduction*. Philadelphia: Fortress Press, 1985.

Kaiser, Otto. *Introduction to the Old Testament*. Minneapolis: Augsburg, 1977. One of the better recent treatments from Germany.

Nickelsburg, George W. E. *Jewish Literature between the Bible and the Mishnah*. Philadelphia: Fortress Press, 1981. A perceptive analysis of the literature in its historical setting.

Pfeiffer, Robert H. *Introduction to the Old Testament*. New York: Harper & Brothers, 1952. An exhaustive discussion from an earlier "literary" perspective.

Soggin, J. Alberto. *Introduction to the Old Testament*. Philadelphia: Westminster Press, 1976. A solid, up-to-date treatment with valuable bibliographical information.

Weiser, Artur. *Introduction to the Old Testament*. New York: Association Press, 1961. A cultic emphasis underlies this comprehensive study.

B. METHODS

Barton, John. *Reading the Old Testament*. London, 1984. A critical assessment of the various approaches to the Hebrew Bible (with special attention to literary and structural perspectives) and the issues they seek to resolve.

Barton, John. "Classifying Biblical Criticism." *Journal for the Study of the Old Testament* 29 (1984): 19–35.

Emerding, Carl E. *The Old Testament and Criticism*. Grand Rapids, Mich., 1983. An evangelical perspective governs this defense of certain types of historical criticism.

Fohrer, Georg, et al., eds. *Exegese des Alten Testaments*. Heidelberg: Quelle und Meyer, 1976. Valuable essays showing how the different approaches to the Hebrew Bible are carried out.

Hahn, Herbert. *The Old Testament in Modern Research*. London, S.C.M. Press, 1956. A conservative discussion, largely out of date today.

The Guides to Biblical Scholarship edited by Gene M. Tucker for Fortress Press are particularly useful—for example, Norman Habel on literary (source) criticism, Ralph Klein on textual criticism, Darrell Lance on archaeological study, J. Maxwell Miller on historical studies, David Robertson on literary criticism, and Robert Wilson on sociological approaches.

C. THE HISTORY OF INTERPRETATION

Anderson, George W. ed. *Tradition and Interpretation*. Oxford: Clarendon Press, 1979. Collected essays issued for the British Society for Old Testament Study purporting to give the present state of the discipline.

Clements, Ronald E. *One Hundred Years of Old Testament Interpretation*. Philadelphia: Westminster Press, 1976.

Frei, Hans W. *The Eclipse of Biblical Narrative*. New Haven, Conn.: Yale University Press, 1974.

Fuller, Reginald C. *Alexander Geddes: A Forerunner of Biblical Criticism.* Sheffield: Almond Press, 1983.

Gunneweg, A. H. *Understanding the Old Testament.* Philadelphia: Westminster Press, 1978.

Hayes, John H., ed. *Old Testament Form Criticism.* San Antonio: Trinity University Press, 1974.

Hyatt, J. Phillip, ed. *The Hebrew Bible in Modern Scholarship.* Nashville: Abingdon, 1965. Collected essays issued by the Society of Biblical Literature.

Knight, Douglas A., and Gene M. Tucker, eds. *The Hebrew Bible and its Modern Interpreters.* Chico, Calif.: Scholars Press; Philadelphia: Fortress Press, 1985. Like the Hyatt volume on behalf of the Society of Biblical Literature, this one discusses the situation twenty years later.

Kraeling, Emil G. *The Old Testament since the Reformation.* New York: Harper & Brothers, 1955.

Rogerson, John. *Old Testament Criticism in the Nineteenth Century.* London: S.P.C.K., 1984. Concentrates exclusively on Germany and England.

Rowley, H. H. *The Old Testament and Modern Study.* Oxford: Oxford University Press, 1951. An earlier volume issued by the British Society for Old Testament Study.

Smalley, B. *The Study of the Bible in the Middle Ages.* Oxford: Blackwell, 1983.

D. OTHER RESOURCES

The Interpreter's Dictionary of the Bible. 4 vols. plus supplementary vol. Nashville: Abingdon Press, 1962 and 1976.

The Jerome Biblical Commentary. Englewood Cliffs, N.J.: Prentice-Hall, 1968. The best single-volume commentary.

Old Testament Abstracts. The Catholic Biblical Society of America and the Catholic University of America: Washington, D.C. A summary of recent publications.

Religious Studies Review. Council on the Study of Religion: Ann Arbor, Mich. Brief reviews of recent publications.

Book List of the Society for Old Testament Study. The Society for Old Testament Study: Leeds. Brief notes published annually on recent works.

Journals
Catholic Biblical Quarterly
Interpretation (Can be read with profit by beginners.)
Journal of Biblical Literature
Journal for the Study of the Old Testament
Vetus Testamentum
Zeitschrift für die alttestamentliche Wissenschaft

Commentary Series
Old Testament Library
Anchor Bible
New Century Bible
Hermeneia
New International Commentary on the Old Testament (evangelical)
Tyndale Commentaries (conservative)

Appendix

A. Characteristics of Apocalyptic

1. Dualism: belief in opposing heavenly powers of good and evil
2. Eschatology: concern for the end of time
3. Pseudonymity: attribution of literature to ancient worthies
4. Visions: dreams and actual visions
5. Numerology: fondness for calculating the date of the end
6. Oppression: evildoers have gained the upper hand in society
7. Astrology: the stars govern one's fate
8. Animal symbolism: representing nations and individuals
9. Angels and demons: corresponding to the two absolute powers
10. Future orientation: the decisive action of the Deity lies in the future

B. The Festivals at Which the "Five Scrolls" Were Read

1. Feast of Weeks   Ruth
2. Passover   Song of Songs
3. Tabernacles (Booths)   Ecclesiastes
4. 9th of Ab   Lamentations
5. Purim   Esther

C. Major Scrolls from Qumran

1. The Damascus Document
2. The Habakkuk Commentary
3. The Isaiah Scroll (two scrolls, one incomplete)
4. The Rule of the Community
5. The Hymn Scroll
6. Wars of the Sons of Light against the Sons of Darkness

7. The Genesis Apocryphon
8. A Commentary on Psalms
9. The Nahum Commentary
10. A Commentary on Isaiah
11. Florilegium (2 Sam. 7:10–14)
12. The Temple Scroll

D. Major Deities in the Canaanite Pantheon

1. El: creator and father of the gods
2. Asherah: mother of the gods
3. Baal: weather god
4. Anath and Ashtart: Baal's consorts
5. Mot: god of summer drought and death
6. Yam: god of the rebellious sea

E. Important Noncanonical Works (Pseudepigrapha)

1. The Epistle of Aristeas
2. The Book of Jubilees
3. The Martyrdom and Ascension of Isaiah
4. The Psalms of Solomon
5. Fourth Maccabees
6. The Sibylline Oracles
7. The Ethiopian Book of Enoch
8. The Slavonic Book of Enoch
9. The Assumption of Moses
10. The Syriac Apocalypse of Baruch
11. The Greek Apocalypse of Baruch
12. The Testament of the Twelve Patriarchs
13. The Life of Adam and Eve
14. The Testament of Job

F. History of Pentateuchal Research

1. Precritical period: Philo, Josephus (noted the strange fact that Moses recorded his own death), Ibn Ezra, (expressed cautious doubts about Mosaic authorship)
2. Philological period: Andreas Rudolf Carlstadt, Thomas Hobbes, Baruch Spinoza, Richard Simon, Jean le Clerc
3. Critical period (Enlightenment)
   a. Older documentary theory: H. Bernhard Witter (1711), different names for God in Genesis; Jean Astruc (1753), sources used by Moses
   b. Fragment hypothesis
   c. Supplementary hypothesis

d. Newer documentary hypothesis: Herrmann Hupfeld (1853), three sources in Genesis (PEJ); Karl Heinrich Graf, laws in Leviticus and Numbers were later than D; Abraham Kuenen, P was late; Julius Wellhausen (1885), popularized the sequence JEDP

e. Newest documentary hypothesis (J_1 and J_2): Otto Eissfeldt, J and L; Robert Pfeiffer, J and S; Georg Fohrer, J and N

f. Form criticism and tradition history: Gerhard von Rad, confessional cultic statements; Martin Noth, tradition complexes

g. Conservative reaction: School of Uppsala (Ivan Engnell), oral transmission; Paul Volz and Kurt Rudolph, denial that E existed; Yehezkel Kaufmann, P was not the latest source

h. Current Debate, strata

G. The Bible in English

Anglo-Saxon beginnings: Caedmon, Bede
John Wycliffe, 1382 C.E.: first complete Bible in English
William Tyndale, 1525–35: New Testament and part of the Old Testament
Miles Coverdale, 1535
The Great Bible, 1539–68
The Geneva Bible, 1560: revision of the Great Bible
The Bishops' Bible, 1568
The Douay Version, 1609–10: Roman Catholic
The King James Version, 1611
The Authorized Standard Version, 1901
The Revised Standard Version, 1946, 1952, 1956
The New English Bible, 1961, 1970
The Tanakh, 1962, 1978, 1982
Today's English Version, 1966, 1971

H. Some Significant Inscriptions and Literary Texts

1. Ebla texts from Tell Mardikh in northern Syria, 2500–2250 B.C.E.
2. *The Tale of Sinuhe* (Egyptian court official who fled to Palestine), c. 1950
3. Egyptian Execration Texts: list Canaanite names and cities from nineteenth and eighteenth centuries
4. Mari documents: early prophecy, nineteenth and eighteenth centuries
5. Nuzi tablets: fifteenth and fourteenth centuries
6. Amarna Texts: letters between Pharaoh Akhnaton and vassals from Syria, Phoenicia, and Palestine, fourteenth century
7. Ugaritic Texts: temple archives from Ras Shamra, discovered after C.E. 1929, Baal worship, 1500–1200

8. Egyptian Royal Inscriptions: on temple walls; Merneptah or Israel stela from c. 1220; Ramses III versus Philistines, c. 1180

9. Assyrian and Babylonian Sources: lists of expeditions by Assyria, Neo-Babylonia, and Persia dealing with the period from 950 until after 587

10. Elephantine Texts: papyri in Aramaic from a Jewish colony in Egypt, fifth century

11. Mesha Inscription: Moabite stone from Omri's dynasty, c. 840

12. Siloam Inscription: records the story of the digging of the tunnel, c. 700

13. Deir 'Alla Texts: Aramaic; tradition about Balaam

14. Hebrew Ostraca: at Samaria, Lachish, Arad

15. Lachish Letters: describe the situation just before Lachish and Jerusalem fell to Babylonians, 587

16. Royal Seals: attached to jars containing provisions for royal outposts, c. 800; seals from the time of Hezekiah to Josiah, 700–600

17. Samaria Documents: official documents from fourth century

18. Qumran (Dead Sea) Scrolls: biblical manuscripts and sectarian documents from c. 200 B.C.E. to C.E. 135

I. Major Periods in Israelite History

Beginnings	fourteenth to twelfth centuries B.C.E.
Judges	eleventh and tenth centuries
Monarchy	1000–587
Exile	587–539
Postexilic period	539–174
Maccabean period	174–63 (Hasmonaean dynasty, 145–63)
Roman rule	63 B.C.E.–C.E. 135

Chart of the Hasmonaean house appears on page 460.

J. The Hasmonaean House

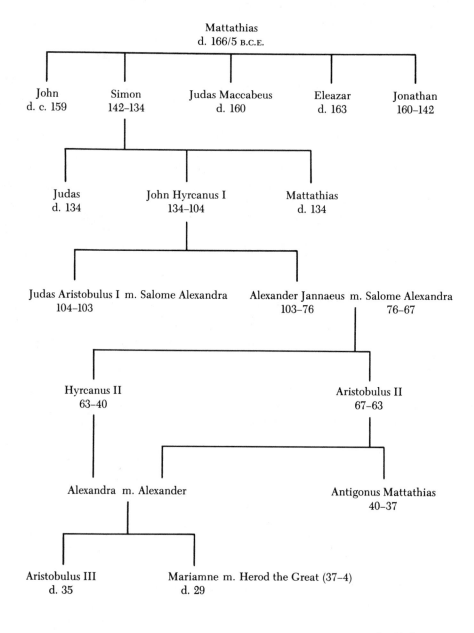

Mattathias
d. 166/5 B.C.E.

John
d. c. 159

Simon
142–134

Judas Maccabeus
d. 160

Eleazar
d. 163

Jonathan
160–142

Judas
d. 134

John Hyrcanus I
134–104

Mattathias
d. 134

Judas Aristobulus I m. Salome Alexandra
104–103

Alexander Jannaeus m. Salome Alexandra
103–76   76–67

Hyrcanus II
63–40

Aristobulus II
67–63

Alexandra m. Alexander

Antigonus Mattathias
40–37

Aristobulus III
d. 35

Mariamne m. Herod the Great (37–4)
d. 29

d. = died
m. = married

Source: George W. E. Nickelsburg, *Jewish Literature between the Bible and the Mishnah,*
(Philadelphia: Fortress Press, 1981), p. 320.

Index